1859:

ENTERING AN AGE OF CRISIS

"There is a practice which . . . I venture to recommend to those of you who are studying history. Take . . . a year and dive straight in at the deep end."
G. M. YOUNG, Today and Yesterday

Queen Victoria opening Parliament, 1859

1859: ENTERING AN AGE OF CRISIS

Edited by

PHILIP APPLEMAN

WILLIAM A. MADDEN

MICHAEL WOLFF

General Introduction by

HOWARD MUMFORD JONES

BLOOMINGTON

INDIANA UNIVERSITY PRESS

This book has been published with the assistance of a grant from the Ford Foundation.

Acknowledgment is made to the Hibbert Trustees and Chatto and Windus, Ltd., for permission to use some of the material from *Darwin and Butler: Two Versions of Evolution*, by Basil Willey.

41173

THE EDITORS AND ESSAYISTS

dedicate this book

to

G. M. YOUNG

author of

Victorian England: Portrait of an Age

"I doubt if he left a page, I am sure he did not leave an essay, which has not startled some fit reader, not so much by the range or the precision, as the appropriateness of the learning revealed—the right detail coming exactly at the right moment—or made him glow with that sense of confident and delighted energy which only the highest genius can communicate. And they who have received it will impart it as they can."

"MAITLAND," *Daylight and Champaign*

*Virtutes autem excellentes et singulares quas
in altero animadvertit in hoc ipso admiramur.*

PREFACE

THERE are already four introductions in this book, and there seems to be no need for another. We know that some people have a distaste for centennials because they provide occasion for collections of essays—and that some people simply dislike collections of essays. It would be a pleasure to discuss this and, incidentally, to put in a good word for the book. But we hope that the book will speak for itself.

Our main reason for writing a Preface is to have a place to thank our wives for aid and comfort; Kay Dinsmoor and Fred M. Kimmey, executive secretary and editorial assistant of *Victorian Studies*, for what was in effect collaboration; and the Research Committee of Indiana University and the advisers, consultants, and subscribers to *Victorian Studies,* whose support has been the foundation of our book.

P.A.
W.A.M.
M.W.

I⊤ is with a mixture of pride and sorrow that we record here that on the original list of contributors to *1859* was the name of the late G. D. H. Cole, one-time Chichele Professor of Social and Political Theory at Oxford and President of the Fabian Society. The enduring profundity, liveliness, and versatility of Professor Cole's mind is partly indicated by the fact that he was engaged in such an enterprise (and how many others?) at the time of his death.

It was our good fortune to be able to persuade Professor J. R. T. Hughes of Purdue University to write his own essay on the industrial and economic history of 1859. In a footnote on page 131 Professor Hughes discusses the relationship of his essay to a synopsis left by Professor Cole.

TABLE OF CONTENTS

PREFACE BY THE EDITORS   7

1859 AND THE IDEA OF CRISIS: GENERAL INTRODUCTION   13
    by HOWARD MUMFORD JONES

I. SCIENCE, RELIGION, AND THE CRITICAL MIND

Introduction *by* NOEL ANNAN   31

Darwin and Clerical Orthodoxy *by* BASIL WILLEY   51

The Limits of Religious Thought: The Theological
    Controversy *by* R. V. SAMPSON   63

Darwin, Pater, and a Crisis in Criticism
    by PHILIP APPLEMAN   81

Technology and Liberal Education *by* GEORGE HAINES, IV   97

II. PATTERNS OF NATIONAL DEVELOPMENT

Introduction *by* WILLIAM O. AYDELOTTE   115

Problems of Industrial Change *by* J. R. T. HUGHES   131

The Individual in the Mass: Mill on Liberty and the
    Franchise *by* R. B. MCCALLUM   147

Party Politics in the Age of Palmerston *by* J. B. CONACHER   163

An International Crisis: The Italian Question
    by DEREK BEALES   181

III. THE CHALLENGE OF POPULAR CULTURE

Introduction *by* J. A. BANKS   199

The Literature of an Imminent Democracy
    by RICHARD D. ALTICK   215

Victims and Spokesmen: The Image of Society in the Novel
    by G. ARMOUR CRAIG   229

The Burden of the Artist *by* WILLIAM A. MADDEN   247

Victorian Reviewers and Cultural Responsibility
    by MICHAEL WOLFF   269

NOTES ON CONTRIBUTORS   290

NOTES   291

INDEX   315

ILLUSTRATIONS

Queen Victoria opening Parliament
  (*Illustrated London News,* 1859).   frontispiece

Head- and tailpiece from the Preface to *Punch's* volume
  for the first half of 1859.   7

Calendar from *Punch's* Almanack Number of Spring, 1859.   15

Title page of the first edition of *The Origin of Species.*   30

Obituary portraits of the Rev. H. L. Mansel and the Rev. F. D.
  Maurice (*Illustrated London News,* 1871 and 1872).   66-67

Caricature of Walter Pater by "Spider."   85

Obituary portrait of Prince Albert
  (*Illustrated London News,* 1861).   96

Return from the Derby (*Punch,* 1859).   114

"The Strike" (Punch, 1859).   143

"The Supporters of the Working Man" (*Punch,* 1859).   146

"Who Will Rouse Him?" (*Punch,* 1859).   162

Map of Italy in 1859.   182

"The Giant and the Dwarf" (*Punch,* 1859).   190

"The French Porcupine" (*Punch,* 1859).   192

"Domestic Economy" (*Punch,* 1859).   198

Title page of the first volume of *Macmillan's Magazine,* 1859. 220

Covers to the October numbers of *A Tale of Two Cities* and
  The Virginians.   242-243

Two illustrations by Ruskin, in *The Two Paths.*   265

Houses of Parliament (S. C. Hall, *Book of the Thames,* 1859).   289

1859:

ENTERING AN AGE OF CRISIS

1859 AND THE IDEA OF CRISIS:
GENERAL INTRODUCTION

HE essays in this collection have been brought together on the assumption that the theme "1859: Entering an Age of Crisis" would give them needful unity. They are intended to survey some of the great fields of human thought and human conduct from the point of view of mid-Victorian England. Inevitably more (though not more important) topics are excluded than are here discussed. For example, no essays deal directly with Victorian science or medicine, painting or architecture, feminism or business. But the book is not an encyclopedia, and the individual contributions are best considered as samplings brought up from the rich variety of Victorian intellectual, political, and cultural strata underlying the apparent placidity of Victorian sobriety, Victorian solidity, Victorian calm. Since every age is an age of crisis and transition, we may expect some dissent from the contributors as to what is critical and what is not. To the nature of crisis as a historical concept I shall come later, but let me first concentrate upon the year.

I

Why 1859? In 1859 Lord Palmerston, a figure who seems to embody Nietzsche's eternal recurrence, once more became Prime Minister. In 1859 there was a small war in China. By 1859 the Indian Mutiny had been put down, the East India Company's long reign was over, and the Crown had succeeded it; Victoria wrote in December 1858 of her great satisfaction and pride in feeling herself to be in direct communication with an enormous empire. Let us, she concluded, "draw a veil over the sad and bloody past." In 1859 likewise John Brown attacked Harper's Ferry, Austria declared war on Sardinia, Napoleon III marched 200,000 men into Italy, won the battles of Ma-

13

genta and Solferino, suddenly abandoned the whole campaign, and signed a truce.

In 1859, however, no Briton knew that Harper's Ferry would be succeeded by Bull Run, Gettysburg, and Appomattox; and news about John Brown, when it came, was simply confirmation of the general truth that the distant Americans were wild and lawless. The Italian business was more serious matter, as Mr. Beales shows in his essay; yet the war clouds lifted and the threat of a general European conflict seemed to be at least postponed. As for China, Great Britain was always fighting a small war somewhere, a job for professional proconsuls and a small professional fighting force. At home, a Reform Bill was the principal topic of debate in the House of Commons, but the country at large was apathetic. The depression of 1857 was over, the world was settling down, and though one should always be a little suspicious of Frenchmen (especially when led by Bonapartes), Catholics, and Americans, any sensible upper-class Londoner might look forward with confidence to peace, prosperity, and progress. Even Ireland was calm.

The key to the importance of 1859, then, is not to be sought particularly in diplomacy, war, or Parliament. Let us look at some books. 1859 was a good year, when a number of important titles came out. Dickens' *A Tale of Two Cities* was published in book form after serialization in his new magazine, *All the Year Round;* and Thackeray's *The Virginians* also completed its serialization in twenty-four monthly parts. A third novel was George Eliot's *Adam Bede,* a fourth *The Ordeal of Richard Feverel.* In 1859 was published Sir William Hamilton's posthumous *Lectures on Metaphysics,* edited by J. Veitch and by H. L. Mansel, whose 1858 Bampton Lectures, attacked by F. D. Maurice, were still the object of much attention. Tennyson published the first four *Idylls of the King,* and FitzGerald printed the first version of *The Rubáiyát of Omar Khayyám*—Tennyson's poetry widely acclaimed, FitzGerald's hardly noticed. Both Ruskin and Arnold published relatively minor works. More important was John Stuart Mill's essay *On Liberty.* And there was a book by Charles Darwin called *On the Origin of Species by means of Natural Selection, or the Preservation of Favoured Races in the Struggle for Life.*

Admirable in its way, Thackeray's novel, filling the historical gap between *Esmond* on the one hand and *The Newcomes* and *Pendennis* on the other, broke no new paths. Dickens' tale of revolutionary Paris inaugurated nothing, echoed Carlyle, and looked backward with complacency upon a French crisis seventy years old. *Adam Bede* confirmed the talent for thoughtful observation and the penetrating

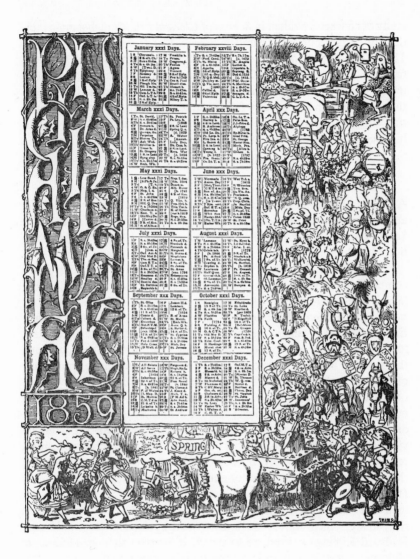

16 HOWARD MUMFORD JONES

study of character evident in *Scenes of Clerical Life,* though a main incident in its plot curiously parallels Scott's *The Heart of Midlothian* of 1818. *The Ordeal of Richard Feverel* alone of these novels looked forward—forward in its style, in its theme, in its assumption that intellect was at once too much and too little. Today the sensitive reader, though Meredith has queerly fallen out, can find in the book anticipation of Meredith's evolutionary triad of blood, brains, spirit, and of his acceptance of the untheological truth:

> Into the bosom that receives the rose
> Shall I with shuddering fall?

A critical reversal of values is implicit in *Feverel,* but it is only implicit, and we must await *The Egoist* (1879) and *Diana of the Crossways* (1885), not to speak of "The Lark Ascending" (1881), for the equation of evolution with health and sanity.

Sir William Hamilton was looked upon as a great philosopher comparable to Bacon, but the notions of consciousness which underlay his work were not going to survive the assault of Mill's *Examination of Sir William Hamilton's Philosophy* (1865). Although neither *England and the Italian Question* nor *The Two Paths* is really central to the discussion of Arnold and Ruskin, Mr. Madden has brilliant things to say about them in connection with his thoughtful examination of the status of the artist. The four *Idylls of the King,* though possibly not quite as central as *In Memoriam,* are, as Mr. Madden points out, much misunderstood nowadays; and the *Rubáiyát* is not quickly to be dismissed. One notes that FitzGerald presents no consistent point of view, not even the point of view of hedonism. In 1859 a highly sensitive reader might conceivably have glossed these famous quatrains as showing the deleterious effect of empire-building upon Christian faith (the British fought a small war against Persia in 1856-57 to protect their interests in Afghanistan and Herat). "The Orient" as a vague, rich, misty something (to be re-discovered by Sir Edwin Arnold and Rudyard Kipling) existed, so to speak, in its own right in 1859 as a philosophy, a style, a rhetoric, an emotional mystery, a cultural complex beyond missionary zeal and Christian complacency; and the *Rubáiyát* is a richly embroidered cloak for a neat bit of dagger-work. History, which is fully alert to economic and political forces—read Mr. Conacher's and Mr. Hughes' essays—is sometimes a little blind to the power of style as a cultural dynamic: though the *Rubáiyát* prepared the way for aestheticism and the decadence, it did not provoke an immediate cultural crisis.

There remain two intellectual triumphs—Mill's *On Liberty* and

Darwin's *Origin of Species.* Mill's essay is a classic to which Western man must always return. It is, and it probably will long be, one of the great expressions of utopian hope. In Mill's universe of discourse the world and men are rational. Men are persuaded by intelligent discussion, their discussions are forever amiable, and whether by some system of concurrent majorities or by Rousseau's general will or by consensus or otherwise, when truth has once been ascertained through informed debate, not only will it prevail, but like Allah it will scatter the misbelieving and black Horde of illogic, repression, propaganda, censorship, and religious and political controls before it with a whirlwind Sword. Like the state in a Marxian utopia these things will simply wither away. But how far off seems Mill's *On Liberty* when it is read from the point of view of Orwell's *1984!* In the sense that Mill looked forward to a perfection that never took shape, one can regard his great essay as a gateway into crisis.

Finally, there is the *Origin of Species,* to which (it is no surprise) one comes as to a crucial, a great volume in the long tradition of British empirical thought of which it is in one sense the culmination, and a volume out of which, in one sense, the current of relativism flows into our time, a current defined and canalized by Darwin as the vague general theory of evolution had never before been canalized. The historical significance of this book is greater than that of any other on our list, and Darwin is therefore the focus or the occasion of more than one of the essays which follow, Mr. Appleman's, for instance, showing the extent of the reverberations. The *Origin of Species,* when it appeared, was the product of twenty-two years of labor and patience—twenty-six if you count from Darwin's departure on the "Beagle." The first edition was bought up in a single day, and there followed, in William Irvine's phrase, convulsions of the national mind. Some specimens of these convulsions appear in the essay by Mr. Willey, and in that by Mr. Wolff. Here, evidently, is crisis.

II

The *Origin of Species* is a rare instance of a scientific work which is also a literary classic. The essays in this collection, though they allude to the matter, do not expatiate on its scientific importance, and, indeed, its scientific importance is so generally understood, there is no need for reiterating what can be found in any encyclopedia. An evolutionary approach is now basic to human thought. It is true that evolution did not originate with Darwin, just as it is true that the final shaping of the book was triggered by Alfred Russel Wallace's parallel statement of the theory, received by Darwin in 1858 and presented to the Linnean Society, together with a summary of Darwin's views, on July 1. These are familiar facts, but since Darwin, fairly or unfairly (but surely through no conscious campaign), has ever since overshadowed Wallace, I suggest that, taking for granted the main outlines of the Darwinian theory, we may well turn to Darwin's qualities as literary performer if we want to understand why this book changed the minds of men.

Contemporary literary criticism is absorbed in discussing poetry and fiction and has taken only the first steps toward setting up standards for judging non-fictional prose. Non-fictional prose has to do with argumentation, with description, and with exposition, the three great purposes of the *Origin of Species*. What is the characteristic excellence of such prose? I suppose its governing principle to be what the French call *ordonnance,* a word for which we have no good English equivalent, but which refers to skill and subtlety in the ordering, the arranging, the weighing of the several parts of the discourse being written. *Ordonnance,* though essential to a good style, will not of itself produce a great style, as the case of Macaulay shows. Order and clarity are the obvious characteristics of a Macaulay paragraph, but the manner is mainly ordinary. Darwin avoids a tinny, a mechanical ordering. He does not as Macaulay does proceed from a topic sentence to a summarizing statement through a series of parallel lines laid down like statements in a Euclidean proof. He is never smart, he is always a responsible writer, and, his purpose being to contribute not merely to scientific research but also to philosophic thought, his prose is in the great tradition of expository prose in English, the tradition of Bishop Butler, whom he admired. He developed a fine ear for cadence at the same time that he developed a sharp eye for detail and effect.

Even as early as *The Voyage of the Beagle* (1839) he combined the scientist's eye with the moralist's power of generalizing. Note how he fuses atmospherical effect and intellectual inquiry in this passage about the "streams of stones" he found in the Falkland Islands:

I have seen, in the Cordillera of the Andes, the evident marks where stupendous mountains have been broken into pieces like so much thin crust, and the strata thrown on their vertical edges; but never did any scene, like these "streams of stones," so forcibly convey to my mind the idea of a convulsion, of which in historical records we might in vain seek for any counterpart; yet the progress of knowledge will probably some day give a simple explanation of this phenomenon, as it already has of the so long-thought inexplicable transportal of the erratic boulders, which are strewed over the plains of Europe.

One can only regret that vile phrase, "the so long-thought inexplicable transportal," but, this aside, how the passage gives both cosmic vision and philosophic speculation in terms any thoughtful reader can comprehend! Chapter Ten of the *Beagle,* let it not be forgotten, contains those descriptions of the Fuegians, "the most abject and miserable creatures I anywhere beheld," which share with Swift's portrait of the Yahoos the distinction of being our most disturbing commentaries upon man as the paragon of animals. The Fuegians were not the much-debated missing links, but the drama of their lives presented in the *Beagle* is a vivid preparation for *The Descent of Man.*

It is canonical and right to admire Darwin's patience as a scientist; I suggest it is time to admire his patience as a writer of prose. If the *Origin of Species* had been as crabbedly written as are most scientific monographs today, it would not in so immediate a fashion have influenced the world. It was bought up and read by laymen, not by specialists only. Its widening influence is the effect not only of its substance but also of its style. This style possesses more than clearness and responsibility; it has other qualities, unexpected, and charming. There was in Darwin, whom most of us know as a venerable Victorian in a beard, a streak of elvish humor. The following, for example, has the flavor of George Eliot telling us about the frequenters of the Rainbow in *Silas Marner.*

I sat one evening in a gin palace in the Borough amongst a set of pigeon-fanciers, when it was hinted that Mr. Bull had crossed his Pouters with Runts to gain size; and if you had seen the solemn, the mysterious, the awful shakes of the head which all the fanciers gave at this scandalous proceeding, you would have recognized how little crossing had to do with improving breeds.

The pigeon fanciers called him Squire and taught him, he gravely adds, "the solace and pleasure derived from the Almond Tumbler." Our scientists, with whom impersonality is a fetish, do not customarily write this way.

The foregoing excerpt is from the letters, but the same dry humor enlivens the *Origin of Species*:

I have seen it gravely remarked, that it was most fortunate that the strawberry began to vary just when gardeners began to attend closely to this plant.

He who believes that each being has been created as we now see it, must occasionally have felt surprise when he has met with an animal having habits and structure not at all in agreement. What can be plainer than that the webbed feet of ducks and geese are formed for swimming? yet there are upland geese with webbed feet which rarely or never go near the water; and no one except Audubon has seen the frigate-bird, which has all its four toes webbed, alight on the surface of the sea.

The gravity in this reference to the dubious Audubon can pass into Shakespearian irony:

Nevertheless so profound is our ignorance, and so high our presumption, that we marvel when we hear of the extinction of an organic being; and as we do not see the cause, we invoke cataclysms to desolate the world, or invent laws on the duration of the forms of life!

This irony can itself take on a powerful, sardonic tinge, as in this passage which Darwin added in a later edition:

It has been said that I speak of natural selection as an active power or Deity; but who objects to an author speaking of the attraction of gravity as ruling the movements of the planets?

Darwin's treatment of his predecessors and opponents has, one knows, been attacked, since, being human, he was occasionally impatient; but one rises from a reading of the *Origin of Species,* it seems to me, with an overwhelming sense of Darwin's modesty of mind:

When a young naturalist commences the study of a group of organisms unknown to him, he is at first much perplexed, to determine what differences to consider as specific, and what as varieties. . . . But if he confine his attention to one class within one country, he will soon make up his mind how to rank most of the doubtful forms. . . . As he extends the range of his observations, he will meet with more cases of difficulty; for he will encounter a greater number of closely-allied forms. But if his observations be widely extended, he will in the end generally be enabled to make up his own mind . . . but he will succeed in this at the expense of admitting much variation,—and the truth of this admission will often be disputed by other naturalists.

Just so, we incline to say; it is precisely thus that human nature works, even among specialists, and we remember that Darwin is not merely a biologist, he is also a moralist, as when, discussing pigeon fanciers, he casually observes: "It is in human nature to value any novelty, however slight, in one's own possession." This writer, we remark, understands not only science but scientists.

Master of the art of rhetorical questions, Darwin with entire fairness of tone can turn the tables on doubters and opponents, a skill especially evident in Chapter Six, "Difficulties of the Theory," which contains among other things the crushing observation:

Some authors maintain that organic beings have been formed in many ways for the sake of mere variety, almost like toys in a shop, but such a view of nature is incredible.

More damaging, however, is this drum-fire of interrogation:

Why, on the theory of Creation, should this be so? Why should all the parts and organs of many independent beings, each supposed to have been separately created for its proper place in nature, be so invariably linked together by graduated steps? Why should not Nature have taken a leap from structure to structure? On the theory of natural selection, we can clearly understand why she should not; for natural selection can act only by taking advantage of slight successive variations; she can never take a leap, but must advance by the shortest and slowest steps.

Mr. Willey in his essay quotes a parallel extract from Darwin's correspondence, but I must, in concluding this analysis of Darwin's stylistic skill, cite two passages for their eloquence. The first is in its implication strongly adverse to Wordsworth; the second restores that grandeur to the universe Darwin's opponents thought the *Origin of Species* was stripping away:

Nothing is easier than to admit in words the truth of the universal struggle for life, or more difficult—at least I have found it so—than constantly to bear this conclusion in mind. Yet unless it be thoroughly engrained in the mind, I am convinced that the whole economy of nature, with every fact on distribution, rarity, abundance, extinction, and variation, will be dimly seen or quite misunderstood. We behold the face of nature bright with gladness, we often see superabundance of food; we do not see, or we forget, that the birds which are idly singing round us mostly live on insects or seeds, and are thus constantly destroying life; or we forget how largely these songsters, or their eggs, or their nestlings, are destroyed by birds and beasts of prey; we do not always bear in mind, that though food may be now superabundant, it is not so at all seasons of each recurring year.

Thus, from the war of nature, from famine and death, the most exalted object which we are capable of conceiving, namely, the production of the higher animals, directly follows. There is grandeur in this view of life, with its several powers, having been originally breathed into a few forms or into one; and that, while this planet has gone cycling on according to the fixed laws of gravity, from so simple a beginning endless forms most beautiful and most wonderful have been, and are being, evolved.

To my ear, at any rate, this, the final passage in the *Origin of Species*, has a persuasive majesty suggesting Raleigh's apostrophe to eloquent, just, and mighty death. The sentences on the contrast between the face of nature bright with gladness and the fact that life lives by destroying life are equally large, powerful, and, as I say, anti-Wordsworthian. Rhetorically they are sound, being *ordonnance* at its finest; intellectually they may be spoiled by Darwin's emphasis upon individual competition and the apparent irrelevance for him of the point of view to be expressed in Kropotkin's *Mutual Aid* of 1902. Nevertheless, the *Origin of Species* is a great, persuasive masterpiece.

III

To come back to the notion of crisis: in its dictionary definition a crisis is a turning-point (usually a point of no return) in the progress of anything; or a state of affairs in which a decisive change for better or worse is imminent. Certainly the *Origin of Species* marks a turning point in the development of our thought about man and the universe—probably a point of no return; but are the hundred years from 1859 to 1959 properly a period of crisis?

The essence of crisis is decision, and decision is supposed to bring about an immediate result. Somebody determines to push, or to put a stop to, a line of thought, or conduct, or expression, and the determination must meet and overcome great obstacles. A political crisis, for example, commonly implies an overturn in the state that sometimes involves imprisonment, exile, or execution. In any crisis, to use James's words, we are facing an option that is living, forced, and momentous. For example, in that momentous year 1917 the Kerensky government was compelled to decide whether it would put down rebellion by force, drawing troops from the front line to do so, and it fell from power. Thus also on 18-19 Brumaire the first Napoleon in another critical situation seized power by armed force and held it. But we also have crises in the history of thought. For example, when in 1656 Spinoza refused to yield either to threat or bribe and continued to affirm his philosophical views, he was excommunicated by the Jewish community and, for a time, banished from Amsterdam, but, so far as we know, he made his decision fully conscious of the obstacles he faced. Again: when in 1632 Galileo published his *Dialogo* after having promised Pope Paul V in 1616 that he would not "hold, teach, or defend" the very doctrines he was promulgating, he made a crucial decision, in a sense created a crisis, and certainly suffered in the sequel.

Neither in 1859 nor in 1871 was Darwin either creating or facing a crisis in these terms. Highly unpopular as his views were in many circles, he was let alone. It is perhaps a tribute to Victorian intelligence that we take it for granted he would be let alone. That is, he was not ostracized and driven out as was Byron in 1816, nor formally banished as was Heine in 1831, nor expelled from the country as was Marx in 1849, nor driven away as was Hugo in 1851, nor self-exiled as a form of protest as was Ibsen in 1864. Nobody tried to suppress his views as Pitt's government suppressed Paine's *The Rights of Man* in 1792, as the court found Moxon guilty of blasphemous libel for publishing *Queen Mab* in 1841, and as another set of officials fined and imprisoned Henry Vizetelly for publishing the novels of Zola in 1889. We can say, then, that Darwin inaugurates a critical age, although he does not, indeed, experience a crisis, nor create one, in the commoner, the more dramatic meaning of the term.

In his admirable appraisal Mr. Annan speaks less of crisis than of shock in referring to the *Origin of Species* and I think he uses the right word. He refers the fundamental conflict to a broader temporal area. For him Darwin is, as it were, a notable episode (a very great episode) in the lengthy conflict between what in a general sense I may call British empiricism and what, again in a general sense, I may call a sacramental view of man and history. The *Origin of Species* was not, says Mr. Annan flatly, "the sole great dissolver of faith in mid-Victorian England," and he points to authors nobody now reads—to Bishop Colenso and to the contributors to *Essays and Reviews*—as being more immediately involved in the controversy. Mr. Sampson's careful elucidation of the points of difference between Mansel, later Waynfleete professor at Oxford and Dean of St. Paul's, and Maurice, deprived of his position at King's College, London, confirms Mr. Annan's interpretation. A crisis need not, in any obvious way, be critical. The heterodoxy of Maurice's *Theological Essays* of 1853 did cost him his academic post, but when he tried to resign as chaplain to Lincoln's Inn his resignation was refused, and from 1860 to 1869 he was the incumbent of St. Peter's in Vere Street in London, no question about his orthodoxy being raised to embarrass the appointment. Perhaps the very flexibility of Victorian institutions—the theme of Mr. Aydelotte's paper—had its virtues as a shock absorber, and what might have led to riots in Paris led to reviews in London. As Mr. Wolff shows, the shaping of opinion was in the hands of earnest journalists rather than of demagogues or heresy-hunters. I think it significant in this connection that, discussing publishing, Mr. Banks characterizes 1859 as a convenient year in an age of that confusion which is the outward and visible sign of pervasive crisis, as well as a year of transition into an age of crisis.

Of course the concept of crisis has its danger: it tends to oversimplify problems. Almost half a century ago, in a book entitled *The New History*, James Harvey Robinson pointed out that there is always an element of the sensational in most histories, especially the kind of history "which does not concern itself with the normal conduct and serious achievements of mankind in the past, but, like melodrama, purposely selects the picturesque and lurid as its theme." Events, he said, should not be narrated simply because they are pleasing or dramatic or highly exceptional. We should not be taught, he further pleaded, to view mankind as in a periodic state of turmoil, and historians should not, by studied neglect, disguise the importance of those lucid intervals during which the greater part of human progress has taken place.

The contributors to this collection have not neglected lucid intervals and sober progress. Mr. Hughes presents no crisis of industrial development in the melodramatic sense. Mr. Conacher finds the meeting of politicians in Willis's rooms in 1859 a significant event, since out of it modern parliamentary Liberalism emerged. But there was no need of conspiracy, for there was no such crisis as that which resulted in the Vichy government. The main difference between publishing in 1859 and publishing in 1959, Mr. Altick tells us, is less qualitative than quantitative—if the Victorians did not confine their reading to literary classics, neither do we confine ours to trash. These papers, each excellent, endorse our notion of the British nineteenth century as a period of gradual adjustment, of flexibility in change, of, in short, the Victorian compromise. But they also, as it were, lay a cooling hand upon the feverish brow of twentieth-century hypochrondria with its haunting belief that men have never suffered as they suffer now, that the human soul is lonelier in 1959 than it was in 1859, that ours is the only genuine Age of Anxiety.

Still, the idea of crisis will not down. Britain was not the whole of Europe nor of Western civilization, yet the *pax Britannia* is central to the nineteenth century, and the *pax Britannia* is no more. From the Renaissance to World War I Western man was dominant; and we now witness the passing of the European age. The bourgeois culture of the Industrial Revolution, best exemplified in English society, was one of the great and powerful cultures of history, dominating an epoch that for originality and energy is comparable to the age of Pericles, the age of Augustus, the age of the Medici, and the age of Louis XIV, but it is transforming itself before our eyes into something else even more exciting though as yet undefined—the welfare state, the aspirin age, the age of the United Nations, the age of Asia and Africa, the age of the total destruction of mankind or of its total triumph. Ours is a critical period in history, even more than were the years between the ending of the American Revolution and the adoption of the Federal Constitution, for our problem is not simply whether a young nation shall endure but whether humanity itself shall survive.

Possibly the historian must belong to the school of Heraclitus and believe that the sole reality is change. Under the smoother actualities of Victorian success in international diplomacy, Mr. Beales points out, there lurked a fatal error. In the problem of Italian unity, which heavily engaged English sympathy, the government, by its policy of neutrality and withdrawal, tacitly admitted that two or three states might be allowed to settle between themselves differences which affect other states. The British believed in self-determination, as, for the most part, they do today, but they expressed their belief by going to international congresses, he says, thus avoiding war in the interests of trade. Unfortunately not even Disraeli could see that the path led straight from the Congress of Berlin to Munich.

Perhaps the greatest failure of the Victorian world was its failure to develop a rigorous, consistent, and modern pattern of education; and I find Mr. Haines' paper on liberal education and technology one of the most illuminating, as his topic is one of the most perplexing, in our book. Mr. Haines raises a fundamental issue for the atomic age. The United States, too, like imperial Germany, has gone in for scientific and technological education, virtually the only kind of education on which the federal government is prepared to spend large sums of money. Shall we, like imperial Germany and Soviet Russia, produce mainly brilliant technologists and mechanicians? Mr. Haines notes that Great Britain emerged from World War I victorious if exhausted; and, clearly, the history of Germany from 1914 to 1945 seems to illustrate the truth that without vision the people perish. Victorian belief in individual worth is, to most of us, preferable to German belief in individual efficiency; and as between the idealism of Mill and the metaphysics of Hegel most Americans have only one choice, and—as Mr. McCallum's essay makes clear—it has also been the choice not only of the England of Churchill but of the England of Attlee. We do not believe in statism, whether of the imperial German or of the Soviet Russian variety. The Darwinian hypothesis tacitly assumed, or at least was made by some of its interpreters to assume, that competition was between individuals or between individuals and their environment, and in so far as this was true, Darwin did not contradict Mill but led directly to Huxley's metaphor of civilization as a cultivated garden to be defended against encroaching wildness. But how does one defend a garden in the modern age? Is it sufficient to give the man with a hoe a liberal education?

IV

Mr. Madden and Mr. Craig both study the problem of individual worth in the Victorian world as this is expressed in the sensitive art of poetry and the scarcely less sensitive art of prose fiction. The Victorian novel seems to Mr. Craig to express the warfare of the individual against the social world, whereas the Victorian poet laureate and his contemporaries seem to Mr. Madden to express a doubt whether the individual is capable of contending against any world. The essays raise nice questions of the philosophy of literary history; but they concentrate upon only one of the arts. I think it would be difficult to say of painting from 1859 to 1959 that it expresses either the dubiety or the uncertainty Mr. Madden finds in Tennyson and FitzGerald; and an age in which Sir Lawrence Alma-Tadema, Sir Frederick Leighton, and John Singer Sargent were fashionable painters can scarcely be accused of lacking either poise or self-assurance. Similarly, if the principal exhibit in Victorian music is the operas of Gilbert and Sullivan, these operas, essentially classical in musical form and in their satiric manner dependent upon a premise of reasonableness that would have delighted Voltaire or Pope, in no way indicate self-doubt: we laugh at what we love. It is not too absurd to oppose to the completed *Idylls of the King* in 1885 *The Mikado or The Town of Titipu,* produced that same year, or to say that one must contrast with Lancelot, the self-tormentor whom Mr. Madden subtly analyzes, the superb assurance of the Japanese Emperor, Pooh-Bah, Ko-Ko, and (Heaven forgive me!) Katisha as well. Gilbert and Tennyson are both eminently Victorian—shall we take the one and reject the other? Surely the Victorian age exists to prepare the world not only for Pound and Faulkner but also for whatever successors to Victorian academic painting and operetta the reader chooses.

I fully agree with Mr. Madden that the official Tennyson of 1859 is not the real Tennyson and that *In Memoriam* and the *Idylls of the King* are neither in the one case a cry across the conquered years nor in the other a celebration of the virtues of the Prince Consort as the first gentleman of England. Both poems, once you strip away conventional judgment and begin to analyze rather than merely read them, express the struggles of an anguished mind to believe that the visible world exists and that the moral world is eternal. Likewise Mr. Craig puts some solid Victorian novels under an X-ray, that modern invention, and reveals unexpected patterns beneath the surface of the plot. Nevertheless, the world of *Middlemarch* and of *Bleak House* still strikes most of us as solid and three-dimensional, and Henry James's notorious dismissal of Trollope as principally a novelist of things is in some sense a description of most Victorian novels. The whole vast problem of literary history arises around us as we speculate.

The history of an art seems to me, at least, one of the most complex and baffling branches of historical writing. Once past the obvious truth that all judgments on history are subjective and the equally obvious truth that the arrangements and proportions of any historical work are as much a projection of the judgments, conscious or unconscious, of the writer, as fiction or poetry, we must yet admit that the political historian deals with documents, that by and large the range in which he may interpret character is limited by evidence and tradition, and that his explication of motive has forever to be checked by results that are registered as evidence in libraries. But, as Mr. Appleman's essay reflects, the meaning of a work of art is a far more flexible, a far more shadowy problem. True, no conceivable ingenuity can turn the *Divine Comedy* into a Protestant document, nor *Hamlet* into a comic play. But *Hamlet* has in our time been adjudged both Shakespeare's masterpiece and one of his failures, and Beatrice has been turned into everything from fantasy to fact. *Don Giovanni* was originally a comic opera; we moderns have made it into both tragic drama and an allegory of man's fate. There must be something in *Hamlet,* the *Divine Comedy, Don Giovanni,* Tennyson, FitzGerald, George Eliot, and the rest to justify the moderns in reading into them their own values rather than the formal values of the age which produced the work. I cheerfully surrender Alma-Tadema and Sir Frederick Leighton to anybody who wants to explicate or defend them; but shall we say of Sargent, who had genius and not merely talent, that he sold out his genius to the nobility and gentry or shall we say that his superb painting of silks and satins satisfied some inward urge comparable to the thirst for decoration that led FitzGerald to disguise his doubts in an elaborate Persian veil and compelled Tennyson to drape the nakedness of his anguish in a style more elaborate than even that of Malory? We owlishly talk about "levels of meaning" in a work of art; which is the true historical one?

There is an obvious connection between the anguish of relativism expressed in FitzGerald and Tennyson, deprived of the sacramental view by the march of mind, and the cautious, yet unshakable, reasoning of the *Origin of Species.* Possibly, of course, if Darwin had never written, the world would eventually have come to the evolutionary, the relativist view of man. Possibly the critical event of 1859 was not, after all, the publication of Darwin's masterpiece. Biological evolutionary theory could not of itself reduce space and telescope time. That became possible only with the creation of automobiles and airplanes, inventions that have not only thrown the peoples of the world into violent contact with each other but have profoundly affected even the transcendental categories of apperception. Rapidity depends upon the inventing and perfection of the internal combustion engine, which in turn depends upon a particular kind of fuel. Possibly this book should not center on Darwin but on a forty-year-old railroad conductor once employed on the New York and New Haven Railroad, who, boring holes in the earth at Titusville, Pennsylvania, on 27 August 1859, at a depth of sixty-nine feet struck oil at its source and proved for the first time the existence of reservoirs of petroleum within the surface of the earth. The long result of time was to wreck the British coal industry, alter the base of naval power, enable industry to expand, automobiles to run, and airplanes to fly, and eventually to change the relation of Great Britain as a great power to the other nations of the world.

I

Science, Religion, and the Critical Mind

ON

THE ORIGIN OF SPECIES

BY MEANS OF NATURAL SELECTION,

OR THE

PRESERVATION OF FAVOURED RACES IN THE STRUGGLE
FOR LIFE.

By CHARLES DARWIN, M.A.,

FELLOW OF THE ROYAL, GEOLOGICAL, LINNÆAN, ETC., SOCIETIES;
AUTHOR OF 'JOURNAL OF RESEARCHES DURING H. M. S. BEAGLE'S VOYAGE
ROUND THE WORLD.'

LONDON:
JOHN MURRAY, ALBEMARLE STREET.
1859.

NOEL ANNAN

SCIENCE, RELIGION, AND THE
CRITICAL MIND: INTRODUCTION

CIENCE is a word for ever changing its meaning in popular imagination. It still conjures up for us, as it did for the Victorians, the romance of man making discoveries and taming Nature, and like them we take pride in our scientific geniuses. They were also proud of their artisans, as we admire technologists, for translating the scientific discoveries into marketable products. But we realize, as they did not, that the development of science and technology rests on a vast base of institutions. We realize what technological effort is required to transform the brain-child of a team of university or industrial or government research scientists into a mass-produced product; what ingenuity and organization is required to market such products; and what complex investment by banks and corporations is needed to finance new projects. We know how scientific invention is for ever changing the structure of industry and transport—still more the welfare, culture, and way of life—of both highly industrialized and under-developed countries. Today science is part of politics. For better or for worse nation-states have begun to invest in science and technology and to organize them as part of the national power complex.

I

A century ago no such picture could have formed in the minds of the Victorians. Mr. Haines tells in his essay of a country in which science had scarcely begun to be taught, and individual initiative and the demand of the market were expected to supply engineers as well as engineering. That even by 1859 science was still neglected in education was partly due to the difficulty of reforming institutions in an age still rigidly respectful of the law and of vested interests. When a

Fellowship at Oxford or Cambridge was regarded as a private chattel, to deprive a man of which would be an act of pillage and the abrogation of the sacred rights of property, how could educational or other resources be re-allocated to take account of the needs of science? Education, moreover, was connected with the idea of a governing class, and the reformers in the 'fifties were thinking in terms of examinations which would test the abilities of a future Indian Civil Servant rather than of training wage-earning technicians or creating a band of physicists or chemists in universities.[1]

Science, then as now, was feared. Today while we see in it the hope of human welfare, we fear it as the agent of our destruction. But it is not the subject itself but the use to which nation-states put it that we fear. In 1859 the Victorians were hardly beginning to take account of the political and international implications of science, but they were deeply suspicious of its effect upon individuals. Science was suspected of being a moral danger. Ruskin pointed to one type of corruption—the corruption of the craftsman. Newman, and after him Matthew Arnold, pointed to another—the impoverishment of the individual's mind if he were permitted to specialize in science and set aside the liberal arts. But in the popular imagination the greatest danger seemed to be whether science was going to contradict the whole tradition of European thought by substituting a totally different account of what life on this planet had been, was, and ought to be. How could the findings of science be reconciled with the history, the morality, the ideals, and the faith of Christian England? The situation was similar to that in the twelfth and thirteenth centuries, when men were forced to reconcile Aristotle to Christian theology. And this time no Aquinas was born to resolve the crisis.

The *Origin of Species* was not, of course, the sole great dissolver of faith in mid-Victorian England, and we would misinterpret the age if we saw it as such. To see the celebrated controversy between science and religion a century ago in perspective we must stand back from the 'fifties and relate Darwin's book to a tradition of thought already long developed. The *Origin of Species* was simply another stage in the development of the positivist tradition—a tradition that owed something to Bacon but first took shape in the writings of Hobbes, Locke, and Newton. For over two centuries it was to be the most consistently powerful intellectual movement in England. Its most original philosopher, Hume, might expose its limitations; the governing class might prefer pragmatic reform and Burkean principles to Benthamism; the Romantic poets and seers from Blake to Yeats pilloried its methods and conclusions. But positivism called the tune and forced other modes of thought to dance to it.

Positivism was both a method and a disposition of mind. It claimed to be scientific because it applied to human behaviour the methods of inductive and deductive reasoning that Newton had hallowed. The interplay of these methods (which John Stuart Mill sketched in his *System of Logic*) was put forward as the soundest way of discovering truth about all subjects. Today we think of knowledge as a set of different subjects, each with its own discipline; but when in 1852 Cambridge, responding to demands to broaden its curriculum, instituted the Natural Sciences and the Moral Science Triposes, the names reflected the implicit assumption that knowledge was a unity. In the nineteenth century, moreover, science meant pre-eminently the discovery of new laws: great immutable hypotheses necessarily replete with profound cosmological implications. There was nothing new in such extrapolation. From Newton's laws not only had a new physical universe been constructed; psychology and even economics and religion were infused with Newtonian inferences. And so, as each new scientific law in Victorian times was propounded, men tried to apply it to society or the universe. Tennyson, whose sensibility was so acutely tuned to the dilemmas of his generation, was of course doing this when he immortalised in *In Memoriam* the relation of thermodynamics to the ancient tale of the loving purposes of God towards man.

There was every reason why such ideas should take root easily. The eighteenth-century tradition of rationalism had assumed that the words "scientific" and "rational" were synonyms. The business of living in society—of choosing between right and wrong, of choosing your objectives, of choosing between different courses of action, of choosing the means to achieve your goals—was described as a rational, and, as men grew wiser, a scientific process. It was irrational to prefer pain to pleasure; it was ascetic or unnatural to aim at unattainable goals; it was superstitious to perform actions, such as rituals, which were not directed towards a specific end. Circumstances, "other people," and the situation in which you found yourself of course influenced your conduct. But you could prevent circumstances dictating to you by acquiring facts about your situation and inferring—scientifically—from them how best to act. What prevented men from doing this? What impeded the march of mind and the progress of civilization? Ignorance, false doctrine, and anachronistic institutions. Here the positivist disposition of mind deeply disturbed the conservatives and the orthodox: they were faced by something much more sweeping and alarming than a movement for political reform.

At the same time positivists recognized that the social sciences could not hold a candle to the natural sciences when it came to making claims that incontrovertible truths had been discovered. The basic premise about society—that its health and wealth rested on the pursuit of rational self-interest—was said to be implicit in Nature herself and to be confirmed by the most striking achievement in all the social sciences—the body of related conclusions about human behaviour constructed by the classical economists. And yet, difficult as it was to refute these conclusions, the abstract and deductive nature of the argument detracted from its prestige. The conclusions of Bentham or Comte or Buckle were not demonstrable to the same degree as those of Lyell. Lyell's work contained hypotheses in plenty but they rested on facts. Was there a branch of knowledge about human beings that could produce facts of comparable strength and validity?

There was indeed. History had suddenly become a much more impressive study and had acquired a new status. The critical study of sources which the Germans introduced became a science in itself and the material on which the conclusions of yesterday were based was exposed, at the worst as surmise, gossip, travellers' tales, and myth, and at the best as documents which carried a meaning for the original writer and his contemporaries quite different from the meaning which had traditionally been assigned to them by the churches and other self-interested parties. The techniques which Barthold Niebuhr had used on Livy began to be applied to the Bible, and it was these techniques, not the general philosophy of the individual historian, that impressed the English clerisy. Strauss, for example, was no eighteenth-century rationalist: his purpose was to expose the shallowness of the old-fashioned rationalist attack on the Bible: but his Idealist interpretation of Roman-Jewish history was insignificant beside the spectacle of his remorseless examination of every fact, every parable, and every incident in the Gospels. This new scientific treatment of evidence put Biblical history outside the orbit of any but professional scholars, and as a result bewildered and enraged the mass of the clergy in mid-Victorian England.

There was, then, a disposition of mind towards interpreting all natural and human phenomena in positivist terms; and it was continually gaining strength. No single thinker ever set out its assumptions and conclusions in their entirety (though Mill came nearer to it than any). Yet already by the 1830's the study of man could not be undertaken analytically without reference to utilitarianism, classical economics, and associationist psychology; and by the 'fifties the positivist interpretation of the history of man began to take a more formidable shape. Lyell's geology was all grist to the positivist mill, and the idea of development—the idea that the world and all that is in it has radically changed over the centuries and that nothing, not even our knowledge of God, is given once and for all and is immutable—was current long before 1859. Darwin confirmed more rigorously what positivism had for long asserted—that the history of the world is the history of progress and that there was no need of supernatural intervention during the ages to account for whatever had happened. The descent of man was incorporated into the positivist cosmology and the picture painted by the new scholars of Natural History was set up to mock the old picture of Creation which the churches implicitly upheld.

And yet we should be equally wrong to minimise the shock made by the publication of the *Origin of Species*. No doubt Francis Newman, George Eliot, and others had lost their faith because they found Christian morality as preached by the churches deficient. No doubt J. A. Froude and Baden Powell were more affected by the Higher Criticism of the Bible than by science. No doubt Lecky or Herbert Spencer or Clough or W. R. Greg or Matthew Arnold or Browning or dozens of other mid-Victorians who moved on their different paths away from belief in dogmatic Christianity were impelled by many reasons. But Darwin remains a crucial name and 1859 a crucial year. The *Origin of Species* became the foundation of a new history of the world. Colenso's statistical enquiry into the arithmetic of the Pentateuch, which so enraged his brother bishops, was influenced by Darwinism as well as by the Higher Criticism. The issue was not simply whether scholars might re-interpret the Bible but whether the beloved story of man's Creation and the Flood was rubbish. Darwin not only offended the Fundamentalists among all Christian communions (and how numerous they were Mr. Willey's essay indicates) but all those attuned to believing in a world in which God was continually at work in a material way—in a world which He planned. Was Natural Selection part of God's design? It might indeed seem so to men who saw the principle at work in the ruthless competition of the early Industrial Revolution in which the weakest capitalists went to the wall and only a prodigious effort of Self-Help on Smilesian lines could lift a man out of the squalor of the slums. But if this seemed morally repulsive, was not Huxley right in claiming that man's sole hope lay in "combatting the cosmic process" and defeating by his own efforts the blind determinism of evolution? A great chasm seemed to have opened between God and Nature. Darwin introduced the idea that *chance* begot order in the world, and today, whether in atomic physics or in the genetical properties of the nucleic acids, chance still rules in terms of any single individual particle, however much the laws of mathematical probability work in respect of any groups of particles. To the Victorians the metaphysical significance of this situation seemed of appalling importance.

As Mr. Willey shows, it seemed to many of them that God had been banished from the world and that the new account of Creation foretold a spiritual and moral destiny for the human race incompatible with the story of God's dealings with man as depicted in the Bible. Belief in Divine intervention in the affairs of men was widespread and disasters in Nature were often held to be instances of God's justly provoked wrath. How could this be if mechanistic blind chance alone prevailed in the order of Nature? Despite the fact that Darwin denied that he intended to trespass on theological pastures, and despite the fact that he was to dissociate his work from Herbert Spencer's adaptation of the principle of evolution, the churches fell upon him. The rumpus perhaps was inevitable, but it turned out to be singularly unfortunate for the churches. As sometimes happens when the established order in society decides to force an issue and crush a lone danger, the dissident suddenly appears to gather strength from the soil itself and emerges as the leader of an army triumphant with banners flying.

The year 1859 was also the year in which Mill published his essay *On Liberty*. In it Mill confused two distinct propositions, but he confused them with incomparable power and fervour. He argued that all repression and restraint is bad because it frustrates human beings, and can be justified only if it can clearly be shown to prevent a demonstrably greater evil; and that only in a free society can men discover the truth and cherish it. The two propositions are not identical, but small wonder that later, with Darwin's experience before their eyes, the new English intelligentsia was convinced that they were. This intelligentsia, which was gaining power as it filled the Civil Service at home and in the colonies, which was providing teachers in the universities and Public Schools, which was editing and contributing to the growing numbers of periodicals that were such a stimulus to Victorian intellectual life, and which was establishing links in the governing class itself but was in no way dependent on aristocratic patronage, was in no mood to be called to order by bishops and country clergymen. When Darwin made his well known comment that Lyell's support for the *Origin of Species* was heroic in view of his age and his position in society, he underlined one of the main theses in Mill's book: the search for truth and hence the means of progress were being impeded not by the laws but by social pressures, such as the risk of losing respectability, or the pillorying and petty persecution of men in the ancient universities, or the requirement that men should be reticent or even prove their soundness by a prudent display of unction. Sometimes today we detect a strained note, an unattractive overemphasis, in the protestations of the mid-Victorian rationalists, but their plea for intellectual freedom was justified and carried all before it, not solely from the rightness of their cause, but because the treatment of Darwin's work was a simple touchstone. That is why 1859 marked a new phase in the development of positivism and led to the outburst of anti-clerical and rationalist books and articles in the 'seventies and to the secularisation of intellectual life.

II

Undoubtedly the churches had become more sharply opposed to science than they had been a century before. Odd as it may sound to speak of an alliance between religion and rationalism in the time of Hume and Gibbon, the theology of Natural Religion was not unsuccessful in harmonising Revelation and Nature. It confidently assumed that the world of spirit and matter were as one, and rested this assumption on verifiable observation. A hundred years after Bishop Butler published his *Analogy* the evidence no longer seemed so clear. The teleological explanation of Nature and the argument from design no longer carried weight. Yet of the dozen other factors that one could mention, which led to the conflict of science and religion, none is as important as the rise of Evangelicalism. The movement that began with Wesley and revived both the Nonconformist communions and the Anglican Church scorned the value of evidences and proofs and wagered all on the conviction of faith. The question was no longer, "How do we believe?" but "Do you believe?" It reduced the Christian religion to "God's scheme of salvation," an historical-theological account of the Fall, of man's universal need for redemption, of Christ's atoning sacrifice, of man's justification in God's sight by faith in this sacrifice, and of an after-life of reward or punishment. It told this story in simple, literal, and personal terms. The transcendent Father, majestic in wrathful justice, could be propitiated by belief in Jesu, the Son, the pitying Saviour, the sinner's friend—an intensely personal and corporeal God. Evangelicalism transformed practical religion and the nation's morality. By the very simplicity of its Christian message it affected the lives of many people who underwent an intense religious experience—even the lives of many of those who disliked the Evangelicals. But this same simplicity rendered it terribly vulnerable to the new weapons in the positivist armoury; and it is not, I think, an exaggeration to see Victorian theology in retrospect as a tireless, and at times almost desperate, attempt to overcome the appalling weaknesses which this simple faith presented to positivist criticism.

It was vulnerable on so many counts. The piercing Evangelical emphasis upon the figure of Jesus was one, and strange as it may seem, this emphasis is theologically dangerous. Theologians are sophisticated men. They are well aware of the dangers of allowing Christians to suppose that the utterances and actions of the Jesus of the Gospels are the main source of a Christian knowledge of God. For centuries they had relied on the constructions of the Early Fathers and the mediaeval Schoolmen to explain how the figure of Jesus was the Word and how through the doctrine of the Trinity He was related both to the Person of God and to humanity. But the human-divine Jesus of Galilee, through whom Evangelicalism stirred the popular imagination, became an historical, rather than a theological, Person. And suddenly the Churches were faced with a new Revelation: the deductive painstaking reconstructions of the historical figure of Jesus produced by the critical study of the Bible. The quest for the historical Jesus had begun. Those who denounced it were fighting a losing battle. Those like the Broad Churchmen who welcomed it were brought up short against the darker eschatological sayings of Christ; they met these difficulties by depicting Christ as a teacher of morality and, in so doing, they often almost humanised away His divinity.

The Broad Churchmen anxiously stressed the higher morality of the Christian faith because Evangelical doctrine had made serious men doubt it. The Evangelical love of personalized religion had led them to treat the Atonement, according to Frances Cobbe, as a "huge commercial transaction between God and man" in which one acquired "a saving interest in the Blood of Jesus";[2] or alternatively it was described in terms of a spectacular trial at the Old Bailey. In 1856 McLeod Campbell published his *The Nature of the Atonement,* in which he tried to avoid the moral difficulty of God appearing to punish Christ by substituting vicarious repentance for vicarious suffering. But such a technical theological study was hardly likely to satisfy those who were revolted by the injustice of the doctrine when presented in its journalistic form and by the equanimity with which so many Churchmen viewed the doctrine of Eternal Punishment.

Furthermore the popular notion of God visiting His punishments upon His erring peoples, so current in a generation that liked to speak of "judgments" falling upon individuals or nations (or even on wicked cities such as Paris), appeared increasingly simple-minded as historiography (whether mechanistic or Idealist) gave other explanations of the rise or fall of civilisations. We have to remember how many were the parsons and the devout whose own brand of proof was to collect scraps of learning that coincided with their convictions and serve them up piping hot: or who used Scripture almost cabalistically and wrenched Old Testament prophesies out of their context.[3] This kind of Biblical interpretation, common among all denominations, made some theologians try to discard allegory. But they at once came up against historical evidence and were asked to explain how precisely God, when He appeared as Christ, put off his attributes of omniscience while retaining those of omnipotence.

What sign, then, was there at this time of an intellectual challenge by the Church to positivism? Among the first Liberal Anglicans, Dr. Arnold and Hare were dead, Thirlwall and Whately preserved episcopal silence, Stanley was a spent force, Jowett was being sniped at in Oxford; and in retrospect the contributions to *Essays and Reviews* show a lack of intellectual vigour and originality. The Tractarian party lay in ruins, its energies now flowing into ecclesiology and ritualism, and its leaders, such as Pusey, as obstinate in their rejection of the new learning as their Evangelical opponents. There was, of course, the solution to these scientific and historical difficulties that the great Tractarian apostate offered: not to come to terms with them at all—to scorn the Protestant reliance on Biblical facts and triumphantly to turn Hume's scepticism upon the rationalists themselves and to argue that all reasoning rested on inferences of little or lesser probability. In 1859 Newman, in his *Lectures and Essays on University Subjects,* admitted that at times Catholics in the past had been led to question the findings of Copernicus or Galileo or other scientists; but that "after a little time" the Church "had never been led formally to explain the [sacred] texts in question or to give them an authoritative sense which modern science may question."[4] Newman denied that there could ever be a conflict between dogma and science: he quoted Macaulay's dictum that no discovery in science could ever affect the arguments for or against Transubstantiation.[5] To those who asked what grounds there were for being dogmatic about religion if its dogmas were incapable of being verified, Newman answered that the truth of Revelation had been attested by great minds and the onus of proof lay on those "who are introducing into the world what the whole world feels to be a paradox."[6] But whatever Newman wrote at this time was ignored. John Bull dismissed him as a sophist and in 1859 he was at the nadir of his influence. The Church of Rome was distant towards its notable convert. It, too, needed to accommodate itself to evolution and Newman had hoped (without success) that it would adopt his *Essay on Development* as its guide: but the Roman Church has not favoured in recent times selecting one particular apologist and resting its case upon his reasoning. It prefers to state as its main argument that reason and faith can never conflict; and where conflict exists, the wrong social and moral conclusions must have been drawn from the study of man or nature. It was to this argument that Newman had turned in 1859, but it was not until 1865 when he published the *Apologia* and Manning became Archbishop of Westminster that there was a sign of a significant counterattack from that quarter.

In 1859 the new defender of the faith was a man whose cast of mind was the antithesis of Newman's sensitive intelligence. He did not play with the paradoxes of scepticism but rather destroyed rational theology with logic. The previous year Henry Longueville Mansel, a witty Oxford High Church Tory, had delivered the Bampton Lectures in which he demolished the grounds for believing that reason could tell us anything about the contents of either revealed or natural religion. The human mind was an inadequate instrument with which to acquire a knowledge of God. That was why Christian Revelation had to be accepted in its entirety. To pick and choose between different parts of it, to allege that this or that doctrine was especially difficult or unacceptable was folly: when all was strictly incomprehensible, why should any part be more or less easy to swallow? Such boldness brought its reward. Hailed at the time as an intellectual triumph, the lectures were pulverised by Mill in 1865 in his *Examination of Sir William Hamilton's Philosophy*. Mansel (who had edited Hamilton's *Metaphysics* in 1859) replied—and his reply showed the future economist Alfred Marshall, who had just taken his degree at Cambridge, "how much there was to be defended."[7]

But in 1859 Mansel had had to defend himself against an attack from another quarter, and Mr. Sampson's essay analyses the conflict between Mansel and F. D. Maurice. It was a really important debate because it marked a turning point in Anglican theology. To J. B. Mozley Maurice " had not a clear idea in his head"; to Jowett he was "misty and confused"; and Mansel exposed his two main weaknesses, a lack of respect for language and an inability to perceive logical connections.[8] Maurice would never admit that in saying something new he was deviating from the old because he saw theology as a polygonal body of truth and not as a multitude of lines which if orthodox were parallel and met in infinity, and if schismatic cut across the parallels. Often he was more old-fashioned than those he criticised: he accepted Genesis as history and spoke of the history of mankind as having lasted for six thousand years.[9]

Yet by 1907 C. F. G. Masterman was already calling him the greatest thinker of the English Church in the nineteenth century. He was an innovator. Until Maurice theology was still a *propositional* exercise: not conducted, of course, with the same rigour the scholastics used, nor appealing with such a ponderous display of learning to the doctors of the church as had seventeenth-century divines, but nevertheless still a branch of learning which relied on making logical connections between different dogmas, doctrines, or propositions which were contained within a rigid metaphysical system. Maurice held that a theologian's task is not to construct systems but to study the nature and being of God and His revelation to men. He did much to free English theology from its slavish obsession with the doctrine of the Atonement. In place of universal depravity he set the conception that the whole human race had been adopted by God, however sinful individual members of it might be. He related religion to society, not in the sense that Feuerbach and the anthropologists were doing, but in the terms of a theologian who used traditional theological language. Language was half of his quarrel with Mansel: he was saying that if the language of philosophy brought Mansel to the barren conclusion that men could not know God and could only repeat certain formulas of the faith about Him, then philosophy was not a suitable language in which to study God. He tried to divorce theology from positivism. Indeed the core of his dispute in 1838 with Pusey over baptism lay in the fact that Pusey thought of baptism as an event in a child's life and not a symbol of God's relation to man: it did not confer a blessing upon an individual, it was a statement that mankind was permanently reconciled to God. What, too, was his well-known criticism of the doctrine of Eternal Punishment—that eternal has nothing to do with time—but another indication that he was taking the language of theology out of range of the language of positivism?

Maurice was not quite alone. On the second Sunday after Epiphany in 1859, at Cambridge, B. F. Westcott preached a sermon before the university on the miracle at Cana in which he maintained that miracles were not a proof but rather a part of Revelation, since they were not to be thought of as facts but as symbols of the Word.[10] Westcott was then not yet thirty-five and at the beginning of a career in which he was, like Maurice, to teach that Scripture should never be interpreted in literal terms. Seen in retrospect the work of the Cambridge trio, Westcott, Lightfoot, and Hort, together with that of Maurice, was far more important in the development of theology than the immediate response in 1860 of the Broad Churchmen in *Essays and Reviews,* for their work led to the infinitely more revolutionary book, *Lux Mundi,* which appeared in 1889 and which echoed biological evolution by its acceptance of the doctrine of Immanence. Nothing, it was argued in this book, was ever new. God always used what men previously had thought to reveal Himself anew; and He made use of all created beings, infidels as well as Christians, to make His message plain. But Immanence was no more than an echo of Darwin. *Lux Mundi* was another landmark in setting the language of theology quite apart from the language of positivism.

III

The most obvious effect of science upon religion was thus to change the character of theology and hence the character of Christianity itself in England. There were other curious by-products. The development of brain physiology made men speculate whether the mind could exist independent of the brain. On a lower level the lively interest in ghosts exhibited by all classes in society was partly due to the mid-Victorian demand that the truth of all supernatural occurrences, and religion itself, must rest on factual evidence. Then, too, began to flourish sects which used scientific terminology—Christian Science, Theosophy, Spiritualism, and the British Israelites. Their emergence coincided with the rise of a large, leisured, ill-educated middle class in which women were becoming more emancipated and more inclined to show their independence of thought—and how better could they do this in that age of ceaseless religious debate than to embrace a "modern" church, which eschewed the old theology and cashed in on the growing prestige of science?

A less obvious, yet far more important, offspring of Darwin's work was the way in which it revolutionised our ideas of Space and Time. It is difficult for us to conceive how fast men's *imagination* in those days was bound by Europe and European history. For almost a century geology and archaeology had been extending the length of world history and as early as 1836 Boucher de Perthes had argued that mankind and extinct mammals were contemporaries. But not until 1859 was this hypothesis accepted by scholars, such as Falconer and Prestwich, and it was to take many more years before such notions were emotionally accepted. The story of mankind was stamped upon the Victorian imagination in the same images as Ghiberti chose for his reliefs on the golden doors of the Baptistry in Florence. It needed to be supplemented only by the story of Greece and Rome, and the rest was the history of Christian Europe, the centre of the world, which brought the blessings of its civilisation to other continents and rescued them from barbarism.

Darwin upset this tidy and self-contained cosmos. He created a vast new time-sequence in which man played a minute part. He linked man to Nature, and organic matter to inorganic matter, in an unbreakable chain. He gave impetus to the rise of anthropology and soon the history of pre-history man was being written. McLennan and Tylor were evolutionists and interested in showing how savage customs and beliefs could eventually evolve into civilised shape, but they could not help bringing to men's minds simultaneously the idea that at different periods in time people had lived in societies with widely different systems of values and beliefs, these in turn being affected by their economy and status and kinship systems. If this was true of the past, it was equally true of the present. Different cultures could flourish simultaneously. Thus the idea of relativism gained fresh currency.

It had, of course, been given currency by Montesquieu; and relativism was implicit in Romanticism. For long the old positivist assumption that men were much the same in every age—though, to be sure, they were progressing from barbarism to enlightenment—held it in check. When Darwin published his book few doubted that the culture of the present was superior to that of the past, and the culture of England surpassed all others in the present. Yet even among the most noted apostles of progress one could find passages which recognised the separate existence and validity of past cultures. There was Macaulay's famous third chapter. There were the Liberal Anglican historians, who had learnt the theory of cyclical change from Vico, and emphasised that different societies were ruled by different codes of conduct. It had even begun to be fashionable to idealise the past: the cult of the Middle Ages was well under way. And in 1859 FitzGerald published the *Rubáiyát*.

Here was the voice of a totally distinct culture propounding different values and proceeding from different assumptions. Who are we to say, FitzGerald seemed to ask, that the civilisation that is held suspended in this poem, is inferior to ours? The *Rubáiyát* should prepare us for an important modification in the Victorian tradition. Within a few years the Victorians had discovered Hellenism. Both Jowett and Pater wrote on Plato: the difference between them is immense. Jowett followed Dr. Arnold in reconciling the classics to the Christian tradition: Pater, Swinburne, and later Hellenists, such as Lowes Dickinson, opposed the culture of Greece to Christianity. At the same time Pater and Symons painted the culture of the Renaissance. No doubt today these pictures seem to portray a Greece that never was and a Renaissance which (so it is foolishly said) never existed. But they recognised that glorious cultures, in some ways superior to our own, had flourished in the past and must be judged in the light of their own standards. Thus a dichotomy in judgment was set up, and this is the subject of Mr. Appleman's essay, which shows how Darwin's influence reaches out into criticism. Pater had read his Darwin and his work illustrates the dichotomy, which is still alive today. Are we to judge things historically, in relation to their age and to the stage of evolution which they have reached? Or are we to judge them against the standard of our own sensibility—or against the culture of our own age—or against perennial standards of what is good and bad? And, if the last, by what right do we assert that these standards are perennial?

IV

When A. W. Benn published in 1906 his *History of English Rationalism in the Nineteenth Century,* he concluded that the work of positivism had been done: little remained now except to wait for the great structure of Christianity, riddled and undermined, to collapse. But Benn's vision of the unbroken ranks of the Victorian positivist army marching into the future faded, not because of any religious revival, but because the ranks broke.

They broke because the Victorian belief in the unity of truth vanished. In the first half of the twentieth century it became less and less possible to relate one kind of intellectual inquiry to another by means of an all-embracing method, or language, or conceptual system. The *desire* to do so, of course, remained, and the continual recruitment to—and defections from—Marxism has shown how strong the desire and the consequent disillusionment have been. The old positivist contention that all questions ultimately were scientific questions and hence could all be answered in the same terms was challenged by the new philosophy of linguistic analysis. Linguistic philosophy, it is true, began by removing religion from the logic of reason: but today it also asserts that there is no difference between the statements of those who deny the truth of religion and those who assert it. The kind of questions which religion answers are unanswerable, but they are not, as Ayer once argued, nonsensical questions.[11] The urgency with which people ask these questions suggests that the answers which religion gives help some people to *accept* the world just as the explanations which science gives help others to *understand* it. Nowadays it is more difficult to attack the religious for believing in individual propositions: they accept complete notions, and all that can be asserted is that others reject them. Religion deals with the hidden and with what can never be seen, whereas in Victorian times it was thought such things could be seen if only man had a large enough microscope or a less sinful nature. The language of modern literary criticism has also helped to dissolve Victorian positivism: its theory of tradition, its emphasis on modes and levels of argument, and its assertion that the validity of a work of art depends not on its "truth" but on the intensity and seriousness of the artist's vision which create a kind of internal logic in the work of art itself, implicitly reject the existence of a single method of eliciting truth.

The revolution in language and logic led to a change in the status of science. Science bowed itself off the stage. Victorian science was determinist science, and scientists were thought to proceed by collecting facts and inferring general laws from these facts. Today scientists are thought rather to invent hypotheses, test them, retain them until they are shown to be false, and abandon only those which *are* shown to be false. Nor do we believe that the world can be made comprehensible only if every true proposition is also logically necessary. The very complexity of science has also dissolved the metaphysical conclusions of many nineteenth-century scientists. The operations of science, multiplying and sub-dividing at immense speed each quinquennium, no longer permit scientists to make large-scale generalisations about the nature of the universe or of human personality. A Jeans or a Carrel or a Hoyle may dogmatise from physics or physiology that God does or does not exist, but no one seriously contends that such conclusions derive from the scientific method itself. The man who attempts to deduce moral or cosmological significance from Heisenberg's principle of indeterminacy or from the left-handed universe of Lee and Yang is in for a rough passage. The linguistic philosophers no doubt struck at the arguments which derived God from morality or ethics from psychology, and in rejecting the old theories of objective ethics they have rejected what was a favourite defence of Victorian orthodox Christianity. But the same philosophers have made especially devastating analyses of the efforts of scientists, such as T. H. Huxley or his grandson Julian Huxley, to derive an ethical theory from evolution. The ruthless separation of factual or descriptive statements from normative statements has undermined any pretensions which thoughtful scientists may cherish to tell us that science ordains that men should behave in any particular fashion.

The other main breach in the old positivism was made by modern sociology. Whereas the Victorian positivists held that actions which were not directed towards a specific end, such as rituals, were irrational, Weber and Durkheim showed that ritual played a part in many different kinds of social behaviour and that religion fulfilled certain functions in society. They gave no comfort to the Victorian rationalists who predicted that as reason spread her wings, religion must necessarily moult. Certainly they were ominously neutral concerning the "truth" of religion; but they turned rather to examine not whether beliefs were true but what role they performed in society. Simultaneously the rise of clinical psychoanalysis immensely complicated the idea of "reasonable" behaviour in the individual. Henceforth there was always a challenge to so-called scientific political theories, whether Marxist or utilitarian, which purported to deduce from studying social relationships or individual psychology how society should be organised and to what goal or goals is should be moving. It is true that it was long before the full implications of the new sociology were recognised. Many writers in the first half of the twentieth century asserted that social problems could in fact be submitted to "scientific" examination: and when this had been done, their "solution" would then be clear. There was much talk of blundering politicians being reduced to the level of public relations officers and of scientists and administrators becoming the real rulers in society. Traditions, customs, and institutions in their present form were asserted to be impedimenta deliberately used to delay the march of science; and the very real advances which had been made in applying statistical and other scientific techniques to social problems admitted of a neutral, correct, scientific solution. These notions were popularised by sociologists such as Lester Ward and scientists such as J. D. Bernal. But today in the West this kind of scientism is a spent force.

In retrospect the Victorian agnostics scarcely seem to deserve the name: they knew so many things. But one of their predictions has come true. Many professing Christians are today in their beliefs agnostic in the Victorian sense. The word "orthodox" has been drained of meaning. Most Christians today, no less than rationalists, eschew dogma. Theology is no longer a series of interlocking propositions and, in its most abstract forms, it tries to dissociate itself as far as possible from reasoning about phenomena. Tillich's famous statement, "It is as atheistic to affirm the existence of God as it is to deny it" is a measure of the change.[12] Assertions about the Divine must be made, if they are to be accurate, in non-worldly language; and since this is impossible, the words such as Love or Spirit, which we use, are almost more misleading than to use none at all. To speculate about a transcendental God is to denigrate God by bringing Him onto the same level of existence as ourselves. A Mansel come to judgment! Ambiguity is today the essence of dogma: a dogma is valuable if it carries a variety of meanings—just as Empson twenty years ago diagnosed his seven types of ambiguity in poetry. Words about the Divine, therefore, are but a feeble analogy to what is Divine. The Christian scheme of creation and salvation cannot accordingly be pinned down to the beliefs which were defined in popular terms and were current during the past nineteen centuries, partly because they were purely an analogy and partly because they are always evolving and changing their shape; and it is argued that while the great Christian dogmas may be said always to have *contained* the full truth, that truth is never in any age fully *explicit*. Some theologians, such as Reinhold Niebuhr, who are aware of the emphasis which literary critics and sociologists place on symbolism, interpret scripture freely in terms of allegory: others, such as Bultmann, want to strip the New Testament of its myths and destroy the ancient cosmology of Heaven and Hell in order to free Christianity from the accusation that its cosmology is intended in any sense to represent what God has really willed the universe to be.

Protestant theologians have moved away from the propositional religion of the mid-Victorians in two other ways. They are prepared to rely on metaphysicians and anti-rationalist thinkers for the logical structure of their theologies. Kant, whose work was in 1859 so strange and so suspect among English clergymen, was the first foreign philosopher to comfort theologians by providing a new basis for distinguishing between scientific and moral reasoning. Today the chasm between the languages which rationalists and theologians use has grown even wider owing to the use which theologians make of Kierkegaard, Heidegger, and existentialist philosophy. It is asserted, for instance, that no criticism of Tillich's epistemology affects his thought since it rest on an analysis of Being, not of Knowledge, and therefore that there is no point of contact between him and his rationalist critics.[13] Rationalists today often discover that their opponents do not assert what rationalists think that they are asserting, and that they can therefore give no precise meaning to what is asserted.

The use which Christians make of history has also changed. In mid-Victorian times the Churches were engaged on the quest for the historical Jesus—a search which was organised, as it were, on positivist terms. The quest ended in a mire of hypotheses. Many Biblical scholars accordingly shifted their ground and argued that the New Testament was not a record of historical facts providing evidence for what happened in Galilee, but a repository of the worship of the primitive Church; and they follow Westcott's hint in his sermon in 1859 that the miracle at Cana, for example, is an allegory of Christ's relation to the water of the Mosaic Law which is transformed by Him into the wine of the new Law of the Spirit. Other scholars, such as Niebuhr or Butterfield, follow Novalis in saying that all history is an evangel to the truth of Christianity. It is a record of the universality of sin in which all men of all countries are alike involved in the curse of Nazism and Communism and of the brutal inhumanity of the age in which we live and for which we are responsible. To try to gloss over this catastrophic human depravity by practising a religion of good works, of social service and of community chests—the religion of organisation man—is futile.

Such immense activity in re-interpreting theology must be regarded quizzically by the Church of Rome. In 1859 Roman Catholicism was only beginning to emerge as an intellectual force in England. Today it would claim that its stand on all these questions remains *quod semper, quod ubique, quod ab [Ecclesia] creditum est.* Pascal, Bossuet, and the great seventeenth-century apologists gave answers to most of the problems of accommodating Roman Catholicism to new learning. Newman's simple lectures in 1859 stated the position clearly enough. Although there may *appear* to be a conflict between science and religion, and even if the hierarchy of the Church speaks strongly and with the full weight of their authority against some innovating scientist, there can be no real conflict: for either the scientific propositions denied are later found to be true and it becomes clear that the hierarchy did not speak in the full sense in which the Church pronounces judgment, or the propositions are found to be masquerading as scientific and are in fact moral and cosmological—in which case the Church is the sole authority on such matters. It is precisely on this clear distinction between what science, using the working hypothesis of the uniformity of Nature, asserts to be for practical purposes true and the moral consequences of pursuing certain courses of action, that the Church of Rome's pronouncements on birth control or on gynaecology are based. In his lecture on "A Form of Infidelity of the Day" Newman warned his audience of the danger that the practical results which continue to be obtained from scientific research were leading men to be impatient of any other kind of thought; whereas Catholic theology alone could give science "meaning."

But it is one thing to say that the logic of science, the scientific method, the new positivism of linguistic analysis and modern sociology, no longer erect a barrier against religion; whether religion still possesses the same power that it had over men's minds is another. How far has society become more secularised in the past hundred years?

As the inheritors of the Industrial Revolution we live in a society which still enjoys the novelty of ever-increasing production and consumption and in which human beings possess an infinitely wider range of choice in the way they spend their leisure hours. A century ago the choices were fewer and religion was for many the main refreshment from work. It had a long lead over other subjects in the art of popularisation; it provided in sermons, books and tracts serious topics for conversation; in its sects it provided lively in-groups with which people could identify themselves; in its hymn-singing, its lectures by missionaries, and its revivalism, it provided entertainment and release from misery for the poor. Some of the working classes felt the influence of religion, the lower middle classes were permeated with it. By belonging to the Nonconformist communions the poor could protest against the church of the ruling class and the rule of squire and parson; and whatever the faults of the Anglican Church in not accommodating itself to the changed conditions of industrialised society, it was trying to perform the functions now undertaken by a dozen government ministries. Victorian culture was one in which religion was a familiar referent and ecclesiastical influence and power was still a reality. Even so there were sectors where religion did not penetrate. Although Marx argued that the working classes turned to salvationist religion because there was no place for them on earth, the "submerged tenth" lived untouched by Christianity. So did a sizeable proportion of upper- and middle-class rakes, Bohemians, demi-mondaines, artists, and *révoltés*. Mudie-Smith and Booth both showed in their surveys how at the end of the century church membership became more and more confined to the middle classes. Part of the losses which the churches today are said to have sustained were never theirs to lose. If it is said that the churches today are themselves secularised, when, if ever, could popular religion withstand the criticism of deeply religious minds? When, if ever, did religion not suffer from the connection between cash and cant and from political compromise and worldly ministers?

And yet it cannot be denied that society is today far more secularised. Some of the causes lie deep in the social changes during the past century. The class war in Europe led the working classes to think of religion as part of the culture of the ruling classes who used the churches to repress them. The sons and grandsons of those who left the churches have not returned. Religion seems only remotely connected to the major political issues of our time; and as governmental techniques have improved men put greater faith in political action to remedy wrongs. Western liberalism envisages a society with many value-systems of which the churches are but one. And whereas the Victorians sought first to regenerate the individual in order to improve society—and hence were concerned for his soul—we approach social problems in a more depersonalised way. "We dimly perceive," writes Norman Birnbaum, "that our disasters are our collective fault. We are individually and collectively helpless before them but a sociological rather than a theological view of causation dominates our thinking about our fate—even if, as is mostly the case, our sociology is false . . . Our social relations are occasional, fragmentary and instrumental: we can conceive no other pattern."[14] Religion, he adds, is a matter of feeling, as well as knowing, and industrialised society represses emotion so that our inner lives are standardised and depleted: dedication, spiritual inwardness, moral concern, and implication in human tragedy are now as a result almost eradicated. Eradicated or not, the life of the spirit is not associated, as it was almost invariably a hundred years ago, with a religious vocation. This in turn is due to the fact that, when all logical distinctions have been made, it is the impression of life as a whole, and the theories which purport to explain phenomena, that incline men towards or away from belief in religion. Many of the notions which men entertain about the nature and meaning of life are non-Christian: indeed David Lack in his recent work on Darwin continually suggests (even though in logic the antithesis is meaningless) that the conflict between the Christian explanation of life and the theory of natural selection is too striking to be ignored.[15] Similarly speculations about the nature and destiny of man are couched in psychoanalytical or historicist terms which deliberately make no reference to other-wordly concerns. The bright clear light in which Heaven was seen in Victorian times is extinguished, and men see it, if at all, through a glass darkly.

On the other side theologians claim that the first stage of secularism—which was the belief that man was lord of all things—is passing away and being succeeded by the second stage of disillusionment as man finds that he is enslaved by an empty materialism. They point to the fact that three out of five Americans belong to a church, and to a revival of belief among the clerisy in Britain. Part of the difficulty in making an assessment lies in the fact that the religion of the present always radically differs from that of the past yet is always being compared with it: the religion of 1759, for instance, was immensely different from that of 1659. In the end one returns to Newman's assertion that those who deny the truth of Revelation are "introducing into the world what the whole world feels to be a paradox." Do we feel it to be a paradox? That is a question which ultimately each has to answer for himself.

DARWIN AND CLERICAL ORTHODOXY

I do not attack Moses," said Darwin once to his friend the Vicar of Down, "and I think Moses can take care of himself. . . . I endeavour to discover facts without considering what is said in the Book of Genesis." But of course, from the orthodox point of view, this was precisely his offence; he ought to have considered what is said there. Darwin himself never admitted that his theory was hostile to religion, and he often disclaimed all intention of trespassing on theological ground. He had never pondered long or deeply upon "such abstruse questions"—they did not interest him; they were an irksome distraction from the main business of his life. "With respect to the theological view of the question," he wrote to Asa Gray (22 May 1860), "this is always painful to me. I am bewildered. I had no intention to write atheistically." Many years later, referring to a sermon against Darwinism recently preached by Pusey ("Un-Science, Not Science, Adverse to Faith" [1878]), he wrote: "Dr. Pusey was mistaken in imagining that I wrote the 'Origin' with any relation whatever to Theology. I should have thought that this would have been evident to anyone who had taken the trouble to read the book . . . I may add that, many years ago, when I was collecting facts for the 'Origin,' my belief in what is called a personal God was as firm as that of Dr. Pusey himself, and as to the eternity of matter I have never troubled myself about such insoluble questions." A year later still he dictated this reply to an earnest German student who had asked for his religious views: "Mr. Darwin . . . considers that the theory of Evolution is quite compatible with the belief in a God." When the German student returned to the charge, Darwin adopted the tactics which had served him so well throughout life in evading unwanted committees, functions, and invitations: he is old, he is out of health, he is preoccupied, and he cannot spare time to answer unanswerable questions. "At no time,"

51

he wrote to another correspondent (in 1871), "am I a quick thinker or writer; whatever I have done in science has solely been by long pondering, patience and industry. Now, I have never systematically thought much on religion in relation to science, . . . and without steadily keeping my mind on such subjects for a long period, I am really incapable of writing anything worth sending."

I

It would be foolish to blame Darwin now for not having exposed to view more clearly the metaphysical foundations of his theory, but this was exactly what many of his critics did in his own time. Darwin well knew his own strength and his own limitations (as the above quotations show), and for him there lay more than a lifetime's work in the accumulation of facts and observations, the "long pondering" of them, and the construction of hypotheses which would explain them better than they had been explained by previous naturalists. So far from being a controversialist Darwin was a country gentleman of ample means, retiring habits, a well-cultivated Victorian valetudinarianism—and, of course, a passion for natural history so obsessive that it crowded everything else out of his life. To a man so obsessed by his chosen topics, and "enjoying" such poor health ("I *never* pass 24 hours without many hours of discomfort"), it seemed perverse, and very inconsiderate, of his critics to insist upon cornering him with abstract arguments for which he had no time and no aptitude. The *Origin* had not been written in order to attack Moses, or the Church, or Christianity; if it had a polemical aim (and it had), it was to expose the errors of other naturalists—whether, like Lamarck, Erasmus Darwin, or Chambers, they were evolutionists on wrong lines, or whether like Linnaeus, Cuvier, or Agassiz, they held the immutability and the "special creation" of species.

Yet Darwin was widely thought to have banished from the world the idea of God as Creator and Designer, and to have substituted the notion of "blind chance," thus undermining the basis of religious belief and the authority of the Bible as part of that basis. Let us first briefly consider how far the *Origin* itself laid him open to these charges.

The *Origin* contains very few explicit references to the controverted topics. Heretical though its tendency might be, it mostly skirts the metaphysical danger-zones at a discreet distance. Such direct references as do occur, however, were seized upon by the critics and placed in the limelight as central exhibits. True, Darwin argues consistently against the view that species were supernaturally "created" (i.e. created by some inconceivable and unexplainable divine act), either "in the beginning" or at many successive geological epochs. Do the "creationists" (and these included, in 1859, the great majority of his *scientific* contemporaries), really believe, he asks, "that at innumerable periods in the earth's history certain elemental atoms have been commanded suddenly to flash into living tissues? Were all the infinitely numerous kinds of animals created as eggs or seed, or as full grown? and in the case of mammals, were they created bearing the false marks of nourishment from the mother's womb?" (In later editions Darwin apologised for implying that his scientific contemporaries *now* believed such things; he has retained this and other passages for their historical interest, to illustrate what scientists believed before he had converted them.) The main burden of the argument throughout the book is certainly that many facts, inexplicable by the theory of special creation, become comprehensible on the theory of natural selection: such facts, for instance, as those of embryonic development (the foetal paradigm of past history) and the existence of "rudimentary" organs (i.e., organs now useless to the creature). "On the view of each organism with all its separate parts," he says, "having been specially created, how utterly inexplicable is it that organs bearing the plain stamp of inutility, such as the teeth in the embryonic calf [which never break through the gum], or the shrivelled wings under the soldered wingcovers of many beetles, should so frequently occur. Nature may be said to have taken pains to reveal her scheme of modification, by means of rudimentary organs, of embryological and homologous structures, but we are too blind to understand her meaning." The special creation theory, he exclaims with unwonted warmth, "makes the works of God a mere mockery and deception; I would almost as soon believe with the old and ignorant cosmologists, that fossil shells had never existed, but had been created in stone so as to mock the shells living on the sea-shore." Were cuckoos "created" that their chicks might eject the other nestlings? ants, to make slaves of other ants? ichneumon flies, to lay their eggs in the bodies of caterpillars? Is it not "more satisfactory" to regard these and suchlike phenomena, not as "designed," but as minor results of a grand law tending to general advancement—that is, the command: "multiply, vary, let the strong live and the weakest die?" The phrase last quoted sums up neatly what Darwin offers in place of special creation. He offers, first, the tendency of all offspring to vary slightly from the parent stock; next the enormous fecundity of creatures, leading to the Malthusian struggle for existence; lastly, Natural Selection. Nature, like man in breeding domesticated plants and animals, takes advantage of the favourable variations, and suppresses the unfavourable; creatures that happen to put forth variations advantageous to them in the struggle, survive and perpetuate themselves; the rest perish.

But what of the manifestations of Design in nature, to which philosophers and divines had for centuries pointed as evidence of the Wisdom of God? What of the exquisite adaptations of organs to their purpose, of which Darwin had read with approval in Paley, at the time of his undergraduate innocence at Cambridge? What, for instance, of that marvellous and intricate structure, the eye? Darwin freely admits the force of this objection; indeed, he could hardly reflect upon such things "without being in some degree staggered," and he confessed to Asa Gray (1860) that "the eye to this day gives me a cold shudder." Yet Darwin will not surrender. Once admit the constant accumulation of favourable slight variations by natural selection, and all is possible. The eye, like all "beautiful adaptations," was not "designed"; it came about, in the struggle for existence, because variations (beginning in this case, with extra sensitivity to light in some part of a primitive lump of jelly), "if they be in any degree profitable to the individuals of a species, will tend to the preservation of such individuals, and will generally be inherited by the offspring." "Nothing," says Darwin with his usual candour, "at first can appear more difficult to believe," and this sentiment was heartily echoed by his critics, theological and biological alike.

Samuel Butler, Darwin's implacable foe, said that Darwin's book had been mis-named, since *the origin* of species was precisely what had been left unexplained. What had to be accounted for was the origin of variation itself, and this Darwin had ascribed to "chance." It was the substitution of chance for design that caused most of the offence; "Nature" selects the useful variations, from the mass of useless ones, when they *happen* to arise. Darwin admitted that he had often spoken as if variation was an affair of mere chance, though he also believed that in nature nothing happens at random, but only according to the strict determination of physical law. "Chance" is a term which "serves to acknowledge plainly our ignorance of the cause of each particular variation." But "chance" means more than this, as the theologians were quick to point out; if a thing happens by chance, it happens without the conscious purpose or design of an intelligent agent.

We know, from Darwin's letters and autobiography, that he never wholly ceased to be "staggered" by the difficulty of conceiving "this immense and wonderful universe" as the product of "blind chance or necessity," though the difficulty faded as his mind turned, by degrees, into "a kind of machine for grinding general laws out of large collections of facts." He said, in old age, that the theistic explanation was "strong in my mind about the time, as far as I can remember, when I wrote the *Origin of Species.*" This may explain his occasional use, in that book, of the words "God" and "Creator," and his attempt, near its conclusion, to reconcile his theory with religion:

I see no good reason why the views given in this volume should shock the religious feelings of anyone. It is satisfactory, as showing how transient such impressions are, to remember that the greatest discovery ever made by man, namely, the law of the attraction of gravity, was also attacked by Leibnitz, as "subversive of natural, and inferentially of revealed, religion." A celebrated author and divine [Charles Kingsley] has written to me that "he has gradually learnt to see that it is just as noble a conception of the Deity to believe that he created a few original forms capable of self-development into other and needful forms, as to believe that he required a fresh act of creation to supply the voids caused by the action of His laws." . . . To my mind it accords better with what we know of the laws impressed on matter by the Creator, that the production and extinction of the past and present inhabitants of the world should have been due to secondary causes, like those determining the birth and death of the individual. When I view all beings not as special creations, but as the lineal descendants of some few beings which lived long before the first bed of the Cambrian series was deposited, they seem to me to become ennobled. There is grandeur in this view of life, with its several powers, having been originally breathed by the Creator into a few forms or into one; and that . . . from so simple a beginning endless forms most beautiful and most wonderful have been, and are being evolved.

There might be "grandeur" in it for Kingsley and a few other stalwart religious liberals and modernists, but not for the general body of believers and their ecclesiastical spokesmen. For them, in spite of Darwin's semi-scriptural conclusion, it meant the banishment of God the Creator and Designer of the world and of all creatures, the overthrow of the Bible, and the triumph of materialism. For—and here was the most dreadful consequence, to which I have not yet referred— if *all* beings were descended from a few primordial forms, or from one—even if it was "the Creator" who first "breathed " life into them —then Man too must be so descended. Darwin had deliberately refrained from emphasizing this inference in the *Origin;* all he had there said was that, by his own and Herbert Spencer's evolutionary theories, "much light will be thrown on the origin of man and his history." But this hint was enough, and in any case the implication of man's pithecoid descent lay near the surface of the whole argument (to be

developed later in *The Descent of Man,* [1871]). It was immediately
assumed by his opponents that Darwin had robbed man of his proud
superiority, levelled him with the beasts that perish, and abrogated all
his spiritual powers—his free will, his participation of the Divine nature, and his hopes of heaven. Darwin's vestigial theism was no comfort
to them; he had not "attacked Moses," certainly; but if he were right,
"Moses" must be wrong.

II

Let us now try to assess the state of opinion in 1859-60 by examining in more detail some of the immediate reactions called forth by
the *Origin of Species.* In summarising a selection of reviews, sermons,
and articles I shall stress mainly (in accordance with the title of this
essay) the religious criticisms, referring only to the scientific objections
in so far as they are relevant to my theme. It will not be possible to
ignore the scientific objections, since it was by trying to represent his
theories as scientifically unsound that many sought to blunt the edge
of his alleged attack on religion. We may begin with Bishop Wilberforce's notorious review in the *Quarterly* (July 1860).

Wilberforce, after complimenting Darwin handsomely on his
powers of observation and lively presentation, goes on to question the
credibility of his theory of natural selection. There is indeed a struggle
for existence, but there is no proof that favourable variations "ac-
cumulate," or that transmutations have ever occurred. With that
ill-starred waggishness which had recently caused his discomfiture at
Huxley's hands (at the British Association in Oxford on 30 June
1860), the Bishop asks "is it credible that all favourable varieties of
turnips are tending to become men?" The new theory, he goes on, is
based on "the merest hypotheses, supported by the most unbounded
assumptions." "Our readers will not have failed to notice," he complacently adds, "that we have objected to the views with which we
have been dealing solely on scientific grounds." Facts of nature cannot
contradict Revelation, for the God of Nature and the God of Revelation are the same. But errors such as Darwin's are not facts of Nature,
they are the idle play of fancy, and as such they must be condemned
when they tend, as they do, "to limit God's glory in creation, or to
gainsay the revealed relations of that creation to Himself." Man's
place in Darwin's scheme is "absolutely incompatible with the whole
representation of that moral and spiritual condition of men which is
[Scripture's] proper subject matter." Darwin has offered us "a de-
grading notion of the brute origin of him who was created in the image

of God." He may have tried to diffuse throughout creation the working and personality of the Creator, but this kind of pantheism is of no avail; "however unconsciously to him who holds them, such views really tend inevitably to banish from the mind most of the peculiar attributes of the Almighty."

So much for the central (and for many years the leading) spokesman and statesman of Evangelical Anglicanism. The leader of the Tractarian party, E. B. Pusey, who at this time joined hands with Wilberforce against "infidelity," had more important things to say. He had no difficulty in showing that Darwin's argument is incoherent when pressed back into that metaphysical hinterland which was Pusey's native country, but which Darwin regarded as the region of insoluble and boring puzzles. For instance, Pusey does not object to "transformist" theories so long as they leave us God in the beginning; and he grants that Darwin, however perfunctorily, has left us the Creator who originally breathed life into a few forms or into one. Darwin, then, is not an atheist. He does not deny God, but he does something worse: he forgets Him. This is worse than denial, for denial at least implies the presence of the mind of the thing denied; whereas it is of the essence of Darwinism to eliminate God, as far as may be, from our thoughts about the Creation and its history. Pusey connects this loss of spiritual perception—the common outcome of modern science, though not of the older science from Copernicus to Newton— with the narrowing effects of specialisation. He quotes from Newman that "any one study . . . exclusively pursued, deadens in the mind the interest, nay the perception of any other"—an utterance strikingly confirmed by the atrophy in Darwin, sorrowfully confessed by him in later life, of the power to appreciate music, poetry, and landscape (and, we may add, the waning of his power to see and to feel any purpose in Nature). Darwin's inconsistency as a theologian is that he first brings in God to avoid the eternity of matter or spontaneous generation, and then eliminates Him "from all interference with the works which he has made"—a procedure "inconsistent not only with God's revelation of Himself, but with any conception of intelligent Theism." We know, of course, that Darwin never gave a thought to "the eternity of matter," and probably did not realise that this was the logical alternative to "Creation." But this same metaphysical unawareness led him also, almost without noticing it, to replace the absent God with a personification of Nature, or even of Natural Selection itself. True, he catches himself out from time to time, and warns us that he is only speaking metaphorically when he talks of Natural Selection "observing minutely," "with unerring tact discovering each improvement for

further perfecting," and so forth. But he returns so habitually to that
way of speaking, that we feel Pusey to be right in accusing Darwin of
having himself introduced, into the teleological vacuum, a power acting
according to design. The sermon I have been speaking of ("Un-Science,
Not Science, Adverse to Faith") was preached after *The Descent of
Man* was published, and Pusey's central affirmation is that man was
made in God's image, and that human evil springs, not from inherited
ape-qualities, but from the degradation following sin.

From the Free Church side there is the article in the *North British
Review* (May 1860) by the Reverend Mr. Dunns. His argument follows similar lines: Darwin's "transformism" is a romance and a myth;
there is no evidence against the immutability of species. Man can
"select" variations in domestic plants and animals, but it is incredible
that "Nature" should be able to do likewise, even if you personify her
after banishing God from the scene. Darwin, indeed, has reverted to
polytheism. In place of God he puts first, the goddess "Natural Selection," who is able to select, but not to produce, the favourable variations. For the latter she is beholden to another deity called "Chance."
And to explain "exquisite adaptations" without referring them to God,
Darwin deifies the Struggle for Life. "Mr. Darwin's work is in direct
antagonism to all the findings of natural theology . . .; and it does open
violence to everything which the Creator Himself has told us in the
Scriptures of truth, of the methods and results of His working."

The liberal Roman Catholic standpoint is represented by a review in the *Rambler* (March 1860), which takes a high scholastic
line, and, while admitting that Darwin is less deserving of the halter or
the faggot than the grinning Voltaire, the whimsical Monboddo, or the
brutal Robinet, rebukes him severely for the mischief he has done. This
reviewer, as is not surprising, brings into action the heavy artillery of
Aristotle and the Fathers. The notion that living beings have been
formed, not by creation for any final cause, but by the survival of accidental improvements—what is this but the Empedoclean teaching
refuted ages ago by Aristotle in the *Physics?* The idea of development
from one primal organism is a piece of ancient heathen mythology,
and, for Darwin's assumption that all "creationism" means irrational
and arbitrary incursions of supernatural power, what said St. Augus-
tine and St. Basil and St. Thomas Aquinas? God conferred upon the
elements the powers which, through cell or egg or seed, enabled them
to evolve into developed beings. Evolution, then, is (as Pusey also had
said) perfectly conformable with orthodox theology; what is heretical,
is that teaching for which Aquinas censured Avicenna, that these

powers were eternally inherent in matter *without* God. It is useless for advocates (like *The Times* reviewer [Huxley]) to say that Darwin must be met on scientific grounds alone, and that, if his hypothesis is physically plausible, we are not to be deterred from accepting it "by the trifling consideration of its incompatibility with any faith in the spirituality of the soul or the creative action of God." Some new La-grange will one day refute Mr. Darwin, and "deliver us from the mental catastrophe of being forced to believe ourselves to be only developed apes."

In another group of reviews, represented by the *Edinburgh* (April 1860, by Richard Owen) and the *North American Review* (April 1860, by Francis Bowen), we find dissatisfaction with Darwin's speculations on scientific rather than on religious grounds. "We have no sympathy whatever," says Owen, "with Biblical objectors to creation by law, or with the sacerdotal revilers of those who explain such laws." And Bowen, after applying to Darwin what Pascal said of Descartes ("It was his ambition . . . to do without God altogether, but he was obliged to suppose the Deity gave the world a fillip to set it in motion; after which there was nothing more for him to do"), observes that he does not expect science to agree with Scripture; he is "ready to call out with the loudest of the anti-Mosaic geologists, *Fiat scientia, ruat coelum.*" But both these reviewers find in Darwin too much unproved hypothesis, too much "proof" along the lines of "the thing may be so for all that we know to the contrary." Similarly Adam Sedgwick (an eminent geologist who happened to be a Christian as well) accused Darwin (*Spectator*, 7 April 1860) of "deserting the inductive track" ("This is not the true Baconian method"); and of repudiating final causes, thus revealing an "unflinching materialism" and a "demoralised understanding." Against these charges Darwin was defended by Henry Fawcett (*Macmillan's Magazine*, December 1860) and W. B. Carpenter (*National Review*, January 1860). Religious veneration, says Fawcett, will not be diminished by the discovery of the laws by which God has actually worked. Darwin has only done in his own field what Newton did in his: he has studied God's methods, instead of speculating about them in pious ignorance. Carpenter, too, thinks that more honour is done to God by the development theory than by the doctrine of catastrophes and dramatic interventions, and echoes Baden Powell's dislike of those who think we "behold the Deity *more* in the dark than in the light." The *Saturday Review* (24 December 1859) has no qualms, but feels that "Mr. Darwin's views will cause painful anxiety to many who will regard them as hostile to the truths of Revelation." Mr. Darwin will have to tackle Man later, and "we shall demur *in toto*" if he then tries to derive the immortal soul materially.

Only fifteen years before the *Origin,* Robert Chambers' *Vestiges of the Natural History of Creation* had provided a dress-rehearsal for the *Origin,* and had been denounced for its "infidel" tendency. Sir Charles Lyell suffered social ostracism for the "uniformitarian" heresy in his *Principles of Geology* (1830-33), and readers of Tennyson, for a decade before the *Origin* appeared, had been familiarised with the more dismal implications of evolutionary science. Geology, in particular, had for a long time been suspect, and "reconcilers" like Buckland and Hugh Miller had been hard at work trying to "harmonise" Genesis with the "testimony of the rocks." Samuel Butler used to complain that many Darwinians spoke of "Evolution" as if it were Darwin's theory, whereas Darwin's theory was merely that evolution had come about mainly by natural selection. Why, then, all the fuss about Darwin? Let Samuel Butler, an *advocatus diaboli* if ever there was one, give the answer:

Less than twenty years ago [this is in *Life and Habit,* 1878] we never met with, or heard of, anyone who accepted evolution; . . . unless it was that some one now and again said that there was a very dreadful book going about like a rampant lion, called "Vestiges of Creation" . . . Yet, now, who seriously disputes the main principles of evolution? . . . It is not he who first conceives an idea . . . but he who makes the people accept the main conclusion . . . who has done the greatest work as regards the promulgation of an opinion. And this is what Mr. Darwin has done for evolution.

III

The year 1859, or should we rather say the period 1859 to 1862, was indeed critical for orthodoxy. At no other time was its fabric assailed, in rapid succession, by three such blows as it sustained first from Darwin, then from *Essays and Reviews* (1860), then from Colenso's *Pentateuch* (1862). To consider the uproar over the last two attacks would take us outside the framework of this essay. But it is relevant to remark that it was not from Darwin, but from the theological liberals (the Essayists and Reviewers, in particular Rowland Williams, C. W. Goodwin, and Benjamin Jowett), and from Biblical Criticism (Colenso and the Germans) that the Scriptures suffered most. Darwin had not directly attacked Moses; Colenso attacked him out of existence; and Jowett enunciated the terrible doctrine that the Bible should be read "like any other book." If therefore we seek evidence of the strength of "fundamentalist" opinion at this time, it is to the attacks upon *Essays and Reviews,* and on Colenso, that we should look. There is no need to repeat here (and space forbids it) the well-known tales of the prosecution of Williams and Wilson in the Court of Arches for "denying the inspiration of Holy Scripture" (and Wilson, further, for "denying the doctrine of Eternal Punishment"), their condemnation, their appeal to the Judicial Committee of the Privy Council, and their acquittal ("Hell dismissed with costs"); or of the persecution of Bishop Colenso, and his (illegal) deposition by the Bishop of Capetown, for revealing the composite authorship of the Pentateuch and its untrustworthiness as a historical record.

The turmoil and consternation produced by these two *causes célèbres* proves abundantly that, whatever the Privy Council might think, the Church as a whole considered itself bound to the traditional Protestant view of the Bible. It will perhaps be sufficient here to remind ourselves of one or two rather less familiar ecclesiastical pronouncements made at this time or soon after. Canon G. Rawlinson, in the Bampton Lectures for 1859 (*The Historical Evidences of the Truth of the Scripture Records stated anew, with Special Reference to the Doubts and Discoveries of Modern Times*), urged that, though historical criticism had revolutionised our views about *profane* history, yet *sacred* history was free from any admixture of error. The New Testament, and the authority of our Lord, presuppose the historical exactness of the Old Testament; hence any alleged "falsity" in the Old Testament would invalidate Christian theology. The Clerical Declaration, organized by Pusey in protest against the decision of the Privy Council, was signed by about half the clergy of England and Ireland (that is, nearly 11,000); it states that the Church of England,

in common with the whole Catholic Church, maintains without reserve or qualification the inspiration and Divine authority of the whole Canonical Scriptures, *as not only containing, but being, the Word of God* [my italics], and further teaches in the words of our blessed Lord, that the "punishment" of the "cursed" equally with the "life" of the "righteous" is everlasting.

Canon H. P. Liddon, in a sermon in St. Paul's in December 1889, could still proclaim that "The trustworthiness of the Old Testament is, in fact, inseparable from the trustworthiness of our Lord Jesus Christ; and if we believe that He is the true light of the world, *we shall close our ears against suggestions impairing the credit of those Jewish Scriptures which have received the stamp of His Divine authority* [my italics again]."

It was against this sort of inflexibility in high (and lower) places that Huxley launched his famous campaign, in which he made the Church appear to be the last (but tottering) stronghold of darkness and superstition, and Darwin to be the herald of final dawn and deliverance. But the science and religion controversy, dragged into the open by Darwin's doughty champion, ended in a truce: religion conceding that it did not stand or fall by the verbal inspiration of the Bible, and science conceding that it could not pretend to offer a complete interpretation of the mystery of existence. Theologians and divines of more enlarged views (men like Kingsley, Stanley, Church, Westcott, Hort, and the authors of *Lux Mundi*), following the lead given long before by Coleridge and Thomas Arnold, fulfilled the prophecy of Jowett, that Christianity must come to terms with modern knowledge or perish. Fundamentalism is not dead, but (in England at least) it mostly inhabits the Protestant underworld. Though the Church formularies remain unaltered, it is now taken for granted by theologians and by the great mass of believers that Christianity rests, not upon any assailable documents or outworn mythologies, but on the facts and needs of human experience.

R. V. SAMPSON

THE LIMITS OF RELIGIOUS THOUGHT: THE THEOLOGICAL CONTROVERSY

HE essential, the only, the deepest theme of world history and the history of mankind, to which all others are subordinate, is the conflict between belief and unbelief."[1] This celebrated historical judgment of Goethe may serve as a pointer to the main intellectual conflict of the nineteenth century. "The real struggle of the day," wrote F. D. Maurice, "will be not between Popery and Protestantism, but between Atheism and Christ."[2] When Maurice spoke in these terms, he reflected not simply the interests of professional theologians, but virtually the whole of educated opinion. This conflict is, of course, still with us; but it no longer looms large. Whether this springs from the conviction that the battle has been fought and "lost," or whether it springs from a more urgent concern with the threat implicit in the loss of moral confidence characteristic of our time, the result is much the same.

I

The controversy which is the subject of this chapter* was not, it is true, concerned with belief and unbelief. Each of the protagonists was a distinguished theologian, the one a future Dean of St. Paul's, the other among the most revered of Anglican priests. The issue that di-

* The books of this controversy are, in order of publication, Henry Longueville Mansel's Bampton Lectures, *The Limits of Religious Thought Examined in Eight Lectures* (1858); Maurice's *What is Revelation? A Series of Sermons on the Epiphany; to which are added Letters to a Student of Theology on the Bampton Lectures of Mr. Mansel* (1859); Mansel's *An Examination of the Rev. F. D. Maurice's Strictures on the Bampton Lectures of 1858* (1859); and Maurice's *Sequel to the Inquiry, What is Revelation?* (1860).

vided them was fundamentally an epistemological question concerning the limits of religious thought with its converse as to the kind of "knowledge" which Revelation may be said to convey. Yet, if no explicit part is assigned to unbelief in the main dialogue, it nevertheless overshadows the entire controversy as completely as the ghost of the King of Denmark dominates *Hamlet*. If it would be premature in 1859 to speak of Christian belief in retreat, there is no doubt that it was on the defensive.* The attack took a variety of forms. On the one hand, the growth of Biblical criticism challenged the authority of the Scriptures, and led to the denial not merely of miracle as history, but also of the fact of inspiration itself. On the other hand, the growing interest in scientific discovery led to the questioning of the possibility of miracle, of the rationality of prayer to request intervention in a fixed natural order, of the egocentricity of the doctrine of Atonement in such a vastly enlarged universe, and of the compatibility of "sin" with scientific determinism.

The initial response on the part of those who felt their traditional beliefs threatened by this ferment of new ideas was to dig themselves in and yield nothing. On the one side was the trend represented by J. H. Newman and the Tractarians, intent upon safeguarding the faith against the concessions of the liberals. On the other hand were the host of provincial clergy, alarmed and angered by the rationalist criticism, but no less fearful of the Papist heresy that Newman's apostasy opened before them. It was in this atmosphere that Mansel emerged in 1858 with his Bampton Lectures, delivered to enthusiastic if not very sophisticated audiences, as the champion of the threatened orthodoxy. In the words of one admirer, "He was, single-handed, contunding a host of unbelievers . . . and sending them flying before him like dust before the wind."[4] His triumph proved in fact to be short-lived. Although the lectures brought him immediate fame, running through four editions in less than two years, they have long remained undisturbed on library shelves, and the very name of Mansel has been forgotten.† This is a pity, for the lectures are remarkable for the cogency

---

* The change which had come about was graphically summarised by that most rumbustious of Regius Professors, Goldwin Smith, writing in 1861. Observing that in the past twenty years, he had seen the wheel come full circle, he proceeded to contrast the former settling of geological issues by reference to "the double nature of a sacrament" with the present tendency to settle moral and spiritual questions by the methods of physics.[3]

† There have been recent signs of a revival of interest. See particularly the lecture by the present Dean of St. Paul's: W. R. Matthews, *The Religious Philosophy of Dean Mansel* (1956). Also in most recent books on Maurice a chapter is given to the controversy with Mansel.

of much of the reasoning, as well as for the lucidity and force of a fine English prose.

Maurice, on the other hand, who was something of a stormy petrel in contemporary ecclesiastical circles and was finally required to resign from his Chair at King's College, London, not for his "socialism" but for his theology, enjoys today a fame and influence possibly greater than in his own lifetime. Notwithstanding what Maurice himself was later generously willing to concede as Mansel's "immeasurable superiority to me as a disputant,"[5] it is Mansel's severely intellectual contribution that lies buried in oblivion, and Maurice's impassioned self-committal that remains an inspiration to Christians. The substance of this controversy is not new. Its affinities with the conflict between Athanasius and the Arians as to the nature of Christ's divinity have been pointed out. In philosophical terms it closely resembles the perennial dispute between realist and idealist concerning the nature of knowledge. If no strikingly novel arguments emerged, the controversy yet retains life from the vigorous clash of personality and temperament involved. This is not to say that the arguments are no longer of interest, but that the dispute has for us today a sociological as well as a theological interest.

It is not to impugn Mansel's integrity or depth of conviction to stress the fact that as a child of the Rectory, and of a family tradition of military distinction and political Toryism, he had grown up with a set of religious and political convictions devoutly accepted and never in their basic premises subjected to rigorous examination. Because of his rigid personality, Mansel's first-class logical powers could necessarily deploy themselves only in contriving as ingenious and internally consistent a formula as possible in order to leave undisturbed the orthodoxies of the paternal Rectory. The strictness of his character and beliefs found expression in a correct but sincere religious devotion coupled with the defence of a rational argument of some ingenuity, and found relief in a rich propensity for common-room wit that was not altogether puerile. Maurice, on the other hand, presents in almost every respect a complete contrast. He, too, was the son of a cleric, but the resemblance goes no further. His father was a Unitarian Minister. So far from there being any settled orthodoxies, religious turmoil was the rule. And when Maurice himself finally announced his conversion to Anglicanism, the father alone remained loyal to a faith which his wife and daughters had long since abandoned. An awareness of the social gulf that yawned between Dissent (and *a fortiori* Unitarianism at this time) and Anglicanism is a necessary qualification for those who would grasp the ultimate roots of this controversy. More

The Rev. H. L. Mansel

directly relevant, of course, was the psychological effect on Maurice of this extreme religious instability in his immediate childhood background. The Anglican dogmas, to the interpretation of which he was destined to make such a notable individual contribution, constituted for him not simply "correct" solutions of certain intellectual problems; they represented the equilibrium of his personality precariously attained from anguished inner conflict. It is merely to express this same truth from a different angle to say that for Maurice Christianity dictated not simply his view of the universe or the meaning of life, but the way in which he breathed and had his being. Unless we mean by "life" just biological existence, it is no rhetorical hyperbole but the bare truth to assert that for Maurice his life was at stake in this controversy.

The Rev. F. D. Maurice

II

To understand the controversy, it is necessary briefly to summarise Mansel's argument. His principal object is to cut the ground from under the feet of those believers who felt obliged on "rational" grounds to tidy up the traditional dogmas, or, to give it a more polite expression, to reformulate on an eclectic basis doctrines vulnerable to Biblical criticism, scientific arguments, and moral sensibilities. Their error, Mansel insisted, was twofold. On the one hand, by misconceiving the proper role of reason, they had succeeded in confusing the twin spheres of reason and faith. And, on the other hand, they had been misled by the justifiable reaction against Paley's comparative neglect of inward, spiritual testimony to underestimate the importance of the external evidences. The second of these two points may be taken first, since, although it is, in terms of the formal argument at any rate, the lynchpin holding together the entire structure of Mansel's faith, he is singularly uninterested in arguing the case. Asserting that the legitimate role of reason consists of an examination of the credentials not of the *contents* of religion but of the authenticity of the external *evidences* of its Revelation, he is content to list baldly and without argument some fifteen reasons why the claims to authenticity of the Christian Revelation are utterly convincing and to conclude that the entire content of Revelation, whatever the intellectual difficulties attaching to any particular element thereof, must be accepted uncritically as the Word.

The objection to this recommended method of making the articles of faith impregnable to criticism is obvious enough. On Mansel's own admission, we are required to accept in obedient humility such doctrines as the Incarnation, the Trinity, the Atonement, notwithstanding the admitted intellectual difficulties attaching to them, because the difficulties are in fact *ultra vires* so far as reason is concerned. In order to make intellectually acceptable this abdication of reason in the field of revealed theology, Mansel has to show that however disturbing and disappointing this may be to us, we really have no choice in the matter, since reason can do no better for us in the field of natural theology. Here too, of its own efforts to obtain a knowledge of God, it runs up against the same difficulties, namely self-contradictions arising not from imperfection in the Deity but from the limits necessarily inhering in human cognitive powers. Accordingly, relying upon the method of analogy—and Mansel consciously drew encouragement from the parallel with Butler's analogy with our knowledge of the physical world in the previous century—Mansel devotes the main substance of his lectures to an analysis of the theory of knowledge in the specific context of natural theology.

There is no need here to repeat the familiar Kantian arguments on which Mansel relied to show the impossibility of human knowledge of things in themselves out of relation to the cognitive faculties, nor his demolition of Kant's attempt to secure immunity from his general rule for the moral "knowledge" of the practical reason. From this premise, he infers correctly that traditional metaphysics, conceived as the science of the Absolute, the Unconditioned, and the Real, is bogus in the sense that it lies beyond the range of possible knowledge. Hegelian dialectic, which claimed that the human reason is at one and the same time able to contemplate both itself and God, leads directly to Pantheism, which, with its logical annihilation of all distinction between truth and falsity, right and wrong, is as destructive of religion as atheism. "There is no resting-place for a Religion of the Reason," wrote Mansel, "but Pantheism or Atheism."[6] Indeed, Mansel is not without the courage of his logic, and comes very close to admitting that if we "would make man's power of thought the exact measure of his duty of belief,"[7] atheism is the most logically compelling position open to us. His only qualification is the weak argument that the very conception of a limit "virtually" implies the existence of a correlative beyond the limit. It is not difficult to understand the alarm of those Christians who felt less confidence than Mansel in the all-sufficiency of the external evidences, when they realised that their sole rational defence against atheism had been reduced to the content of the adverb "virtually."

If then Reason is impotent to demonstrate the existence of the Infinite, does it follow that scepticism is as admissible in theology as it is unavoidable in metaphysics? Within the confines of natural theology, are there no grounds for any kind of religious belief? Mansel's answers to these questions are not simply negative. In the first place, we cannot ignore the persistence of the conviction that the Infinite must exist. Secondly, we cannot but be aware of significant intimations in the shape of the psychological experience of the feelings of (a) dependence and (b) moral obligation, which together have constituted in religious life the source of the traditions of prayer and expiation respectively. At the same time, we should be on our guard lest we be tempted to infer more than we are entitled from the existence of such intimations. The feeling of awe or dependence in itself tells us nothing of the nature of God, and would justify superstition equally with religion. Even the apologists' familiar "universal consciousness of sin" implies only that the Deity has moral attributes of whose contents we can have only the most rudimentary conception. In short, these twin elements of the religious consciousness are relevant to a sociological explanation of the continuity of religious institutions in human society; they do not invalidate the thesis concerning the limits of human knowledge. On the contrary, they are bound by precisely the same restrictions as is consciousness in general.

Nor, Mansel insists, are these limits in any way transcended by the knowledge we have of God through the Revelation whose evidences prove it to be authentic. The perfect and personal God, of whose existence we have inward intimations, discloses to us through Revelation not His real nature in Himself. *Speculative* knowledge of God's essence is as inaccessible through Revelation as it is through reason's unaided efforts. Our darkness is illumined by Revelation to the extent of permitting us *regulative* ideas of the Deity, which however unsatisfying to our intellect, are nevertheless accommodated by God to the limits of our merely human understanding, and suffice to guide our behaviour. If we do not know what God *is*, at least we are told in what manner we are to think of Him. We must, for instance, believe in the Incarnation, for this is revealed. How this phenomenon was possible, we cannot know, for this is not revealed.

It is not difficult to understand why Mansel has been forgotten. He unites in the style and character of his beliefs qualities that are rarely found together, and which accordingly are liable to impress one as perverse. An agnostic method which evoked the approval of men like Spencer and Huxley could not but give ultimate offence to most Christians. And similarly, Mansel's fundamentalism on the question of Biblical authority was bound to alienate those sympathies aroused by his positivism. Nevertheless, even from the Christian point of view, there is surely a good case for suggesting that Mansel has been unduly neglected. If the main stream of Christian apologetic has passed him by, appeal is still widely made to the argument from analogy, for example, although in rather different form. The analogical argument has enabled theologians, confronted with charges of anthropomorphism, to attempt to disarm their critics by admitting the charge. Since all knowledge is inseparable from the knowing agent, in what sense is theology more anthropomorphic than philosophy or science? Indeed, idealist philosophy, which was in the ascendant at Oxford in the latter part of the nineteenth century, encouraged theologians to neutralize anthropomorphism in theology by asserting a theomorphic doctrine of human personality.

Again, the thoroughgoing positivism of Mansel's theory of knowledge is in no wise incompatible with a deeply religious sense of awe or humility in the presence of the unknown at the frontiers of knowledge. In modern positivist terms, to insist that statements which are neither analytic nor amenable to verification by sense experience are not significant leaves open the question of the status of theological statements. It may be inferred that such statements are necessarily nonsensical or that religious intimations are inexpressible except in antinomian terms. The persistence of the religious impulse in certain familiar forms may with Freud be explained in terms of unresolved childhood neurosis. Or it may with Mansel be given a very different status: "Das Schaudern ist der Menschheit bestes Teil."*

* In this respect Mansel's approach to religious belief might profitably be compared with the work of a modern writer who has made a considerable im-

Nevertheless, when due recognition has been made of the depth of Mansel's own religious sensibilities, it must be admitted that his position was open to the most serious objections from the orthodox Christian standpoint. Orthodoxy would readily have agreed that a God who is understood is no God at all, that a transcendent God cannot be directly apprehended by a finite mind, that much remains unknown and unknowable "behind the veil." There was no wish to claim that the whole truth had been revealed to man, but most Christians considered it absolutely necessary to insist that what had been revealed was authentic knowledge of God as He truly is. The essential question at issue for them turned on the status of Revelation. And this was the point at which Maurice launched his attack. Apart from his contention that the deity must be a personal God, Mansel's unknowable God was as abstract a logical entity as Newton's *opifex mundi,* an entity so stripped of anthropomorphic attributes as to render it immune from rational criticism. A deity so conceived offers cold comfort to those who yearn for knowledge of a God to whom they can pray, who stands committed to certain universal principles, who can be counted upon as an ever-present father, protector, counsellor, and friend. These people see the living, active, and most intimate core of their existence exchanged for a bleak, logical abstraction useful for employment in dialectics. Maurice, in a letter to Kingsley some years after the Mansel controversy, admitted that his own polemic on that occasion had beeen conducted with less calm than was fitting. But he immediately added in extenuation, "But I did feel then and feel now that it is the most important controversy of our time; and that all others must depend upon it."[8]

III

Although Maurice was quite incapable of doing battle with Mansel on his own ground, nevertheless, when the storm had passed, he

pact on Christian opinion. Although Mansel's work was in a different field, his assumptions are very similar to those of Rudolf Otto; and we may be sure that Mansel would have warmly approved Otto's empirical attempt to analyse the nature of man's "creature consciousness" when in the presence of what he termed the *mysterium tremendum* when the boundaries of possible knowledge had been reached. In all Mansel's writing there is conveyed a strong personal sense of the dependence and awe of the individual human soul before the majesty of the inscrutable, Unknown and Unknowable God. The following sentence from Otto could as well have occurred in Mansel's Bamptons: "If a man does not *feel* what the numinous is, when he reads the sixth chapter of Isaiah, then no 'preaching, singing, telling' . . . can avail him" (Rudolf Otto, *The Idea of the Holy,* English transl. [1923], p. 63).

emerged not without honour. There was not only passionate sincerity on his side; there was substance to his case. If he exposed himself unnecessarily to severe and merited rebuke, the castigation administered was of a different order from that inflicted by Newman on the hapless Kingsley.

Maurice is seen to better advantage in private correspondence and in his sermons than in polemic; and the nub of his case against Mansel is nowhere better stated than in a personal apologia to his father in 1832. He is referring to what he sees as the dilemma in the hearts of the prophets, a conflict which is his own, and which can be resolved in only one way without doing violence to the inmost conviction of his being. "God, they knew, must be forever the Unsearchable, the Mysterious. They would not for worlds He should be anything else; for it was the glory of Judaism that their God was not a visible, intelligible idol, but an incomprehensible Spirit. Yet they longed to behold Him, and to behold Him so as they could understand Him."[9] This seeming contradiction, he admits, presents us with a difficulty and leaves us with a sense of mystery. It is awareness of this mystery of the heart, with its persistent demand for the reconciliation of the elements within the paradox, which has characterised "enlightened" men in all ages. There is, he affirms, only one solution that will still the heart's longing and satisfy reason's unease. "If the Infinite Incomprehensible Jehova is manifested in the person of a Man, a Man conversing with us, living among us, entering into all our infirmities and temptations, and passing into all our conditions, it is satisfied; if not, it remains unsatisfied."[10]

The core of the difference between Mansel and Maurice turned on the issue of the status of our "knowledge" of the Incarnation. On Mansel's theory of knowledge, we seem bound to affirm with the positivist (in present-day terminology) that statements of the kind we make about the temporal world, clothed in temporal language, cannot be made about a non-temporal God. On the other hand, Mansel as a Christian *must* make such a statement at the point of the Incarnation. This statement he seeks to immunise from rational attack by claiming that God's revelation in Christ, although the last and fullest revelation, is analogous to previous revelations clothed in symbols borrowed from human consciousness, and is, moreover, not a direct manifestation of God as He truly *is*. For Mansel, the Incarnation, "the manifestation of God *in the flesh*" is "the assumption of a nature in which the manifestation is adapted to human faculties and limited to a mode in which man is capable of receiving it."[11] To Maurice this was anathema. For him, the Incarnation is the complete manifestation of God the Son, who has from all eternity been united with God the Father. This revelation is the means whereby man may know the primal unity which is of the essence and perfection of God, and which underlies reality and alone makes possible our knowledge of that reality. His case is less an argument than an impassioned affirmation; and no paraphrase can give an adequate impression of the force of its imaginative impact. It was not simply that he felt that Mansel's doctrine would lead to a belief in the Bible being substituted for detailed study and assimilation of its message as an inseparable part of "adverbial" Christian living. He felt much the same sort of anger that Kierkegaard directed against "the professor-scientific type" of Christianity and for much the same reasons. Truth is not knowledge of certain propositions, mental conceptions arrived at in a context divorced from the act of living; it is an avowal of the committed spirit of the inward conviction. "Yea, he who defends it [Christianity] has never believed in it. If he believes, then the enthusiasm of faith is . . . not defence, no, it is attack and victory. The believer is a victor," wrote Kierkegaard.[12] "For are there not some persons who preach Faith instead of preaching Christ?" asked Maurice.[13] And elsewhere in praising Jonathan Edwards for his affirmation that the religious thinker cannot rest content with consciousness as his goal, he wrote, "Nothing will satisfy him but *being*. He must rest in One who is; in One who is deeper than his consciousness; if he does not, that will only deceive him."[14]

IV

In an important sense, there is no common meeting ground between Maurice and Mansel. In response to Maurice's assertion that man is possessed of a faculty which enables him to apprehend that which *is*, Mansel challenges Maurice either to state the content of the knowledge that is claimed of the essence of the Infinite, or to demonstrate how in view of the notorious divergence of different individual intuitions we are to distinguish between true and false intuitions. To such a challenge, Maurice can of course make no direct reply. Fundamentally, he rests his case on the appeal to personal experience, which by its universality is susceptible of being shared by all men. The belief in God and the Christian Revelation is squarely grounded in the nature of religious experience. Although Maurice was in no sense an irrationalist, and indeed in one passage in *The Kingdom of Christ* specifically warns against mysticism as something to which "religious men in all ages have been prone,"[15] it is nevertheless clear that there was a strong mystical element in his own nature. The following passage taken from his reply to Mansel, while it describes the experience of mystics of previous centuries, could scarcely have come from the pen of one who was not himself familiar with the kind of experience in question. "At one crisis of their lives they were aroused to feel that they wanted something else than a religion, or a philosophy of religion. One whom they could not see, or who they thought was afar off, seemed to come very nigh to them, to question them about themselves, to bring not their acts and words merely, but *them*, the doers of the acts, the speakers of the words, into His clear and piercing light. The process was terrible. Out of it they emerged different men."[16]

The emphasis on spiritual illumination, a marked feature of the Nonconformist and later the evangelical tradition, was closely matched by a reluctance to ground religious belief exclusively upon external evidences. And whatever misgiving Maurice might have felt concerning the danger inherent in Mansel's position of divorcing theology from the study of the scriptures, it is clear that he, too, was apt to be little interested in the results of critical and historical Biblical research. Neither Mansel nor Maurice is in the least typical of those whose main interest at this time was exemplified in the controversy over the issues raised by *Essays and Reviews* in 1860. But Maurice's impatience with a preoccupation with evidence sprang from motives akin to Coleridge's. "Make a man feel the want of it [Christianity] . . . and you may safely trust it to its own evidence."[17] This attitude among those of devout temperament became even commoner after the close of the century. G. Lowes Dickinson, for example, spoke for many of his generation when he announced his intention of seeking elsewhere than in history to provide a valid foundation for "whatever is really essential in religion."[18]

The difficulty is that when religious belief chooses to rest its claims to truth exclusively on psychological grounds, it lays itself open to the objections which Mansel himself made so forcefully against Maurice. When a personal experience not common to other men is put in evidence, before admitting the evidence as relevant to the issue of truth or falsity, it is necessary to investigate the authority of the person citing the experience. We have no need to resurrect the vehement accusations levelled by Mansel against his antagonist as reasons why he personally could place no confidence "in the credentials of the messenger."[19] But we are bound to raise the question as to why Maurice was such a fierce controversialist, when his opponents were men of integrity, courtesy, and distinction. Maurice never actually alienates our sympathy because of his transparent sincerity and depth of conviction; it is nevertheless necessary to insist on the truism that no man has a monopoly of conviction. And Mansel had in previous controversy with Maurice proved himself to be a generous opponent.[20]

Maurice could have been under no illusion as to the effects of such phrases as "Of all outrages upon philosophical method, and upon ordinary English justice . . . the most flagrant"[21] or "whether it is equally admirable as coming from a Clergyman and a Gentleman, I leave to the author's conscience."[22] Maurice's apologists have generally experienced a certain embarrassment* in handling this aspect of Maurice's polemical style, on which Maurice's reference in a private letter to "Mr. Mansel's Carlton Club and Oxford common-room yawn"[23] throws an interesting sidelight.

Appreciation of Maurice's true greatness should not be permitted to inhibit our analysis of his weaknesses. Maurice evinces a good many symptoms of an inner conflict of which he had only the most limited awareness. John Stuart Mill, who was a shrewd judge of character and who knew Maurice well at one time, attributed to "timidity of conscience" the fact that "there was more intellectual power wasted in Maurice than in any other of my contemporaries."[24] The self-depreciation of the following mode of argument, to which Maurice not infrequently resorts, is not simply distasteful; it exhibits the pathos of unconscious arrogance. "You see how rude and poor my way of arriving at the force of this word is . . . I know that Mr. Mansel's account . . . must strike every one as far more profound and philosophical than mine . . ."[25] or again, "Mr. Mansel, well aware as he is of his own popularity and my unpopularity . . ."[26] He combined an excessive severity towards his own failings with an urge to something closely akin to martyrdom, judging by the desire he once expressed to "earn any of the hatred, which the godly in Christ Jesus receive, and have a right to."[27] It is surely significant that the central issue of the Mansel controversy is identical with that of the crucial letter to his father in which he sought to justify his final abandonment of his father's Unitarian faith. It is clear from what he himself has told us that he felt a measure of guilt both

*Both Dr. H. G. Wood in 1950 and Dr. A. M. Ramsey in 1951 have repeated the story told by Maurice's son in the *Life* (1884) to the effect that Maurice, who had not himself heard Mansel's Bampton Lectures, got an unfortunate impression of them from an account given by Dr. Thomson in conversation. Dr. Ramsey (the present Archbishop of York) in his *F. D. Maurice and the Conflicts of Modern Theology* (1951), p. 72, writes, "But Thomson described the lectures to Maurice as 'the most unalloyed Atheism that had been heard in England for generations'." Yet Dr. Thomson (then himself Archbishop of York) wrote in a letter to *The Times* (3 Feb. 1885), "Kindly give me space to deny that I ever used words so foolish and so utterly unjustifiable." He pointed out that it was inconceivable that he could have used such language of a respected friend, and that he had in fact reviewed Mansel's Bamptons in quite different terms in the *Saturday Review* at the time.

concerning his conflict with his father and over the shame he felt over his Unitarian origins from "mere, vulgar, brutal flunkeyism"[28] as well as from ecclesiastical feelings. To his mother, who was made very miserable through "the most unnecessary fears about all who were dear to her,"[29] he remained always very closely attached. The evidence is necessarily sketchy, but it all seems to point in the same direction; namely, that Maurice's dialectical pugnacity was compulsive and had its roots in unconscious conflict and concordant self-unsureness at a profound psychological level.

It is, of course, indisputable that the truth or falsity of theological statements is independent of the findings of psychological analysis; but it is also true that *in so far as* anyone claims personal experience as the ground of the truth of a religious statement, he necessarily invites very close scrutiny of his authority for such a claim. Each must judge for himself the relevance of the above analysis of one facet of Maurice's character to the problem of assessing the nature of Maurice's religious experience. It is not suggested that analysis of character conflict is an automatic dissolvent of religious belief, or that the "true" role of religious belief must necessarily be diagnosed as a protection against neurotic affliction. In the last resort, Maurice's whole life stands as his authority; and many will doubtless continue to find this in itself sufficient testimony. It is, however, suggested that on balance his personal authority was ultimately weakened by his conduct of the Mansel controversy, notwithstanding his undoubted courage.

V

No discussion of this important controversy should close without some mention, however brief, of its relevance to the mid-Victorian discussion of the status of moral judgments and to subsequent developments in the philosophy of religion. Mansel held, as against Kant, that the moral sense is an *a priori* category of the human mind no less than the intuitions of time and space. He concluded from this that reason has no access to absolute moral standards any more than it has to a knowledge of the Absolute. He further concluded that it is inadmissible to reject Revelation on rational grounds as inconsistent with standards of merely human morality. And with the characteristic courage of his logic, he chose God's instruction to Abraham to sacrifice his son in expiation as the example to point his argument. Or again, if exception be taken to the doctrine of Eternal Punishment on moral grounds, we need to be reminded of the presumption of supposing that we may have knowledge of the relation of Sin to Infinite Justice. To inquire how far any professed revelation is compatible with the Infinite Goodness of God is a task exceeding our rational competence.

The short answer to this argument was made in imperishable form by John Stuart Mill, and cannot be improved upon.* In *What is Revelation?*[30] Maurice's attempt to refute Mansel is ineffectual, but in the *Sequel* he shows that he had a profound awareness of something that is of supreme importance and that lay beyond the severely conservative, formalistic grasp of Mansel's positivism. Maurice is attempting to elucidate the meaning of that idea to which humanity through many ages has consistently, however falteringly and imperfectly, shown such stubborn readiness to respond. Many names have been and will be tried to catch and focus this yearning of the human heart, Human Rights, Humanity, Brotherhood. "They found," he wrote, "there was something in every man which *might*, by God's mercy, be aroused, which *might* testify to him of his own rebellion. We want that assurance more than ever; there is great danger of our losing it."[31] The note he strikes here is peremptory and urgent, and carries with it an authority that no man can gainsay. With the passage of a century the authority assumes added poignancy to a generation whose dangers are greater and whose time is less.

Still, philosophy of religion has undergone such changes of method and emphasis in the course of a century that it is only by indirect means that the Mansel-Maurice controversy can be fruitfully related to the present-day debate. There is a greater disposition to tolerate difference of opinion, partly maybe because Christians are no longer conscious of themselves as a majority in the culture they inhabit, partly because of a greater awareness of the difficulties of persuading a generation steeped in scientific empiricism. It may be that the significance of the 1859 controversy will ultimately be seen as the reaction to an attempt to restate the Christian faith through the vehicle of contemporary philosophy. To Maurice, Mansel's employment of positivist theory of knowledge as a framework for his theology constituted an indefensible opportunism. Similarly, today some Christians look with anxious misgiving upon attempts to employ existentialist philosophy as a means of winning acceptance of the Christian case. The fact that some of Maurice's warmest admirers are to be found among the non-existentialists suggests that fear of anything akin to philosophic opportunism may provide a stronger link with Maurice than existentialism itself.

It was suggested at the outset that among the greatest intellectual changes since 1859 is the diminished importance attached to the belief-

* "I will call no being good who is not what I mean when I apply that epithet to my fellow creatures, and if such being can sentence me to hell for not so calling him, to hell I will go."

unbelief controversy. It might well be argued today that the conflict between a theistic system of belief and a nontheistic system is not one that
need disturb disputants on either side. It is true that a theistic system assumes the reality of a transcendental realm of the spirit, while a nontheistic system holds that the values of love, equality, equity, reason enjoy such reality as they do only in so far as they have been developed
by evolutionary man striving to achieve a meaningful life. But both
systems of belief share a profound concern with moral and spiritual
reality. "But it is also no illusion but uncontested fact," wrote Susan
Stebbing, "that here and now we know that hatred, cruelty, intolerance
and indifference to human misery are evil; that love, kindliness, toler-
ance, forgiveness and truth are good, so unquestionably good that we
do not need God or heaven to assure us of their worth."[32] Is it not this
kind of awareness, with the unqualified self-committal that is entailed,
which is crucial in determining the quality of a human being? Maurice,
although his protest was under inadequate intellectual control, was undoubtedly a committed man in the fullest sense. But so is Jean-Paul
Sartre. "For the secret of man," he writes, "is not his Oedipus complex
or his inferiority complex: it is the limit of his own liberty, his capacity
for resisting torture and death."[33] Although ostensibly this is an empirical psychological observation, it is clear that it expresses something
more, a conviction concerning the nature of the ultimate dignity of
human life. But the supporting metaphysic is atheistic. The fact that
Sartre's rebellion sometimes strikes a note harsh or strident with anger; the fact, we might think, that he lays on the individual a burden
of responsibility that exceeds what is reasonable; these are criticisms
whose source need not be traced to his denial of God. No doubt, compared with the conditions of life in sheltered precincts (in the Carlton
Club and the senior common-room of Maurice's allusion, for instance),
the French Resistance constituted a privileged situation for those who
were able to undergo their experience of the nature of liberty; but
every privilege exacts its price.

At the root of theistic religion there is generally found a conviction, embedded in profound emotions, that man's brief hour has a
significance that is more than contingent, and reflects a harmony with
the ultimate principles of the universe. And those who feel themselves
to be living always in the presence of the Eternal will doubtless reveal that their conviction communicates itself discernibly to their
every behaviour. But those who do not lay claim to such awareness
are not debarred from understanding the impulse that lies behind the
adoration of the Magi, the emotions stirred by the quality of holy
simplicity in Dostoievsky's Prince Myshkin, or from evincing the

speechless, impotent protest of the horrified human soul confronted by the spectacle of Auschwitz or Hiroshima. We need not be theists to make our response. Nor in Matthew Arnold's "crowded streets" is it the theist alone who knows

> A longing to inquire
> Into the mystery of this heart which beats
> So wild, so deep in us—to know
> Whence our lives come and where they go.

Yet, when all has been said, it surely remains true that the differences between theism and agnosticism, between belief and unbelief, are not unimportant. From the agnostic standpoint, two important points suggest themselves. (1) In science, if facts are found to be at variance with the hypothesis, it is the hypothesis that must be revised. In religion, if facts are found which accord ill with the hypothesis, it is the explanation of the facts which must be revised to reconcile them with the hypothesis. The method of science has the merit that it accustoms us to confront the possibility of having to entertain very painful hypotheses where they are the only ones reconcilable with the facts. (2) François Mauriac wrote recently, "Of what use is it in politics to be right and to be always beaten? The Christian faith is sufficient to satisfy my demand for the absolute. In politics I am a pragmatist."[34] For those of less moral courage than M. Mauriac, in modern society where the pressures toward social and political conformity are so all-pervasive, may there not be great dangers in such a dualism? What for Mauriac may be a buttress, may for his neighbour prove an alibi.

And from the Christian standpoint, there remains the crucial importance of the issue which, notwithstanding their deep antagonism, ultimately unites Mansel and Maurice. Both were agreed that the "historical" events from the Incarnation to the Resurrection cannot just be treated naturalistically by techniques adequate to our investigation of all other historical phenomena. But for Mansel these questions were mysteries impenetrable by human reason; they were matters for absolute faith. Maurice, for his part, was so moved by the living testimony of the life and person of Jesus Christ that he felt unable to consent to any theory, epistemological or theological, which would have denied to his experience the status of "knowledge." So earnest was his conviction that the Christian Revelation was *essential* truth that to concede Mansel's argument would have been to abandon himself to universal scepticism. We who can accept neither of these positions and have committed ourselves to doubt rather than to faith do so, not

because we believe we can demonstrate the correctness of our unbelief, but because in the impossibility of knowledge we are morally and
aesthetically most convinced by the vision of man, standing without
illusion, without fear, without guilt, to face with dignity and courage
the unknown.

PHILIP APPLEMAN

DARWIN, PATER, AND A CRISIS
IN CRITICISM

*If we are at a moment of crisis in criticism, it is good to
know what has brought us to it . . .*

HAZARD ADAMS in the *American
Scholar* (Spring, 1959)

AVING made the proper bows to the insights of Kropotkin
and pointedly turned one's back on both the misconcep-
tions of Lamarck and the legerdemain of Lysenko, one need
not argue the point that biological evolution became a scientifically
established fact only in 1859. And one can assume a universal agreement that the philosophical implications of the *Origin of Species* were
both wider and deeper than anything since Copernicus. In the interior
of this civilized area of considered assent, however, I suspect that
there are many unexplored territories needing a new kind of investigation, both patient and bold. Everyone will admit, for instance, that
evolution has "affected" all of us—it has come to shape the very way
our minds work—but this consideration has not greatly informed
the writing of Darwin "influence studies," which have been typically
descriptive rather than analytical, reporting external likenesses or
copyings rather than examining fundamental influences.

The criticism of literature is one of those important areas of human experience affected by Darwin, and it will furnish my instance,
the critic Walter Pater. I shall attempt here to establish that Darwin's
influence on Pater was more significant than is usually assumed; that
this influence led Pater's literary criticism toward two antithetical positions, the impressionistic and the historical; that contemporary criticism has suffered from a similar counterpoise (between the historicism
of "scholars" and what I shall call the impressionism of the "New
Critics"); and that criticism can profit from an examination of Pater's
case.

81

I

Pater had gone up to Oxford in 1859, the "year of earthquake"; as it turned out, all of Pater's undergraduate years at Queen's were shockers: Lyell's damage to Genesis had long since been done, of course, but now Colenso attacked the whole of the literalist's Pentateuch, and the "Seven Against Christ" caused desperate concern among the old guard for the sacrosanctity of all of the Scriptures. The most severe tremor of Pater's undergraduate years, however, was caused by the publication of Darwin's *Origin of Species,* for it simultaneously particularized and universalized nineteenth-century predilections for relativism. Even without the *Origin,* relativism would of course have had a brisk sale in the nineteenth-century marketplace of ideas, but given the *Origin,* competitors were the more relentlessly crushed. Pater, at Queen's, discussed Darwin with his fellow students,[1] with results that were soon to be evident in his thinking and writing.

Pater's first published essay was a discussion of Coleridge (1866); it is clearly the work of a man impressed with the *Origin of Species.*

Modern thought is distinguished from ancient by its cultivation of the "relative" spirit in place of the "absolute." Ancient philosophy sought to arrest every object in an eternal outline, to fix thought in a necessary formula, and the varieties of life in a classification by "kinds," or *genera.* To the modern spirit nothing is, or can be rightly known, except relatively and under conditions. *The philosophical conception of the relative has been developed in modern times through the influence of the sciences of observation. Those sciences reveal types of life evanescing into each other by inexpressible refinements of change.*[2]

Pater had "buried himself in" the philosophy of Heraclitus, Plato, and Hegel at Queen's,[3] but this passage is nonetheless outright empiricism,[4] and the empiricism, furthermore, of a man who has pondered his Darwin.

"It is no vague scholastic abstraction that will satisfy the speculative instinct in our modern minds," Pater went on. "Who would change the colour or curve of a rose-leaf for that . . . colourless, formless, intangible being Plato put so high?"[5] What this attitude means for criticism is clear enough. Pater the post-Darwinian wanted to examine "not the truth of eternal outlines ascertained once for all, but a world of fine gradations and subtly linked conditions, shifting intricately as we ourselves change . . ."[6] It is the duty of the critic, then, "by a constant clearing of the organs of observation and perfecting of analysis, to make what we can of these."[7] (Later in life, Pater put it this way: "In Dante's minuteness of touch there was in fact something of that art of miniature painting . . . Our own delight in it, the welcome we give to minute detail of that kind, uncompromising 'realists' as we needs must be, connects itself with the empirical character of our science, our philosophical faith in the concrete, the particular."[8])

Seven years after the "Coleridge" essay, in the Preface to Pater's first volume, *Studies in the History of the Renaissance,* the full meaning of this empirical, evolutionary view of art is made specific: "Beauty," he said there, "like all other qualities presented to human experience, is relative . . ."[9] This constitutes the challenge for the post-Darwinian critic: once it is admitted that one's perceptions and judgments are relative, beauty itself, which is a "quality presented to human experience," must become relative. The task of the critic, then, is accordingly limited, restricted to subjective statements about particular objects. "To define beauty, not in the most abstract, but in the most concrete terms possible, to find not its universal formula, but the formula which expresses most adequately this or that special manifestation of it, is the aim of the true student of aesthetics."[10] This is the underlying assumption, Pater implies, the starting point, for all post-Darwinian criticism, and he takes his stand firmly upon it: "To regard all things and principles of things as inconstant modes or fashions has more and more become the tendency of modern thought."[11] In an evolutionary world, he proposed that men are obliged to live by "impressions, unstable, flickering, inconsistent, which burn and are extinguished with our consciousness of them."[12] So that life is, indeed, only a "series of moments"; "to a single sharp impression, with a sense in it, a relic more or less fleeting, of such moments gone by, what is real in our life fines itself down. It is with this movement, with the passage and dissolution of impressions, images, sensations, that analysis leaves off . . ."[13]

Anyone even slightly familiar with Pater's work knows that this line of thought will lead to the much-quoted passage on the critic's temperament:

What is this song or picture, this engaging personality presented in life or in a book, to *me*? What effect does it really produce on me? Does it give me pleasure? and if so, what sort or degree of pleasure? How is my nature modified by its presence, and under its influence? . . . What is important . . . is not that the critic should possess a correct abstract definition of beauty for the intellect, but a certain kind of temperament, the power of being deeply moved by the presence of beautiful objects . . .[14]

This is a part—the flamboyant part—of Pater's critical thought; as such it frequently finds its way—along with those other heady clichés of Pater scholarship, the "Mona Lisa" passage and the remarks on burning with a hard, gemlike flame—into textbooks and anthologies. (The recent Wimsatt-Brooks *Literary Criticism: A Short History* [New York, 1957], for instance, "represents" Pater by the "gemlike flame" passage, the above passage on "temperament," and some re- marks on form.[15]) But the part is not the whole, and it seems to me unfortunate to cut Pater thus to a limiting "impressionist" pattern, for in so doing he is denied both his true complexity and the relevance his critical thought could have for our own time.

Pater was more than an impressionist: he was also, and frequently, a historical critic. And just as the *Origin of Species* was an important shaping influence upon Pater's impressionism, so his historicism was also (paradoxically) substantially shaped by Darwin's great work. The word "evolution" was frequently on Pater's tongue: he wrote of the historical "evolution" of the most disparate things—of the state, of the human spirit, of grace, of fictional character, of drama and other works of literature, of sculpture, and of architecture.[16] Pater saw himself as a student of process, of a changing, developing world. He called himself at one time a "student of *origins*" and spoke of the "stages" of art and poetry.[17] In his first book he had asserted that "There is . . . an element of change in art; criticism must never for a moment forget that 'the artist is the child of his time'";[18] and in a late essay he pointed out the necessity of placing a document "as far as possible in the group of conditions, intellectual, social, material, amid which it was actually produced if we would really understand it."[19] Although Hegel inspires this comment, and Heraclitus automat- ically comes to his mind, Pater indicates that there is also—and powerfully—in the background "Darwin and Darwinism, for which 'type' itself properly *is* not but is only always *becoming.*" "And the Darwinian theory," he goes on, "well! every month is adding to its evidence. Nay, *the idea of development . . . is at last invading one by one, as the secret of their explanation, all the products of mind . . .*"[20] Thus Pater from first to last maintained a conscious linkage between the force of the evolutionary idea and the necessity for the historical approach.

This general evolutionary-historicism underlies Pater's historical criticism in particular, and those scholars who have recognized this complexity in Pater's criticism[21] have sometimes seen it as one term in a basic dualism that required metaphor to describe adequately. Sir

Caricature of Walter Pater by "Spider"

Maurice Bowra, seeing in Pater both the "aesthete" and the "thinker," put this dualism in terms of "a friend of Circe" on the one hand, and "his bulldog breed" on the other;[22] and Lord David Cecil pointed to Pater's "apple green tie" and his contrasting "broadcloth" as symbolic of the same dualism.[23]

The "friend of Circe" and the "apple green tie" in Pater represent his much-publicized tendency toward aestheticism and impressionism. The "bulldog," the "broadcloth" side of Pater is what anthologists and historians have not given full credit to: that is, his historicism. Recently the very existence of Pater's historical criticism has been, in fact, denied: "During the latter part of the 19th century," says the Wimsatt-Brooks *History,* "the aesthetic movement . . . took a contemplative, static view of individual art works and so was antihistorical."[24] For Pater this comment could hardly be more wrong. He recognized that historicism was the characteristic method of his time, and he thought this quite proper. "Nothing man has projected from himself is really intelligible," he said, "except at its own date, and from its proper point of view in the never-resting 'secular process'." And again: "every intellectual product must be judged from the point of view of the age and the people in which it was produced."[25]

Thus Pater could speak of the poetry of Homer as the product, "the almost mechanical transcript of a time, naturally, intrinsically, poetic, a time in which one could hardly have spoken at all without ideal effect,"[26] and he could call Ronsard's poems "a kind of epitome of his age."[27] Pater spoke of the style of an age, the spirit of an age, and the temperament of an age, and pointed out how these affect the art of their times.[28] His particular criticism of certain earlier scholars was that they were not historically minded: "They lacked the very rudiments of the historical sense, which, by an imaginative act, throws itself back into a world unlike one's own, and estimates every intellectual creation in its connexion with the age from which it proceeded. They had no idea of development, of the differences of ages, of the process by which our race has been 'educated'."[29]

Walter Pater, then, represents a critical dilemma, a dilemma fostered by his empiricism in general and his awareness of Darwin in particular. The horns of the dilemma are his impressionism and his historicism, each of which, to be consistent, requires the exclusion of the other. For if one undertakes to be an "impressionistic" critic, to ask, "What is this work of art to *me*?" then one has in fact forbidden oneself to assume also the mantle of historicism and say, "Every intellectual product must be judged from the point of view of the age and people in which it was produced." Faced with the dilemma of having to give up the one or the other, however, Pater could not choose. I propose that this indecision was a natural result of his Darwinian conditioning and that this is, as I hope to show, a significant fact. But I propose also, as I turn to a brief discussion of contemporary criticism, that this indecision was actually a saving grace for Pater's criticism—and that criticism in our time can profit by understanding this and by understanding the Darwinian roots of its own dualistic concerns.

II

"The past century has seen critic after critic quarrel with every assumption or method of modern criticism, including every type of knowledge that might be brought to bear on literature . . ." "Criticism . . . is no better than a Sunday park of contending and contentious orators, who have not even arrived at the articulation of their differences." "Although the archaeological and quasi-scientific and documentary study of literature is still the dominant one in our universities, it is clear to everyone that scholarship is on the defensive and is ready to share the rule with its antagonist [criticism]." The speakers are Stanley Edgar Hyman, T. S. Eliot, and Lionel Trilling, respectively,[30] and although they are not talking about exactly the same thing, the consistent tenor of their remarks bears upon what I am about to say. For the theory and practice of criticism have been under unprecedentedly close scrutiny during the last century and have, in the last forty years or so, been the subject of much intense debate and the object of much sincere expostulation.

Debate over literary theory has never caused storms of popular controversy and the crisis under discussion is no exception; it has managed nicely to contain its tempestuousness within the pages of academic and "highbrow" periodicals. Nevertheless, like so many issues which seem to be "only academic" (in both senses of the term), this debate has been an important one, for it concerns a significant area of human experience and in that area it has probed some fundamental questions. For those whose business is criticism, the situation is familiar enough, but a brief review is no doubt proper in a book of this kind. Easily the keenest and most interested controversy among critics in the last quarter of a century has been that between the scholars or historians of literature on the one hand, and, on the other, those critics whose emphasis is on literature *"as* literature." The "scholars" are described by one of the "critics" as being men who

know the threads of factual and intellectual history which connect some English poet with the incidents of his own life, with the "thought" and "interests" of his age, and with contemporary and earlier poets in the same "school" or "tradition." It will probably occur to us that they seem ordinarily to stop with knowing these connections; they do not use their historical learning for the literary understanding of the poet, and so the rather disparaging tone in which they are often referred to as simply "historical scholars."[31]

The "critics" do aim at this "literary understanding"; for my example of those so concerned I shall take that vaguely-associated group of American critics known as "New Critics"* (and particularly from among them Cleanth Brooks, Robert Penn Warren, and W. K. Wimsatt, Jr.).

These men frequently emphasize their attention to the literary work as such rather than to what have been called "extrinsic"[32] matters. One of them, Mr. Wimsatt, has gone so far as to assert that "the critic is not interested in questions of authenticity."[33] His analysis of the "intentional fallacy" has become a keystone of the New Criticism; here it is briefly summarized by Brooks: "to ascertain what Marvell the man thought of Cromwell, and even to ascertain what Marvell as poet consciously intended to say in his poem [the "Horatian Ode"], will not prove that the poem actually says this, or all this, or merely this. . . . There is surely a sense in which any one must agree that a poem

---

* Two other men who have been influential in insisting upon criticism as "literary understanding" are F. R. Leavis, whose antagonism to "mere" scholarship has been frequently and vigorously stated (see, e.g., The Common Pursuit [1953], pp. 9-10, 33, and 35), and Ronald S. Crane, whose early (1935) distinction between the scholarly and the critical methods is the most thoroughgoing one I am aware of.

> The essential thing about the understanding to which the literary critic aspires is that it is understanding of literary works in their character as works of art. It is not criticism but psychology when we treat poems or novels as case-books and attempt to discover in them not the art but the personality of their authors. It is not criticism but history or sociology when we read imaginative writings for what they may tell us about the manners or thought or "spirit" of the age which produced them. It is not criticism but ethical culture when we use them primarily as means of enlarging and enriching our experience of life or of inculcating moral ideals. It is not criticism but autobiography when we content ourselves with stating our personal preferences with regard to them or the adventures of our souls in their presence. Criticism is not any of these things; it is simply the disciplined consideration, at once analytical and evaluative, of literary works as works of art. ("History versus Criticism in the University Study of Literature," English Journal, XXIV [1935], 654.)

Both Leavis and Crane, however, are historical scholars in their own right, and it would therefore be unjust to use them as examples of a single pole of the dualism I am trying to develop.

has a life of its own, and a sense in which it provides in itself the only criterion by which what it says can be judged."[34]

Brooks has been perhaps the most insistent of the New Critics— theoretically, at least—on this point. To treat poems, he says, "primarily as poems is a proper emphasis, and very much worth doing. For we have gone to school to the anthropologists and the cultural historians assiduously, and we have learned their lesson almost too well. . . . I have been primarily interested in the specific view taken in the particular poem, and interested in how the attitude of the poet was made to inform the poem—and not primarily interested in historical or psychological generalizations about the poet's mind."[35] Throughout Brooks's writings the words *"as a poem"* repeat themselves like a theme, a watchword. Like other New Critics, he attempts to judge and to judge "objectively." "For better or worse," he says, his judgments "are rendered, not in terms of some former historical period and not merely in terms of our own: the judgments are very frankly treated as if they were universal judgments."[36]

Working upon these assumptions, the New Critics have examined the "structures" of poems, their "textures," their "tensions," their imagery and symbolism, their diction, their rhythms, and so on, and have produced analyses of which they are understandably proud. "Critical writing like this is done in our time," John Crowe Ransom exclaimed over a quotation in *The New Criticism.* "In depth and precision at once it is beyond all earlier criticism in our language."[37]

The "scholars" readily admit that "extrinsic" researches are not themselves the end-products of literary study. Geoffrey Tillotson, a distinguished scholar, makes the point without embarrassment: "The student who has acquired the historical knowledge but has nothing else to show is, of course, no critic: we call him a scholar."[38] On the other hand, the scholars insist, one cannot properly be a critic of any literature of the past without "extrinsic" knowledge. Their argument with the textual critics is basically an ontological one: "The question is always arising: What is the real poem? Is it the poem we now perceive? Is it the poem the author consciously intended? Is it the poem the author intended and his first readers read?"[39]

The historical scholars' answers are categorical, though not uniform. F. W. Bateson emphasizes the poet's "first readers": "to understand a poem's meaning to-day we need to be able to identify ourselves as far as possible with its original readers, the poet's contemporaries, whose ideal response to the poem in fact constitutes its

meaning."* Tillotson is no less insistent, though his emphasis is different: he makes "the bold assertion that the original meaning of a word
in a great poem is the only one worth attending to. . . . To read later
emotions here and there into a poem is a tedious error in criticism
. . ."⁴⁰ He puts a strong case for this attitude in discussing a great critic
of another age: "I have referred to Dr. Johnson's dissatisfaction with
that famous speech of Macbeth which, because it employed the 'low'
words *blanket, dun* and *knife,* struck him as ludicrous. In our turn
we see Johnson as ludicrous. When we discover the reasons for Johnson's laugh, ours changes to regret that a critic should have allowed
such merely contemporary reasons, however forceful, to throw away
anything of 'Macbeth' for him."⁴¹ A printed work is only "sacrosanct,"
then, Tillotson says, in a very particular way; that is, "sacrosanct for
what it originally was: not for what it may accidentally have become
by the time that it is our turn to examine it. What is sacrosanct is not
the appearance of the work at any point on its curve of fame, but the
work as it lay complete before that curve began its rise, the work as
it lay complete under the sabbath eye of its author."⁴²

With these as basic assumptions, it is clear that two things are
necessary. One is the (historically) accurate text of the work; the
other is a "feeling" for the author's "age." David Daiches has summed
up the "scholar's" case forcefully:

If, in seeing *Hamlet,* we appreciate its dramatic structure and its poetic magnificence while, at the same time, seeing it as the work of Shakespeare the
Elizabethan, are we being aesthetically wicked? A work of literary art,

---

* *English Poetry: A Critical Introduction* (1950), p. 78. Cf. the notable
controversy between Bateson and John Wain in *Essays in Criticism,* II (1952),
105-114. Wain, taking issue with Bateson's historically-derived interpretations of
a number of phrases (especially "dark Satanic mills") from Blake's "Jerusalem,"
complains that "The lines themselves would never, in a thousand years, yield
this meaning; it has to be supplied from the outside." Bateson replies, "Aesthetically [Wain's] interpretation [of "dark Satanic mills" as "a nineteenth-century
textile factory"] may perhaps be preferable to Blake's, but if so it derives its
beauty from the historical accident that Mr. Wain was born *after* the Industrial
Revolution, whereas Blake was born before it. There can be no question of
Blake or his original readers giving 'dark Satanic mills'—in however muzzy or
subconscious way—the sense that Mr. Wain prefers. . . . It is not, of course, a
crime to rewrite Blake [but then] a literary classic is made the pretext for what
is essentially an original creation." Wain then offers a compromise position: that
the critic should "create and maintain a balance between the 'original' and the
'developed' significances, and by this difficult act . . . recognize that subtle tension which is the mode of existence of a work of literature." But Bateson remains adamant: "In the last resort, Blake's readers must choose between Samson's mills [Bateson's proposal] and the steam-driven textile factories."

which, because of its richness, its use of so many elements of expression, can be so many things at once, is often, also, a work of history and of auto-biography and of moral philosophy; and its impact on us is the more profound because it is all these things. In appreciating a work of art, we have only one ear cocked for "internal consistency," for the purely "formal" aspect.[43]

Clearly we have arrived at an impasse. It is one which I have in a sense contrived, for the rival manifestoes are not often juxtaposed, these days, so starkly and uncompromisingly as I have just done. Very recently, Jacques Barzun has even denied that there is any operative difference between the two groups.[44] There is nevertheless real usefulness in stating the opposing views at their most single-minded, for one can arrive at no proper arbitration without first knowing accurately the basic demands of both parties to a dispute.

III

The significance of Pater's dilemma to twentieth-century criticism is perhaps already obvious, and it will surprise no one if, to draw my moral, I align Pater's historical criticism with the work of the men I have referred to as "scholars." To parallel his impressionism with the New Criticism, however, might be, as Matthew Arnold once put it, to knock some astonished heads together. Relevant and important similarities there are, though: the tendency to deny the historical; the tendency to stick with those facts which are important "to *us*," to write "from a point of view";[45] the tendency to emphasize the critic's "sensibility" (a term that takes us back through Eliot to Rémy de Gourmont and thereupon to Pater and the Aesthetic movement[46]); and the tendency to arrive (sometimes almost triumphantly) at insular conclusions about literary works.

This last is a serious charge, and I feel obliged to expand upon it. That Pater's criticism was "personal" needs no further comment. Yet his aim was always to find the "formula" of an author's work—an example of the way in which the "objective" frequently tempered the "subjective" in his criticism. Pater's dilemma, I have proposed, involved the logical incompatibility of his impressionism and his historicism; yet, curiously, Pater did sometimes profit by this dilemma. His success is apparent in many of his most valued essays, but the abstract method which underlay this success is nowhere so obvious in his published work as it is in an unpublished draft of a letter to him from "Michael Field" (ellipses indicate cancelled readings):

we enjoy the lectures & care to follow you as you become the contemporary of Plato . . . Your . . . historical criticism is in deep . . . accord with our newly-awakened interest in the Present—as the point where life flashes into meaning & . . . an attempt to seize the vitality of its own present in any moment of the past . . .[47]

Clearly this is an expansion of what Pater meant when he spoke of the "historical sense" which "by an imaginative act, throws itself back into a world unlike one's own." It is this attempt to "become the contemporary" of the authors he studied that is so frequently over-looked, but which makes Pater a model for what I am about to propose.

Pater has long been a whipping-boy for twentieth-century critics who pride themselves on being "objective" in their work. But paradoxi-cally these very critics have, all the while, been making a case for a critical neo-subjectivism. For criticism cannot exist without context. Whether we choose the author's environment as the context for critical assumptions, or simply use our own, these assumptions are neverthe-less inevitably made in context. Thus when Cleanth Brooks asserts that his critical judgments are "universal," he is in reality expressing a pious wish rather than committing the critics of the twenty-first cen-tury to his position.

If I may put the whip in the hand of the victim for the moment, I would suggest that Pater, while insisting upon seeing with his own eyes, attempted to train his vision to see what the object made it proper to see; whereas the New Critics, in their attention to the object "as object," have tended to ignore insufficiencies in their viewing apparatus. Pater's "objectivity" has thus been too often underestimated and the New Critics' "subjectivity" has not, I believe, been enough remarked upon.

Responsible men in the camps both of the scholars and of the New Critics, however, are now satisfied that the claims of each deserve seri-ous consideration by the other. This revelation has been taking place gradually over a period of years, and it displays, in microcosm, a gen-eral rule of many serious and reasoned arguments: that whatever the bitterness of the disputants, as the position of each side is stated, re-stated, refined, and insisted upon, the other side recasts its arguments, admits (albeit sometimes in disguise) parts of the opponent's argu-ments into the formerly puristic position, and ends by realizing that the two are, after all, agreed upon many essentials and opposed chiefly in matters of emphasis.

Such has been the progress of the scholar-New Critic debate. Brooks and Warren's valuable textbook, *Understanding Poetry*, may serve as a barometer, the reading of which was low indeed in 1938, when the authors denounced biographical and historical materials, among other things, as "substitutes for the poem" and "confused approaches to the study of poetry," and called for emphasis "on the poem as a poem." But twelve years later the weather of criticism was less blustery: "the critical attitude [has] entered into hundreds of classrooms," Brooks and Warren reflected, and they adapted themselves to this new condition: "though we continue to insist upon the need for a sharp focus upon the poem itself, we have tried to relate criticism to other literary studies. Specifically, we have attempted to view the poem in relation to its historical situation and in relation to the body of the poet's work."[48]

Earlier this year Hazard Adams remarked that "The appearance of histories of criticism by new critics, and even historical analyses of the new criticism, come as somewhat of a shock."[49] The shock can hardly be genuine, however, for the moderating climate has been evident for some time now. Brooks, for instance, proposed to a professional literary association more than ten years ago that "the critic needs the help of the historian—all the help he can get . . ."[50] And Wimsatt has more recently expressed his concern to "define and vindicate the role of history in criticism."[51]

What I want here to suggest, in view of this amiable tendency for each of these antagonists to recognize the claims of the other, is that we have not yet reached a reconciliation sensitive enough for the complexity of the subject. Surely such a mechanical relationship as that suggested by words like "the role of," "the help of," and so on, are not what is needed. One does not, in the study of literature or the arts, simply build a foundation of the blocks of scholarship and then erect upon this foundation a structure made from the timbers of criticism. What criticism needs to develop, I propose, is a pervasive and abiding "sense of the past." Literature, even that written yesterday, is a historical phenomenon, and this is a fact as important to the critic as to the scholar.[52] A comment of Trilling's is relevant: "In the New Critics' refusal to take critical account of the historicity of a work there is, one understands, the impulse to make the work of the past more immediate and more real, to deny that between Now and Then there is any essential difference, the spirit of man being one and continuous. But it is only if we are aware of the reality of the past as past that we can feel it as alive and present."[53]

In our time awareness of the "reality of the past as past" is inevitably conditioned by Darwin's revolutionary proposals of 1859. Loren Eiseley's recent book, *Darwin's Century* (New York, 1958), makes this point more convincingly, I think, than it has heretofore been made:

In Darwin's century . . . the unique and unreturning nature of the past began early to evince itself. . . . Without anyone's being able to say just why,
the struggle for existence which people had been examining for a century
or more was suddenly seen by a few people almost simultaneously to be a
creative mechanism. Basically—and this reached great intensity after Darwin—man was adjusting himself, not just to time in unlimited quantities,
but rather *to complete historicity, to the emergence of the endlessly new.*
His philosophy was to include, henceforth, cosmic as well as organic
novelty. It is not enough to say that man had come into possession of time,
or even of eternity. These he had possessed before in other cultures, but
never with this particular conception of on-goingness. *To see and to re-
create the past, to observe how it has come to mold the present, one must
possess the knowledge that all things are new under the sun* and that they
are flowing in the direction of time's arrow never to return upon their course
—that time is noncyclic, unreturning, and creative.[54]

Not only Pater but other post-Darwinian critics have, now and
again, reflected this awareness. The American critic Lewis E. Gates
spoke, in 1900, of the critic as separated from his object by "a vast
gulf of time," but achieving, by "imaginative sympathy," not simply
the artist's original "mood," but a more complex response which depends upon "all the gains the spirit has made since the earlier age."[55]
And T. S. Eliot stressed the idea of aesthetic "contemporaneity" in a famous essay of forty years ago, "Tradition and the Individual Talent."
Coming perhaps closer than anyone else to the truly post-Darwinian
sense of the meaning of time in criticism, Eliot stressed "a sense of the
timeless as well as of the temporal and of the timeless and of the temporal together" as the proper background for "aesthetic, not merely
historical criticism."[56] Trilling's more recent essay, "The Sense of the
Past" (1942) is a still more full-bodied development of the point I am
trying to emphasize. The poem, says Trilling, "is the poem as it has
existed in history, as it has lived its life from Then to Now, as it is a
thing which submits itself to one kind of perception in one age and another kind of perception in another age, as it exerts in each age a different kind of power. This makes it a thing we can never wholly understand—other things too, of course, help to make it that—and the
mystery, the unreachable part of the poem, is one of its aesthetic elements."[57]

This complex of related ideas has not made spectacular headway,
but it is a hopeful sign that it is at last invading the critical quarterlies
themselves. Writing in a recent (1958) *Kenyon Review,* Roy Harvey
Pearce calls for a "new" historical criticism which would "establish
between ourselves and the literary work a direct, existential relation-

ship. . . . This historicism assumes that the past, by virtue of its very pastness, becomes an aspect of the present. In effect, a literary work carries the past into the present . . ."[58] All of these voices imply that "the poem" is the first and ultimate object of scholarship, but nevertheless they remind those who speak of a poem as "having a life of its own" that the life of one poem is not the life of another, and that, when critics put the poem on the couch for analysis, they must remember that it is important to find out what happened during its childhood and throughout its life.

A critic must be constantly aware of both his responsibility to history and the promise of history when considering an aesthetic product, or his attention to other, more "intrinsic" matters will yield less than it might. This proposition was as much the case before 1859 as it is in 1959; but I hope my exploration of Pater's critical dilemma has helped to establish that since the philosophical revolution of the *Origin of Species*, our recognition of the problem has been made both more inescapable and more auspicious. From simple beginnings, Darwin wrote in concluding the *Origin*, "endless forms most beautiful and wonderful have been, and are being evolved." This concept, so commonplace in 1959, is what broke upon the world-mind of 1859 with such shock and such revelation; it was one of the reasons Pater's criticism became neither a vapid impressionism nor just one more variety of nineteenth-century historicism. Pater's "attempt to seize the vitality of its own present in any moment of the past"—as "Michael Field" put it —is the critic's response to the *Origin*, just as its counter-statement represents Darwin's scientific, descriptive awareness translated into the evaluative terms of Pater's scholar-criticism: "there is something verily worth having, and a just equivalent for something else lost, in the mere effect of time . . ."[59]

There is a fusing agent in the theory of evolution, a welding power that blends present with past in causal and meaningful relationships and forces us to be more aware of the multiplicity and yet the interrelation of all sorts of experience. The post-Darwinian critic simply does not have the option of being "either" isolated and personal "or" historical and traditional; nor may he stack the one on the other like building blocks. If any metaphor will do at all, it is what Eiseley calls Darwin's "sweeping vision" of all forms of life: we are "all melted together."[60] The responsible critic must keep past and present, tradition and texture, history and imagery "melted together," for it is not any one of these alone, but all of them at once, which make the power and richness, the value, of the work of art.

The Prince Consort, who died in 1861, was one of the few men in high places who was alert to England's need for scientific education.

GEORGE HAINES, IV

TECHNOLOGY AND LIBERAL EDUCATION

N SEPTEMBER of 1859 Prince Albert, the Royal Consort, presided at Aberdeen over the meeting of the British Association for the Advancement of Science. Educated on the Continent, the Prince had early recognized the threat which the development of scientific technology by the Continental universities presented to Great Britain's industrial leadership. In his presidential address, one of his last public utterances, he noted that in the past science had had to beg for any assistance given by the government. He continued:

> We may be justified in hoping that by the gradual diffusion of Science, and its increasing recognition as a principal part of our national education, the public in general, no less than the Legislature and the State, will more and more recognize the claims of science to their attention; so that it may no longer require the begging box, but speak to the State like a favoured child to its parent, sure of his parental solicitude for its welfare; that the State will recognize in science one of its elements of strength and prosperity, to foster which the clearest dictates of self-interest demand.[1]

But the hope of such paternalism by the state in Britain was at that time vain. Science, its technologies, and even education were still regarded as undertakings for individuals, voluntary societies, or the churches, and the danger to the state from their neglect, which the Prince perceived, was ignored save by a few. With the bitterness of hindsight, Sir Richard Gregory, the editor of *Nature,* wrote in 1928: "How vastly different the course of British history might have been had the Prince Consort lived, say, another twenty-five years."[2]

In the decades after Albert's address Prussia consolidated the states of Germany into the Second Reich. The competition which the new empire offered in power and in all that contributes to power in the modern world—in education, science, and technology, in industry and trade, in imperial aggressiveness and war-making capacity—precipitated the crisis for Great Britain which the Prince had foreseen. Distrustful of any centralized supervision of their affairs, and devoted to permitting individuals the freest possible choice in ordering their lives, the English people faced an educational dilemma.

The dilemma stemmed from the conflict between the need in a liberal democracy for an education that would enable men to think for themselves as individuals and citizens and on the other hand, the growing demand on the part of the state for professional and technical men who would require a highly specialized training. The dilemma was not peculiar to Britain; it was common to all democratic states. But it became critical for Britain and France first because of the challenge posed by Germany. Since 1914, as one state after another in Eastern Europe and Asia has adopted Western technologies but rejected liberal democratic ideals, the same dilemma has become critical for all the states of the West. What was yesterday a crisis for Britain and France is today a crisis for all liberal democratic nations.

I

Historically, the principal promoters of education have been the churches, the dynastic state, and the liberal democratic state. Roman Catholicism had fostered and spread education; Protestantism had universalized it. Eventually the dynastic state protected and utilized education for its own purposes as a training for the officials of justice, the civil service, medical service, the army and navy. In the eighteenth century the democrats of France and the United States conceived of the educational "ladder," an education graded from the primary school through the university, designed for all men and open to all. The French Revolutionaries founded a national school system, an Ecole Normale, and an Ecole Polytechnique to propagate the democratic conception of the state and to advance a knowledge of science and technology. Napoleon returned the schools to the Church and closed the Normale, but continued the Polytechnique.[3] The state had preempted the sciences and technologies for its own use.

Later in the century, when the power of Germany had become evident, Lord Acton remarked that in organizing the University of Berlin for the Hohenzollern state of Prussia Wilhelm von Humboldt had "forged the link between science and force."[4] No lover of force, what Acton probably had in mind was more precisely stated a few years later by a less critical admirer of the Germans. John Theodore Merz, himself educated in a German university, wrote: "The German nation may pride itself on possessing . . . the most powerful and best equipped army . . . With greater pride it may boast of having trained in the course of centuries the largest and most efficient intellectual army . . . Wherever the progress of learning and science requires a large amount of detailed study inspired by a few leading ideas, or subservient to some common design and plan, the German universities and higher schools supply a well-trained army of workers, standing under the intellectual generalship of a few great leading minds."[5] Suggestive as this is, it may yet be inquired: in what new sense had learning become power?

Any concentrated concern with theory, as theory, may be of intense intellectual interest, but intellectual interests are of social importance only as they become the guides or auxiliaries of social action. In the mid-twentieth century the tremendous power generated by technologies founded on the theoretical sciences is clear. But this sort of power is relatively recent. It is true that the idea of acquiring power through theoretical scientific knowledge was current in English and Continental thought from at least the time of Bacon and Descartes, and the technological application of scientific theory was frequently, if intermittently, made earlier than in the nineteenth century, but only then did the rate by which theoretical knowledge was transformed into technologies and inventions become sufficiently rapid to assume major social importance. The tempo of this process was so remarkably accelerated in the course of the last century that Whitehead declared the greatest invention of that century to be "the invention of the method of invention."[6]

Until the 1850's, invention had proceeded side by side with scientific investigations with only occasional overlappings. The early inventions were largely, though not exclusively, the product of trial-and-error artisans; science, on the other hand, was the product of independent theoretical speculators and inspired amateur experimenters. The method of using one in conjunction with the other continuously and purposefully had been but slightly developed,[7] since the method of invention implies an organized and systematic investigation of the implications of scientific principles in order to determine their possible use for specific economic or social ends.

Several things are prerequisite to this. First, there must be a body of established theory from which the implications can be deduced. In the middle of the nineteenth century a large body of new principles was being established. Second, there must be both a body of sound technical procedures and extensive laboratories for the training of large groups of men in the theoretical principles as well as the standardized experimental procedures. These men are the technologists. From among them a few men of genius may emerge, but for the most part they remain technologists. Since rather less abstract imaginative power is demanded of them than of workers at the highest theoretical level, more can qualify. Working in groups under intelligent direction, tenacity and some imagination will enable them to obtain such results as are possible within any given theoretical framework. During the second and third quarters of the century the technological procedures were being rapidly standardized and laboratories constructed, not only in the universities and technical schools but also for the very purpose of founding industries based on the new technologies. Finally, there is required a still larger body of men capable of supervising and applying the newly discovered techniques in industry. These are the technicians, and since less abstract imaginative power is demanded of them than of either of the former groups, even more can qualify. The technologists and technicians together constitute what in Merz's words the German universities and higher technical schools were especially designed to produce: "a well-trained army of workers, standing under the leadership of a few great leading minds."

Although early starts in developing the method of invention had been made by the English, Scots, Dutch, and French, from whom the Germans gained their earliest insights, it was the Germans who brought the method to perfection.[8] This was not a cultural accident; the process appears as a characteristic off-shoot of German culture. When the scientific influences from the West entered the Germanies, the latter were rigidly institutionalized societies. The more important cultural institutions, especially of Prussia, reflected the organizational imprint of the army, and the army accustomed the nation to the pattern of hierarchic rank and systematic gradations of authority and obedience. The Prussian bureaucracy, developed in the late seventeenth century to supply the army, remained "the most enduring achievement of the absolute monarchy" and "survived all the revolutionary changes of the nineteenth century." Though the missions a bureaucracy is called upon to perform and the nature of its training are obviously different from that of an army, the similarity of the structural organization is apparent.[9] With the army, the bureaucracy represented the model of professional services in German civil life.

These two great state institutions necessarily exerted a strong impress upon the people, for no German failed to come into continual contact with one or the other. Both inculcated the necessity for training and the advantages of education in a hierarchy. Both inculcated that respect for titles, rank, and authority so characteristically German. The rigid class structure had the same effect, and this was again reflected in the educational system with its lines of division between the *Volksschulen* and continuation or trade schools, the *Realschulen* and higher technical schools, and the gymnasia and universities. State-supported and state-supervised, with all teachers, from the elementary schools through the universities, trained members of the state bureaucracy, this carefully graded system was based upon compulsory education to the age of fourteen, followed by two years of military training, and often by subsequent trade or technical instruction.[10]

The systematic gradation of ranks with corresponding duties and responsibilities was promoted also by another important element in German culture: German idealist philosophy. What lay perhaps at the heart of this culture, other than the dynastic will, was an overwhelming belief in the necessity for order, for systematic arrangement, flowing from an ineradicable faith in the importance of theoretical knowledge as a guide to practice, a faith taught by every major German philosopher.

All of these, the army experience, the bureaucratic regime, the markedly class structure of society, the carefully designed system of education, a belief in the systematic unity of knowledge, contributed to a cultural situation favoring the invention of the method of invention. When the German students learned in Leyden, Paris, or Upsala of the experimental method and with it the need for weight and measure, upon their return to their own universities they sought at once to formalize or systematize this new method of study, to create true disciplines in the German sense (*Wissenschaften*), in which students might be accurately trained to become their assistants in research and train yet others.*

By the third quarter of the century all the world acknowledged German supremacy in science, technology, and scholarship. To her university laboratories and seminars went the best students of America, the Continent, and England. The rapidity of German industrial development was one of the world's wonders and it was particularly notable in the industries dependent upon technology and engineering. Her military strength was unrivalled. By the end of the century the British were well aware of the challenge posed by the Germans.[11]

---

* It was not a mistaken wit who dubbed Justus von Liebig's teaching laboratory, founded at Giessen in 1824, which became the model for such laboratories the world over, "a factory for the manufacture of chemists." That was, in fact, its greatest significance; it was the educational equivalent of the production line in industry. (See Sir William Tilden, *Famous Chemists* [1930], pp. 191-192; cf. Merz, I, 188 and note.)

How alien all this was to the English of the 1850's! By comparison England then had nothing remotely deserving the name of a national system of education. Her universities were composed of undergraduate colleges. Her numerous original men of science were, except for a few trained on the Continent, usually brilliant amateurs. Scientifically trained technologists were rare. Only the foundations were being laid for a professional bureaucracy and there were few recognized professions of any kind.[12] The army, in which commissions were still purchasable, was without a general staff and was hardly an army in the Continental sense.

II

The "era of reform" of the middle decades of the century represented in Britain an effort to adapt the practices and institutions of the past in such a way as to fit the needs of the new industrial techniques. This was crucially important to the British because of the industrial competition they had to meet from the United States and Germany. An unexpected result of the Great Exhibition of 1851, for example, was the recognition of the high quality of American technical enterprise by British engineers. They looked with astonishment upon three of America's mass-produced items which were soon to capture the English market: the sewing machine, the revolver, and the mechanical reaper. The next year the American firm of Colt established a plant in England, equipped with American machinery, to manufacture revolvers. The British engineer Sir John Anderson commented: "It is impossible to go through that works without coming out a better engineer."[13] In 1853 George Wallis, an official of the Department of Art and Science, and Joseph Whitworth, a leading engineer and iron manufacturer, were commissioned to attend the New York Industrial Exhibition. Visiting many factories, they were particularly impressed by the machine tools used in manufacturing interchangeable parts at the Springfield Armory and elsewhere. English purchases of small arms and of the machines for making them promptly followed. The American invasion of English industrial life had begun.

Among the reasons advanced by British observers for America's great technical progress, one was to be repeated year after year "as fundamental in its industrial growth":[14] the practical education "which was common in America," and especially in New England. A writer in the *Edinburgh Review* in 1853 (XCVIII, 190) inquired, "If America with all her accessions from natural growth and immigration, cannot afford to lose the mine of intellect hidden in the popular masses . . . can England, comparatively stationary in growth and population, afford such loss?" Whitworth and others were convinced that England could not and urged the establishment of a national system of compulsory education.

What was called the "great Education question" was not new in Britain in the 'fifties; it had been under discussion since the reform movement of the 1820's. But for nearly three decades the only steps taken were half-measures. Beginning in 1839, the Government annually contributed funds to the two voluntary societies, Anglican and Dissenter, which operated elementary schools. An occasional master, such as Thomas Arnold, made reforms in the Public Schools; a few of the colleges of Cambridge and Oxford were improved by the masters and tutors. University College, London, and King's College, London, were founded, though the hopes of the Utilitarian and Scottish founders of the former to establish a teaching and examining university on the model of the University of Berlin were frustrated by the creation of the University of London as simply an examining and degree-granting body.

Obstruction to educational reform resulted partly from religious rivalry, partly from the inertia and complacency of most educational authorities, partly from class snobbery, and partly from the real ignorance of even the best educated of all classes of the implications of the rapidly advancing technologies and sciences. A few—political radicals, Nonconformists, and men educated in Scottish universities—urged reform and extension of education because of the glaring deficiencies. A very few, such as Edward Bulwer (later Bulwer-Lytton), having glimpsed the importance of scientific technology, supported Charles Babbage, William Brewster, and other scientists in urging greater attention to the sciences. But after the Great Exhibition a new awareness of the importance of education for a technological industrial society placed the whole question in a new and more critical context.

If technical competition was to be feared from the West, technological competition was also to be feared from the East. Immediately following the Great Exhibition Prince Albert drew the attention of the Commissioners for the Exhibition to the danger of Continental competition.

The improvement in locomotion, the increased means offered by science . . . have lessened the peculiar local advantages of certain nations . . . The nations most likely to afford a public recognition of this fact are those whose fuel and raw materials are chiefly derived from other lands, and who can therefore only carry on a successful competition by continually economising and perfecting production by the applications of science. It is accordingly in those countries, as in France and Germany, that we find entire systems of education devoted to those who are charged with industrial pursuits. . . .

But as in England the progress of science is daily equalizing more the distribution of raw materials, and depriving us of those local advantages upon which we may have been too much accustomed to depend, it is an obviously growing necessity that it should afford its manufacturers the means of acquiring that knowledge without which they cannot long keep foremost in the struggle of the nations.[15]

Already, as Chancellor of Cambridge University, the Prince had stimulated educational reform there. He had aided in founding the Royal College of Chemistry where, under the direction of the German August von Hofmann, a whole generation of English chemists received their training. The success of the Exhibition, in no small part due to him, furnished him with a new opportunity. With his aides Henry Cole and Lyon Playfair, he founded a Department of Science and Art under the Privy Council, and made a permanent organization of the Commissioners for the Exhibition of 1851 to promote scientific education.[16]

However, the Department of Science and Art, like the Department of School Inspection under the Privy Council, could do little within the inadequate schools. The schools were too few in number: thousands of children were wholly without education; attendance was irregular; and students left at too early an age.[17] But the necessity of educating the masses to assist the country's industry, to combat "juvenile delinquency," and to prepare for the immanent extension of the suffrage, already under constant agitation in Parliament, became widely recognized.[18] Strongly influenced by the American example, associations to promote free, compulsory, non-sectarian elementary education were founded—significantly in the industrial centers of Manchester and Birmingham.[19] After numerous bills to promote elementary education failed of consideration, a Royal (Newcastle) Commission was appointed in 1858 to investigate the subject. In 1859 Matthew Arnold was in France and Mark Pattison in Germany to study the schools for the Commission.

When action was finally taken by Parliament to provide elementary education, it was due, more than has been generally understood, to the need and demand for technical instruction for the workers. In the 1860's Matthew Arnold noted the widespread demand.[20] And if the Education Act of 1870 awaited the Reform Act of 1867, it awaited also the Report of the Select Committee on Scientific Education, resulting from the Paris Exhibition of 1867 when British goods "were beaten in everything."[21] Following its report, public meetings were held in the principal cities of Britain to promote technical education. In introducing the Education Bill of 1870, W. E. Forster, after noting the examples of the United States and Germany, argued that elementary education was a necessary preliminary to technical education for the workers.[22] That a major purpose of the bill was to achieve this is further supported by the fact that it simply arranged for public provision of elementary education, where it was not already available, for the laboring population. It was not designed to replace existing facilities, nor to provide for the middle or upper classes.

Though as early as the 1850's the need for a compulsory and national system of education was urged, not until A. J. Mundella's Act in 1880 was the former achieved. As for a national system, even of the Act of 1902 a recent English historian of education observes: "Although it would be an exaggeration to claim that the Act created a national system of education, yet one can justifiably assert that it laid the foundation on which a system could be built."[23]

The greatest advance made during the second half of the century in education beyond the elementary level for the working class was the provision of technical training schools. Usually night-schools, these were founded as employers awoke to the necessity of meeting foreign competition. To have met the critical need for a scientific and technological education, which the Prince Consort and a few of his collaborators clearly saw by 1859, much more fundamental alterations in secondary education would have been required than any made at any time during the century.[24] In July of 1902 a committee, appointed by the London County Council to investigate the application of science to industry, reported "That the main causes of the relative failure of British manufacturers in the chemical, optical, and electrical industries were (a) the lack of scientific training of the manufacturers themselves and their inability to recognize the importance of scientific assistance; (b) the defective condition of secondary education and the lack of sufficiently prepared recruits for advanced technological training . . ."[25] Part of the responsibility for this must be attributed to the educational ideals of Oxford and Cambridge. For the great Public Schools, which principally prepared men for the two ancient universities, adapted their program largely to that end, and they set the standards of secondary education generally.[26]

III

The concept of liberal education originated, both as theory and practice, in the colleges and universities founded under religious auspices. Based on a study of the Christian faith in some one of its varieties, and upon Greek and Latin literature, college or university education was designed for an élite of class, intellect, or wealth. Its ideal was the preparation of men for positions of leadership in religion or the professions. But where the professions or guilds ceased to control standards of admission or established their own separate training institutions, as in Britain and the United States, and as training for the ministry ceased to be the principal object, liberal education increasingly implied an education limited to training for general intelligence. In the words of John Henry Newman, "This process of training, by which the intellect, instead of being formed or sacrificed to some particular or accidental purpose, some specific trade or profession, or study or science, is disciplined for its own sake, for the perception of its own proper object, and for its own highest culture, is called Liberal Education."[27]

Under the dominance of the Anglican Church, Oxford and Cambridge in the early nineteenth century only indifferently forwarded this ideal aim. The university professors had been almost eliminated from the educational program by the colleges, through their control of large endowments. Celibacy was required of the college tutors, whose hopes for advancement resided principally in securing a church living. Subscription to the Anglican creed was required for matriculation at Oxford and for degrees and emoluments at Cambridge. Greek and Latin, with mathematics and a little "natural philosophy," a theoretical study of the natural world, constituted the curriculum.[28] The products of this education were clergymen, who occasionally became scholars, and amateurs able to adapt their talents with varying degrees of success to anything or to nothing.

Support for the curriculum appeared between 1830 and 1860 in the Tory statements of Adam Sedgwick, William Whewell, J. H. Newman, and E. B. Pusey.[29] They sought in part to revitalize university education from its eighteenth-century complacency and neglect. But a larger part of their intention was to counter the efforts to compel basic changes by Utilitarian radicals and their Scottish allies, and by the Broad Churchmen or Liberal Anglicans. Since the universities were a part of the Establishment, the question of university reform usually took the form of a conflict among the Churchmen.

As with Coleridge and Thomas Arnold, the Liberal Anglicans found stimulation in German scholarship in philosophy, history, philology, and Biblical criticism.[30] Their knowledge of German work and German universities made them critical of their own, especially of the lack of professional standards of research and criticism and of professorial teaching. But it made them conscious, too, of the role of the universities in the national state, to which, as well as to the students and the church, the universities, as the center of its intellectual resources, had a responsibility. "There is nothing I less wish than to see Oxford turned into a German . . . University," wrote Benjamin Jowett. "On the other hand, is it at all probable that we shall be allowed to remain as we are for twenty years longer, the one solitary, exclusive, unnational Corporation . . .?"[31]

When in 1850 a Dissenter and Radical moved in the Commons that a Royal Commission be appointed to inquire into the state of the universities, and Lord John Russell finally complied, the Liberal Anglicans had triumphed.[32] The Commissions recommended reforms, and action was taken. After the new regulations became effective in 1857, some of the worst institutional abuses were eliminated and the intellectual life of the colleges was generally stimulated. Thereafter, the two ancient universities at least provided ambitious boys of the upper and upper middle classes with an education designed to produce capable public servants. The immediate result was an increase in the matriculations at both universities, the number for the first time rising to and surpassing levels which had been attained two centuries earlier.[33] Something was done for Dissenters, but very little for the improvement of science instruction, although both had been recommended by the Commissions.[34] And, as Mark Pattison noted, one particular abuse, the system of idle fellowships, which had existed before as an irregularity, was legitimized, and the financial resources of university education were allowed to drain away for another quarter of a century.[35]

Not only the universities, but many professions as well, were reformed in the 1850's. The Crimean War, marked by the use of new technical instruments, the railroad, telegraph, steamship, iron-plated ships, the rifled gun, resulted in revolutionizing the supply, sanitation, and hospital services. The professionalizing of the nursing and hospital services was a direct consequence: Florence Nightingale's *Notes on Nursing* and *Notes on Hospitals*, the basic texts for training professionals in the two subjects, were both published in 1859.[36] But nursing, hospital, and supply services were only dramatic instances of a general failure of administrative procedures everywhere apparent in the conduct of the war by gentlemen amateurs.

After many years of effort, an approach to order was begun for the medical profession by the Medical Act of 1858. A first move toward professionalizing public administration was made for the Indian Service in 1853, a reform which also benefited from the interest and advice of Jowett. Two years later a Civil Service Commission was established by an order in council to examine candidates for a number of other services. A Superannuation Act in 1859 "extended and strengthened the new system" by confining pensions to those admitted to the service by the Commission, though completion of the reform, its extension to all the services, awaited another order in council in 1870.[37]

The professional reforms multiplied the need and demand for education. With the institution of examinations for public administrative offices, education which would provide equal opportunities for all was demanded.[38] The requirement for expert knowledge had begun its ineluctable advance, and the critical educational issue had become clearly defined. In 1858 a writer in the *Edinburgh Review* (CVII, 100) stated it succinctly.

> The Continental theory, which has received its most complete realisation in Germany, relegates the course of general study to the gymnasia altogether . . . The English theory . . . sacrifices learning *as a profession* entirely, and has thus been in no small degree the cause of the gravest defect which mars the social organisation of our country. Why have we in England no learned class . . . ? The reason is to be found in the very undeniable fact that in our highest educational institutions *we regard learning as always a means, never as an end*.

Such a concern for national consequences was, however, rare among educational theorists. In *University Subjects,* published in 1859, Newman, while repeating his support of liberal education as a mental discipline, ignored the state in the interests of the Roman Church. More often in the mid-century, education was viewed solely for its benefit to the individual. Representing a secular utilitarianism, Herbert Spencer's most important contribution to educational theory, "What Knowledge is of Most Worth?" appeared also in 1859.[39] Though he thought self-preservation the primary end of education and the sciences the only efficient means to that end, the struggle for existence was in his eyes wholly an individual matter. It was not the survival of either society or the state that concerned him.

Matthew Arnold would not have been a true son of his father had he not viewed education in the light of the needs of the nation and state. Criticizing the English in comparison to Continental education, he wrote:

> Our dislike of authority and our disbelief in science have combined . . . to make us leave our school system to take care of itself . . . Under such auspices . . . it does nothing to counteract the indisposition to science which

is our great intellectual fault. The result is that we have to meet the calls of a modern epoch, in which the action of the working and middle class assumes a preponderating importance and science tells in human affairs more and more, with a working class not educated at all, a middle class educated on the second plane, and the idea of science absent from the whole course and design of education.[40]

And he argued strongly for state support and state supervision of an organized system of education, and for a more generously conceived liberal education, including the sciences. Yet the emphasis in the bulk of his writing was on the cultural development of the individual as the primary aim of education.

As the *Origin of Species* is a landmark in science, something of the same can be said with respect to scholarship of *Essays and Reviews,* published the following year. Both became centers of debate for both challenged the right of conservative authority to limit speculation and investigation. If by the 1860's instruction in a few subjects in the universities had improved, professional scholarship received little encouragement and instruction in the experimental sciences followed largely the old pattern. Even the oldest of the professional disciplines, law and medicine, were still neglected. In 1859 there were few teaching laboratories either in the universities or hospitals; those in existence were suitable only for the most elementary teaching or restricted to the use of the instructor and his assistant. Instruction in the sciences was usually by lecture and demonstration.[41]

Demands for more attention to scholarly research had been made by Jowett, a contributor to *Essays and Reviews,* in the 1850's. A decade later Mark Pattison, another of the essayists, Charles Appleton, J. R. Seeley, Goldwin Smith, and others, attacked the indifference to serious scholarship in the universities.[42] After 1867 the spokesmen for the scientists, Lyon Playfair, Benjamin Brodie, J. Norman Lockyer, T. H. Huxley, H. E. Roscoe, and E. Ray Lankester demanded more, and more effective, science instruction in the interests of industry and the state. The scientists who, following the lead given by the Prince Consort, saw mostly clearly the importance of meeting the German challenge supported the study of the humanistic disciplines, but the long neglect by the universities and by English education generally of the experimental sciences made their stress on the sciences and technologies inevitable and necessary. Aided after the Austro-Prussian War and the Paris Exhibition of 1867 by a few industrialists such as Mundella and Bernhard Samuelson, these scholars and scientists, German-trained or German-influenced, succeeded at least in improving and expanding scientific and professional instruction and research by bringing about further reform in the two ancient universities, by stimulating the founding of city colleges and technical schools for the lower middle class and the workers, and by awakening the industrialists and politicians to the danger of the German competition.[43]

Starting in the 1850's with backward and inadequate educational institutions and traditional programs of instruction, the British were caught in the educational dilemma of the liberal democratic states. Concerned with universal values and the development of the individual, they clung to their ideal of liberal education and defended the individual against total absorption in his social function. But when compared to their major competitors, they only inadequately met the need for specialization and the need to develop every child's capacities to the utmost in order to supply the varied demands of a modern state and society for efficient personnel.

Writing of technical education for the working class, a London County Council officer of education observed: "Germany is aiming at benefiting the nation by training all workers through definitely specialized courses. Britain has organized so that individuals may secure what they think best for their own advancement."[44] That was in 1913. In 1916 the distinguished British scientist Sir William Ramsay, thoroughly acquainted with both British and German education, while severely critical of the former, wrote: "Although the methods employed have been lamentably defective, it must be acknowledged that the democratic ideal lay at the bottom of English education . . . On the other hand the German aim has been to create an efficient machine . . . We are learning now . . . how efficient this system is in war; in German hands it bid fair to be equally successful in commercial war . . . Stated tersely the difference in the two ideals is that between individualism and collectivism."[45] In the same year Whitehead observed: "English education in its present form suffers from a lack of aim . . . It has not decided whether to produce amateurs or experts.[46] That was the consequence for Britain of the liberal democratic dilemma in education.

IV

If in 1945 the British emerged from their long struggle with Germany broken and bankrupt, they emerged also victorious and honored. And much as the United States contributed to the ultimate victory and to Britain's recovery, that contribution was made in the last analysis because of the similarity of American ideals to those the British had sought to preserve in their liberal education.

Without the power of spiritual ideals, a society's life is barren and rudderless; without technological, material power, the ideals of a society cannot prevail. It is the function of the state in education to see that all young men and women are trained to the utmost limit of their capacities in the special techniques necessary to the work of the world and defense of the state. It is the function of liberal education to open the vision of all youth to the beauty, glory, and terror of the universe, to impart to their minds and hearts a conception of a good life as their culture has envisioned it, and to enable them to make distinctions and judgments for themselves. A liberal, democratic education builds still on a belief in the right of every educated individual to choose voluntarily the values he will seek to realize. No single concept of the good life is fixed to which the whole society is committed. The realm of ends is the realm of freedom, and each individual is encouraged to seek within the broadest possible social limitations his own vocation and his own ideal goal in the belief that in doing so he will most effectually contribute to the ultimate good of mankind. That is an essential of what has been called the "Open Society."

Its antithesis, the "Closed Society," is one in which a specific end has been designated as a goal to which all members are committed. All the activities of the society are then subordinated to the chosen end and must contribute to it. The arts, sciences, philosophies, and all economic and political life become mere instruments or technologies designed for its attainment.[47] The inevitable result is a power structure. And whatever the chosen end, whether it be religious, economic, or political, any great society so committed constitutes a threat to the very existence of societies pursuing other ends.

Since 1859 the actors have changed, but the character of the crisis has not. Students of education in the Soviet Union find nothing which can in Western terms be called an education: there is only the training of manpower under complete control of the central authority.[48] Yet we shall misjudge that system, and our own necessity, unless we see that the teaching of the accepted dogma, omnipresent at every level of that training, is the debased and distorted substitute in a Closed Society for the liberal education of the Open Society. Today Communist education represents an extreme development of the hierarchic, bureaucratic, professional training which a century ago seemed peculiarly German. The difference in degree—and it is great—is a measure of the difference in the intensity of the conflict at every level.

Fortunately the West is today both better equipped institutionally and more aware of the crisis than was Britain a century ago. But the dilemma remains. Like the British, Americans believe in the personal right to choice of ends and in the distribution of responsibility and power among many subsidiary corporations and local groups. But to cooperate in the preservation of the democratically-organized state which protects the Open Society, and perhaps even to become subordinate in some respects to it, must be the recognized duty of its subsidiary institutions and corporations whose very existence depends finally upon the central government.

This is the context in which educational questions must be resolved in our day: the questions of financial assistance to education by the national government, the character of elementary and secondary education, of who shall go to college and what kind of college, of general education or specialization. In 1859 only a handful of men in Britain were able to free themselves from the fetters of the past and to perceive the overriding necessity of the crisis. And those few proved unable to solve satisfactorily the democratic dilemma. To sacrifice liberal education to the necessity of the hour is to betray the ideals of the liberal democratic society and to impoverish all, including the technologists and technicians. But to neglect the efficiency of a national personnel which requires expert knowledge and skill threatens ultimate disaster. The educational dilemma Britain faced in the crisis which emerged a century ago is the dilemma faced by all liberal democratic states today.

II

Patterns of National
Development

THE DERBY—THE RETURN.

John Bull: "Now then, show your ticket! Three hundred and two! You can't get through with that!" (The three hundred and two seats in the House of Commons won by the Conservatives in the 1859 election were to prove too few to maintain Derby and Disraeli's Government.)

WILLIAM O. AYDELOTTE

PATTERNS OF NATIONAL DEVELOPMENT: INTRODUCTION

HE four essays in the second section of this volume approach by different avenues the central problem of the structure of Victorian politics. The purpose of this introduction is not to retraverse the ground they cover, but to raise some questions about how their topics fit into this large context. These questions are, specifically: (1) for Mr. Hughes' essay on industrial change, the political reflection of that change in the class basis of politics and the composition of Parliament; (2) for Mr. McCallum's essay on John Stuart Mill, the movement for Parliamentary reform to which Mill's theories were in part at least designed as a contribution: (3) for Mr. Conacher's essay on party politics, the constitutional and party framework in which Palmerston was able to carry out his policies; (4) for Mr. Beales' essay on the Continental crisis, the general relationship in this period between foreign and domestic policy.

I

Mr. Hughes' essay indicates that many of the complexities of a modern industrial economy were already present in 1859. Yet it is evident that the changing economic structure had, by that year, affected the social basis of politics a good deal less than might be expected. It used to be said that the Reform legislation of 1832 abolished the rotten boroughs, put an end to the practice of appointment of Members of Parliament by individual patrons and, at least in its ultimate effects, handed over political power to the "middle classes." The perspective of time has changed our emphases and greatly qualified this interpretation. The ineluctable fact, which it is almost impossible to reconcile with the older view, is that the social composition of the House of Commons was relatively little altered by the Reform Act. Such analyses as have been made, including the searching essay published by Bernard Cracroft in 1867,[1] reveal an enormous numerical preponderance of the landed gentry and the relatives of the nobility, and a Parliament much closer in its social composition to the eighteenth century than to the twentieth. The important though small group of business and professional men in the House of Commons was not significantly larger than it had been before 1832.

The influence of the "middle classes," so far as it existed, must have derived, not from Members of Parliament, but from pressures exerted by the electorate upon them. There is every reason to suppose that public opinion had greater weight in politics in the mid-nineteenth century than ever before. The Reform legislation, if it did not change the membership of the House, at least created a situation that must have restricted the liberty of action of men sitting in it. Waves of popular feeling could have a powerful effect on the decisions of governments: some examples of this will be given in the last section of this essay. The statements and actions of contemporaries, both politicians and party managers, attest the power of public opinion, the need to cultivate it, and the regard that had to be taken for the popular view.

Yet, though the importance of public opinion was generally acknowledged, it is less clear whose opinion this was. The Reform Acts of 1832 had created a very limited constituency. The previous electorate of about half a million was increased to 813,000, one in every 29.8 of the population. Even by 1867 this electorate had grown to only just over a million; the act of that year nearly doubled it. Nor were the opinions of this body of voters, of course, anything like unanimous. Even in the boroughs the £10 householders (enfranchised in 1832) can scarcely have been a homogeneous entity. They were a legal abstraction, a political myth, and it would be hard to show that they possessed any real community of opinion or interest. A still different point of view was vigorously expressed by the tenant-farmers in the counties, who pushed the interests of agriculture more aggressively than was always welcome even to the landed magnates representing them in Parliament, and who continued to exert a powerful influence on politics through the middle years of the century.[2]

Not only was the electorate relatively small in size and diverse in composition but also its power over Parliament was subject to certain limitations. Radical efforts to make Parliament more directly accountable to the electorate, by shortening its maximum duration, had conspicuously failed. More important, it is difficult to think of direct popular control emerging from a General Election in which half the constituencies might be uncontested. Still more important, elections in many constituencies were affected, and often governed, by an intricate network of personal influence. It was still regarded as normal practice that a man's tenants should vote as he directed. Norman Gash has estimated that over forty pocket boroughs survived in England and Wales alone, in addition to other boroughs that regularly returned members of particular families and still others where influence, if not controlling, carried great weight. Electors in general showed themselves extraordinarily ready to accept the recommendations of their betters, especially when they were accompanied, as they still frequently were, by bribery or treating.

The small size of the electorate, the diversification of its interests, and the continuation into the mid-nineteenth century of much of the electoral structure and customs of a former age suggest that it is simplistic to regard Parliament as under the control of a single outside interest. Popular feeling was beyond question influential, but there are grounds for holding that it was most effective when exerted, not in opposition to influence, but in alliance with it.[3] Men at the time were impressed by a public opinion stronger than any that had been seen before. To us, looking back and comparing the situation one hundred years ago with the present, the striking thing is the degree to which popular control was still hampered and restrained.

The political power of the landowners was far greater than can be accounted for by the narrowly based Parliamentary constituency. Though their position in the counties, where they also controlled local government, was paramount, the counties were still greatly underrepresented on either an electoral or a population basis, despite the additional sixty-five seats which they had acquired in 1832. Landowners sat not only for counties but also for boroughs, and not only for pocket boroughs but also frequently for large, popular, industrialized constituencies, where their wealth and social position were apparently regarded as guarantees of integrity and conscientiousness.[4] Their strength lay not merely in the character of the electoral system, but also in their firmly entrenched social position, in certain advantages they derived from the state of the laws governing the holding and inheriting of land, and in the undeniable fact that they were as a class immensely rich. The figures in the "New Domesday Book," the Parliamentary return of owners of land published in the middle 'seventies, provide a startling revelation of the concentration of landed wealth in the hands of a relatively small number of people. Agriculture was in a prosperous state: in fact Lord Ernle has singled out the time from 1853 to the end of 1862 as the "golden age" of high farming.[5]

Radicals had hoped, after the repeal of the Corn Laws, to proceed to further measures against the landed interest such as reform of the electoral system or abolition of what seemed the special legal privileges of the landowners. These efforts encountered for the next twenty years almost complete failure. The very success of the movement against protection militated against them. Peel in 1846 had deprived the opposition of its most powerful weapon, the "emotive symbol" of the bread tax, and thus, as was apparently his intention, helped to pave the way for a continuation of aristocratic rule.[6] In the prosperous mid-Victorian era the prestige of the landed class reasserted itself. Attacks upon it made little inroad upon its impregnable position and tended often to recoil upon their authors. John Bright's fulminations against the "oligarchy" in his public speeches of 1858 resulted merely in his failure to receive an invitation to join Palmerston's Cabinet in 1859. Palmerston explained to Cobden that Bright had made himself impossible by his wild speeches: "it is not personalities that are complained of; a public man is right in attacking persons. But it is his attacks on *classes* that have given offence to powerful bodies, who can make their resentment felt."[7] Palmerston's proposal soon after to make Bright a Privy Councillor brought from the Queen an emphatic refusal based in part upon "his systematic attacks upon the institutions of the country."[8]

Eminent business and professional men, the group that might most effectively have challenged the position of the landowners, either failed in the effort to do so or did not even make the attempt. Some of them, such as Bright and Cobden, preserved a sturdy independence in the face of the established social order and continued, though to little effect, to advocate radical change. Others proved imitative rather than rebellious, seeking to advance themselves or their families within the existing system rather than to impose a new one. In many cases, though by no means invariably, their social ambitions were realized.*

* Sometimes they married into the aristocracy, as did Sir Josiah John Guest, the great iron manufacturer, or Henry Broadwood, who was a brewer and a member of the piano-manufacturing family. More frequently they were able to marry their daughters to the sons of the socially eminent. They bought country estates and some of them even became M.P.'s for their counties, a privilege supposedly reserved to the old established class.[9] Sending their sons to Public Schools hastened the process of social amalgamation and thus helped to give the second generation of the new class a stamp which made it indistinguishable in externals from the old. Baronetcies, and even peerages, were bestowed not only on lawyers but also on banking families such as the Smiths (Baron Carrington, cr. 1796) and the Barings (Baron Ashburton, cr. 1835), and in the 1850's even on a cotton manufacturer, Edward Strutt (Baron Belper, cr. 1856).

Class barriers, though formidable, were not insurmountable and the territorial interest, though a privileged group in society, was not a closed caste. Its power to assimilate newcomers was undoubtedly an additional source of its strength, since those best able to dispute its authority could also hope, with reasonable expectation of success, to rise into its ranks.

Finally, perhaps too much has been made of the conflict of interest between the landed classes and the business and professional classes. Agriculture and business were to a certain degree interdependent: agricultural prosperity in the 1850's was in part based on the transportation provided by the new railways and on the new markets created by the larger incomes derived from industry. James Caird, after his survey of English agriculture in 1850-51, concluded that "in the districts where the increase of manufacturing and commercial enterprise and wealth has been greatest, there the rent of the landlord, the profits of the tenant, and the wages of the labourer have most increased."[10] These influences contributed to weaken the tension between landlord and businessman, to increase their community of interest, and to induce them to make common cause politically.

II

Mr. McCallum describes Mill's growing concern during the 'fifties with the representation of the people. This was also, at the time, a topic of some Parliamentary concern. After 1832 no Government proposed a new Reform measure for twenty years. In the period 1852-66, however, five Government Reform Bills were introduced, three by Russell—in 1852, 1854, and 1860—one by Disraeli in 1859, and one by Gladstone in 1866. Although these proposals were mild in comparison to the far-reaching Act of 1867, and the "fancy franchises" (special franchises for various educated or property-holding groups which appeared in the Bills of 1854 and 1859) seem today a little absurd, these Bills did envisage considerable changes. But they failed to attract adequate support, and the temper of Parliament on the Reform issue seemed apathetic. Despite these appearances, however, the mood of Parliament was gradually but unmistakably changing. This can be shown by an analysis of the divisions on Reform over a period of time. During the thirty-five years between the two Reform Bills, Radicals kept the issue alive in Parliament by a series of motions at fairly regular intervals. These proposals, though none of them resulted in legislation, are historically useful for they can be made to

120 WILLIAM O. AYDELOTTE

yield an index of the development of opinion. A comparison of the figures on these divisions shows a clear trend, from overwhelming opposition in 1837 to near acceptance by the beginning of the 1860's.*

By 1860 Reform had been proposed from all sides of the House of Commons and every important member of the House had supported some Reform measure. It was generally accepted and freely admitted in debate by both Conservatives and Liberals that the question would have to be settled. The Bill of 1860 was withdrawn after its defeat, Russell was elevated to the peerage the year after, and no new Government measure was proposed until 1866. But this was only an intermission, due largely to the unusual political circumstances of Palmerston's last ministry, and it was clear enough which way the tide was running.

It is not altogether easy to account for this change. Clearly it was not due to pressure from below, which Parliament had vigorously resisted in the Chartist days when it was strong, but which was negligible in the 'fifties and early 'sixties. "The apathy of the country is un-

* The nadir of the Reform cause seems to have been 20 November 1837, when Thomas Wakley moved to amend the address by making it promise juster representation to the people. His motion provoked Lord John Russell into making his "finality" speech (that the Reform Act of 1832 made the final changes in the Constitutional framework) and secured only twenty supporters against 509 opponents, or less than 4 per cent of the votes cast. During the years 1839-52 Reform made a better showing. Sir Hesketh Fleetwood's motion in 1839 for a £10 householder franchise in the counties obtained 28 per cent of the votes, and three motions by Sharman Crawford in 1842-44 for a reform of the representation varied in the narrow range of between 23 per cent and 24 per cent. Four motions to the same effect by Joseph Hume in the years 1848-52 varied in a range of 19 per cent to 28 per cent. The percentages were astonishingly consistent, whether the number of votes cast was large or small.

Locke King's proposals to assimilate the county to the borough franchise in the years 1850-61 did considerably better, and show a gradual rise from 39 per cent in 1850 to a height of 48 per cent in 1857, nearly half the House. Twice, in 1851 and 1858, he even secured a majority, though these cases were each due to a political fluke and do not seem characteristic of the trend. Edward Baines' motions for a £6 householder franchise in the boroughs in the years 1861-65 varied in the small range of 43 per cent to 44 per cent.

As for the Government measures, we have no divisions on the bills of 1852 and 1854, but Disraeli's Bill of 1859 obtained 47 per cent of the votes on the second reading, and a motion to go into committee on Russell's Bill of 1860 got a vote of 48 per cent. These two votes are strikingly similar to each other and to the vote of 47 per cent on Locke King's motion of 1861: the three proposals were supported to almost exactly the same degree though they were made respectively by a Conservative, a Whig, and a Radical, and the Parliamentary forces deployed behind them were quite different. Gladstone's Bill of 1866 secured a bare majority on its second reading.

deniable," Russell wrote to Palmerston on 16 November 1860, "nor is it a transient humour. It seems rather a confirmed habit of mind. Four Reform Bills have been introduced of late years . . . For not one of these has there been the least enthusiasm."[11] It was the upper classes, not the lower, who took the initiative in the Reform movement of the 'fifties, and it is a little hard to understand why, in the absence of popular pressure, they should have done so.

The change may have been due in part to political expendiency. Herbert Bell believes that this was the consideration that weighed most with Lord Palmerston. Palmerston, though he declared himself "a great advocate of reform" in an election speech in 1847, had shown very little sympathy for the Bills of 1852 and 1854. Yet he promised a Reform Bill after the General Election of 1857, though he fell from office in 1858 before he could introduce it. He attacked Disraeli's 1859 Bill because it did not lower the borough franchise, despite the fact that this was the very point against which he himself had been adamant until that moment. He also seems to have done what he could to secure the passage of Russell's Bill in 1860. Palmerston's new line derived, his biographer thinks, from his wish to further the amalgamation of Whigs, Liberals, and Radicals into a workable political party. His announcement on 20 March 1859 of his conversion to a broader borough suffrage was intended as a peace offering to Russell and the Liberal Reformers.[12]

It was also important that a number of circumstances had contributed to take the sting out of the Reform issue, and to make it appear less threatening than it had been in the 1840's. The easing of social tensions, in a period of rapid industrial growth, gave grounds for less apprension about the dangers of a working-class vote, particularly the vote of the limited section of the working classes that would have been enfranchised by any of the proposals of 1852-66. The patent economic conservatism of skilled labor suggested that its inclusion in the political nation would hardly represent a threat to property and that it might be possible, as actually proved to be the case, to bring it under the leadership of one of the two traditional parties. An additional mitigation was provided by the mildness of the Reform proposals which Governments laid before Parliament in the years 1852-66, and this applies also to Disraeli's original Bill of 1867. These projects were limited in scope and attempted either "lateral" extension of the suffrage to bring in more voters of the kind that presumably already existed, or a strictly limited "vertical" extension to give the franchise to those voters who would presumably be safe. Even the motions of Radical Members in the 'fifties were moderate in comparison to the sweeping measures offered by Sharman Crawford and Hume in the 'forties.

All this emerges in clearer perspective if we bear in mind that the proposals for Reform in the 'fifties and 'sixties were not conceived by their sponsors as steps towards democracy. The interpretation of nineteenth-century political history as a gradual unfolding of the democratic principle is a rationalization after the event. The fears inspired by Chartism gave democracy in this generation the connotations of mob rule, ignorance, corruption, and, above all, a threat to the rights of private property. Even those who advocated Reform repudiated the democratic label. Disraeli, reporting to the Queen on the moderate Reform Bill introduced by his Government on 18 March 1867, informed her that there was "no spice of democracy" in it.[13] John Bright, who was characterized by Charles Newdigate Newdegate as "a bigoted advocate of democracy,"[14] described his position himself in the following words: "I do not pretend myself to be a democrat. I never accepted that title, and I believe those who knew me and spoke honestly of me never applied it to me."[15] Bagehot, in his study of Parliamentary Reform published in 1859, went out of his way to demonstrate the absurdity of the democratic case. Mill, in his essay on the same subject published in the same year, argued that "no lover of improvement can desire that the *predominant* power should be turned over to persons in the mental and moral condition of the English working classes."[16]

The arguments used to justify Reform in the years around 1859 were of a very different chaarcter. Their main burden was utilitarian: improving the moral character and intellectual efficiency of Parliament. The criterion of a representative system was the personal character of the M.P.'s it sent up, and changes in the franchise were justified only to the extent that they would lead to the selection of an even better body of men. Constitutional government was primarily government by discussion in which decisions should be taken, not because of the compulsion of a majority of the nation, but on the basis of wisdom or a common sense of national interest and duty. The "tyranny of numbers" should be avoided. It was necessary to have instead a "balance of classes," to secure representation from the different social and occupational groups, not in proportion to their numbers, but in such a way that the interests and wishes of each could be fully expressed without any of them predominating over the others.[17]

These points can be found not only in the discussions of 1859 but also in the Reform debates of 1832, where they were used by both the supporters and the opponents of the Bill. They appear even in the eighteenth century. In fact they closely approximate what Samuel H. Beer describes, in the categories he has set up, as "the Old Whig theory of representation."[18] Though this was an eighteenth-century doctrine, it had a long life and still formed the guiding rationale of many Members of Parliament even after 1859.

This line of reasoning could be used in the 'fifties and 'sixties, as it was in 1832, either to support or to oppose a change. The utilitarian argument, the mainstay of the Reformers, was turned by Robert Lowe into the strongest case against Reform presented in Parliament during this period. The danger of the tyranny of numbers, of a mass of new electors who would submerge the intelligent and independent voters, was as great for Russell when he was proposing Reform as it was for Palmerston when he was opposing it. Palmerston was anxious not to "overpower intelligence & property by ignorance and poverty." Russell, defending his Bill on 13 February 1854, quoted and endorsed Fox's declaration of 1797 that any system of representation was defective which brought out those whose "situation and condition" took from them "the power of deliberation."[19] The efficiency and good management of the working classes in organizing their unions proved to R. H. Hutton that they would be responsible voters but proved to Robert Lowe that, precisely because of their effective organization, they would be dangerous members of the political community.

After the lapse of a hundred years the arguments used in the Reform debates of 1852-66 appear weak and ambivalent, less a philosophy of Reform than a thinly veiled attempt to avoid the issue or to prevent the movement from coming to any concrete result. Yet they appealed to men who were anxious to avoid what they thought would be the unfortunate consequences of complete democracy or who feared the preponderance of numbers and the domination of a mass vote. Nor were these arguments wholly ineffectual. They formed the basis for interesting if unsuccessful preliminary proposals, and they did something at least to prepare the way for the important Act of 1867.

III

Mr. Conacher's account of the complexities of party organization illustrates that the political system inaugurated by the legislation of 1832 was one which contemporaries found difficult to operate. Peel believed, and he was by no means alone in this opinion, that the Act provided an inadequate basis for the administration and had seriously weakened government. For some this was a lesson to avoid further concessions. The Queen expressed in 1851 the fear that the Reform proposals Russell was considering might strengthen the democratic principle and by this means weaken the executive still further.[20] For others, especially by the 1850's, when elections were inconclusive and the House of Commons delicately balanced, the chronic weakness of Governments holding office only through a division of their enemies or through a coalition of not always harmonious factions provided an argument for further Reform. The third Earl Grey, for example, in a tract advocating Parliamentary Reform published in 1858, argued that a reshuffling of the electoral system would produce a more decisive and manageable situation in Parliament.[21]

Yet probably the explanation of this instability lies deeper, not so much in the statutes as in extraconstitutional arrangements, certain features of the British political system which, though formally unknown to the constitution, are nevertheless essential to its successful operation. To induce a large group of men to work effectively and constructively together is no easy matter, and various practical devices had to be adopted to make Parliament function successfully. The mid-nineteenth century might be regarded as a transitional period in the sense that the old methods of handling the House of Commons had disappeared or become impracticable, while new ones were as yet inadequately developed. The structure of patronage and influence by which politics were managed in the eighteenth century had long been ebbing away. What finally replaced these old devices was the system of tightly organized political parties without which, as many observers have pointed out, modern British politics would be unworkable.

Similarity of nomenclature can be deceiving, and it is only too easy to read into the history of the nineteenth century the monolithic party structure that we observe in the twentieth. Actually British political parties in the mid-nineteenth century were very unlike what they have become today. It is true that the Reform legislation did provide, contrary to the expectations of some, a mighty stimulus to party organization. It created a situation where parties were increasingly necessary for carrying on the business of the House of Commons, while its registration clauses made organization of the electorate for party purposes an urgent matter. In the decades following 1832 there appeared registration societies, constituency organizations, the great political Pall Mall clubs, central party agents who did not sit in Parliament, and central offices under the control of the party whips. Independent Members had been decreasing in numbers even before 1832, and by 1841 men without at least a formal party label had almost disappeared from the House.

All this, however, still amounted to very much less than the party organizations of the twentieth century. Parties did not yet have a real life outside Parliament and did not constitute, as they necessarily do now, a mechanism for bringing the mass voters into the political community. Although independent Members had, on paper at least, almost disappeared, in practice the looseness of party organization and the strength of local support in their constituencies gave Members of Parliament not connected with the Government a liberty of action and an influence in the House of Commons that would be unthinkable today. There was no Liberal Party in the sense of any clear organization, but only a loose general connection through which leaders could maintain contact with different groups and sometimes induce them to work together. In 1859 an attempt was made to patch things up when Russell and Palmerston agreed to leave the choice between them to the Queen, each consenting to serve under whichever of them she might summon to form a government. The reconciliation, which was solemnized at the meeting at Willis's Rooms on 6 June, opened the way for Palmerston's return to office a few days later. Yet Palmerston even in his last ministry from 1859 to 1865 relied perhaps as much on the unwillingness of the Conservatives to turn him out and on their support against his own Radical followers as on the so-called Liberal Party as a whole.

The revival of the two-party system was hailed by various observers at different dates, for example in 1852, 1857, and 1859. In each case, however, what materialized could be described as a two-party system only to a limited degree. Throughout the period between the two Reform Acts the two-party system was more apparent than real, and both the main parties were deeply divided. Parties were still too immature, too rudimentary in structure, too loosely organized and controlled, to provide adequate support for a firm government.

Although we do not yet know how far voting on issues followed party lines, it is clear enough that each party contained within itself major divisions of opinion. On the other hand there was considerable common ground between the moderates of both sides, and the two principal parties borrowed freely from each other. Whigs as well as Tories participated in the opposition to Free Trade, political reform, and factory legislation. Conservatives, on the other hand, on more than one occasion adopted and made political capital out of causes previously sponsored in the main by Whigs or Liberals, as with Corn Law repeal in 1846, Jewish emancipation in 1858, or extension of the suffrage in 1867. Taper's famous definition of a "sound Conservative government," "Tory men and Whig measures," strikes close to home. At first sight it seems odd that Parliament in 1866 rejected a Liberal

Reform Bill because it went too far, and in 1867 accepted a Conservative Reform Bill that went much farther. Yet the paradox lies only on the surface; it is less apparent if these events are considered in context.

IV

Public interest in the Italian question, of which Mr. Beales writes, was pronounced, and indeed foreign affairs occupied a much larger share of public attention in the years after 1850 than in the period just before. There is space here merely to offer a few speculations about the relation of attitudes on foreign policy to the ambiguities of domestic politics which have already been noted. The question, to put it in a different way, is whether there is any sense in which we can refer to a Liberal or a Conservative foreign policy. There are one or two aspects of British external relations in this period which suggest the possibility of such a comparison.

The issue of constitutional reform made its appearance in the foreign as in the domestic field. In the mid-nineteenth century Britain notoriously supported the cause of constitutionalism in Europe, particularly in Spain, Portugal, and Piedmont, as it had earlier in Greece and Belgium. It might reasonably be conjectured that those who favored constitutional improvement in one area would favor it in the other, and that this liberal orientation had been imparted to British foreign policy by those pressing for domestic reform at home. This, however, was palpably not the case. Palmerston, who was at first cool to Reform and later a reluctant and opportunistic supporter of it, was the single man most prominently associated with the support of constitutionalism on the Continent.[22] Nor does this aspect of British foreign policy appear to have been regarded as a monopoly of the Whigs or Liberals. Thus Lord Malmesbury, who had been Foreign Minister in Derby's Conservative Cabinet of 1858-59, declared in 1861 that "the general principles" of both parties in foreign policy were "the same, by which I mean that we wish always to support constitutional governments, and to support and encourage them as much as possible."[23]

In one notable instance this Liberal policy was reversed. Throughout the nineteenth century all foreign ministers of both parties showed a tenacious unwillingness to raise the question of constitutional reform in the Ottoman Empire. As Harold Temperley pointed out in an important article some years ago, the central objective of British policy in the Near East was to uphold and strengthen Turkey, and an attempt to liberalize the political institutions of that country was apparently not regarded as consistent with this basic aim. The British did press for humanitarian reforms, with some hope of achieving them, though with little ultimate success. However, this was in part at least for home consumption, to obtain the support of British public opinion for a pro-Turkish policy. As Palmerston cynically put it on 21 May 1852, "Our power [of maintaining the Turkish empire] depends on public opinion in this country and that public opinion would not support us unless the Turkish government exerts itself to make reforms." The realism of British policy in Turkey suggests that, when British interests were really at stake, abstract sympathy for constitutionalism did not weigh heavily against concrete strategic realities.[24] It does not, however, provide a touchstone for domestic politics since both parties, on different pretexts but with extraordinary unanimity, followed the same policy.

But there was a still deeper issue of foreign policy on which there did develop a marked cleavage of opinion. In some respects the middle years of the century promised well for the development of improved international relations. The Free Trade movement had scored brilliant successes and was regarded by some of its most eminent sponsors as being the first step towards a still greater objective, the achievement of international peace. Just before the Crimean War Richard Cobden and John Bright, with a few other like-minded men, threw themselves into the effort to moderate the war-fever. Bright's pacifist stand during the war, greatly increased his reputation in the House of Commons. These events seemed to indicate some progress in the development of an atmosphere of international good will.[25] They were offset, however, by the deeper current of suspicion and distrust towards supposed enemies, internal as well as external, that runs through the middle decades of the nineteenth century. The fantastic apprehensions of a French invasion and the needless antagonizing of successive French Ministers, who apparently wanted nothing so much as the maintenance of friendship with England, affected unfortunately the relations with one of the principal countries with which the British had to deal. Russophobia developed at a time when, according to J. H. Gleason, "the basic foreign policies of the two nations were, if not identical, at least complementary." Its revival in the 1850's and the crystallization in the popular mind of certain stereotypes about Russia had an important bearing on the origins of the Crimean War.[26] Public opinion on foreign affairs in this period was anything but pacific or judicious. One eminent diplomatic historian speaks of the "irritable susceptibility," and "the jumpiness, the insularity, the aggressive tendencies of public opinion in the mid-Victorian era," and describes it further as "singularly misinformed and unbalanced" and "touchy, exacting and unreasoning."[27]

Sentiments of this kind could also appear in a less obvious guise. The first two volumes of Macaulay's account of how well England had managed her revolution were published in 1848 when the other countries of Europe were presumably mismanaging theirs. His book brought him an immense popular vogue which, though well-deserved, was perhaps not unconnected with its implicit chauvinism. It fits the pattern that Macaulay admired Palmerston above all living statesmen, an admiration that was apparently reciprocal, for it was Palmerston who procured Macaulay his peerage in 1857.

Feelings of hostility towards "outsiders" could also be directed against religious minorities in England such as the Roman Catholics or, to a lesser extent, the Jews. The hysteria over the "papal aggression," the restoration of a Roman Catholic hierarchy in England in 1850, stirred militant Protestantism to vigorous action and reached a point where it even became difficult to carry on the government. Expressions of anti-Jewish sentiment and vulgar stereotypes about the Jewish race can be found throughout the century in, among other places, Cobbett's *Weekly Political Register, Punch,* various novels and plays, and even the prejudices of the sovereign.[28] The contempt and disregard shown in this period for "colonial" peoples such as the Indians or the Chinese seems a part of the same pattern. Macaulay's superciliousness towards Indian civilization is evident from the famous minute of 2 February 1835 advocating English rather than Arabic and Sanskrit in India's state system of education. A similar contempt for Chinese civilization was expressed later in the ironical laughter which greeted Roebuck's statement in the House of Commons on 3 March 1857 that the Chinese were a civilized people of a peculiar kind. They were peculiar, Roebuck continued, in that they had not applied their intelligence to the art of war. The evidence for their being civilized, he said, could be found in the Blue Book regarding the bombardment of Canton which had been laid before the House. "Compare the truculent manner in which the English papers are written with the papers of the Chinese. Mark the courtesy and intelligence which distinguish the latter, and let any impartial person—if such is to be found on the face of the earth—say which is the civilized man and which the barbarian."[29] With the support of Roebuck, Gladstone, and others, Cobden's motion censuring the Government for its behavior in the affair of the *Arrow* and the bombardment of Canton passed by a majority of sixteen votes. Palmerston at once dissolved Parliament and secured a resounding electoral victory. The fact that he could win immense popular support for his outrageous policy in China in 1857, and then be turned out of office a year later after having acted with moderation over the French Minister's suggestion that refugees harbored in England were behind Orsini's bomb attack on Napoleon III, is a sinister indication of the state of public opinion in that period.

It is tempting to try to find in these currents of feeling the key to the relationship between foreign and domestic issues. The xenophobia which Palmerston so skillfully exploited appears to bear closely on the three topics discussed earlier, the domination of Parliament by the landed class, the ambivalence of Parliament in regard to political reform, and the instability of mid-century politics. So strong a public appeal could, presumably, be used to bolster weak governments. It could also serve, for a class established in power and reluctant to grant political concessions, as a means of diverting popular attention from the question of Reform. This is the relationship between foreign and domestic policy that Bright thought he perceived when he wrote to Cobden towards the end of 1859: "The Reform question here is an ugly one for our oligarchy. A war with France would, in their eyes, be a cheap price to pay for a few years' respite only from the hated Reform."[30] Similarly, Disraeli described Palmerston as "the Tory chief of a Radical Cabinet," pursuing a "turbulent and aggressive" policy abroad "that his rule at home may be tranquil and unassailed."[31]

Yet these judgments, though persuasive at first sight, do not go to the heart of the matter. The facts will not support a theory of a simple and direct relationship between aggression abroad and reaction at home. On some questions of foreign policy there was substantial agreement in the House of Commons. When men disagreed, this division often did not follow party lines. On the motion to censure Palmerston's policy in China in 1857 a split occurred within each of the two main parties. Reformers were not always for peace. Bright was an exception among the Radicals in opposing the Crimean War; most of them, like Roebuck, were strong for it.[32] Nor were anti-Reformers invariably militarists and imperialists. Robert Lowe, perhaps the most effective opponent of Reform in this age, came to hold a position in foreign policy close to Bright's. It would be hard to show that foreign and domestic policy were connected in the sense that a man's position on one clearly indicated his position on the other. Instead, one finds a variety of combinations of attitudes. An aggressive foreign policy could fit into either a Conservative or a Liberal context; a Radical could be either a pacifist or a jingo.

Issues of foreign policy, rather than being related to domestic causes, often transcended them. Expressions of national self-assertiveness, however uncalled-for, and fears of threats from outside, however preposterous, aroused responses of an emotional intensity seldom attained by such sound but dry objectives as the franchise, sanitation, or improvement of the Civil Service. Thus it was Palmerston, despite his regency air and his cheerful indifference to Reform, who was regarded by contemporaries as the embodiment of the national spirit, while the Radicals, who detested him and bent their efforts to constructive change, never attracted in the 1850's anything like the same degree of popular approval. Palmerston's strength in the country was based not only on his great abilities but also and more on his careful and skillful cultivation of good relations with the press and his appeal to the public on the ground of national pride. In the use of these methods he came closer than the Radicals to anticipating the political ways of the twentieth century. Appeals to national sentiment, far from losing their power with the advance of Reform, became increasingly effective as the progress of enfranchisement broadened their potential basis. Ironically, the very changes to which Palmerston was indifferent or unfriendly ultimately provided greater scope for the exercise of the techniques of political agitation with which his name is principally associated. His career had in certain respects a very modern aspect, and the circumstances of his extraordinary political success formed a precedent for the future, although one that was not entirely reassuring.

J. R. T. HUGHES

PROBLEMS OF INDUSTRIAL CHANGE

T IS my purpose in this essay to describe in general terms several of the most important problems which faced Britain in 1859 rather than to present a complete economic survey of that year.* All of the problems treated below were related to Britain's harrowing experience with the business cycle. No two business cycles are completely alike in their origins, but some created problems which have not been dissimilar to those of other periods. Thus some of the problems of 1859 resemble those of 1959, and some of the solutions changed the course of British economic history. These will all be noted as we proceed.

I

The year 1859 was one of uneven recovery from the crisis of 1857 and the deep depression of 1858. After nearly a decade of vigorous but discontinuous expansion and technological advancement the whole unwieldy edifice of the British economy had been rudely

* The late Professor G. D. H. Cole left a very brief synopsis of his intended essay. As I have made no special study of those areas of social history and political theory where Professor Cole excelled, I have produced instead an essay in economic history based upon my own work in the period of the 1850's. There was one point, however, in Professor Cole's synopsis which I could not resist following up even though he did not enlarge upon it. This was the connection between the London builders' strike of 1859 and the formation of the First International. In a part of the essay below I therefore make this one excursion into social history, holding firmly to Professor Cole's intellectual coat-tails, and in this I beg the reader's indulgence. If I have failed to do Professor Cole's ideas justice, that is my own fault. Of course I assume full responsibility for all parts of my essay; but for discovering a connection between the London builders and Karl Marx I wish to give full credit to Professor Cole.

shaken.[1] The main economic problems of 1859 are perhaps best understood as problems of adjustment to these developments. In 1859, as after any great "boom" in economic activity, a changed economy was emerging from the broken shell of the old. Some new techniques and institutions had to take their place in the economy, and some of the old ones needed finally to succumb and be abandoned. The 1850's had been generally, until 1858, an age of unprecedented industrial growth. This was not an era without its problems, but these had seemed, in large part, to be essentially ephemeral. After nearly thirty-five years of falling and low prices, industrial disorders, and dangerous social strife, the long gestation period of Victorian capitalism seemed to be over, and British industry had finally achieved a rate of growth which apparently removed or alleviated the worst social evils of the Industrial Revolution. Following the collapse of Chartism in 1848 came the great gold discoveries in California and Australia, monetary expansion, and a vast growth of domestic investment and overseas trade. The economic troubles of the first half of the nineteenth century had vanished, "as if by magic."[2] For most of a decade, until 1858, the attainment of that "progress" so dear to the hearts of the laissez-faire economists seemed to be inevitable.

With the advantages of hindsight, the historian might now see that, after the brilliant sunlight of the 'fifties, by 1859 new shadows were lengthening across industrial Britain. For the economy which emerged in that year from the 1857 crisis and the subsequent depression was destined soon to experience the cotton famine of the early 1860's and persistently high unemployment in the later 1860's, and would finally tumble into the "climacteric" of slower rates of growth in the "Great Depression" of the 1870's. Moreover, even if the historian knew of these events, he could, looking at 1859, already perceive a great change which had come with the end of the boom of the 'fifties. The recovery of 1859 hardly touched certain sectors of the economy (some of which would never again enjoy their former importance), there was a marked shift in the direction of overseas trade and the export of British capital, and the trade unions were stirring again after the relative quiet which followed the end of the great cotton strike in 1853.

There was no obvious wave of the future in sight in 1859, but a historian more confident of the "lessons of history" than is the present one, might well be tempted to identify an historical watershed in that year. Among the major adjustments (each of which will be treated below) that British industry made to the ending of the boom of the 'fifties, one was made in 1859 which merits some general remarks here. In a single industry, building construction, labor strife was followed by organization: the London Trades Council. With this a new chapter opens in the political history of British trade unionism. Political action by the workmen soon led to the direct involvement in trade-union affairs of an obscure German author who happened to bring out a major work on industry and economics in 1859. Thus (the confident historian might argue) did the "forces of history" conspire to change the path of human development. From the London builders' strike and the London Trades Council it was a short step for British workmen to activities which greatly assisted the founding of the First International. Karl Marx was invited out of the obscurity which followed the defeats of 1848 to draw up the Inaugural Address and Statutes of (what began as) a *bona fide* international organization of working men.[3]

The present writer balks at connecting these events in a directly causal fashion. But it was British industry's problems of change and adjustment, after all, which produced both the great builders' strike of 1859 and those Parliamentary inquiries into industrial conditions in the 1830's and 1840's which formed the empirical substance of Marx's *Zur Kritik der politischen Ökonomie*. The latter work, though published in 1859, doubtless had little or no direct effect upon the events of that year. Nor did its author influence any of the actors in those events. But, as already noted, some of those actors were led by the consequences of 1859 to give Marx much-needed support.

These days any economic historian who seriously embraces the heresy of "economic determinism" is likely to have his hat blown off by the laughter of his colleagues. It is not my object in what follows to invoke this old philosopher's stone. But it may be that, a century after the London builders' strike, there is a lesson in the tangled consequences of that event for us all to ponder. Industrial change, in Britain in the 1850's, or in America in the 1950's, releases powerful forces, some of which may find far-reaching political expression. By 1859 such forces were leading British workmen back toward political action. It was not that such political action necessarily led to the support of revolutionary movements. The London Trades Council, after all, helped to found the Trade Union Political Union, and thus ultimately was a founder of the National Reform League.[4] It was perhaps only a perverse turn of events which led leaders of the Council also to assist in the formation of the International Working Men's Association and thus to strengthen at a critical juncture Marx's chances to change the course of history. But one cannot help considering how much better off the world's capitalists might be today if London's master builders had given their men a nine-hour day back in 1859 and let it go at that. The price of defeating the London builders in 1859 has proved in the end to be a very high one for the world's capitalist institutions. On this showing the virtues of long-term "enlightened" self-interest would seem to be very great indeed. The problems of industrial change tend to be resolved—one way or another.

II

Britain's problems of adjustment in 1859 can be better understood if the reader remembers that Britain was the leading industrial nation at that time, and had been rapidly developing toward even greater concentration on industry. According to the 1861 census,[5] the United Kingdom's population was roughly twenty-nine million compared to about twenty-seven million in 1851, an increase of less than 8 per cent.* The average rate of population increase in England and Wales had slowed down to 1.14 per cent per annum in 1811-21. Hence the great expansion of output which came in the 1850's was not accompanied by the population increases which had characterized the Industrial Revolution. There had been, however, no evident labor shortages in the 'fifties in spite of the sharp drop in the rate of population growth; this was no doubt partly due to the great internal migration of labor from the underemployed countryside into the industrial cities in the 1840's and early 1850's.[6] In the Western countries urbanization has been a phenomenon related to, and partly caused by, industrialization. Britain at the mid-nineteenth century was the most urbanized country in the world and was rapidly becoming even more urban than it was.† The 1850's had been a period of rapid growth of ur-

* More than twenty million of the 1861 total were in England and Wales, just over three million were in Scotland, no fewer than 5,798,967 (one might say "still") lived in Ireland, and 100,000 British people lived on the smaller isles. In addition, more than two million had migrated from the British Isles in 1851-61. Thus in this period Victorian Britain had a population almost equal to that of the United States.

† The population of London in 1861 stood at 2.8 million (larger than the nine most populous American cities combined had been the year before), having increased 18 per cent over 1851. Glasgow had a population of 477,000, a gain of 44 per cent over 1851. Liverpool and West Derby combined had a population of 460,000, an increase of 18 per cent compared to 1851; Manchester had a population of 441,000, 40 per cent more than in 1851. The smaller industrial cities had also gained more rapidly than had London, or the country taken as a whole; for example, Birmingham, with a population of 296,000, was 27 per cent larger than in 1851; Leeds had 207,000, an increase of 20 per cent, and Sheffield,

ban and industrial population and all that implied in terms of dependence upon factory employment and the festering social blights of urban life.

The same concentration on industrialization in Britain was apparent in the breakdown of occupations. By 1861 eleven million, or just over half of the populations of England and Wales, lived in twenty-nine industrial towns and cities of more than 50,000 (the same figures for the United States in 1861 were sixteen towns and cities with about 10 per cent of the population); and, of nearly eleven million persons over twenty years of age, 34.1 per cent were employed in industry compared to only 14.6 per cent in agriculture. The main occupational groups (evidently these data include *all* ages employed)[7] were: 590,-000 engaged in building construction, 450,000 in mining and quarrying, 700,000 in metal working, engineering, and shipbuilding, 1.5 million in textiles, 516,000 in tailoring and boot- and shoe-making, and just over three million in agriculture. Thus England and Wales (and no doubt also Scotland, although I have no separate Scottish data) by the end of the 1850's had clearly been transformed from a mainly agricultural and rural country into a mainly industrial and urban one so far as employment was concerned.[8] In terms of contributions to the national income at current market prices, this transformation no doubt occurred considerably earlier.[9]

Considering how large the increase in the physical output of goods and services was compared to the rise in the population,* one might

---

with 185,000, had gained 37 per cent over 1851. (All comparative American data in this essay are taken from *Historical Statistics of the United States* [Washington, D.C.], 1949.)

* The expansion of trade and industry in the 1850's might be better appreciated by similar comparative data (where they are available). Such data tend to underscore the growth of industrialization already noted. The "declared value" of exports of British and Irish commodities was £135.8 million in 1860 (U. S. exports of its own commodities in 1860 totaled about £65 million) compared to £71.4 million in 1850 (*Statistical Abstract for the United Kingdom*). In the same period the "real value" of imports (net of re-exports) was £181.9 million (the comparable U. S. figure was £69 million)[10] compared to £91.0 million in 1850. Consumption of raw cotton was 2.5 million bales in 1860 compared to 1.5 million in 1851 (Thomas Ellison, *The Cotton Trade of Great Britain* [1886], Table 3). Textiles made up about 57 per cent in value of total exports and about 30 per cent of imports. By 1861 the British cotton textile industry employed 452,000 (the U. S. cotton textile industry employed about 115,000 compared to 331,000 in 1850, with 282,000 nominal horse power of steam engines compared to 71,000 in 1850. The number of power looms in cotton textiles had risen from 250,000 to just under 400,000 and the number of spindles increased from twenty-one million to over thirty million in the same period. Other branches

readily see why many of the troubles of the earlier decades seemed to disappear "magically" in the 1850's. There is no magic for removing economic troubles quite so effective as a rate of industrial growth which outstrips the growth of population—depending upon the distribution of income, of course. On a straight per capita basis industrialism was clearly "paying off" for Britain by the 1850's. Not only was Britain still *the* industrial power of the world, but the main phenomena of ur- banization and rapid growth of output which accompanied British in- dustrialization were becoming even more marked than they had been in the more famous period of the Industrial Revolution. The 1850's had been one of enormous industrial growth compared to earlier de- cades, absolutely, per capita, and in terms of rates of growth.[10a]

But no industrial system, however beneficial, is without its prob- lems; and acute economic problems had developed in the period, which tend to be obscured by such aggregated data. These problems figured prominently in the adjustments of 1859. By the end of the 1850's it was clear that one of the results of such industrial advance had been a greatly increased consumption of foreign supplies of foodstuffs and raw materials. This of course had been anticipated by the liberal economists who for so long had urged Britain to pursue total specializa- tion and trade on the basis of comparative advantage. No doubt there were great benefits, especially to the poorer classes, in the cheaper food- stuffs and raw materials. Abolition of the Corn Laws in 1846 and the reduction of protective tariffs in the new era of Free Trade assured that such would be the case and that imports would be freely available at world prices. But these were not always stable and all troubles were not removed. During the deficient harvests of 1859 and 1860,[11] prices

---

of the textile industry had registered similar advances in the period (*Factory Returns, Accounts and Papers*, XLII [1850], 745; LV [1862], 23). Coal pro- duction in 1860 stood at eighty-four million tons (the U. S. mined about fifteen million tons) compared to about fifty-one million tons in 1850 (*Report on the Coal Supply*, Statistics appended to the Report of Committee E, *Accounts and Papers*, XVIII [1871], C. 435-II, vol. 3), while the output of pig iron was 3.8 million tons (U. S. output in 1860 was 919,770 tons) compared to about 2.2 mil- lion tons in 1850 (*Statistical Abstract* for 1860; for 1850, A. D. Gayer, W. W. Rostow, A. J. Schwartz, *The Growth and Fluctuations of the British Economy 1790-1850* [Oxford, 1952], I, 302n.). Gross traffic revenues from the railways were about £28 million in 1860 compared to only £13 million a decade earlier. In the same period the mileage of British railways (an innovation more than two decades old by 1850) had risen from 6,621 to 10,443. Even after the depression in shipbuilding which followed the Crimean War, 212,000 register tons of sail and steam shipping were built in 1860 compared to 134,000 tons in 1850, and the total of Britain's tonnage employed in foreign trade increased by nearly half in the single decade (*Statistical Abstract*).

of corn rose and supplies were relatively tight, cutting into real wages. Moreover, the tendency of British industry's productive capacity, raised continuously by competitive innovation, to create excess demand for imports of raw materials (driving up their prices) was troublesome, and could, as it did in 1856-57, contribute to sudden losses of bullion by the Bank of England and to cripplingly high rates of interest[12] (see below for the effects of these on mortgages). That august institution, acting under the direction of a "whole catena of authorities"[13] as an ordinary commercial bank since the Bank Act of 1844, was not famed for its prescient wisdom in such circumstances. Thus the "new" economy of the Free-Trade era had not been altogether relieved of some of its older problems and some new ones had been added. It is a mistake to assume that Britain's rapid industrial development in the 1850's had been frictionless; the economy continuously created new problems as it provided solutions to the old ones which had disappeared by "magic."

Moreover, prices had, on the average, risen more than 25 per cent over the decade,[14] limiting advances in real wages; and the weakness of the trade unions after the end of the great cotton strike contributed to a decline in the growth of money wages. In fact, average money wages actually declined slightly from 1855 to 1860 after having risen by some 16 per cent in 1850-55. Tucker's index of real wages of London artisans stands at only 55.9 (1900 = 100) in 1860 compared to 58.0 in 1850. Real wages of other occupational groups seem to have done better: Wood's index of real wages is 101 in 1860 (1850 = 100) after having fallen to 90 in 1858.[15]

It is important to recall that it is not just per capita income, but rather the distribution of income, which determines the extent to which the gains from industrial advances are shared by most of the population. Given the radically unequal distribution of incomes in Victorian England, the data for real wages hardly could be expected to reveal the kinds of advances shown by the data for increases in physical output. Unequal income distribution, while it no doubt played a crucial role in determining the availability of investible funds at home and for the vast overseas investments of the Victorian economy, also was a source of discontent at home. It probably added to the willingness of British workmen to "go political" again (see below) after the events of 1859 in order to achieve better conditions. In addition, there were problems of profound structural adjustments which were thrown into sharp relief by the 1857 crash and its aftermath. If the worker had his problems, so did the industrialist in 1859. Moreover the spread of specialization and division of labor as industrialism advanced increased the degree of interdependence between the various sectors of the economy, so that the effects of industrial dislocations tended to be more and more far-reaching.

III

Of the problems of adjustment in 1859 perhaps none was more unexpected than the shift in the flow of trade and capital toward India and Asia generally. After the Mutineers were crushed in 1858 the Crown assumed the government of the subcontinent and the East India Company's long reign was over. Although there had long been Indian development projects for the London investor, the new Government of India, aided by the renewed disenchantment with American investments in the wake of the 1857 crisis, effected a decisive shift in the flow of British overseas investment toward the Empire.[16] By 1859 the effects of this were evident in the trade figures: 22.2 per cent of British exports went to Asia compared to 20.5 per cent to North America. This change in the direction of exports had first appeared in 1858, but it might then have been ascribed to the depression in America. In 1859, with recovery underway, the new pattern held. Except for 1866 and the extraordinary American expansion of 1871-73, exports to Asia were henceforth, and throughout the Victorian era, greater than those to North America.[17] Only the relatively stable European market consumed more British products than did Asia. The new pattern (supported much later by Imperial Preference) held until the Second World War. The focus of overseas investment and trade was shifting to the Empire, providing Lancashire with a long new lease on life.

In 1859 cotton textiles, as was usual after cyclical downturns, led British industry to recovery. But this time it was the shift in markets already noted and not just the usual American expansion which buoyed the spirits of the Manchester mill owners. At the beginning of 1859 Manchester sensed the new order of its affairs:

We began last year with unparalleled commercial depression and gloom, and with the drawbacks of a crisis the effects of which were seriously felt in all branches, and before its close we are dazzled by the splendour of the prospect which unexpectedly breaks in upon us from the East.*[18]

* The declared value of exports to India in 1857 was £12.2 million; in 1859 the figure was £20.8 million (*Statistical Abstract*). Dazzling indeed. The cotton mills worked at full capacity in 1859, and in spite of the troubles of excess capacity which had plagued textiles in 1856-57, mill owners responded with a tremendous burst of new investment. Between 1856 and 1861 (the only years for which official data exist) the use of steam power in cotton textiles rose from roughly 88,000 h.p. to about 282,000 h.p. Employment in cotton textiles in-

The cotton industry's adjustment problem after the 1857 crisis was a relatively simple one: response to booming demand by heavy new investment. In this case the lessons of the great boom of the 'fifties were meaningless. Extensive investment in textiles in 1851-56 had produced raw-material supply shortages, excess capacity, and voluntary short-time in the mills.[20] But the 1857 crash and the prolonged depressions in cotton textile manufacturing in France[21] and in the United States had released cotton supplies for British use. Moreover, in spite of the appearance of sporadic strikes, the labor question in cotton textiles had been temporarily settled by the defeat of the workers in the great cotton strike of 1853. In 1856 and 1857 the mill owners had successfully introduced short-time working, with little opposition from labor, and had successfully reduced their stocks. In 1859, with no significant labor problems and no stocks to draw upon, the return to full capacity output was rapid in cotton textiles.[22] With booming Indian demand in 1858-59, investors ignored warnings of over-production. One sector of the economy at least had only to enjoy a new boom. Lancashire, riding the changing tides of overseas trade, faced a new and expanding market in Asia,[23] a market which survived the cotton famine of the early 1860's and continued as a mainstay for British cotton textiles for most of a century.

Lancashire's happy experience in 1859, however, was only partially shared in other sectors where serious structural changes had to be dealt with. One of the most striking of these adjustments came in the iron industry. Prices of wrought and pig iron had been falling steadily since the Crimean War, when demand had bid up prices sharply. The great wave of investment in iron in the 1851-53 boom had been succeeded by a further period of high investment in 1854-55 under the pressure of wartime demand, so that excess capacity and falling prices had bedeviled the industry even before the crash in 1857.

During the period from 1850 to 1855, high and rising prices had stimulated innovation and experimental investments. A critical area for such investment had been the opening out in Yorkshire of the Cleveland "yellow band" iron ores, using taller blast furnaces and the hottest blast yet seen in England.[24] In 1850 there had been only thirty-

---

creased by no less than 73,000 and wages rose substantially (*Factory Returns, Accounts & Papers*, 1857 [session 1] XIV [7]; 1862, LV [23]). In 1857 and 1858 there was probably little investment in cotton textiles, due to the depression in 1857 and excess capacity which needed to be utilized in the 1858 recovery. (In 1861 the cotton famine was upon Lancashire, and there must have been little new investment in that year.) It is little wonder that observers were alarmed in 1859 and 1860 at the extent of the investment boom in the cotton industry.[19]

eight blast furnaces in the North of England; by 1857 there were 101 furnaces in the Northeast (that is, Northumberland, Durham, and Cleveland, the North Riding of Yorkshire).[25] A whole new iron industry had developed in the Cleveland district, pioneered by the famous partners, Bolkow and Vaughan, and had provided a cheap ore for the Northeast iron masters. South Staffordshire, the ancient seat of the iron industry in England, was now destined to be displaced by a more efficient area, the development of which had occurred entirely during the great expansion of the 'fifties. In 1857 South Staffordshire had 180 blast furnaces, and, with such a massive investment in old equipment, still held a slight lead in pig iron production in England with 657,000 tons compared to 499,000 tons in the Northeast. During the 1858 depression (which struck the iron districts especially hard) the South Staffordshire district still held its slim lead. But by 1859 the writing was on the wall for all to see. Over 60 per cent of South Staffordshire's furnaces were out of blast compared to 28 per cent in the Northeast and just under 30 per cent for the United Kingdom as a whole. By then, the combined output of South Staffordshire and Worcestershire had fallen to 475,000 tons compared to 618,000 tons in the Northeast.[26] By 1865 the Northeast had surpassed even Wales and Monmouthshire, and was making 21 per cent of the United Kingdom's pig iron, compared to 9 per cent a decade earlier.[27]

The 1857 crisis had struck Staffordshire especially hard, bringing down a large bank, and in the 1858 depression unemployment was severe.[28] By the end of 1859 the Staffordshire iron masters knew its causes:

The serious fact which manifests itself more and more is the growing competition of districts where the manufacture of iron is being newly developed, and where the abundance and nearness to the surface of the minerals give great advantage to the proprietors of the new undertakings.[29]

Staffordshire was finished as England's leading producer of pig iron. In Britain in 1859, as in the United States a century later, the struggle to recover from an industrial depression involved the abandonment of old methods and the inevitable decline of less efficient areas. The preceding boom had nurtured more efficient techniques and newly developed resources, which, in the strenuous competition of contracted markets, drove the old-timers to the wall. The business cycle, then as now, was no respecter of tradition.

There were other industries whose difficulties in 1859 were mainly variations of those which faced the iron industry. In coal mining, for example, a great investment boom in the Crimean War period had raised output rapidly in the middle 'fifties and prices had declined steadily from 1854 all the way to 1858.[30] Output fell in 1857, reaching a trough in 1858. By 1859, when output recovered, there was no strong revival of investment (only eight new collieries appear in the data in 1859, compared to 197 in 1855 and 236 in 1856).[31] The industry was plagued by excess capacity and it was 1864 before a strong revival of new collieries appeared.

Excess capacity was also the lot of the shipbuilding industry in 1859. The Californian and Australian gold discoveries had been accompanied by a sudden and massive rise in demand for shipping space, both for commodities and for emigrants. Following immediately upon that, demand for shipping to the Near East in the first year of the Crimean War (1854) was even heavier. Freight rates rose radically (as much as 200 per cent in some cases) and, with the additional war demand, shipbuilding capacity was increased to the extent that over 323,000 register tons were built in 1855, compared to 204,000 a year earlier, and 134,000 in 1850. By 1855 freight rates were already falling and with the introduction into the shorter routes of the new steamships, sailing ships were displaced, and the British shipbuilding industry faced excess capacity with large-scale unemployment. The year 1859, therefore, was not a year of recovery for British shipbuilding, but actually marked the lowest construction total—186,000 register tons —since 1852. In fact it was not until 1863 that the level of construction achieved in 1855 was seen again in British shipyards.[32] The adjustment problems of excess capacity in capital-goods industries in 1859 recurred in later decades; excess capacity could not quickly be overcome in the early stages of a recovery which followed a major boom.

The situation in building construction was somewhat different. Here, in one industry at least, the high rates of interest which prevailed from 1853 to 1857 had constrained investment. Mortgages, bearing relatively low rates of interest, could not be readily negotiated during the "tight money" period. It was argued that with bank deposits yielding as high as 5 and 6 per cent and with loans realizing similar yields, there was no incentive for lenders to become encumbered with low-yielding mortgages.[33] Construction was clearly hampered by high interest rates but it is difficult to say how much, as data are scarce. In Birmingham, for example, barely 800 houses were built in 1856 compared to 2,784 in 1853.[34] Moreover, high interest rates on short-term money also reduced the marketability of the securities of local governments which might have financed public improvements. By early 1857 it was reported from Birmingham that "few, if any, public works are in progress, and at no former period did so many tramps pass through the town in search of employment."[35] Even before the 1857 crisis widespread unemployment seemed to have become endemic in the building trades. In London estimates of unemployment among the building artisans ran as high as 25 per cent. Mass meetings were held at Smithfield and Somerstown with speakers proposing government aid for the unemployed. As early as January 1857 a protest meeting at Smithfield was attended by an estimated ten to twelve thousand unemployed. It was estimated that in the parish of St. Pancras alone unemployment in the building trades reached five thousand.[36] It is no wonder that there were few important strikes for better conditions in the building industry before 1859; jobs were relatively scarce and there was little prospect of improvement so long as interest rates remained high, and widespread unemployment prevailed in the building trades.

Moreover, in the building industry, as elsewhere in the 1850's innovation was disrupting older, more settled usages, and altering the character of the market. An organizational innovation of far-reaching consequences had brought large-scale building "developments" onto the scene. As the size of building projects grew in the 'fifties so had the organizations which undertook them. Such organizations, with greater command over capital than the small-scale builder could mobilize, were able increasingly to achieve internal economies of scale through the application of machinery in crucial areas of building construction—machinery which displaced manual labor. Master builders had come to rely upon the money market for large-scale financing, borrowing funds equal to "20 or 50" times their own resources. By thus tapping directly the central source of loanable funds, the master builders could put up whole blocks of houses in anticipation of demand, making them, and selling them, like shoes. In the middle 'fifties, however, these operations had been curtailed to some extent, the masters being unwilling to engage in many large-scale development projects under the burden of high interest charges on the funds they needed to borrow.[37] Although there is little quantitative evidence relating to the impact of these new arrangements on the market for building labor, it is clear that the bargaining positions of individual workmen must have deteriorated vis à vis the master builder who had now become a large-scale developer, contracting at one time for whole gangs of workmen. By 1859 there were in fact six master builders who employed as many as 1,500 men, and the largest 100 master builders together employed 28,000 of the 38,000 London building workmen, compared to some 9,000 employed by the 450 smaller building firms.[38] Certainly this consolidation on the employer's side of the market made joint action against the the work-

THE STRIKE, A SUBJECT FOR THE CONSIDERATION OF THE REAL WORKING MAN.

Committee Man and General Talker: "What I say, my boy, is Hold Out!
Hold Out—and we'll soon bring the Masters to their Senses!"
Worker: "Ah! It's all very well for *you* to hold out—*you* live at a Public
House, and get plenty to eat and to drink—meantime, *we* are next to
starving."

men easier, and, as we shall seee, in 1859 the masters joined hands
against the demand for the nine-hour day.

Since the building industry had been depressed during the tight-
money period up to the end of 1857, the advent of lower interest rates
in 1858-59, if it did in fact stimulate a renewed demand for building
workmen, also gave them an opportunity to press for better conditions.
The result was the great London builders strike and, ultimately, the important organizations noted earlier. Here was a delayed-action adjustment to the expansion of the 1850's. The demand for a nine-hour day
had been around since at least 1853 when the London masons pressed
for it. In 1856 the Manchester building trades had won a Saturday
half-holiday, and by 1857 the London Carpenters had asked for nine
hours.[39] In 1858 a Joint Committee of Carpenters, Masons, and Brick-
layers was organized to agitate for the nine-hour day. After a buildup
which included "trade and general meetings, lectures, discussions, letters in newspapers, and the extensive circulation of a 'prize essay' . . .

repeated appeals by earnest and respectfully worded addresses, and deputations of working men, to several of the large building firms . . . ," the workmen did not succeed. By demanding ten hours' pay for nine hours' work, the men in fact were seeking a pay increase on the order of 10 per cent under the guise of "spread-the-work" demands. The masters sometimes treated them "harshly and rudely," received deputations with "silent contempt," or, in several cases, simply discharged the men in the deputations. It was an incident of the latter nature which touched off the builders' strike in 1859.[40]

Messrs. Trollope, a large firm of master builders, were struck against in order to: (a) force them to rehire a mason who had been discharged for presenting a nine-hours memorial, and (b) force them to grant a nine-hour day. The strike began 21 July 1859. The master builders of London rallied to Messrs. Trollope and no less than 225 builders resolved to:

> Close their own establishments until the "strike" against Messrs. Trollope should be abandoned, and not again to open them to any operative who should not give a written pledge, not to belong to ANY society that in any way directly or indirectly interfered with the rate of remuneration, the hours of work, or any other arrangement between employer and the employed.[41]

The introduction of the "document" (a yellow-dog contract) set both sides for a long strike. All the large-scale London master builders, those employing more than fifty men, joined in the lockout. In the end neither side won. In February 1860, after meditation, the men gave up the nine-hours demand and the master builders withdrew the "document."

The strike taught the London workers two important lessons: first that considerable solidarity existed between the various trade unions of Britain (£23,000 had been contributed as strike support by trade unions which were not directly involved);[42] and, second, that the trades societies needed a central organization which could mobilize that solidarity when it was needed, both for strike support and for political action. The result was the establishment in 1860 of the London Trades Council "to watch over the general interests of labour, political and social, both in and out of Parliament."[43] It was this organization of good, solid, British working men, agitating for political reform and improved conditions, whose leaders assisted, almost inadvertently, in the launching of, and for a time supported (although the Council itself never officially joined), an international organization which would, they thought, provide a means of international communication for "the purposes of regulating the hours of labour and assimilating wages."[44] A curious launching platform for the First International! The International Working Men's Association (founded 28 September 1864) had its statutes drafted by Karl Marx. He was well aware of (and, one suspects, saw the supreme irony of) the modest aims of his British colleagues and sponsors, and at first traveled incognito (or as nearly as he could) with regard to the doctrines of 1848, hoaxing the British while disseminating revolution abroad.[45] The hoax lasted (effectively) until 1872. As it turned out, there was no proletarian uprising in Britain, nor even in Germany. But, in the event, it was not too far from London to the Finland Station. As Lenin wrote later, it was the revival of "democratic movements" at the end of the 1850's and the establishment of the First International which, after the events of 1848 and the years of defeat and hardship that followed, enabled Marx to return to "practical activity."[46]

IV

In the history of British economic development, great expansions and contractions of economic activity typically left deposits of basic industrial change which became the foundations for subsequent expansions. These changes, whether they were improved techniques, transformations in the character of markets, shifts in the location of industry, or the appearance of new political alignments fostered by industrial changes, were, by adjustments in the direction of flow of productive resources, accommodated by the economy. It was the accumulation of such adjustments which enabled Britain to realize the lasting benefits of "progress" in the form of higher man-hour productivity. The attainment of such benefits was rarely painless. In 1859 some of the obvious adjustments appeared to be relatively simple (cotton textiles), some were painful indeed (the shift of supremacy in the English iron industry to the Northeast), some basic changes came about largely because of political action (the rise of the India trade), and some incidents which initially appeared to be purely "economic" had in the long run fantastic political consequences (the London workmen and Marx). For the economic historian, the identification, classification, and evaluation of such developments is a treacherous pastime. "Things" are all mixed up in history. Surely, for example, it took more than a Marx to produce a Lenin, and more than a Lenin to create a Soviet Union out of Old Russia. Moreover, it could certainly be argued that Marx would have influenced the course of history without any assistance from the London workmen. Yet all these events were tied together by connecting threads, some of which seem to be disarmingly simple to separate out for evaluation, even though they are all part of the same story of economic development and change, and, in the larger measure, of the totality of the flow of human events. It is the unhappy lot of the wretched historian, economic, social, or other, to try to understand the way the threads combined to make a single piece of cloth. In 1859, after one great period of industrial expansion in Britain had given way, and a new one was in its infancy, some important threads were partly visible.

THE SUPPORTERS OF THE "WORKING MAN"

The working man is supporting, from left to right, Palmerston, Russell, and Bright.

R . B . MC CALLUM

THE INDIVIDUAL IN THE MASS:
MILL ON LIBERTY AND THE FRANCHISE

T WAS in February 1859 that Mill's essay *On Liberty* was published. Then he prepared for the press his *Thoughts on Parliamentary Reform,* the substance of which was written five years before when the question had come before the public. Disraeli's Reform Bill, defeated on 31 March 1859, made it especially relevant. It was not until 1861 that he published his essay on Utilitarianism and his *Considerations on Representative Government.* These important works were still in the future but they proved to be entirely consistent with his general political philosophy. The *Representative Government,* so far as it is concerned with the franchise, shows no difference in principle from what he published in 1859.

I

The world was turbulent in 1859, but Great Britain, it might be thought, had less to fear than most nations. In spite of a somewhat unstable situation in Parliament, her internal security and public order were remarkable. After the wars with revolutionary France there had been for a time some dangerously insurgent movement in the period of so-called Tory reaction. But the word "reaction" was somewhat misplaced; the Government was conservative but did not seek to put back the clock as did·many governments in Europe—for some decades with success. Parliament prevailed over the Crown; the liberty of the press, in spite of some infringements, was preserved. It was an age when the strongly conservative government in London could honour the critical writings of James Mill on India: one of John Stuart Mill's biographers, Mr. Packe, observes that despite the harsh strictures of James Mill's

History of India "on the government of India by the East India Company, and its saturation in radical sociology, . . . James Mill was enabled to apply for a subordinate place in the India House itself."[1] Where in other countries exile, prosecution, or at best disregard in complete obscurity would have been the fate of the political critic, the Mill family grew up in comparative comfort, able to consort without peril in a free-thinking, free-speaking coterie of what the Russians later were to coin a name for, an intelligentsia.

A political crisis had come in 1831 and 1832, but the conservative elements bent and yielded to avoid revolution and civil war. The deep secular wisdom of the Whig leaders who won their way to power had found a mean, a working compromise, in the famous Reform Act of 1832. In the 'forties the new régime of the reformed Parliament was put to the test. The radical middle classes and the political intellectuals in economics showed their power against the land-owning interest in their struggle for repeal of the Corn Laws. A more dangerous force was Chartism. Here was a plan for extreme democracy which horrified all but the most advanced democrats. But in 1848, when so much of Europe was in revolt, the Chartist movement shot its last bolt. The power of the established, possessing classes was demonstrated and organised and the expected revolt passed over. But those who had lived through the crisis were unlikely to forget the danger; every Londoner who in 1859 was thirty years of age or more could remember as an adult the scare of 1848—extreme democracy had seemed very near and very dangerous.

What was there in 1859 to make thinking Englishmen fear as they looked into the future? For one thing, the country had engaged in a war with Russia that had shed little glory upon the military system. Afterwards by the slow process of commissions and committees the military organisation was surveyed and later it was reformed. Secondly, this was a period in which the House of Commons was not divided very rigidly into parties and majorities were small. The Reform Bills then mooted proposed to alter the basis on which the all-powerful Commons were elected. There was no great popular agitation or violence, yet everyone knew that if the franchise were widely extended it might be dangerous; the change could not fail to be important. What would its effects be? That was the question to which men like Mill were turning their minds.

It must be remembered that in British constitutional practice everything depended on the House of Commons, which had the power of designating the Queen's Ministers, the real executive government. It could, as had been shown and was to be shown again, prevail over the opposition of the House of Lords. Against the determined resolve of the Commons there was no ultimate defence. Those who feared royal or aristocratic tyranny could be assured of that. But there were other dangers. Suppose that the House of Commons became the creature of a rude and ill-educated electorate? Suppose that the most balanced, the most informed and educated and intelligent sections of the nation were to be submerged by a mass opinion concerned only to vent its bitter prejudices and pursue its short-sighted interests? It could happen. In France the population seemed to accept gladly the rule of a despotic Emperor. From America came news of a growing populism in politics, universal suffrage, direct election of judges, an inordinate bias against men distinguished by lineage or property. The successors of Jefferson and Washington were coming to be designated by rowdy mass conventions. All this was alarming to traditionally minded Englishmen, even to those who considered themselves liberal and progressive.

Here we must obeserve some important differences between British and American government. The right to vote meant something different in each country. The United States was a federation: electors had the duty of choosing their rulers both within the sovereign states of the federation and in Congress, and this duty was not double but manifold. American electors commonly had to choose many officers, governors in the several states, often other officers such as sheriffs, district attorneys, and, most important of all, by what had become in practice direct election, the President of the Republic himself. In England in 1859 and in England today there is representative government; there is no direct democracy. This essential difference between the two systems of self-government is often overlooked by students. The relevance of it is that in England in 1859 the question of the extension of the franchise really posed only one question; who would elect the House of Commons? Whoever had this power had the effective government of the country eventually in their hands. The local electors in the towns, who were in general those who paid the rates (local taxes), elected no mayors or officers but only the town councils, and their powers were much restricted. The counties were still without elected local councils, which were not set up until 1888, although there were local boards elected to administer the poor law, health regulations, and other matters. Great Britain was, as the famous jurist F. W. Maitland has put it, "a unicellular state." There was one residuum of political power, Parliament, and that power lay in the House of Commons. In the context of the British Constitution the anxious question of how far Britain could dare to go on the road to democracy was narrowed down to the question of who should elect the House of Commons? To the American, with his written constitution and his balance of political authority, the power of the electors and their influence over the Commons was an unchecked and terrifying power. It is no wonder then that men like Mill and Bagehot were anxious.

II

Mill turned to the question of who should elect the Commons in his *Thoughts on Parliamentary Reform,* which, as we have seen, was worked out about 1854 and published as a pamphlet in 1859. The Reform proposals put forward by Russell but abandoned at the outbreak of the Crimean War had occasioned his first articles, but Disraeli's Reform Bill made their republication timely. In spite of such stirring events as the Crimean War and the Indian Mutiny abroad, the factors governing the Reform question had not greatly altered at home. Mill was concerned with general principles of political right and also with the complexity of English Parliamentary elections. The much-vaunted reform of the electoral system carried out in 1832 was by no means systematic nor entirely rational. The largest boroughs, such as Glasgow and Manchester, returned only two members. Many small market towns returned the same number. The counties or shires, the most ancient and primordial divisions of English government, recognised and effective before the Norman Conquest of 1066, were each units returning two members; but the larger counties had been subdivided to increase their representation (but never to an extent proportionate to their population). Scotland, Wales, and Ireland differed in some respects from England, and single member constituencies, often very unequal, were more common there.

The most peccant element in the present state of representation is not the smaller number of electors taken in the aggregate. They are too few doubtless, and they will always be too few while any are excluded whose admission will not deteriorate the quality of the mass. . . . But these are not crying evils. They might be removed without making any very material difference, either in the composition of the House of Commons or in the inducements acting on its members. The most serious mischief is, not only that a fraction of the community have the right to vote, but that the majority of the House is returned by a very small fraction of that fraction. The small boroughs, those which number from 200 to 400 electors, are the seat of all the evils which the Reform Act was intended, and was believed to annihilate.[2]

He then goes on to examine this problem with a degree of detail which is now only of historical interest, but he ends up by urging a matter of high principle.

The expenses of an English Parliamentary election were great and were one of the main deterrents to men of moderate or little wealth seeking a career in politics. Then and for long after, the expense of elections did much to give British political life its aristocratic flavour. The expense was twofold; there was the expense of propaganda, which in the mid-Victorian period included a good deal of bribery in many places; there was also the fact that the expenses of the returning officer and his officials, the actual mechanism of the poll, was borne by the candidates and not by the public purse. The expenses of propaganda, Mill hoped, could and would be defrayed by a committee supporting the candidate, as happened when he himself put up for the City of Westminster. Otherwise, he observes, it is only too likely that the member elected will not be the best man but the best rich man available. The actual expense of holding the poll, he urged, should be defrayed by the public purse. Propaganda expenses should be made public. These two reforms have in due course been carried out, but it was a long process. A long series of Acts dealing with the expenses of elections and corrupt practices culminated in an Act of Parliament of 1883, which even then did not put an absolute end to bribery and absurd over-spending. The placing of the returning officers' expenses on public funds was delayed until the Act of 1918 which at last established adult male suffrage and partial women's suffrage. This slow process illustrates very well the weight of conservatism that rational and radical thinkers like Mill had to contend with.

Having dealt with these important technicalities, Mill in characteristic fashion comes down to the basic principles of representation. His first assumption is that every adult human being (he used the word "adult" and not "male") should have by the suffrage a portion of influence on the management of public affairs. Even if it were admitted that in this or any other country a large part of the public are not fit for political influence, their exclusion seemed to him a very great evil. Governments and individuals must strive to make progress in increasing the proportion of people who may be given political power. For, and here we have the essence of Utilitarian democracy, "it is important that every one of the governed should have a voice in the government, because it is hardly to be expected that those who have no voice will not be unjustly postponed to those who have. It is still more important as one of the means of national education. A person who is excluded from all participation in political business is not a citizen."[3] But, he goes on, "ought everyone to have an equal voice? This is a totally different proposition, and in my judgment as palpably false as the other is true and important."[4] At this point Mill's views on the mechanism of democracy become merged in the thought of his greater work, *On Liberty*.

III

While the pamphlet on the problem of the extension of the franchise in Great Britain was no doubt read by a few keen and attentive students of British politics, *On Liberty* was, and remains, of general application. A recent biographer of Mill, Miss Ruth Borchard, describes its effects: "It was at once likened to the *Areopagitica*, Milton's noble piece on the liberty of unlicensed printing of two hundred years earlier. It had an electric effect on the ardent men and women of the younger generation. 'I do not know whether then or at any other time so short a book ever instantly produced so wide and important an effect as did Mill's Liberty in that day of intellectual and social fermentation,' John Morley wrote of it. This book, essentially aristocratic though it was, proved to have an immense democratising influence where feudal snobbery lingered so tenaciously in all social relations."[5]

So challenging a book could not fail to produce much antagonism. We know that it enraged Carlyle, to whose authoritarian spirit it was anathema. A more restrained but formidable criticism of it came from the jurist Fitzjames Stephen, whose work, published later under the title of *Liberty, Equality, Fraternity,* remained perhaps the best-reasoned answer. Catholic and High Church theologians had little concern with such arguments as Mill's except as they showed forth the dangerous spirit of infidelity and individual judgment as opposed to the divine authority of the Church. But Miss Borchard points out its important influence on the ardent men and women of the younger generation. For many years before 1859 there had been little leadership in the field of political thought for the radical and forward looking. In economics and in applied politics the general philosophy of the Utilitarians had come to be widely accepted and was furthering the general cause of laissez faire. But Mill's *Liberty* at once had something of the aspect of a gospel. For several generations it was a prime classic in British universities and was on the shelves of all men wanting to be thought well-educated. It was translated into many languages; within two years it was translated in Russia, where it found fruitful soil. If today it does not have quite the celebrity and influence it had in the decades following its publication, it is still a book that students of political thought neglect at their peril. What was its message?

Its significance has varied according to the reader and society receiving it. Miss Borchard has called it "essentially aristocratic." There is much truth in this, for in his *Liberty* as in his other writings Mill is suspicious of the doctrine of mere equality; his fear of the power of society in general, of the brute mass of opinion, gives rise to a warning against demagogic tyranny. In this respect, what he says in the *Liberty* does not conflict with the passage we have already quoted from his *Parliamentary Reform*: the doctrine that all should have an equal share was palpably false. Disraeli also thought so when in his Reform Bill of 1859 he proposed the famous but never-to-be-adopted "fancy franchises." Yet the spirit and tone of Mill's book is democratic in that readers were inclined to see the justification of the liberties which they desired rather than the warnings against the abuse of popular liberties. Several generations of Indians as well as peoples in other parts of the British Empire found in the *Liberty* a bible of resistance to imperial domination. Mill had said in a pregnant phrase, "there is no such thing in morals as a right over others." This was a great solvent of imperial aristocratic and caste dominion whether at home or abroad. In 1947 the British rule in India came to an end by the handing over of power without strife between British and Hindu, an event made possible not only by the fact that the Indians had learned the lesson of the illegitimacy of dominion over others, but also—much harder and rarer—by the indoctrination of the political conscience of the British, by Millite liberal principles, to doubt their right.

IV

Whatever the effects of Mill's book in countries where there were whole peoples and communities hoping for liberation, in countries like Britain or America, where there was representative government and a rule of law, the principal message of the book was its insistence on the freedom of the individual—the basic principle of Utilitarian thought. The Utilitarians believed that the only sure and real centre of experience was the individual person, his pain and pleasure, his hopes and passions, his reason and his interest. In the name of Utilitarianism, especially when distilled into the famous formula of the greatest happiness of the greatest number, one can go far on the road to collectivism, and Mill in his later days was not without some sympathy with socialism. But while government control in the general interest might be desirable, the beneficiaries of that control must be, according to Utilitarian principle, the individual persons within the community concerned. You may or may not be to some degree a collectivist; but you must not believe in the existence of a collectivity, a nation, a class, or a civilisation, or culture which is to be invested with a greater reality than the individuals who compose it. Thus the individual Utilitarianism of which Mill was the greatest exponent was, and even now remains, resistant to concepts of collective rights whereby the state is more than the sum of the individual citizens.* In the Western mind it has acted as a kind of antibiotic against the fevers and nightmares of state-intoxicated prophets. Although the strange forms which the demons of collective tyranny were to take in the twentieth century were not imaginable by the men who lived in 1859, men were then still living who had been young when Napoleon reigned and men were born who were to survive as elder contemporaries of Hitler and Stalin.

To young Englishmen of the day, like John Morley, Mill's writings came mainly as a call to fight for progress through individuality. In retrospect we may think of the year 1859 as a period of great freedom from the restraints of state power. Taxation and other forms of government interference were mild by modern standards. But we must remember that 1859 was not 1870. Palmerston, not Gladstone, ruled the land. There was still in the future the repeal of the paper duties, called taxes on knowledge, the opening up of the old universities of Oxford and Cambridge to others than those who professed the Anglican faith, and the opening of the Civil Service to competitive examination. Radicals therefore still had much to complain of: in social life the arrogant assumptions of the aristocracy; in political life the limitation, by legal or practical discrimination, of entrance to Parliament by young men of no fortune or without powerful patrons; in the realm of thought and religion a stifling spirit of conformity. As Mill saw clearly in 1859, it is not always or most obviously the burden of state control that weighs most heavily on human freedom. "When society is the tyrant—society collectively over the individuals who compose it—its means of tyrannising are not restricted to the acts which it may do by the hands of its political functionaries. Society can and does execute its own mandates."[6] Mill attributes the power of society over the individual to "the magical influence of custom."[7] He does not altogether despise the uses of custom, but he fears its power. "The likings and dis-

---

* This makes it contrary to Burke's theory in his more mystical and conservative moods, to the complex of theories associated with the name of Hegel and his many disciples, to Marxism and communism, to the conceptions of history favoured by Spengler and Toynbee, in which by some arbitrary division of time and space something called "a culture" can be isolated and invested with attributes. These mysticisms and hypostatisations cannot survive in the mind of those who accept Mill's fundamental position.

likings of society, or of some powerful portion of it, are thus the main thing which has practically determined the rules laid down for general observance, under the penalties of law and opinion."[8] He feared the threat to individuality which the conformity of the average man tends to impose on the more exceptional one. He used as a motto for his essay a quotation from Wilhelm von Humboldt's book, *Spheres and Duties of Government*: "The grand, leading principle towards which every argument unfolded in these pages directly converges, is the absolute and essential importance of human development in its richest diversity."

We must not exaggerate the number of Englishmen who worried about this in 1859. Mill's writings, powerful as they were, passed over the heads of many of the upper classes of society who would have been merely amused at the idea of learning how to live richly and in diversity from the trim, parsonical little prophet of Bentham's dull gospel. Mill's appeal was to what we would now call the intellectuals; there it was strong and the thinking and reading men were either roused to opposition, like Fitzjames Stephen, or filled with enthusiasm, like Morley. In general, thoughtful Victorians like Meredith and Swinburne, Matthew Arnold, Spencer, and Huxley were exasperated by the Philistine conservatism or the dull self-satisfaction of the average Englishman, whom they sought in their various ways to shock and galvanise. Mill's call for a fair field for reason and hard, individual thinking was welcome to them. They rejoiced that Mill had put in so clear and memorable a fashion the claim that there must never be any presumption in favour of an alleged truth because of the multitude of its supporters. Since 1859, generations of boys have read with glowing enthusiasm that famous passage in the *Liberty* which begins with the words, "Mankind can hardly be too often reminded that there was once a man named Socrates."[9] Here is the classic statement of the case for the value of the individual judgement made more eloquent by the other historical examples which the author cites. All who in some aspect of their life have felt oppressed by the stifling conformity of their environment have heard this clarion call.

From the first, however, the dogmatic assertion of the sovereignty of the individual aroused strong criticism. It made Carlyle, for example, furious. And ever since then it has been a matter of high debate in political philosophy. To some schools, as we have seen, it was a denial of the right and reality of the power of the community in which and by which alone an individual could lead a civilised life. Certain schools of psychology, tending to think of individual minds as "bundles of tendencies," have frowned upon it. Modern anthropology has made us think of the helplessness of the individual apart from the group which has formed his life and thoughts. Mill was not unaware of this limitation of his concept, that it can operate only in certain states and times in history. "Liberty, as a principle, has no application to any state of things anterior to the time when mankind have become capable of being improved by free and equal discussion. Until then, there is nothing for them but implicit obedience to an Akbar or a Charlemagne, if they are so fortunate as to find one."[10] But Mill thought, and with reason, that the age that Britain and the Western countries were entering was an age of sufficient maturity for the right of self-determination to be extended. But while this status of responsible individuality must be claimed for the people in general and not merely for a select élite, the problem in practical politics, in constitutional organisation, was how to protect individuals and minorities from the brute mass of majorities. In his thoughts on the extension of the franchise Mill kept this constantly in his mind.

To thoughtful liberals like Mill the phrase "liberty and equality" was little more than a jingle. Equality might well be the enemy of liberty, and it was self-deception to suppose it otherwise. Mill had the courage to run against the general radical view which was hostile to fancy franchises, to the weighting of the power of some electors as against others. He wrote, "There is a wide interval between refusing votes to the great majority and acknowledging in each individual among them a right to have his vote counted for as much as the most highly educated person in the community; with the further addition that under the name of equality, it would really count for vastly more so long as the uneducated outnumber the educated. There is no such thing in morals as a *right* to power over others; and the electoral suffrage is that power."[11]

He tries therefore to find abatements and mitigations to the sheer power of mass voting. He does not do this by checks and balances between the different organs of the state as an American might have done. In the unicellular state of Great Britain such a course was impracticable. In the eighteenth century the jurist Blackstone had stated that the King-in-Parliament could do anything except make a man a woman or a woman a man. The new masters of Parliament were not likely to accept any less power than their more aristocratic predecessors. Mill's abatements of pure democracy were threefold. First comes a plurality of votes. He rejects property or income as a basis and falls back on education, which "can be tested directly by much stronger presumptive evidence than is afforded by income, or payment of taxes or the quality of a house a person inhabits."[12] He gives as a minimum qualification for any vote, "the greatest amount of education which can fairly be regarded as within the reach of anyone."[13] After this test there would be a plurality of votes on an elaborate scale, which we need not here recite. The second safeguard he proposed was vote by the old open franchise as opposed to secret ballot. Here he was at odds with most declared democrats of his time, but he stuck firmly to his position that the vote was a trust and not a right and must not be exercised in secret. Thirdly he hoped to mitigate the brute power of the majority by proportional representation, for "Even the government of mere numbers requires that every number should tell in proportion to its amount ... there is no true popular representation if three fifths of the people return the whole House of Commons and the remaining two fifths have no representatives. . . . a Parliament may be obtained by universal suffrage which may represent the bare majority of the people and again when this Parliament proceeds to legislate it may pass laws by a bare majority of itself."[14] The essential thing to notice is that Mill was on guard against the notion that when all are enfranchised the majority of the voters must have unfettered power. He could have no sympathy with the doctrine of fifty-one per cent and the devil take the rest which threatens representative government in some of the new countries of the British Commonwealth and is accepted with equanimity by the people of Britain itself. Mill, who was prepared to defend the rights of a Socrates against the totality of mankind, could not tolerate such crude and thoughtless empiricism.

Looking back a hundred years from 1959, we may now ask how the expectations of people like Mill have been justified or falsified. There is now full adult suffrage, male and female. No plural suffrages such as he advocated have been created. What was called plural voting, persons voting in more than one constituency because they had residence or property in it, has been abolished. Voting is still by the simple relative majority and if one organised party can obtain the votes of half the electorate, or perhaps even less, it may have a safe majority in Parliament and a secure tenure of power. Minorities are helpless unless concentrated in some particular area. Electoral districts are practically equal. For forty years past there has been payment of members. There are no property qualifications for candidates. All the clauses of the Great Charter have been passed into law except the demand for annual Parliaments. What have the masses done with their overwhelming power?

In some respects they have used their power, as was feared, against the wealth of the few. The system of taxation in Great Britain strikes hard at the rich. Death duties take the greater part of all estates whether in land or money. At the highest it is 80 per cent. Income tax at its highest is 89 per cent. Mill's salary before retirement from the India Office was £2,000 and would now, as earned income, be taxed at 25 per cent. If we multiply it by five to meet the present day rise in costs and call it £10,000, the rate of tax would be 60 per cent. In the name of socialism a fair part of the productive system has been compulsorily taken over by the state power. The predatory aims of democracy may be said to have been fulfilled. But have they? The process has been constant over fifty years and the biggest leaps in taxation have not come from a violent proletarian demand but because of the need to pay for two exhausting wars. Moreover the industries acquired for public ownership were taken at a fair valuation. When Demos is in an insurgent and predatory mood things are done less mildly.

But even if we concede the despoiling of the rich by the power of the enfranchised masses, these are only the formal facts. In a way that would have astounded fearful conservatives and hopeful radicals, the English social system has survived with remarkable vitality. Its aristocratic flavour, its traditionalism and class-consciousness, can still infuriate well-disposed American visitors as well as suspicious Russian Communists. The monarchy survives in all its splendour and is secure in popular affection. The House of Lords, diminished in power, is still there (and it was ninety-seven years after Mill in his *Representative Government* had advocated a chamber of statesmen by merit that the rank of Life Peerage was introduced). The Church of England and the Church of Scotland are still by law established. Titles, hereditary and for life, are still bestowed; eminent leaders of Trade Unions are knights, as well as politicians and generals. The select schools where the sons of the wealthy are educated with a consciousness of their superiority, although challenged, still survive.

But these may be outward survivals. If we are to apply Mill's test to the state of Britain under democracy we must ask whether the better elements of the population, as he would have called them, are ruthlessly crushed by a Philistine and thoughtless mob? Do we see, in Humboldt's words, "human development in its richest diversity"? That is harder to answer. People at all times, and "individualists" least of all, are disinclined to see the marks of genius in their contemporaries. Perhaps there are not the giants of thought and imagination that there were in Victorian days: Darwin, Dickens, Gladstone, Tennyson. Certainly in social and political studies there is no one to be compared with Mill himself. But in whatever way Britain fails favourably to impress the world, it can hardly be because the masses have brutishly suppressed the better elements. The first years of this century saw British scientists, inventors, and writers very prominent in the world. It may be that the products are not now so good but it will require time to judge of that. The question for the sociologist is whether the government and society are devised and directed in such a way as to encourage individual talent and progress. Or has English democracy failed in what Mill would have considered the primary test of its capacity: has it failed to educate its members?

The answer must be that it has not. In the end, after long delay, England was stung into a great zeal for education. Tired of the boastful sermonizing of Scotsmen, Americans, Germans, and others, England put her educational house into order. Free public education was followed by the growth of efficient secondary schools or high schools, many of them old foundations rejuvenated, many new creations. England, which in 1800 had only two universities, has now fifteen, as well as many other new centres of technical or higher education. And the educational system of England is so arranged that the talent of the nation is skimmed off at an early age and sent to superior schools and to the universities, largely at the public expense. We can imagine Mill approving of such devices. Foreign observers from countries more consciously dedicated to democracy, from America and Russia, are often quite shocked by the cold-blooded intellectualism of this process, and there are signs of revolt against it in England also. It may be that the ordinary man and woman may revolt against the deliberate creation of an élite.

But will it? It is hard to say, for English social development has a way of defeating the expectations of social theorists. Mill pinned his hopes on education widely diffused through the community. It may be that they have been realised, and that even the less educated elements have come to learn that the physical requirements of a comfortable life, to put it no higher, are dependent on the nursing of an educated minority. But as to his fears that the majority would use its power thoughtlessly to crush diversity, talent, and knowledge, they appear to date to have been falsified. We may ask why this is so.

The answer perhaps is that Mill, while a great political thinker, was a poor sociologist. He was too withdrawn, too reclusive, too limited not in his reading but in his personal life, to understand the nature of his fellow citizens. His father had given him an extraordinary education, private, intensive, precocious. He had striven to bring him up free from "vulgar modes of thought." He had succeeded all too well. Mill had never been to school or college or university. He knew little of the bonds of association that tie most men together. He had never been to church. It was not until he was thirty that he seriously read

the New Testament. The simple pieties of life as well as the more exalted religious moods were outside his experience. He knew little of
English social life outside the very select coterie of intellectuals with
whom he associated. The social world as described in Trollope's novels
was more or less unknown to him. Nor did he compensate for this by
experience of the life of the working classes. He could plead their
cause on occasion; he could censure them and still keep their respect,
but he knew little of how they felt. Neither his Scottish ancestry nor
his sound knowledge of Ireland's problems left him with anything of
the feel of the national spirit of either country. It may be said that he
was defective in the sensibility necessary to understand what elements
kept society together.

Some examples may be given. Patriotism and traditionalism, love
and respect for the throne and dignity of the English state, by far the
oldest of any in Europe, does not appear to have aroused his admiration or his interest. He was also much amiss in his estimate of the
power of religion. Not only the established Church but all the smaller
sects have survived, new sects have appeared, and Roman Catholicism
has grown in power and numbers. In another way Mill fully failed to
estimate the use which so many of the newly enfranchised voters would
make of their new status. While in his pamphlet on the franchises
he reflected on the bribery rampant in the smaller boroughs, like many
others in politics, he underestimated the tenacity with which these
self-regarding habits would survive and what a long task it would be to
eliminate them by legislation. Instead of using their votes to crush their
social masters they settled for a tip. Nor does it appear that he fully
estimated the extent to which chauvinism, soon to be called jingoism,
would unite the masses with most of the classes, leading them to denounce Gladstone and the Little-Englanders, to shout Majuba and
Khartoum, to mourn more over Gordon slain than benefits withheld.

It may also be suggested that "the people" could be kept from
dangerous courses by being amused and entertained. About the middle of the second half of the century, amusement and sport, from being
a matter of local games and fairs, became of national interest, fully
reported, discussed with excitement. More than one generation of
grim, reforming radicals were driven to despair by the indifference
of the populace whom they tried to teach and to deliver, by their
jaunty enthusiasm for things which had nothing to do with wealth
or power or politics, by what Chesterton was to call "God's scorn
for all men governing." Here was a "vulgar mode of thought" that a
few years' normal schooling might have taught the great savant.

Mill, if he could survey the world today, would tremble as many of us do for man's rational integrity. He would forebode the growth of some kind of para-proletarian mediocrity. In America, which he so much admired, he would fear the cult of social conformity, he would frown at an educational philosophy that gave pride of place to social adjustment, how to fit into a society and not how to develop as a man, if need be in spite of society. In eastern Europe he would see the signs of something much more alarming, democracy so-called, without free elections, without liberty of thought or publication, everything ordered and enacted by a self-perpetuating group of political janissaries, a party and doctrine apparently in power for all foreseeable time and commanding the resources of science and technology. But where democracy had come by extension of the suffrage under the rule of law he would on the whole have some grounds for comfort and assurance. But wonderful as was his work as a political thinker, the evils which he feared have been averted not by the use of his prescribed safeguards but by forces in human nature which he was by temperament and education little fitted to understand.

WHO WILL ROUSE HIM?

The British Lion is being prodded by, from left to right, Bright, Disraeli, and Russell.

J. B. CONACHER

PARTY POLITICS IN THE AGE OF
PALMERSTON

Let your Reforms for a moment go,
Look to your butts and take good aims,
Better a rotten borough or so,
Than a rotten fleet or a city in flames!

TENNYSON[1]

HE poet laureate probably expressed the views of a good
many of his fellow countrymen in 1859 when he penned
these lines. Foreign affairs loomed larger than domestic in
contemporary eyes, but as it turned out the fears and apprehensions
concerning Britain's safety were much exaggerated. The year 1859
is less important in the political than in the intellectual history of Britain. Indeed its domestic history is for the most part depressingly
barren. The decade from the accession of Palmerston to the premiership in 1855 to his death in 1865 was one of political doldrums presided over cheerfully and complacently by an ageing but popular
statesman who symbolized what was still the predominant feeling of
confidence.

I

In the view of the *Annual Register*, 1859 was a frustrating year in
Parliament. Although a variety of reforms were considered, no legislation of any importance was completed except the estimates and
two bills dealing with Indian affairs. "The only advantage gained from
the party conflicts, by which the time of Parliament was occupied,"
the *Register* judicially concluded, "was that the state of public opinion
and the relative strength of parties were more thoroughly ascertained,
and thus the ground was cleared for those important operations in
the direction of financial reform, and of constitutional changes, to
which the expectation of the public pointed as the work of the ensu-
ing year."[2]

Parliamentary reform had been discussed for a decade and would

163

have to wait another eight years for solution, but financial reform would follow immediately on the final juncture of Gladstone with the Liberal party. For, in retrospect, we may say that the most important event in the political history of 1859 was the final absorption into the Liberal Party of the remnant which continued to support Peel after the Tories split over repealing the Corn Laws. Indeed, to be more precise, one might say that the juncture of Gladstone and his friends with the party of Palmerston and Russell was an important step in the transformation of the old Whig into a new Liberal party. To appreciate the significance of this event it is necessary to examine the state of party politics in the years preceding 1859, and to clarify what is meant by the term "political party." First of all a political party should exist with the purpose of becoming the basis of government; secondly, it should be composed of members sharing common principles and traditions; thirdly, it should possess some definite form of organization inside and outside Parliament. For lack of one or more of these essential requirements the modern political party could not come into existence until after the Reform Act of 1832. From that time the first of these requirements is generally acknowledged, but the questions of common principles and of organization are more involved.

It is instructive to find that in the 1850's men looked back to the 'thirties as a time of sharp party distinctions. For instance in 1856 Gladstone wrote an anonymous article in the *Quarterly Review* on "The Declining Efficiency of Parliament" in which he recalled nostalgically "the good old days of party government before the breakup of 1846." "Ah! those were times indeed," he wrote. "What close running! what cheering! what whipping in! no loose fish! no absentees; if a man broke his leg before a great division, it was a kind of petty treason. What harmonious meetings then in the dining rooms of party leaders!"* Even making due allowances for the exaggeration of a frustrated Parliamentarian looking back on the good old days of his political youth, we find in this article ample evidence of a degree

---

* *Quarterly Review,* XCIX (1856), 527. In an earlier paper which he did not publish Gladstone had noted the decline of parties after 1846. "The great characteristic of this singular state of things," he wrote, "is that political differences no longer lie between parties, but within parties. The most Conservative Liberal and the most Liberal Conservative not only are near one another; but probably the one of these two persons (and they both represent a class) who retains the Conservative designation is for every practical purpose, though his traditions and associations are the other way, the more Liberal of the two. Indeed on some great questions such for instance as Public Economy and Colonial Policy, the Peelites, who have never parted with the name Conservative, are much more in harmony with the strong advanced Liberal party than the Whigs" (British Museum, Add. MS. 44,745, ff. 198-199).

of party development with respect both to principles and to organization in the generation following 1815. After the victory of Free Trade in the late 'forties it became more difficult, however, to find any clear-cut line dividing parties. It may be admitted that it is difficult to distinguish between parties in the 1850's, but there were differences, some perhaps potential rather than actual. The Liberal's traditions and outlook still differed from the Conservative's. He was less afraid of change, readier to defend civil liberties, to make concessions to non-Anglicans, to extend the franchise, and to recognize popular national movements abroad.[3]

Although the passing of the great Reform Act did not effect much immediate change in the social composition of the House of Commons, it did make the average Member more sensitive to public opinion and consequently General Elections became more significant as a possible means of changing the government. For this reason the need for party organization outside Parliament increased, but actual development came slowly. Both parties appointed party agents to take charge of this work, and encouraged the growth of constituency associations and the business of registering the new voters. Thanks to the organizing genius of Francis Bonham, the party agent who enjoyed Peel's full support, the Tories, or Conservatives, as they now called themselves, were the more immediately successful.[4] Their opponents, although numerically greater in the 'thirties, were still a ramshackle coalition of aristocratic Whigs and Canningites, moderate Liberals, various brands of Radicals, and Irish Repealers. The Protectionist rebellion against Peel in 1846 brought about the collapse of Bonham's carefully constructed electoral machinery, but with the appointment, in 1853, of Sir William Joliffe as Chief Whip, and of Disraeli's friend, Philip Rose, as party agent, the Conservatives once more began to take the lead in this field. The Liberals had to wait until the appointment of Sir Henry Brand as their Chief Whip in 1859 before they could compete in the matter of extra-Parliamentary party organization.

The Conservatives also took the initiative as early as 1832 by founding the Carlton Club as an unofficial party headquarters to which by 1859 about two thirds of the Conservative peers and Members of Parliament belonged.[5] The Whig-Liberals reluctantly followed suit with the foundation of the Reform Club next door to the Carlton, but less than half the Liberal Members of Parliament belonged to it in 1859.*

* *Parliamentary Companion* (1859). Dod lists as members 145 Whigs, Liberals, and Radicals from the Commons and only 23 from the Lords. Brooks's, with older traditions and more exclusive socially, had a membership of 128 Lib-

II

But even with some organization, problems of leadership provided a drag on the development of both the major parties in the 'fifties. Palmerston's presence at the head of the Liberals proved an especially embarrassing obstacle impeding the normal course of that party's evolution. He had long been an outsider in the Whig-Liberal camp, and in the end circumstances had made him its leader almost accidentally. Lord John Russell, Liberal Prime Minister from 1846 to 1852, had lost the confidence of most of his followers by his conduct in dismissing Palmerston from office in 1851 and again when he deserted his colleagues in 1855, and was consequently unable to form a government when the Aberdeen coalition collapsed in the latter year. The war made Palmerston the obvious man in the eyes of the country and so with varying degrees of enthusiasm most of the Liberals accepted him, but when peace came he was bound to put a cramp on any party calling itself Liberal. One thinks of his smiling rejoinder to a young colleague inquiring about legislation for the coming session: "Oh, there is really nothing to be done. We cannot go adding to the statute book *ad infinitum!*"[6] His conservatism in domestic affairs and his forthright championship of British national interests abroad made him, in fact, an acceptable Premier to many Conservatives. According to Herbert, "the regular old-fashioned country gentlemen who are not Londoners enough to have come within the vortex of the Carlton are Palmerstonian *pur et simple.*"[7] Indeed, to Distraeli's chagrin, Derby was long content to leave Palmerston in office for fear of something worse.

The fourteenth Earl of Derby, an aristocrat of great wealth and social position, a celebrated Parliamentary debater and a tough political fighter, was the only possible Conservative leader after the schism of 1846, but he lacked the qualities of ambition and dedication normally necessary for successful party leadership. In 1856 Lord

---

eral M.P.'s. and 14 peers, few of whom were members of the Reform. In the article already quoted Gladstone made an amusing reference to the proximity of the two clubs: "He who turns from Pall Mall towards the Park between the Reform and the Carlton Clubs will perceive that each of those stately fabrics is mirrored in the windows of the other; and it may occur to him with horror or amusement, according to his temper, that these mutual reflections of images set up in rank antagonism to one another, constitute a kind of parable, that offers to us its meaning as we read with conscience and intelligence the history of the time" (*Quarterly Review,* XCIX [1856], 562).

Malmesbury prodded him into writing a letter on party affairs that revealed these weaknesses: "We have been so busy shooting that I have had no time to give to politics," he confessed in explanation of his carelessness in correspondence. He freely admitted the disorganization of the party, but was rather surprised that it was not worse! He alluded to Disraeli's unpopularity and as for himself admitted: "I *never* was *ambitious* of office, and am not likely to become more so as I grow older."[8]

Although most Members of Parliament called themselves either Liberal or Conservative by the 1850's and received notices from one or the other of the party whips, it is difficult to be precise about numbers at any one time; there were always those who hovered on the fringes, perhaps temporarily alienated from the party leadership of the day.* An examination of the *Parliamentary Companion* for 1859 prior to the election of that year suggests that there were some 379 members who might be classified as belonging to the Liberal party, of whom 341 called themselves Liberals. Only twelve are classified as "Whig," a term that no longer carried any official significance, but merely denoted the old-fashioned right wing of the party. (The clique of aristocratic leaders who are commonly dubbed "Whig" all called themselves "Liberal" by this time.) Another fourteen are listed by Dod as "Radical Reformers," but most of the Radicals now accepted the name of Liberal. Since there was no clear line dividing the Radicals from the main body of the Liberals and since there were so many different types of the species—philosophical, humanitarian, Manchester school, and independent—it is impossible to give any exact estimate of their numbers, but we may put them in the neighbourhood of one hundred, the number who supported Locke King's Reform motion of 1851 against the party leadership in the previous Parliament.[9] While most Radicals were agreed in their opposition to aristocratic privilege and in their championship of Free Trade and Parliamentary Reform, they were often divided on foreign affairs. Here the Manchester men, Cobden and Bright, were apt to find that they had more in common with the Peelites than with the Radicals of the Roebuck variety. There were also a number of Liberals who preferred Russell to Palmerston and who voted with most of the Ra-

---

* Indeed it has been said with some truth that this was the age of the independent member, and Mr. John Kenyon has suggested to me that the development of party organization at this time was as much an attempt by party leaders to counter the strength of these independents as it was to organize the constituencies. See *Saturday Review*, III (1857), for an article on "Independent Voting and Party Government."

dicals and the Peelites to put Palmerston out of office in 1858. Finally we may note the group known as the Irish Brigade, who had acted independently of the main party since Russell's ill-conceived Ecclesiastical Titles Act of 1851, but their numbers had dwindled away to about a dozen by 1859 and they ceased to operate as a separate force after the election of that year.[10]

It is also a difficult task to count the Conservatives in the 1850's, although they do not fall into as many categories as their opponents. Dod lists 222 "Conservatives" and fifty-five "Liberal-Conservatives" on the eve of the election of 1859, but Disraeli, ignoring the latter category, counted 260 safe Conservatives in this Parliament.*[11] Only a handful of these Liberal-Conservatives, however, were Peelites proper, for the most part survivors of Peel's great ministry. In the days of the Aberdeen coalition (1852-55) they had numbered as many as forty, but no attempt had been made to resurrect this group as a party when the coalition broke up. The Peelites of the later 1850's were simply the ex-Peelite ministers of Aberdeen's Government along with a few personal and unsolicited followers.† The triumvirate of Graham, Gladstone, and Herbert, all close friends and former Cabinet colleagues, sat together on the front bench below the gangway on the Government side of the House of Commons from 1855 to 1858. These three and Edward Cardwell, who had resigned with them in 1855 from a post outside the Cabinet, met frequently with old Lord

* Nine of Dod's "Liberal Conservatives" are listed as "Liberals" by The Times after the election, but the bulk of the group had no intention of breaking with the party, although perhaps temporarily dissatisfied with its leadership. Some of them might have been those Conservatives who were content to see Palmerston as Prime Minister, but the majority were probably heirs of the Peel tradition and would have welcomed Gladstone's return to supplant Disraeli in the House of Commons.[12]

† Gladstone vividly described their position in his anonymous article on "The Declining Efficiency of Parliament": "Among the anomalies and solecisms of the Lower House in its present condition, one of the greatest, without doubt, is the position of those gentlemen who pass by the appellation of Peelites, and who, ejected from office by their scruples and difficulties with respect to the Sebastopol Committee, have since maintained an attitude which the country, as represented by its press, plainly considers to be equivocal. Moreover it is plain that, among all the outliers from the great parties, none, not even Lord John Russell, so powerfully tends to prolong the existing state of general weakness, and the relaxation in party organization. Not that they are powerful either in their numbers or in the general favour, but that by their traditions if not by their characters, they happen to have points of contact and of sympathy, rather marked in their character with gentlemen sitting on both sides of the House who own no general political connection with them" (Quarterly Review, XCIX [1856], 565).

Aberdeen, their revered former chief, now living in virtual retirement.[13] All four were noted for their ability as debaters and administrators, the combination that made Peelites such desirable Cabinet material when any Prime Minister designate of the 'fifties was scratching for a team.

Graham, Herbert, and Cardwell were by this time virtually independent Liberals. Gladstone, the most important of the four, was the enigma. Everyone recognized that he had the greatest gifts, but many of his best friends feared that he was throwing them away; personal ties and his lively distrust of Palmerston drove him towards the Derby camp, but whenever the gate was opened he hesitated, put off by what he saw within, and withdrew. The result was four years of bitter frustration: from February 1855, when he resigned from Palmerston's newly formed first ministry, to June 1859, when he joined the second. In 1857 he gave vent to his pent-up emotions by drafting (but not publishing) "An Indictment of Lord Palmerston" in the form of an open letter to Lord Aberdeen, the device he had used in 1851 to denounce the Neapolitan atrocities. Condemning Palmerston's prolongation of the war, his illiberal fiscal policy, and his lack of Reform legislation, Gladstone accused him of forsaking the true policy of Liberalism, and here we begin to perceive the secret of Peelism:

> In fair competition fifteen years ago, Sir Robert Peel, then the trusted head of the Conservative body, carried away from his Liberal opponents the prize of more vigorous administration and of superior zeal for practical reform. . . . Disinclined, I believe down to the latest hour of his life, to organic changes, he sought to attach the people to our political institutions and the present structure of the representative system by letting them feel its increased benefits.[14]

Thus it may be seen that even in 1857 Gladstone had the makings of what would later be called a Gladstonian Liberal, and his flirtation with Derby from 1856 to 1859 was due only to Palmerston's repudiation of the principles and policies which were to be the essence of Gladstonian Liberalism. The flirtation came to nothing because in fact, despite some nostalgic attachments, Gladstone was no longer a Conservative at heart and he knew that he was *persona non grata* to many in the Conservative party. There were some Conservatives who would have liked to see Gladstone oust Disraeli from their leadership in the Commons, but Gladstone doubtless realized that Derby was too far committed. This realization must have made his decision easier, although he would never admit, even to himself, that Disraeli's position was the decisive factor. On the other hand he would not join the Liberal party until he felt he could turn it towards Liberalism as

170 J. B. CONACHER

he understood it. Heartened by his continued attacks on Palmerston, the Conservatives in office made renewed overtures to Gladstone in 1858 and finally in early 1859, but all to no avail. Gladstone could not be persuaded to act alone, to desert his old colleagues and enter a Cabinet of strangers. If he ever wished to hold office again, therefore, he would have to make his peace with the Liberals.

We may conclude then in light of the tests which we have set that, while "party" clearly existed in the 1850's, the dividing lines were blurred and organization was incomplete, with the result that party leaders could never be certain of the exact number of their followers after a General Election until a vote had been taken in the House of Commons. It would take years and at least one more Reform Act to achieve anything like the modern ideal, but the events of 1859, by reuniting the old Whig leaders and disposing forever of the problem of the Peelites, were to be an important preliminary in any movement toward that goal.

III

The continued existence of a minority government in office from February 1858 to March 1859 without serious challenge vividly demonstrates the political chaos of the times. The second Derby-Disraeli administration had come into being in February 1858 only as a result of disunion among the Liberals, and it had been kept in office for a whole year by the tacit support of some ninety-odd independent Liberals, Radicals, Peelites, and Irish who were opposed to Palmerston's return. As the price of office the Conservatives had to agree to measures such as Jewish emancipation, which they normally would have opposed, and so left themselves open to charges of political inconsistency and infidelity. The curious debates on Indian affairs in 1858 in particular reflected this strange state of affairs. The Conservatives were forced to bring in an India Bill they did not really want. Some of the absurd provisions of their original Bill gave the Opposition a wonderful opportunity of driving them out, but the Liberals were not yet ready to settle their own differences. Russell let the Government down lightly by suggesting that the Bill should be replaced by resolutions that eventually became the basis of the India Act of 1858.

The session of 1859 opened on 3 February in an atmosphere of deceptive calm. The speech from the Throne dwelt complacently on the general quiet at home and abroad. No direct reference was made to the affairs of Italy, but a measure of Parliamentary Reform was forecast.[15] These two important issues were to bring about the fall of the ministry.

Framing the main headings of a Reform Bill was a favourite intellectual pastime of the politicians of the period. But Bright was the only important Member of Parliament who approached the subject with crusading fervour and his aim was avowedly to upset the aristocratic bias of the constitution. Russell and Graham, the surviving members of the famous committee that drafted the first Reform Bill, were anxious to see a second, but for different reasons. They recognized the justice of the argument for some working-class representation and regarded an extension of the franchise as inevitable sooner or later. They wanted to settle the matter before the demand became too extreme, and Russell was no doubt personally ambitious to have his name associated with such a settlement. Some of their political associates such as Herbert and Argyll were moderately interested and ready to discuss the terms of a Reform Bill, but the majority looked upon it with varying degrees of coolness and treated it as a political manœuvre. These were the circumstances under which the Conservative Government's bill was introduced on 28 February. As another survivor of the great Reform Ministry, Derby himself was open-minded on the subject, while Disraeli was always ready to propose the unusual. They were both aware of the issue's electoral possibilities, but they had a difficult time convincing the Cabinet and lost two ministers before doing so. Their critics professed to be scandalized by the sight of an anti-Reform party bringing in a Reform Bill, and Reformers saw little merit in a bill that failed to lower the borough franchise. The Bill was ill-conceived from the Administration's point of view because it was too conservative to excite the public, yet it made some of the Conservatives uneasy and rallied the different sections of the Opposition. Bright's criticisms were to be expected, but it had been hoped that the Peelites, Russell, and other independent Liberals might continue to support the Ministry for tactical reasons, and even that Palmerston and the right-wing Whigs might settle for such a moderate solution to the Reform issue. But Russell was not ready to play second fiddle in any Reform orchestra, and developments in Italy had revived his traditional suspicion and mistrust of the Tories. For similar reasons Palmerston too was ready to oppose them, making the proposals for a uniform franchise his pretext.

Palmerston shrewdly allowed Russell to take the lead and show himself over-ambitious for office by moving a set of resolutions embodying his views as to the principles on which a Reform Bill should be based. The ageing Greville, nearing the end of his long diary, was equally caustic about the tactics of both parties, the Conservatives for their inconsistency in bringing in any Reform Bill, the Whigs for the dishonesty of their arguments. He regarded "the whole state of affairs with indescribable disgust and no small apprehension," and contrasted it bitterly with the situation in 1832 when "the interest was intense, the whole country in a fever of excitement, the Press rabid, the clamour for Reform all but universal, party feeling running tremendously high."[16] Greville was too hard on the politicians, perhaps because he secretly envied them. Their approach to the problem was largely political, of course, but many of them did believe that, no matter how unpleasant Reform was, something had to be done about it. Moreover, their jockeying for office was not merely ambition. It is not improper in Parliamentary politics for the "outs" to believe themselves more capable of looking after national affairs than the "ins," and in 1859 foreign affairs alone gave ample cause for the Liberals to hold this view. It is interesting to note that in the debate Herbert and Stanley, speaking on opposite sides, both expressed the view that the old system of party government was pretty well at an end. "Some years hence," said Herbert, "what man will ask, 'Who was Prime Minister in 1859?' "[17] Herbert's friend Graham was nearer the truth a few months earlier when he wrote to Lord John Russell: "New events will give rise to new combinations. I shall not live to see them, at all events I am too old to enter into them. But if parliamentary government be prolonged in this country, I am satisfied that it must rest on the basis of party."[18]

IV

The outcome was the defeat of the Government on 31 March by 330 to 291, despite the support of Gladstone and of several independent Liberals. This was followed by a surprise dissolution and although in the subsequent election the Conservatives gained some 24 seats, their total was only 302 as against 353 for the Liberals.[19] Greville judged that the General Election had "manifested the indifference of the Country to all parties and to all political ties and connexions." "In the last General Election," he observed, "the cry was all for Palmerston, in this there has been no cry for anybody, neither for Palmerston nor Derby, and less than all for J. Russell or Bright."[20]

It remained to be seen whether the various sections of the Liberal Opposition could be brought and kept together in a common front. For more than a year the Conservative Government had remained in office with well under 300 supporters, but this was because of the aversion of the independent Liberals to Palmerston. Having put Derby in office by their action on the Orsini vote, they had felt constrained to give him a chance. The dissolution, however, had broken the spell. Almost all the Liberals were highly critical of it, and a new Parliament would have none of the scruples of the old one about keeping in office a minority government that had been put there by a vote of the old House of Commons. The question remained whether Palmerston and Russell, the rival claimants for the premiership, could bury their differences.

In the meantime Derby and Disraeli were making the last of their innumerable attempts to attract independent support, Liberal or Peelite. Disraeli was ready to try anything—to approach Palmerston with assurances on foreign policy, to entice the Irish Brigade with prospects of patronage, to rally Roebuck and some Radicals by more talk of Reform, and even to push Derby into yet another approach to Gladstone—but all to no avail.[21]

In the Liberal camp the pieces at last began to fall into place. Austria's ill-judged demands on Sardinia and the arrival of ex-Neapolitan prisoners in England had helped to arouse English public opinion to sympathy with the Italians and had induced Palmerston to come out strongly in favour of Italian independence in a revised election speech at Tiverton. The indispensable requirement, of course, was the reconciliation of Palmerston and Russell, and the ground had been prepared by their co-operation on the latter's Reform Resolutions in the House of Commons.[22]

It was quite in character for Lord Granville, one of the younger Whig peers who was normally on good terms with everybody, to initiate the reconciliation by urging Palmerston to get in touch with Russell. Palmerston sent Sir George Cornewall Lewis, a highly respected Whig baronet and former editor of the *Edinburgh Review,* to see Russell and discuss the wisdom of a want of confidence motion. Russell undertook to consult his Peelite friends, Graham and Herbert, who impressed upon him the necessity of framing a motion that would command the support of all the 350 Liberal members and warned him that his own absence from a Liberal government would be fatal. Russell declared his anxiety to dispel the idea that differences between him and Palmerston stood in the way of the formation of a Liberal government, but declined "to accept office without power," either as Prime Minister or as leader in the Commons. On 20 May, Palmerston visited Russell on the latter's invitation and the two rivals reached agreement on a number of important points: Reform, foreign policy, and the desirability of a want of confidence motion. They also agreed that any new administration must be formed "on a broad basis," but Russell

ominously insisted upon "reserving" his "entire freedom." For the
next two weeks he remained "in a very unsettled state of mind." Herbert, Graham, and his brother, the Duke of Bedford, all pressed him
to be reasonable, but with no immediate success.

It is interesting to note the way in which both factions among the
Whigs sought the good offices of Herbert and Graham to heal the
breach, and that both Palmerston and Russell insisted that Peelite
participation in any Liberal government was essential. Herbert suggested that "the two rivals should agree to serve together as the Queen
may direct" and call a meeting of the whole party to determine their
course. "They [the Liberals] are very independent in habits and feelings," he told Lord Granville, "and the time is gone by when they will
vote like a flock of sheep for whatever some half dozen men may
concoct in a library." Granville urged these proposals on Palmerston,
who accepted them, and finally after much hesitation Russell did so
as well.

It was widely held that the balance of power lay with some thirty
Radical Reformers who looked on John Bright as their spokesman.
Consequently, on 3 June, Russell paid a visit to Bright and his colleague,
Milner Gibson, and told them that he and Palmerston proposed to
issue an invitation to a party meeting and were anxious to secure Milner Gibson's signature as a Radical sponsor. Bright and Gibson considered it a "satisfactory" interview and agreed to the proposal.[23]

The great meeting was held at Willis's Rooms (formerly Al-
mack's) on 6 June and attended by 274 Liberal members, a large number considering that the session was only beginning on the following
day. The meeting got off to a good start when old "Pam." climbed onto
the raised dais and turned around to help little Johnny Russell up by
the hand, to the delight of the assembly who broke into "a droll burst
of cheering."[24] The meeting was addressed by Palmerston, who dwelt
on the weakness of the Government's foreign policy; by Russell, who
deprecated the continuance in office of a minority government after
an election; by Bright, who agreed to sink old differences if some
attention were paid to the men below the gangway when a Liberal
government was formed; and by Herbert, who strongly urged resolute
and united action by all the Liberals.[25] According to Herbert's account, Russell promised that "if the Queen sent for Pam. he, Johnny,
would cheerfully co-operate with him in the formation of a Government—broad basis, etc.,—and then Pam. whispered to him, and he
added as much for Pam."[26] It was a remarkably harmonious meeting
and only three members[27] opposed the proposal to move a vote of
want of confidence in the Conservative Government.

When Parliament assembled on the following day the newly united Liberals immediately moved their vote of want of confidence. Disraeli[28] spoke first for the Government but warned his followers to keep silent in the hope of a quick division before the Liberal forces were mustered. "The country party received the order of the day with military obedience," recorded *The Times,* "and the whole phalanx prepared to march into the lobby, but determined not to say a word." There was great scurrying around on the part of Lord John, drumming up speakers for the opposition "in order that Palmerston might be able to defer his speech late enough to justify an adjournment to Thursday."[29] Disraeli's little ruse failed, and when the division finally came on 12 June the Government was defeated by 323 to 310 (excluding three pairs and the tellers). Gladstone and fourteen Liberals voted for the Government, but eight of those supporting the Opposition were Liberal Conservatives in Dod's classification.[30]

V

Gladstone's position throughout the crisis was an anomalous one. He had only arrived home from his comic opera adventure in the Ionian Islands in March. On the way back he had noted preparations for war in Venice and Turin and had visited Cavour, who easily aroused his old pro-Italian sentiments. His distrust of Malmesbury as a foreign secretary at such a crucial time and the Conservative Government's reputed sympathy for Austria were obviously important factors in governing his course in the months to come, but he did not see his way immediately to break with the Government that he had been supporting. (Gladstone had a penchant for doing things the hard way that would have warmed the heart of Mark Tapley.) He accepted the Conservative Reform Bill complacently on the grounds that an early and moderate solution to the problem was desirable and he refused to be shocked at the spectacle of an anti-reforming party introducing such a measure. He continued to write for the Tory *Quarterly Review,* although what he had to say about Italy in the April number was a shock to many of its readers.[31] He was also critical of the dissolution and after the election discouraged renewed overtures from Derby.[32]

The Liberals, despite past bruises, included him as a possibility in all their tentative Cabinet making. Lord Aberdeen wryly acknowledged Palmerston's pro-Italian speech at Tiverton as a "brilliant stroke," because it had "secured Gladstone." It was a clever forecast, but he kept the Liberals on tenterhooks until the end. "One very unfavourable symptom is that Gladstone hangs back," Russell wrote to Graham on 26 May. "If he will not vote a want of confidence will he accept office in the new Government?"[33] Gladstone told his friend Herbert that his position was "a very odd one" since he was in full agreement with Russell and Palmerston on the question of Italy and distrusted Malmesbury's conduct of foreign affairs. He wrote:

> Under such circumstances, it will not be pleasant to me to have to give a vote which will appear to mean confidence in the Government. . . . Such, however, seems likely to be my fate. For I have not brought myself to think that a man who has been acting as I have wholly out of concert with Opposition, can safely, I would almost say can honourably, *enter* Opposition, so to speak, by a vote of such sweeping and strong condemnation as a vote of no confidence must always be, and, of course, intended for the resumption of office. This personal difficulty I have intimated to Ellice, to Wood, and last night to Lord Palmerston, who broke ground with his usual good humour, at his party, on the subject of the coming vote.

He would, he said, have voted for a moderate motion disapproving of the dissolution.[34] It is doubtful if bluff old Palmerston could follow the intricacies of Gladstone's strange conscience any more than could Sir Robert Peel years earlier when the young Gladstone resigned office over the Maynooth grant although he privately supported it! Yet his obvious anguish probably helped to reassure the Liberals that they would secure Gladstone in the end.

Why, it may be asked, were they so anxious? It was a hard question to answer for disappointed Whigs such as Lady Clarendon, who shortly afterwards wrote in her journal: "Why he who voted in the last division with the Derby Ministry should not only be asked to join this one, but be allowed *to choose his office,* I cannot conceive, or rather—I *can* conceive because I know it is for his power of speaking. They want his tongue to help and they dread it in opposition."[35] She might also have remembered his ability to draw up a budget to catch the public imagination. In the end Gladstone gave the Government his silent vote, but it was the last time in his long life that he would enter a Conservative lobby. Thirty-five years with the Liberal Party lay ahead of him.

VI

After the defeat of the Derby Government, the Queen unsuccessfully attempted to foil the two old stagers whom she detested by calling Lord Granville, who in fact had been caretaker leader of the party for the preceding year.[36] Palmerston agreed to lead in the House of

Commons under Granville but Russell declined to join, explaining, according to Granville "that with Lord Palmerston he would only have to consider who was to have the first and who the second office in the State, that with me [Granville] he should only occupy the third, and should not feel that he had sufficient security either on foreign affairs or on Reform."[37] So Granville threw up his commission, which was hopeless from the start, and the Queen was forced in the end to recall her old *bête noire*. Palmerston, brisk as ever and obviously delighted with the way the cards had fallen into his hand, immediately drove to Pembroke Lodge to call for "the little man's" assistance and to offer him his choice of office. Russell inconveniently chose the Foreign Office, which forced Palmerston to withdraw a previous offer to Clarendon, who accepted with good grace but declined any other post. Thereafter the old rivals ("the old Italian masters," a wit dubbed them) worked harmoniously together until death finally removed Palmerston from the scene in 1865, leaving Russell one last twilight session as Premier before he finally retired.

Palmerston's second ministry of 1859 is sometimes considered as the last of the old aristocratic Whig Administrations, a mere reshuffle of its predecessors. Herbert, himself the son of an earl, told Graham, "I fear we must run the risk of three Dukes."[38] In addition there was the brother of a fourth duke, four other peers, and two sons of peers, and three aristocratic baronets. Nevertheless Palmerston and Granville were the only ministers to return to the same offices that they had left the previous year and all elements who participated in the meeting at Willis' Rooms were represented. Bright was pleased when he first heard that office would be offered to Milner Gibson and Cobden. "We have succeeded in breaking down the exclusiveness of the family party, and this is something," he wrote in his diary. On the other hand he expressed relief that he had not been offered office himself since he did not see how he "could join Palmerston for whom I have felt so much contempt," and he would now be free to continue to talk about the exclusiveness of the Whigs! "Better teach the people something good for the future than resign oneself to work institutions already in existence." He added rather smugly, "Few men can do the former; the latter is but a matter of routine."[39] History was to prove that Bright was temperamentally unsuited to be a minister, but Russell explained to him politely that it was his recent speeches which had precluded an invitation on this occasion. When it became apparent that there was not a secretaryship of state to spare for the Radicals, Bright became indignant that "the chief offices are to be given to the old place-men, and the crumbs to the representatives of the Independent

Liberals."[40] When Cobden returned to England a few weeks later he refused the Board of Trade which was offered to him, but Gibson accepted it.[41] Charles Villiers also represented the advanced section of the party, but scarcely the middle classes, in the Cabinet.

The Peelites came into the ministry *en masse,* but as individuals who now merged into the Liberal Party. Gladstone became Chancellor of the Exchequer, destined to be the strong man of the Government and Palmerston's successor; Newcastle Colonial Secretary, by way of atonement for his rough treatment in 1855; Sidney Herbert Secretary for War, and Cardwell Irish Secretary, both able administrators and Parliamentarians in the best Peelite tradition. The Duke of Argyll, Lord Privy Seal, was Peelite by origin, although he had remained with Palmerston in 1855; and so was the Earl of Elgin, the Postmaster General, whose career had been official rather than political. Graham declined office on account of age and health. The six remaining posts went to orthodox Whig-Liberals,[42] while many old Whig officeholders were perforce left out.

Gladstone, it may be said, backed into the Liberal party. Even though his decision disappointed some of his friends and annoyed some of his critics, it now seems to have been a sensible, almost an inevitable one. He had closed the door on Derby, and the participation in the Willis's Rooms meeting of Herbert, Russell, and the independent Liberals with whom he had co-operated against Palmerston in the previous year now held out promise of a new deal. The Palmerston Cabinet of 1859 was in fact very different from the despised administration of 1855-58 and there was important work for Gladstone to do. We may be surprised to find him confidently asserting: "Never had I an easier question to determine," but it was in his nature once he had made up his mind to be emphatic. To his friends who needed explanation he put it on the grounds of Reform and foreign policy. Derby had lost his chance to settle the former by his ill-advised dissolution, while in foreign policy he was now "in real and close harmony of sentiment with the new premier, and the new foreign secretary." He also felt that in finance there was much useful work to be done, "and that is was time that he put an end to the mischievous situation" created by his continued "isolated position, outside the regular party organization of parliament."[43]

The new Government was unpopular in Parliament and in the clubs[44] and many anticipated its early breakup. Yet it survived without upset longer than the previous ministries of Russell, Palmerston, or Aberdeen. It was not a great ministry, but it was important in that it marked the end of an era and made possible the transition from Whiggism to Liberalism. The alliance in Willis's Rooms of old Whigs, Liberals, Radicals, and Peelites was preserved despite many stormy passages and gave birth to the Gladstonian Liberal party of the coming era. The final absorption of the Peelites and the reconciliation of Russell and Palmerston removed two of the biggest obstacles that had thwarted the normal development of the party system. The extension of the franchise, the most belated sequel of the reunion, would in time remove yet another obstacle. The most important result of the Peelite wandering in the political wilderness since 1846 was to lead Gladstone eventually into the Liberal Party, but ironically the group that had stuck together so long in adversity was soon broken up once their goal was achieved. Aberdeen, Graham, Herbert, Newcastle, Canning, and Elgin all died within the next four years, but even before Herbert's death, Gladstone was discovering that politically he had more in common with Cobden and Bright than with his old friends of Oxford days. It was this discovery that made Gladstone the predestined leader of a new Liberal party and that led Palmerston in his last years to say, "Gladstone will soon have it all his own way and whenever he gets my place we shall have strange doings."[45]

VII

In the field of politics 1959 is a far cry from 1859. How shocked the respectable mid-Victorian Member of Parliament would have been had he been able to foresee a House of Commons where the implications of manhood suffrage were taken for granted on both sides and where the benches on one side were largely filled by members drawn from the working classes. A century ago it would have been inconceivable that the Opposition's chief spokesman on foreign policy should be an ex-coal miner, much less that the Foreign Office would be directed for five years by an ex-drayman. To Gladstone, whose budget of 1860 was in the neighborhood of £70 million, a budget of over £5,000 million would have been as fantastic an idea as a trip to the moon.

Nevertheless on closer examination one is struck by the element of continuity in British political institutions over the past hundred years. If anything was settled in the year 1859 it was that the parliamentary system, advancing along the road to democracy, would do so within the framework of a two-party system. This system has been challenged on several occasions since then, but it has survived and taken deep root. Indeed it is so effectively organized in Britain today that some independent critics in the old radical tradition deplore the loss of liberty to the independent Member that is involved. A Cobden or a Bright would undoubtedly have agreed with the recent strictures of Mr. Michael Foot,[46] but it may be presumed that Gladstone and Disraeli would appreciate the logic behind the party development that has taken place since their day.

The Liberal Party that was emerging a century ago has, it is true, virtually disappeared, but its inheritance has been zealously assumed by Labour. Despite nominal preoccupation with the nationalization of industry, the latter party stands by many of the same principles that inspired nineteenth-century Liberalism, especially with respect to foreign affairs. By its nature the party of the left faces greater difficulty than does the party of the right in holding together the various elements that compose it. This was true in 1859, but the coalition that emerged in that year held together after a fashion for sixty years despite the gradual disappearance of the Whig element which really had no place in a modern party of the left. The modern Labour Party has a similar problem in holding together the uneasy alliance of trade unionists and cooperativists, doctrinaire socialists, and old Liberals which make it up. For better or for worse it has met the challenge by imposing a much higher degree of party discipline than Members of Parliament would have accepted in the past.

It may be questioned whether the standing orders of the Parliamentary Labour Party binding all members by party decisions[47] are really necessary for the proper working of the two-party system, but the effectiveness of that system is clearly reflected in the British political scene of the 1950's, where a General Election always holds the immediate possibility of a well-organized Opposition being transformed into a powerful Government. Regular sample polls of the electorate enable the public (and the politicians) to see which way the electoral wind is blowing at any given time. The imagination boggles at the idea of a Gallup poll anticipating the outcome of an election in the 1850's.

The importance of 1859 in British political history must not be exaggerated, of course, but we have seen that it is a date of some significance in the history of British political parties. Its events ensured the emergence of a Gladstonian Liberal party with traditions and principles that have in part survived to the present day, and they contributed to the development of a healthy two-party system, which has been an important factor in British political stability in the twentieth century.

DEREK BEALES

AN INTERNATIONAL CRISIS:
THE ITALIAN QUESTION

HROUGHOUT the year 1859 Europe was in crisis: from late April until early July, France and Piedmont-Sardinia were at war with Austria in Italy; before April an outbreak was expected; and after July a resumption. This essay is concerned with the crisis itself and with England's reaction to it.

I

On 21 July 1858 Napoleon III, the Emperor of France, and Count Cavour, the Prime Minister of Piedmont, had met for eight hours at Plombières to plan a war against Austria. The report of their conversation sent by Cavour to his King, Victor Emmanuel, lays bare the plot: "The Emperor began by saying that he was determined to support Sardinia with all his strength in a war against Austria, provided that the war should be undertaken for a non-revolutionary cause which could be justified in the eyes of diplomacy and still more of public opinion in France and Europe." Such a pretext was found, though with difficulty: it was decided to exploit the chronic discontent in the Duchy of Modena, an Austrian satellite state. Then:

Turning next to examine the means of ensuring a happy issue out of the war, the Emperor observed that we must try to isolate Austria and to deal only with her; hence his great concern that the war should be motivated by a cause which would not alarm the other Powers and which would be popular in England. The Emperor seemed convinced that the one we had adopted answered this double purpose. The Emperor is absolutely confident of the neutrality of England; he recommended us to make every effort to influence public opinion in that country to force her government, which is its slave, to undertake nothing in favour of Austria. He relies equally on the Prince of Prussia's antipathy to the Austrians to keep Prussia from pro-

Italy in 1859

nouncing against us. As for Russia, he has the Emperor Alexander's formal promise, several times repeated, not to oppose his designs on Italy. If the Emperor is not deceiving himself—and I am rather inclined to believe he is not from all he has told me—the question would be restricted to a war between France and us on one side and Austria on the other.

If France and Piedmont should be victorious, Austria's Italian provinces, Lombardy and Venetia, would be taken from her and annexed to Piedmont. With the removal from Italy of the influence of Austria, her satellites would be fatally weakened, and Piedmont could expect further gains in the North. There might also be erected a Central Italian Kingdom based on Tuscany. The Pope was to be left in possession at least of the City of Rome; the King of Naples would remain undisturbed. If all went well, the resulting four states would be federated under the presidency of the Pope. France was to receive Savoy and perhaps Nice from Piedmont; and Prince Napoleon, the Emperor's cousin, was to marry Princess Clotilde, Victor Emmanuel's daughter.[1]

In the short run, and in general, Napoleon's calculations proved remarkably accurate. Austria was duly goaded into aggression, though not by the exploitation of discontent in the Duchy of Modena; she remained isolated until the end of June; and she was defeated. But in July, when Prussia seemed to be on the point of joining Austria, Napoleon suddenly made peace, before his army had conquered Venetia. He met the Emperor of Austria at Villafranca, and persuaded him to agree to Piedmont's annexing Lombardy, but to no other territorial changes. So, although the inhabitants of Tuscany, Modena, Parma, and the Romagna had taken advantage of the war to rebel against their rulers, it now appeared likely that the old régimes would be restored. Gradually the tense situation changed. The revolutionary governments of Central Italy succeeded in maintaining themselves, and the peoples declared for annexation to Piedmont. But at the end of 1859 it was far from certain that Austria would tolerate this outcome.

No present-day historian can forget that the Franco-Austrian War was the first stage in the unification of Italy; that the unification of Italy helped to prepare the way for the unification of Germany; and that these two achievements, taken together, established in Europe the uneasy balance of power which invited a catastrophe like that of 1914. But it is necessary to try to forget. It would not be proper to join historians who have rejoiced at what is seen in retrospect to have been the first stage in the unification of liberal Italy, nor, on the other hand, to lament the establishment of a dangerous precedent for Bismarckian *Realpolitik* and a step on the road to Armageddon. The focus in this essay must be the aims, hopes, and fears of the men of 1859 themselves, and the significance for them of the year's events.

Italian unification was not considered a practical aim in 1858 and 1859. The followers of Giuseppe Mazzini, Italy's great prophet of nationalism, had been discredited by the repeated failures of their attempts at unification by revolution. Despite the boldness of the Plombières scheme, and although Cavour pointed out to Victor Emmanuel that under its terms Piedmont would effectively control the whole peninsula, there was then no hint that Italy might soon be politically integrated. And for some months after Villafranca unification appeared more remote still.

At first sight the Plombières plot does seem to be an exercise in pure *Realpolitik*. But in fact something like it was a necessary stage in any practical scheme for the emancipation of Italy, and was recognised as such. Because Austria dominated the peninsula and buttressed its

rulers in their refusal to make any concessions whatever to their subjects, liberals had no alternative but to work for her ejection from Italy.
Of the Italian states only Piedmont would help them; Piedmont could
not succeed without an ally; and the only available ally was France.
Though unification appeared impossible, Plombières gave hope of
emancipation. And it was a hope which, in varying degrees and in
different ways, both Cavour and Napoleon III shared. There is little
reason to believe that Cavour was working for the unification of Italy,
even as an ultimate goal, at any time before the middle of 1860; and
he often thought more of the aggrandisement of Piedmont than of the
liberation of Italy. But there is no doubt that he was something of a
nationalist and something of a liberal. He was more ready than most
Piedmontese to ally with nationalists in other parts of the peninsula and
to see his own state incorporated in a united Italy. He identified himself with moderate Italian nationalism when he resigned in disgust at
the terms of Villafranca; and he resumed office only when it became
feasible, in January 1860, to encourage the nationalists of Central
Italy to defy those terms. He was by no means a scrupulous constitutionalist and parliamentarian. But he was more scrupulous than some:
he did try to justify his more high-handed actions, by alleging the
national emergency.[2] Napoleon, on the other hand, was certainly not a
liberal. But, as a former revolutionary, he had a streak of genuine
nationalist idealism in him. He did not wish to see Italy unified, but
he wished her to be independent. He was also anxious both to overthrow the European settlement of 1815, the principal object of which
had been to contain France, and to defeat Austria, his country's traditional enemy. A victorious war, particularly if it resulted in the annexation of Savoy and Nice, would gratify French patriotic feeling and
enhance his own and his dynasty's prestige.[3] Like Cavour, he was using
Italian nationalism to further dynastic ends. But, as also with Cavour,
that was not the whole story.

The pact concluded at Plombières, then, was an early example of
the alliances between monarchs and nations which were characteristic
of the third quarter of the nineteenth century, in marked contrast with
the period 1815-50 when nationalists were normally republicans. But
it was not a typical example, since the monarchs' sympathy with the
nationalist ideology was genuine, and some connexion between nationalism and liberalism subsisted.

It was also part of the Plombières plan to appeal to international
morality. Here the plotters were entirely cynical. They thought it essential to find a respectable pretext for war, since only then would
Austria remain isolated. Between Plombières and the outbreak of war

their diplomatic manoeuvres were directed towards "the definition of Austria as the aggressor."[4] They made much play with proposals for "disarmament"—what is now called demobilisation—and with projects for a European Congress to settle peacefully the questions in dispute. Verbal hypocrisy nearly proved insufficient. In mid-April Austria was reported to be willing to disarm, provided that other Powers did the same. France reluctantly joined England in pressing Piedmont to agree to follow suit, which she did on 19 April. Napoleon and Cavour seemed to have lost the game.

On the same day, however, Austria sent an ultimatum to Piedmont demanding that she disarm unilaterally. This colossal blunder put Austria manifestly in the wrong and ensured the success of the war plot. Her motives are not wholly clear. It looks as though she expected to receive support from England and Prussia—probably only moral support from the former, but material from the latter. When Austria sent off the ultimatum, she did not know that Piedmont had agreed to disarm in company with other Powers, and so she did not anticipate the hostile reaction it evoked. She may even have believed that Piedmont would comply with it. But, more important, she thought war was virtually inevitable. She knew that if a Congress were held on the Italian Question, she would find herself in a minority and be forced to make concessions. Russia was determined to spite her; Prussia resented her rivalry in the German Confederation; and England sympathised with some of the grievances of Italian liberals. Austria preferred the possibility, even the probability, of defeat in war to the certainty of defeat at the conference-table. She had had to mobilise partially at the beginning of the crisis; she could not afford to keep up this military effort much longer. She decided to fight while she could. On Austria's side the war was a preventive war.[5]

Villafranca was a transaction only slightly less conspiratorial than Plombières. As before, the conspiracy was primarily directed against the Concert of Europe. A localised war was terminated by localised peace negotiations. Napoleon made it appear to Austria that Prussia and England were ready to mediate on the basis of much greater Austrian concessions than he himself would ask. The French Emperor feared the intervention of Prussia on Austria's side. Curiously enough, the Austrian Emperor also feared it, since he realised he would have to give way to Prussia in Germany as the price of her support. So the two Emperors came to terms between themselves. True, they proposed to allow a European Congress to ratify their agreement. But they had no intention of submitting any further questions of importance to its decision.[6]

Napoleon at Villafranca had been conspiring also against his ally. The situation in Central Italy was getting out of hand, and the Emperor blamed Cavour for encouraging the rebellions there. But by the end of the year he was again indulging his sympathy with nationalism. He sanctioned the publication of a pamphlet called *The Pope and the Congress* on 22 December, which advocated the reduction of Papal territory to a small area around Rome itself, and also the acceptance of the principle of non-intervention in Italian affairs—in other words, the recognition of the revolutionary governments of Central Italy and the definitive exclusion of its former rulers. This was sufficient excuse for Austria to refuse to countenance the proposed Congress. It was therefore abandoned.

The Italian crisis, then, raised exceptionally clearly two of the perennial questions of international politics: first, can the promotion of an ideology be reconciled with a power-policy; second, should two or three states be allowed to settle between themselves matters which affect other states?

II

By the beginning of 1859 the plans of Napoleon and Cavour, though kept strictly secret, had been fathomed by most observers. The crisis proper may be said to have started with Napoleon's remark to the Austrian Ambassador on New Year's Day: "I regret that our relations are not so good as I would wish them to be."[7] This caused a great stir. But stronger hints followed. The marriage of Prince Napoleon and Princess Clotilde, for instance, took place on 30 January—a very clear indication of the existence of a Franco-Piedmontese alliance. What, then, was England's position?

As Napoleon predicted, England remained neutral. Her policy was first fully stated in despatches of 10 and 12 January to the other four Great Powers and to Piedmont. France, Piedmont, and Austria were urged to caution; Russia and Prussia were asked to join in mediation. England admitted that the Italians had genuine grievances: there were garrisons of both Austrians and French troops in the Papal States; both the Pope and the King of Naples misgoverned their territories. By comparison, in fact, Austria's administration in Lombardy and Venetia, recently somewhat liberalised, was altogether admirable. But in any case war would not solve the Italian Question. It might well, either by strengthening Austrian influence or substituting French, make its solution more difficult; or it might promote revolution, which neither side could desire. Negotiation was the only satisfactory means of ameliorating the condition of Italy. England herself would do anything she could to facilitate negotiation, but (though she did not inform every Power of this decision) she intended to maintain her neutrality "at all events and as long as possible."[8]

She did not deviate from this general line during the year. She gave positive advice, but took no positive action. Only once did she offer to commit herself materially: she told France in March that she would join with her in a guarantee of Piedmont against Austrian attack. But France backed out when England seemed in earnest. Otherwise, England refused to be tied: two requests from Austria for a guarantee were rejected before the war, and numerous less explicit French overtures both before and after it.[9] England's first recommendation to all other Powers at all stages was to keep the peace. Before the war she worked to prevent war; during the war she worked to localise it; after the war she worked to prevent a resumption. In this cause she even went so far as to warn Russia and France that they would not be allowed to extend hostilities to the Baltic and Adriatic without English retaliation.[10]

There was, however, a considerable modification in the emphasis and tone of her advice during the year. This was partly because in June Lord Derby's minority Tory Government was replaced by Lord Palmerston's Whig Government. But it was largely the simple result of changes in the international situation. At first Malmesbury, the Tories' Foreign Secretary, squarely blamed France and Piedmont, particularly Piedmont, for the crisis: "It is impossible, indeed, for any impartial person to agree with Count Cavour in seeking to justify the military preparations of Sardinia by the menacing attitude assumed by Austria. If the attitude of Austria imposes on Sardinia the present necessity, the language and conduct of Sardinia are, in the opinion of Her Majesty's Government, chiefly to blame for that attitude."[11] The Austrian ultimatum, however, caused Malmesbury to alter his tune. By sending it, he said, Austria "forfeits all claim upon the support or sympathy of England."[12] During the war his policy tended to assist France and Piedmont, because his main concern was to keep the conflict localised. But he treated their conquests as temporary and unfortunate.[13]

Russell, who took office in June as the Whigs' Foreign Secretary, wrote his despatches in quite a different style:

> Be their divisions and boundaries arranged as they may, it is the firm persuasion of Her Majesty's Government that an Italy in which the people should be "free citizens of a great country" would strengthen and confirm the balance of power. . . .

I must not omit to state that any settlement of Italy would, in the eyes of Her Majesty's Government, be incomplete, which did not effect a permanent reform in the administration of the States of the Church.

Every one knows that Rome and the Legations have been much worse governed by the Pope's Ministers than Lombardy by Austrian Archdukes, and that would be a partial and unsatisfactory arrangement which struck down the rule of the latter, and left the former in all its deformity.[14]

Much of the tenor of this despatch might have come from Malmesbury. There is the same concentration on the Papal States and something of the same reluctance to consider territorial changes necessarily related to internal improvements. But Russell was able to welcome the embryo "great country," because the new Government could acknowledge accomplished facts more easily than the old Government, committed as the latter had been to an obsolescent policy. Even though Russell did not take any more positive action than Malmesbury, his whole policy was more forward-looking, less conservative. He quickly announced England's disapproval of the Villafranca terms. He insisted that the principle of non-intervention in Italian affairs must be accepted before England could take part in the proposed Congress. He recommended that those parts of Central Italy which had declared themselves in favour of annexation to Piedmont should be allowed their way. Yet he was not entirely uncompromising: in a despatch of 26 November he informed France that, as a second-best, England would not oppose the establishment of an independent Central Italian Kingdom.[15] But this was his only retreat from the principle of self-determination. Personally, Russell, together with Palmerston and Gladstone, the Chancellor of the Exchequer, would have been prepared to give much stronger advice, and even to back up words with deeds; and in private these statesmen made their inclinations clear enough to foreign envoys. But the rest of the Cabinet, strongly encouraged by the Queen and the Prince Consort, prevented Russell committing the country to his own views in his official despatches.

Before the war and in its early stages, England was pessimistic; afterwards, optimistic. At first she doubted whether the plans of Napoleon and Cavour could contribute to Italian freedom; and she doubted also whether they were intended to. Villafranca, though in itself it belied the promises of the Emperor, seemed to open up the possibility of assisting liberal Italians without furthering Napoleon's ambition. Thus, England's policy reflected her basic interests. As a great imperial Power outside Europe and a great commercial Power within it, she could only desire the preservation of peace on the Continent. Her pre-eminence depended on the maintenance of some sort of

European balance of power; and, as long as the balance was not seriously threatened, she would not need to intervene in Continental struggles herself. The Italian crisis did not lead in the event to a disadvantageous adjustment in the balance, and England was relieved on other grounds not to be forced to take part. She was nominally the close ally of France, but traditionally she was Austria's ally. She sympathised with Italians' liberal aspirations, but not with their anxiety to overthrow the 1815 settlement. She was not, in fact, especially attracted to either side.

According to Napoleon at Plombières, the English Government was the slave of public opinion. Certainly the shifts of policy seem to have coincided more or less with shifts of opinion. The Italian crisis overshadowed domestic matters, as external questions often did between about 1848 and about 1866, and the issues it raised were widely discussed. The immediate reaction at the beginning of the year was strongly anti-French. As Gladstone wrote in an article in the *Quarterly Review:* "A sentiment not unlike that which excited this country during the Russian war was enlisted on behalf of Austria. . . . [This] was not due to any love for the Austrian Government or system, but to mistrust of Louis Napoleon, and to an impression that his words to [the Austrian Ambassador in Paris] savoured of that very spirit of *brigandage* which Russia had shown six years ago. . . . Italian interests were viewed in England, not as they are in themselves, but as the ministerial instruments of French or rather of Napoleonic ambition."[16] This attitude was largely shared by the most prominent members of the Whig Opposition. Even Palmerston, though he believed that Austria's retirement from Italy would be "an unmixed good," thought it "would be too dearly bought by the calamities and dangers of such a war as would be necessary for its accomplishment."[17] The English in general did not accept the fact that the Italian Question was more than a matter of local reforms. They clung to the conviction that it could, and should, be solved by peaceful change within the existing Italian state-structure. In Gladstone's words, "The relief of Italy is an honourable end, but it must not be sought by unholy means."[18]

Opinion began to shift a little before the Austrian ultimatum. *The Times* suddenly became more sympathetic with Piedmont at the beginning of April.[19] When Disraeli in the House of Commons on 18 April claimed that Austria had behaved well and Piedmont badly, Malmesbury could not help noticing "a very strong Sardinian feeling . . . & nothing is required to make it blaze forth but the smallest act of injustice by Austria."[20] Naturally the ultimatum produced a revulsion. To quote the Queen, it "entirely changed the feeling here, which was

THE GIANT AND THE DWARF.

"BRAVO, MY LITTLE FELLOW! YOU SHALL DO ALL THE FIGHTING, AND WE'LL DIVIDE THE GLORY!"

It was clearly *Punch*'s opinion that Napoleon III hoped for dynastic glory
through the efforts of Victor Emmanuel's little kingdom
of Piedmont-Sardinia.

all that one could desire, into the most *vehement* sympathy for Sar-
dinia."[20a] In the first months of the year it had seemed conceivable that
England might take Austria's side, since the public was so firm against
France. But, although rumours of an alliance between the two great
English bogeys, France and Russia, were causing general alarm at
the end of April, Derby assured the Queen "that no Government which

could be formed in this country could hope to carry public opinion with it in taking an active part, as matters now stand, against France and Russia."[21]

Malmesbury had been determined to "stand clear before the public of the rascality going on at Paris,"[22] but the ultimatum made this pose seem wholly inappropriate. The Tories found themselves identified with the apparent aggressors. They did their best to live it down. Derby described the ultimatum as "criminal"; Malmesbury damped the Court's pro-Austrian hopes.[23] The Opposition had seized on the Government's weakness and was trying hard to exploit it. But there is little evidence that the result of the May General Election was greatly affected by the country's preoccupation with foreign affairs. All candidates were by this time in favour of neutrality. It would be curious to find that the Election had been much affected, because in fact the Tories gained about twenty-five seats. There might have been a serious clash in Parliament, and, when it came to the drafting of the Queen's Speech, the Government was still anxious to dispel the impression that it was pro-Austrian. Derby told the Queen: "The charge now made against your Majesty's servants, by the opposition Press . . . is that their neutrality covers . . . designs in favour of Austria; and any word in your Majesty's Speech which should imply a doubt of the continuance of strict impartiality, would, undoubtedly, provoke a hostile Amendment, which might very possibly be carried in the Sardinian sense."[24] This peril at least was avoided; the Government was defeated on a general motion of no confidence. Though its management of foreign policy was a contributory factor in its downfall, the main cause was simply that it was a minority government, dependent for its survival on the continued divisions of the Opposition. These divisions were healed in May and June, partly again because of the foreign situation, but largely for other reasons.

During the autumn opinion moved in favour of the Italians. At the end of the year Palmerston and Russell thought it opportune to propose a close alliance with France on Italian affairs, Gladstone agreeing that public opinion would now support such an alliance.[25] The Cabinet declined to take the risk, although at least one of the objectors, the Duke of Argyll, the Lord Privy Seal, was confident that the country was very sympathetic.

Suspicion and jealousy of France [he wrote] has, till very lately, been the prevalent feeling and has completely overborne the sympathy which, otherwise, would exist for Italy.

Lately—since the peace, this feeling has been subsiding. I am satisfied that if Austria attempted violence again in Italy, the feeling for Italy

L'Empire c'est la paix

THE FRENCH PORCUPINE.

He may be an Inoffensive Animal, but he Don't Look like it

Punch, like Tennyson, clearly distrusted Napoleon III's claims of good will toward England.

would immediately rise in this country, and help the government in its course.[26]

It is plain that the Government's more radical policy, as far as it went, accorded with the attitude of the public in the latter half of the year.

Englishmen felt considerable sympathy with the Italian cause, but two other feelings dominated their outlook on the Italian crisis. The stronger was distrust of France, the roots of which went very deep in history. Napoleon III had revived it by his *coup d'état* of December 1851 which ended the Second French Republic, an event which seemed to Englishmen to be the climax of the absolutist and Catholic reaction after the 1848 revolutions. It evoked an invasion panic in England. During the Crimean War England and France were allies, and Russia became the principal bogey. But in 1858-59 hostility to France mounted again. Its most remarkable manifestation was the Volunteer Rifle Club movement, to which on 12 May a War Office circular gave official sanction. It aroused great enthusiasm, and by February 1860, 60,000 men had been enrolled.[27] The movement was unmistakably anti-French. Its mood was well expressed by Tennyson in his poem "The War," which was published in *The Times* on 9 May. The second verse is especially apposite:

> Be not deaf to the sound that warns!
> Be not gull'd by a despot's plea!
> Are figs of thistles, or grapes of thorns?
> How should a despot set men free?
> Form! Form! Riflemen form!
> Ready, be ready to meet the storm!
> Riflemen, riflemen, riflemen form!

According to the Prince Consort, the movement showed that "popular instinct teaches the man in the street who his enemy is and of what the Italian war is merely the first Act."[28]

Concern about national defence was general. For many months the Admiralty had been disturbed by French naval preparations. Iron-clad ships were commissioned by France earlier than by England. At the beginning of 1859 France had eight on order, whereas in June 1859 England had ordered only one. But by the end of the year, despite a delay due to the change of government, four were under construction. There was in addition a great increase in the expenditure on wooden ships, the object being to attain parity with France and Russia combined. It was not long before coastal fortifications too had to be remodelled.[29]

Associated with this movement, strangely enough, was an agitation for non-intervention. All this martial ardour was defensive. At the time of the General Election meetings were held all over the country in favour of neutrality. Malmesbury was hardly exaggerating when he informed Prussia that neutrality "may be said to be the only [point] in which the English people appear to be at the present moment absorbed."[30] The diarist Greville recorded: "The sentiments of people here are of a very mixed and almost contradictory character, for they are on the whole anti-Austrian, anti-French, and though more indulgent to the Sardinians than they deserve, not favourable to them. The most earnest and general desire is that we should keep out of the mêlée."[31] This determination to remain neutral was partly the result of the two opposed forces, anti-French feeling and pro-Italian feeling. But it was more than that. The belligerent mood which had produced the Crimean War was giving way to a more isolationist outlook. And "moral force" was being seen as an effective substitute for physical force. As Clarendon, a former Foreign Secretary, said: "The public generally are satisfied with the Foreign policy and think we stand well, and that nothing is to be done but to leave the Italians to themselves."[32]

Democracies have particular difficulty in forming their foreign policies. If mid-Victorian England was not a full democracy, she was near enough to that condition to share many of its problems. On the whole, she overcame them during this crisis, and her policy seemed successful in the outcome. For most of the year there was substantial agreement between the Government and public opinion on the main questions at issue. Although there were serious differences of emphasis between Government and Opposition from April to July, a definite breach of the principle of bi-partisanship was avoided. On the other hand, the change of Government demonstrated the advantages of a party-system, in that it made possible a greater degree of flexibility in foreign policy than could easily have been achieved otherwise.

England's policy seemed successful. She had been advocating the application of the principles of self-determination and non-intervention to the Italian situation. At the end of the year both these principles were on the point of general acceptance. But the achievement was not really England's. It was the armed force of France which decided the issues. Englishmen, both statesmen and public, tended to underrate the importance of power in international policies. They did so at the beginning of the year, when they assumed that the Italian Question could be solved without territorial changes; they did so at the end when they imagined that, by giving moral support to Central Italian patriots, they were thwarting French designs. This was the attitude, stated by the Lord President of the Council, Lord Granville: "While many of the Cabinet entertain insuperable objections to our engaging ourselves to give material assistance, all or nearly all are ready to agree to great moral support to France and to strong moral pressure upon Austria in order to prevent armed interference in Italy; in short, that independent and unfettered policy by which [Russell] has hitherto succeeded in preventing Italy from being bullied either by France or Austria."[33] Contrast the view of the Piedmontese Minister in London: "The strongest partisan of the English alliance could not fail to notice that it is tending to become sterile and unproductive, while we must think twice before we alienate a benefactor who protects us with fifty thousand men."[34] The experts, Palmerston and Russell, knew that a more active policy was needed. That the need was not immediately underlined by events was due to the good will of Napoleon III. England was fortunate that in the Italian crisis she was dealing with so sentimental a militarist, solicitous of the English alliance and sympathetic with Italian nationalism.

Napoleon and Cavour did not succeed in satisfying England that it was possible for foreign Powers to reconcile the promotion of an ideology with a power-policy. For herself, however, she contrived to pursue a policy in harmony with both her interests and her sympathies —though a rather negative one. She never had to make a choice between the two. When it is merely a case of giving advice, it is not difficult to have the best of several worlds.

By her neutrality England tacitly admitted that two or three states may be allowed to settle between themselves matters which affect other states. She was ready to go into Congresses and to mediate, though not with great enthusiasm; but she would not take action strong enough to impose her views.

III

Within another year the unification of Italy was all but completed. A new constitutionalist Great Power had been created. England's moral support had won the gratitude of the new nation-state. These results deeply impressed contemporary liberals, and have impressed many subsequent historians, as triumphs of enlightened and progressive statesmanship, particularly on the part of Cavour and Russell.

That is not the whole story. In the first place, it is doubtful how much control Cavour exercised over the swiftly-moving events of these two critical years, and also doubtful how much he desired unification. England was fortunate that she succeeded so well in associating herself with accomplished facts. When irresolution prospers, men are ready to call it flexibility. Second, to take a different point of view, Cavour's motives were very mixed and his methods exceptionable. It was by no means obvious that England should not oppose him. At no stage in the process of unification was the Concert of Europe consulted; and it was partly as a consequence of this neglect that international relations became more anarchical in the next decade, giving Bismarck his opportunity.[35] It was also partly as a result of the Italian crisis that England was psychologically unfit to face the developments of that decade. The real influence of Russell's policy was overrated, and a tendency grew to believe in the efficacy as well as to appreciate the convenience of non-intervention. While international tension increased, English interest in foreign affairs waned. For the present, England was in a position to ignore Europe's squabbles. She was still incomparably the greatest Power, though weak on land; as long as some sort of European balance was maintained, she could afford to dispense with allies, to be as perfidious as she cared to be. But in the long run, in other circumstances, this isolationist attitude was to prove dangerous.

The reader will have little difficulty in finding modern parallels to these situations and instances of these problems, and in drawing from the Italian crisis morals for the present day. As long as power-politics continues, statesmen will go on trying—though the attempt can never be completely successful—to reconcile the promotion of an ideology with the pursuit of national interest. The most Machiavellian politician cannot dispense with propaganda, he must weigh in his calculations the advantages of morality, and may be forced in the last resort to subordinate interest to ideology. The purest idealist needs the support of practical men, must adapt his message to appeal to them, and may expect to see it perverted to obnoxious ends. Again, situations will continue to arise in which two or three Powers seek to settle by themselves matters of wider concern, leaving the other affected Powers to decide between intervention and acquiescence. But no parallel can be at all exact. The rough balance between the two world-blocs of 1959 is entirely different from the European balance of 1859, and no Power can now feel so detached as England then felt. Though wars may still be limited, the risks involved are incomparably greater. Each shift of forces makes necessary a fresh approach.

III

The Challenge
of Popular Culture

DOMESTIC ECONOMY.

Newly Married Daughter (whose Husband's income is, if anything, decidedly limited). "—And see here, Papa dear, we are getting on so beautifully with our Furnishing! We bought these lovely Gold and Silver Indian Elephants at a sale the other day, and only gave Fifty Pounds for them, wasn't it cheap? We only want a little Cracked China to make the Room quite comfortable!"

J. A. BANKS

THE CHALLENGE OF POPULAR CULTURE:
INTRODUCTION

Consider these people, then, their way of life, their habits, their manners, the very tones of their voice; look at them attentively: observe the literature they read, the things which give them pleasure, the words which come forth out of their mouths, the thoughts which make the furniture of their minds.

MATTHEW ARNOLD, *Culture and Anarchy* (1869)

MATTHEW Arnold's advice to his readers was meant to make them attentive to the cultural poverty of those "Philistine" Englishmen who believed that greatness and wealth were synonymous terms. It is, however, advice which may equally well be applied to the contemplation of any group of people: for only by knowing the whole way of life which shows itself in everything they say and do, can we determine what their cultural standards are. This is the sense in which we understand the expression "popular culture"[1]—the way of life of a great number of different people capable of being reached through the medium of literary and artistic works— and the challenge of popular culture is the challenge offered to the makers of opinion and the disseminators of ideas by the sheer size and general nature of their public.

All this is commonplace enough and a familiar feature of our own time. What is perhaps not so well known is the extent to which a hundred years ago writers were struggling with the same problem. The four essays which comprise this section of the book deal severally with this theme. Mr. Altick opens with a description of the publishing world of 1859 and draws many striking parallels with today. Authors, editors, and publishers alike were faced at that time, as indeed they are now, by a large and diversified body of readers for whom they may be truly said to have provided a "literature for the millions." In part, of course, this was due to the great growth in population. Whereas in 1750 there had been only about 6¼ million in England and Wales,

in 1850 there were eighteen million, an increase which had taken place
at an ever accelerating rate—by 47 per cent from 1750 to 1800, but
by 95 per cent from 1800 to 1850.[2] Our own figure of 43¾ millions
may seem very much larger, but the comparison becomes less striking
once we realize that the rate of growth has slackened off—81 per cent
for 1850-1900, 34 per cent for 1900-50.[3]

A consciousness of so many people was, then, one of the phenomena of 1859; and although literacy was not universal there was already a sizeable public for printed matter which was growing rapidly.
It consumed a very varied fare—novels, periodicals, encyclopaedias,
poetry, religious tracts, compilations of curious facts, newspapers—
in effect everything which is bought today: and if it was not a very
critical public, at least its eagerness to buy his products took from the
author the anxiety of having to find a patron to maintain him while
he went ahead with his work. For the first time in English history
there existed a literary market which could maintain a fair body of
professional writers in ease and even in luxury.

Mr. Craig then takes up the major preoccupations of the novelists
who were confronted by this new public. He finds in their work a basic
sociological interest, not in the traditional sense that the sociological
novel deals with the problems of the underprivileged, but in the sense
that people are often "victims" of social pressures they do not fully
comprehend. Their consequent bewilderment is heightened often by
their inability to make themselves understood; and it is of some interest to consider the extent to which concern for these problems in 1859
was a reflection of the writer's own predicament. In the eighteenth century there had been no special difficulty about communication: authors and readers were both members of the same literary or cultural
community; but by the middle of the nineteenth century the social circumstances of the literate had begun to present an appearance of considerable diversity; and it is possible that his own self-consciousness
of being part of a massive society which was not at all easy to grasp
had increased the writer's sensitivity to the similar plight of others.

This consciousness of being at a loss, of existing in an alien
world, emerges particularly clearly in those works of Tennyson and
FitzGerald which were published at the same time as the *Origin of
Species*. In his essay Mr. Madden deals with these, along with less
well-known publications by Arnold and Ruskin, and points out that,
for the artists and writers of 1859, the treatment of hope and despair,
joy and anguish, is fundamentally close to that treatment in works
published today—as contrasted, for example, with the Romantics.
This feeling of alienation, to be sure, was not necessarily defined in

social terms; it was projected outwards to an indifferent and virtually hostile universe; but we should not overlook the social roots from which it sprang. The burden of the artist was the burden of the individual in the modern mass society.

Mr. Wolff then concludes the book with an account of the part played in 1859 by the group of literary intermediaries who spanned the gulf between the outstanding thinkers and writers and the ordinary man. Selecting a wide range of weekly, monthly, and quarterly periodicals serving the main political and religious positions of the day, he describes the reception they gave to the most important works published in 1859. His point is that they demonstrate the extent to which a large and growing body of popularisers had appeared, who in their own way made a serious contribution to the great debates from which the nation took its lead and without whom there was a danger that the contact between the makers of opinion and the public generally would have become attenuated to the point of extinction.

The impression which emerges from the four essays is that 1859 was not only a year of transition to an age of crisis but also a date in an age of confusion which had begun earlier and continues today. The evolution of a new semi-literate public and the approach to a mass democracy had created a problem for which as yet no solution has been found—how can we preserve and promote individuality in a mass society? It is not merely a question of numbers or the scale of operations. Part of the confusion of our time, as of 1859, derives from the sheer diversity of such a society and from the different types of individual identity which it makes possible. Popular culture in the widest sense of the term—in the sense of the patterns of belief surrounding everyday experience—is far less homogeneous now than it was in 1859 and was far more heterogeneous then than it was in 1759. If we are to understand the reception offered to the makers of opinion and to the creators of art a hundred years ago, we must understand what was happening to the people who were trying to appreciate the message they hoped to convey. Let us consider these people, then, their way of life, their habits, their manners. In this fashion we may come closer to the thoughts which made the furniture of their minds.

I

An English family consists of a few persons, who from youth to age, are found revolving within a few feet of each other, as if tied by some invisible ligature, tense as that cartilage which we have seen attaching the two Siamese. . . . Domesticity is the tap-root which enables the nation to branch wide and high. The motive and end of their trade and empire is to guard the independence and privacy of their homes. Nothing so much marks their manners as the concentration on their household ties.

R. W. EMERSON, *English Traits* (1856)[4]

Emerson's description of the English men and women of his day might easily have been written in 1959. For it is precisely as home-worshippers that we think of the Victorians. Whenever we read the novels of a hundred years ago or turn over the pages of old issues of *Punch,* we are immediately impressed by the way in which the family appears as the central point of reference. Although its members no longer worked together as they had perhaps a century earlier when England was still largely rural, they nevertheless thought in family terms; and their family prayers in the morning and their family readings and concerts in the evening provided the ritual whereby their consciousness of kinship was preserved. Indeed, if we would quarrel with Emerson at all it would be over the numbers involved; to us Charlotte M. Yonge's eleven Mays and thirteen Underwoods are perfect complements for the round of domestic events she portrays.[5]

It is against this background of a large family and intense family life that we must set the writing covered by the essays in this part of the book. Novels were read aloud to the assembled company and the monthly-magazine "improving" article as well as the latest item in the serial had to be designed with this in mind. It necessarily set a premium on propriety, and the author could expect to be reprimanded by his readers should he depart too radically from the accepted mode. The books which in Trollope's phrase were "in the hands of all readers" had a special place in instruction: "it is from them that girls learn what is expected of them, and what they are to expect when lovers come; and also from them that young men unconsciously learn what are, or should be, or may be, the charms of love."[6] The popular novelist, then as now, was aware that he must please if he would be read, but he was also aware that his public was a family public with a special concern that a story for family reading should not bring a blush to the cheek.

Yet, for all that, the Victorian of 1859 was not blind to the fact that in the streets there walked "that unhappy being whose very name is a shame to speak."[7] References to the "Great Social Evil," as Mr. McGregor has pointed out,[8] were not meant to indicate that working-class housing was deplorable, or that the sanitary condition of the manufacturing towns was appalling, or that the lives of agricultural labourers were poor, nasty, brutish, and short; they meant that there were at least 8,000 prostitutes in London alone and that there were many more outside.[9] The writers for the many new periodicals which Mr. Altick in his essay shows to have been the most talked-about aspect of publishing in 1859 had to pick their way with care. For although Mrs. Gaskell aroused no fury with *Lizzie Leigh* in 1850—perhaps because Lizzie was portrayed as a reformed character who had suffered for her sin—the storm of protests which followed the publication of *Ruth* in 1853, showed only too clearly that the reading public was not yet ready to accept the unmarried mother as the proper heroine for a book.[10]

The explanation for this unwillingness to face in word what was an obvious feature of Victorian life and which has laid the Victorians open to the charge of hypocrisy[11] seems to lie in their special attitude towards the home. "It was much more than a house where one stopped at night for temporary rest and recreation—or procreation—in the midst of a busy career. It was a place apart, a walled garden, in which certain virtues too easily crushed by modern life could be preserved, and certain desires of the heart too much thwarted be fulfilled."[12] In maintaining this conception of home, "sweet Home," the novelists and writers for the periodical press had their own particular role to play. They were expected to extoll its qualities and play down its shortcomings, and they were expected to perpetuate the view that the basis of all morality was to be found in a devotion to the ideal of Christian domesticity, especially as that displayed itself in its more puritanical attitudes toward sex.

It is hardly surprising, therefore, to find that the more sensitive of them, striving to understand what Mr. Craig in his essay calls "both the throb of the heart and the order of society," could not be satisfied with so simple a recipe. The *Westminster Review* might complain that it did not feel itself "brought any nearer by the experience of Richard Feverel to the solution of that great social question about the sowing of wild oats,"[13] but at a time when so few contemporaries were prepared publicly to connect the "Sin of Great Cities" with the growing tendency of middle-class men to postpone marriage for reasons of worldly prudence and convenience,[14] it was of some importance that the issue was raised in this form at all, even if Meredith could not solve it. The more common approach was to ignore it altogether or to treat it simply in terms of the prostitute and hence to dispose of it by branding her as a social outcast.

The more perceptive of the social commentators, that is to say, especially amongst the women novelists, were uneasy about the moral position of the view that if a man "found a woman already spoiled, he did not do her any harm, poor creature"[15] and put forward the alternative theory that "when a man's spoiled his fellow-creature's life, he's no right to comfort himself with thinking good may come of it; somebody else's good doesn't alter her shame and misery."[16] The class barriers were beginning to break down and middle-class men could not continue for much longer to maintain that the common prostitute from another social class was made of a different clay from that of the pure and innocent girls of their own class whom they were destined eventually to marry. By 1859 Victorian England had already started on the long road towards the single standard of sexual morality which a hundred years later seems almost accepted.[17]

Perhaps the feminist movement itself had some influence. The *Englishwoman's Journal* was founded in 1858, and the Society for the Employment of Women, which was to do so much for the single woman during the next twenty years, was established in 1859. By this time "Lord Brougham's little corps of lady orators, preaching strong-mindedness"[18] had already begun to read papers on education and on the employment of women at the Annual Congresses of the National Association for the Promotion of Social Science. But as yet the reformers had done little to affect the current relationships between husband and wife, or between men and women generally. Indeed, if anything, events of the 1850's seemed to be making matters worse rather than better; and the Matrimonial Causes Act of 1857, which might be said to have inaugurated a century of family law reform,[19] by making divorce easier for men than for women set the seal for the time being on the double standard of sexual morality.[20]

This is not to deny that important changes were taking place in family relationships; it is to assert that they were proceeding largely independently of the efforts of social reformers. There can be no doubt that by 1859 the standard of living which middle-class men and women had come to look upon as appropriate for a civilised existence marked them off from the previous generation. As one social critic put it: "A young man must plunge into married life at full gallop; begin where his father ended. He must have a house replete with elegancies, with plate, pier glasses, pictures, and all the paraphernalia of a drawing-room of fashion; and he must be prepared to give an extensive entertainment, once or twice a year, to all with whom he is on speaking terms; or if he will not do this, if he will not be bound down by such conventionalism, he must submit to sink his status in society, and be considered a plebeian and a boor by his former associates."[21]

Moralising complaints of this kind, although frequently made, had apparently no effect. More money than ever before was spent on setting up home and providing it with a staff of servants. Friends and acquaintances were invited more often to "little dinners" where wine was commonly drunk. Often a horse and gig or chaise was regarded as a *sine qua non* for the up-and-coming young man, and his wife was expected to spend much more time and money on her toilet and to take on "the architecture of perfection"[22] which would transform her from a mere wife into a perfect lady. None of this, of course, would have been possible if middle-class incomes had not been rising rapidly at this time; but for all that, middle-class aspirations outran the middle-class capacity to pay, and a *Times* correspondence in 1858 discussed quite seriously whether a young man could afford to marry on £300 a year.[23]

Longer courtships had, in fact, become customary in this class. Young men, accepting the maxim that it was

> not manly to allure a girl
> From peace, and comfort, and sufficiency,
> To a sad, cheerless hearth, and stinted board[24]

preferred to wait prudently for the "proper" time to marry—a time which the handbooks told them should be when "worldly circumstances . . . present a reasonable probability of increase."[25] For such men, seeking a career in London or some other great city, the Clubs with their smoking-rooms and dining facilities, provided a home away from home.[26]

Thus, for young middle-class men at least, two features of their time were conspiring against the attractions of home life which were so prominently extolled in the periodicals. On the one hand, they were offered the charms of the Club with its freedom from parental constraints, which Florence Nightingale described vividly as interfering severely with personal independence.[27] On the other hand—and more important—they were expected to follow a career wherever it might lead, and at this time it often led to the great cities and abroad. Indeed, as middle-class occupations became professionalised, the call of the career resulted increasingly in the sons of the family leaving home as mere boys to go to the newly re-organised Public Schools, the "mint for the coining of Empire builders" as they have been called.[28] The search for identity, dealt with in Mr. Madden's essay on the burden of the Victorian artist, reappears in the middle-class family, with the difference that the question is not "What am I?" but "What shall my son be?"[29] That a career of some sort should be found and that money should be spent on educating him for it were beyond dispute, but which was the best line to pursue was one of the puzzles of the time.

In these circumstances it would seem that middle-class parents

were posed a dilemma which their parents had not been obliged to face
when they were young. They saw that it was necessary, if their sons
were to succeed, that they should send them away from home to pre-
paratory and to Public School and then let them follow a career in
London or abroad, wherever opportunities should present themselves;
but at the same time they also saw dangers in this course. Not only was
a highly competitive existence probably suspect in itself, but away from
home there were other possibilities of demoralisation: the sowing of
wild oats might lead to "a life of vice." It is hardly to be wondered at,
therefore, that the emphasis on the virtues of domesticity and on the
concept of the home as a "walled garden" quickened even as this pattern of domestic life was breaking down.

For the girls who remained at home, moreover, changes were
occurring in the customary nature of the domestic routine. As the
middle classes found their incomes rise, they employed larger numbers
of domestic servants, especially of the more specialised kinds—house-
keepers, cooks, housemaids, and nursemaids—to carry out tasks which
previously had been performed by members of the family themselves.
The young ladies became ladies of leisure, spending their day paying
calls, looking at prints, doing light and remarkably intricate needle-
work varied by an occasional game of backgammon or a glance at a
magazine. Such activities, although advocated by the family oracles
like Isabella Beeton,[30] were deplored by the feminists and others like
Florence Nightingale, who having herself experienced a sense of their
futility, declared that the main charm of reading novels for girls in
such circumstances arose from the fact that they provided an avenue
of escape into a world of fantasy where the heroine could satisfy her
high moral and idealistic sentiments, untrammelled by family ties and
the too-close supervision of her mother.[31]

Indeed, Florence Nightingale and other young middle-class ladies
like her exemplified the dilemma of their time. On the one hand they
were exhorted to idealism by pulpit and printed sermon and on the
other they were prevented from finding ways of fulfilling their ideals.
Out of their frustration arose a demand that opportunities for chari-
table and social work should be increased,[32] or alternatively that they
should be allowed to take up fields of employment as yet only open
to men.[33] In a few years their perplexity would find its echo in a novel
written by a man. "What should a woman do with her life? . . . Fall
in love, marry the man, have two children, and live happy ever afterwards. I maintain that answer has as much wisdom in it as any other
that can be given;—or perhaps more."[34] The fact that Trollope's "solution" showed that he had failed to understand the problem posed by

the "flock of learned ladies" he wished to confute, and the fact that it was of little relevance to the 72,500 single women of his day who could never hope to marry even if *all* the men of marriageable age were to select a bride, need not detain us here. What is important is that he could create a character who was put out by the issue. "What am I?" and "What shall I be?" had become as significant for the young middle-class woman of the early 1860's as it had for the young middle-class man, even if as yet parental concern had not moved far beyond the search for an eligible son-in-law at a time when young men seemed disinclined to marry.

During the next twenty years, and throughout the rest of the century, the family was due to undergo a regular process of change to become the small family it is today. The pattern of family activities, too, was to change as the walls caved in and horizons broadened. Gradually, family prayers and church-going *en famille* which appear to have been more prevalent in the 1850's than they had been twenty years before,[35] fell into disuse. Whether this was due to the growing worldly wealth of the middle classes and growing materialism on their part, or whether it was due to the scientific and religious debates which have been dealt with earlier in this book, or whether it was simply due to a general decline in family sentiments and family-organised activities as domestic patterns changed, it is difficult to say. Perhaps it was due to a mixture of all three. But whatever its cause, it is clearly symptomatic of the general domestic restlessness of 1859 which set the makers of popular culture a task the dimensions of which they had never had to face before. The essays which go together to form this section of the book show how they tackled it.

II

Time was when the words "middling class" conveyed to the understanding a definite idea that there was a class that divided the upper and lower portions of society; but in these days, when such a miserable pride prevails in those classes whose incomes just keep them from poverty, it becomes difficult to say who does, or who does not, belong to the middling class. Of course the rich banker's wife, whose town house is in Russell Square, and whose husband has a "villa" in one of the suburbs, and whose wealth enables her to load her dinner-table with plate, and welcome those who honour her with their company, only on account of the luxurious style of living to be met with there, belongs to the middling class. A clerk with 300 l. a year would be most indignant if classed with any other rank than the one just named. We must therefore designate the class we now address as the "genteel" classes—we mean those whose annual incomes range from

200 l. or 300 l. to 500 l. or 1,000 l. These classes of the community are perpetually endeavouring to identify themselves with the ranks just above them. To do this, all sorts of contrivances, many painful private sacrifices are made by the heads of families who have become affected with the absurd mania of vying with those who are better off than themselves. And when every unworthy, mean art has been practised, much private privation undergone, and the desired end is attained, and the man with 500 l. a year gains an *entrée* to the better-appointed house of his neighbour of 1,000 l. a year, he deceives no one, but probably excites the secret contempt of the very individual to whose level he thinks he has raised himself by spasmodic, anxious efforts. . . . There are thousands at this very time who are striving in this miserable race.

> *Meliora: A Quarterly Review of Social Science in its Ethical,*
> *Economical, Political, and Ameliorative Aspects* (1859)

Modify the style of writing, change the allusions, make allowance for the progressive devaluation of the pound, and this statement by an anonymous commentator in 1859 might easily pass as applying to 1959. Just as we often think of the Victorian age as one in which class barriers were more clearly drawn than they are in our own time, so many Victorians themselves believed that the society marked by clear-cut divisions along class lines lay in their past. If, therefore, the writers for the people were confused by what was happening to the walled gardens that constituted domesticity, they were even more confused by what was happening to their public generally. Democracy, as Mr. Altick puts it, was imminent; but it was a very special type of democracy, marked not by equality as such but a "tendency" towards equality.

It is important to emphasize that the literature discussed in the essays by Mr. Craig, Mr. Madden, and Mr. Wolff in this section of the book was almost entirely the literature of *this* public. It is also important to emphasize that the changes in family life described in the previous part of this Introduction were changes in the family life of *this* part of the community. The young working-class man, to be sure, had the pub to go to in place of the club, but his family did not expect him to leave home in search of a career. The young working-class woman, indeed, was much more likely to do this, for it was she who was employed below-stairs by the growing servant-keeping class; and in any case, whether she went out to work or not, the woman of the working-class was expected to conduct her household affairs herself.[36] The conditions of family life for this class were very different from those described above and offered few opportunities for family readings or concerts even where the members were literate or musically-minded. Nor was a change a prominent feature of family life at this time; that was to come much later. Thus, in so far as there was a challenge of popular culture in 1859 it was a challenge made by and for those of a certain level of education, and the kind of education any individual might obtain was largely determined, then as now, by the demands made upon him by the social characteristics of the occupations to which he aspired. The tendency towards equality, showing itself in the form of striving after gentility, differed according to the extent to which individuals could be successful in this unequal race; and the kinds of literary fare they would consume would depend, it seems not unreasonable to suppose, upon the tastes they had developed at home, at school, and in the course of making a living.

Seven broad classes comprised this community. At the top there were the leisured gentlemen. Still largely depending upon land ownership for the source of their income and in some cases actively engaged in farming it, these were the people who ruled the country—locally as Justices of the Peace, and nationally as members of a legislative system which was conducted by amateurs. It is true that the Reform Act of 1832 had given some share in this government to the rising new middle classes; but "for a generation after the Reform Bill, the benches on both sides of the House were still occupied by country gentlemen, and people of the social standing of Cobbett, Cobden and Bright were stared at as oddities."[37] It is true that by the time of the repeal of the Corn Laws in 1846, agriculture had begun to take second place in the economic policy of the nation; but the rents of land continued to rise and landlords "were still piling up on an ever vaster scale structures which survive too often as an embarrassment to their descendants of to-day."[38] In 1859 the great aristocratic families, the lesser country families, and the families of leisured gentlemen generally still played a most important role in the life of England, and their activities, whether on the hunting field or in the Cabinet, provided a novelist like Trollope with much of his inspiration.

Next to them in importance and often closely connected to them by birth or marriage were the professional gentlemen. The term perhaps needs some explanation at this point, since it is necessary to distinguish between professional gentlemen and another of our seven broad classes, the professional men, just as it is necessary to distinguish between gentlemen and working farmers. The latter, analogous, distinction was perhaps made most clearly by Levy in 1904 for the benefit of his German readers: "the first rides, hunts and pursues various kinds of sport, as do his sons, while his wife enters local society and his daughters learn music and painting. The working farmer is to be found with his sons in the field among his men, probably in his shirtsleeves, and his wife and daughters help with the milking, in the dairy or with the poultry. Pipes, cider and wooden chairs take the place of cigars, wine and drawing-room furniture."[39] The distinction was thus less economic than social, and this was as true for the professions as for farming. In 1840, for example, the Bar was said to be composed for the most part of "Young men, belonging to respectable families—to that minor aristocracy which is interposed in England, between the patrician gentry and the middle or tradesman classes. There are some indeed to be found in its ranks, whose origin is more lofty."[40] But the legal profession was not homogeneous in this respect. Attorneys came from "the inferior branches of society. There are, doubtless, a great number of highly respectable men, respectable both from birth and connexion, and, to a certain degree, from education: men of high honour, and of very extensive information. But looking at the profession generally as a class, I should say that it consisted certainly of inferior men, both in point of station and education."[41]

By "education," of course, Sir George Stephen did not mean "academic ability." He meant an acquaintance with the classics and "good breeding." Thomas Hughes has provided us with the perfect vignette here. His Squire Brown, it will be recalled, did not think primarily of his son's academic prowess or what Arnold might do to foster it when he was considering sending him to Rugby—"If only he'll turn him out a brave, helpful, truth-telling Englishman, and a gentleman, and a Christian, that's all I want," he declared; and Tom, once there, was not slow to assert that he wanted to be "A. 1. at cricket and football, and all the other games" and to leave behind him "the name of a fellow who never bullied a little boy, or turned his back on a big one."[42] Intellectual pursuits as such were not highly prized. Gentlemen gave more weight to "manliness" than to brainpower; and it is clear that the literature which would appeal to them, whether they were leisured or professional, would not demand much of them beyond an occasional reference to Virgil, Cicero, and Horace in the Latin, a little Homeric Greek, the Bible, the first six books of Euclid, and some French—the typical fifth form Public School curricula.

On the other hand, many a professional *man* about this time was struggling to make his way as a gentleman, since "everybody thinks it is his *duty* to try to be a 'gentleman'."[43] In the process the intellectuals of socially obscure origins tried to redefine the term to meet their own special needs—"To have been to a public school was not a necessary qualification; but to have been to a university, or by some means to have acquired higher education or professional status, was."[44] By 1859 the new intellectual "aristocracy" of today had not yet come to be recognized as a power in the land and intellectual achievement was not regarded as a sufficient cause for admitting its possessor to have the necessary gentlemanly quality; yet the straws were already in the wind. The Medical Act of 1858, which set up the General Medical Council with its registration only for doctors who could satisfy the minimum qualification requirement, very quickly resulted in the virtual control by the profession over the standard of teaching at university, medical school, and hospital; and set a pattern which other professional men strove to emulate throughout the next hundred years. The establishment of an association like the British Medical Association, founded in 1856, with its own distinctive "ethic" of service to the client and to the community was the first step of this new professionalism; and one by one bodies of engineers, architects, dentists, and schoolteachers set up their associations, published their journals, and sought to create an examination system which would provide objective criteria by which to judge a man's fitness to practise.

All this, however, lay in the future. For the time being professional men were not quite acceptable socially, although they were to be preferred to the fourth of our classes—the *parvenu* captains of industry. These were still classed with tradesmen and "shoppy" people, in spite of the obvious wealth of some of them, and a demand for education on their part was uncalled for. As Mrs. Gaskell's Margaret Hale put it: "What in the world do manufacturers want with the classics, or literature, or the accomplishments of a gentleman?"[45] In another generation this attitude would change and businessmen would be accepted by London Society for their *"possession of some form of power over other people,"*[46] but in 1859 success in business, except in banking, was no guarantee of social acceptance and if a manufacturer's son was sent to Public School it was most unlikely that he would want to return to the family firm. Yet businessmen had a thirst for knowledge of a special kind. They were interested in the technology of their trade and in political economy. They also sought an ideology, or philosophy of industrialism, which would justify their place in the scheme of things, and men like Ure and Smiles, Cobden and Bright came forward to champion them as founders of a new prosperity for mankind.[47] It is to be expected, therefore, that the literary fare which would satisfy them would be different again from that of "gentlemen," as theirs differed from that of the intellectuals, and all three differed from that of the working farmers who in any case remained on the whole hostile to "mere book-learning" for a long time to come.

In the big cities, especially in the ports, there was another large and growing class for which the novelists and writers catered. These were the men who kept the financial records and were responsible for correspondence, filing, and routine office matters in the counting houses. Usually of "respectable family," the clerk often had advantages not possessed by the businessman. "His hours of business, ten to four or five, leave much time for recreation; his salary enables him to dress in the fashion, to enjoy many an agreeable evening in the ball-room, at the opera, or other places of public amusement."[48] His education was often superior to that of the industrialist and although he was warned that a knowledge of the classics or of literature was not what his employer wanted, it was to be some time before book-keeping, accounting, and office procedure generally were sufficiently systematised to make direct instruction in their mysteries a specialism. The clerk of 1859 accordingly was likely to have tastes which neither his occupation nor his income could satisfy. Balanced precariously just above the working class, the clerk was noted for his snobbishness and his pretensions, for his exaggerated middle-class morality which was displayed prominently to mark him off from those lower in the social scale.[49] His education was unlikely to be intellectual, therefore; nor was it likely to be technological in the sense that this term might be applied to the industrialists; almost certainly it would be "fashionable," since the clerk would be anxious to learn how the well-to-do behaved, and it may be presumed that the Ward and Lock series of booklets on morals and manners found a ready sale in this market.

It is not clear socially how clerks had formerly been recruited; but by 1859 many were themselves the sons of clerks and of the less prosperous professional men, fallen on hard times. Some of them were the sons of the "respectable" working class and this may have been one reason for their anxiety to dissociate themselves in dress and speech from the labourer who was illiterate and worked with his hands. Certainly this tendency was prevalent amongst the teachers of the poor who all came from working-class families and who form our seventh, and last broad class. Having achieved their position by much hard work, they considered themselves both intellectually and socially superior to the people from whose ranks they had come and whose children they taught. They were, it is true, socially more isolated than any class in the community: their salaries were no better than the average clerk's, they had all the attributes of a profession, yet their "fellow" educationalists, the teachers in the private schools, regarded them with distaste, claiming that "the status of the certified master is far beneath that of the independent middle-class educators."[50] They nevertheless looked upon their occupation as a profession and had professional journals to read, which marked them off clearly from the literate working men and the clerks who in point of social status were closest to them.

Leisured gentleman and gentleman farmer, professional gentleman, professional man, working farmer, industrialist, clerk, and schoolmaster: each had his own special needs to be catered to by the publishing world, even if their wives, coping with the problem of how to manage home and servants, were likely to want their own distinct—but in the class terms we have been using so far, largely undifferentiated— fare. Some specialisation there must necessarily be, just as there was specialisation in the education and training associated with the different social destinies each way of life entailed. By 1959 we have become accustomed to a mass society diversified and specialised along these lines, but in 1859 the idea was sufficiently novel to cause some confusion for those who were seeking to bridge the gap between the thinkers of the day and those who would eventually make use of their thought.

But, if this middle-class public was differentiated in these respects, it was still largely unified in its social evaluations. The life of the leisured gentleman was as yet most highly prized. Samuel Smiles might formulate a philosophy of useful and creative activity as the sure basis of the truly gentlemanlike character, but popular esteem accorded to the leisured existence the really desirable and even charismatic qualities. Accordingly it was the activities which went with such an existence which received most acclaim—hunting, shooting, travel abroad, dining well, entertaining and being entertained in company. People on the fringes of this society looked enviously upon it and aspired to become part of it. What made it all very confusing for the social commentators, moreover, was that every day fresh opportunities seemed to be offering themselves for men and women of comparatively humble origin to obtain the necessary income whereby they might acquire the paraphernalia of gentility. Provided that they were silent about their grandfathers they might yet pass for ladies and gentlemen.[51]

Amongst the literate working class, on the other hand, conditions were very different. The Age of the Chartists was only just passing away and this, as so many of them were aware, had been a Bleak Age.[52] Better times had come but there were few opportunities for the individual workingman to get ahead by his own efforts. The renewed vigour of the associations which workingmen organised—trade unions and co-operative societies—showed the direction events would take. Self-help for the people of this class could only be co-operative self-help.[53] "If you long for social elevation—if you desire to live and to die free, and to leave freedom to your children—come forward nobly, generously, wisely, in support of that society, which, suffering for the defence of its own rights, is standing between you and oppression, shielding you from degradation and forwarding the progress of labour."[54] There was no question of a "miserable race" to identify themselves with the class above.

Education in the three R's was, of course, far from universal; and "the ignorance in which the great mass of the working classes is sunk, is frequently and bitterly lamented by the few intelligent working men that exist among them, and who in vain labour to impress the mass with the importance of disciplining the feelings and passions, and of cultivating the intellects. The truth of the above will be, perhaps, more readily credited when we state, that out of 550 members of the Mechanics Institution . . . only 50 can be said to belong to the working class."[55] Neither for the purpose of emulating their wealthier neighbours nor for the subjects themselves were they interested in literature, art or science. Instead the tastes of the literate workingmen were catered for by a mass of cheap publications "regularly venting forth the nauseous details of seduction, crime and horror." Newspapers, we are told, "noted for strong party sentiments, lengthy police and criminal reports, and a liberal number of the pest advertisements of the quack doctors, are the most freely taken. The *News of the World* is the greatest favourite . . ."[56] Radical in politics, increasingly free-thinking in religion,[57] working men in 1859, "uninformed" and "informed" alike, appear to have preferred the dramatic and the colourful in what they read, perhaps as a counter to the almost universal drabness surrounding their everyday lives. This public, different again from the "genteel" or "middling" classes, had its own set of popularisers, composed very largely of people nearly as ignorant as itself.

It is hardly surprising that the makers of opinion, faced by this large and heterogeneous public, working-class and middle-class alike, were confused. It is hardly surprising that they found the problem of communication with an audience which by their standards was semi-literate, greater than they could solve. Small wonder, then, that a new group of interpreters had arisen to bridge the gap and to attempt a definition of personal identity in the midst of social diversity! Small wonder, too, that the more sensitive thinkers were oppressed by the questions: "What is man?," "What am I?" It is the task of the essays which follow to discuss in greater detail these perplexities of 1859 as they showed themselves in literature. The challenge of popular culture represents the demands of the mass on the individual in an age of hope mixed with despair.

RICHARD D. ALTICK

THE LITERATURE OF AN
IMMINENT DEMOCRACY

Grant that the old Adam in these persons may be so
buried, that the new man may be raised up in them.

—THE BOOK OF COMMON PRAYER

HE English people in 1859 were entering a new age of popular culture, and they were fully aware of it. "An immense
number of new and powerful processes," wrote a contributor to the January *Blackwood's* as he led into one of the year's most
repeated platitudes, were "converging to one great end." Popular education, despite grievous inefficiency, low aims, and lack of funds,
was making headway. Books were, from a practical standpoint, more
than ever necessary: to ply his trade, the eighteenth-century cobbler
needed no alphabet, but now the man who manufactured shoes in
Northampton had to be literate to survive. The oppressive newspaper
stamp tax had been abolished four years earlier. The electric telegraph
had given newspapers the fascination of immediacy, and other revolutionizing inventions had made possible the cheap large-scale production of all kinds of reading matter, as well as the means of repro-
ducing illustrations, so that he who ran, even if he could not read,
could enjoy the pictures. This, proclaimed the oracles, was the age
of "the universality of print, the omnipotence of ink."[1]

Admittedly, people as far back as Dr. Johnson's time had been
exclaiming over the increase in the number of readers, and the March
of Mind was one of the most publicized social phenomena in the period stretching from the 1820's to mid-century. But it was only in
the 'fifties that the familiar phrase "literature for the millions" ceased
to be mere hyperbole.[2] In 1859 there existed a many-leveled reading
public with divisions and tastes strikingly similar to those of the mass
public a century later. Catering to it was a book trade which, despite

the eradication one evil winter night in 1940 of the Paternoster Row the Victorians had known, survives today, essentially unaltered in structure or method. And even in 1859 there was a chorus of protest or pessimism—or, at best, gentle melancholy—over the developing democracy of print. Thoughtful men were already lamenting the debasement of traditional literary culture.

But here the resemblance between 1859 and 1959 abruptly ends; for in the earlier year lament was still tempered by hope. Belief in progress was never stronger than in the year of Darwin. In the orthodox Victorian creed, progress was an undoubted metaphysical force which it was the duty and privilege of a reforming society to assist in every possible way. Education, cheap books and papers, and free libraries could refine the taste and enlarge the intellectual capacities of the common man, making him a thoughtful, well informed, socially responsible citizen, receptive to good literature and impatient with all inferior varieties. Substantial progress had lately been made in respect to certain of his social habits: drunkenness was declining, the deposits in savings societies were increasing, domestic sanitation was gradually improving. Why, then, should he not also, in those other realms of mind and taste, "Move upward, working out the beast,/And let the ape and tiger die"?

I

It was an article of faith that man could move upward. What in fact were the signs of the times? One at least (looking back after a hundred years) was most hopeful. The reading public of 1859, unknowingly put on its mettle by the appearance in a single year of a remarkable group of books destined to become "classics," responded in a fashion that posterity is bound to applaud. The great books of 1859 were immediately recognised as great, with two exceptions, *The Ordeal of Richard Feverel*, which had an indifferent press and a small sale, and *The Rubáiyát of Omar Khayyám*, which had to await discovery in a penny-remainder box, two years later, by a prospector who thereupon carried the book to Dante Gabriel Rossetti. But *Adam Bede*, published on 1 February, went through eight printings before the year ended, for a total of almost 16,000 copies: a remarkable record in that day of small, relatively expensive editions.[3] The *Idylls of the King* appeared late in June, and sold 10,000 copies in a single week, a feat that raised the Laureate to a commercial eminence hitherto occupied only by Martin Tupper.[4] The *Origin of Species*, which had the popular appeal neither of fiction nor of narrative poetry, was a best-seller in its own class. Its first edition of 1,250 copies was exhausted on publication day, 24 November. "I sometimes fancied," Darwin wrote, "that my book would be successful, but I never even built a castle in the air of such success as it has met with." With incredulous underscoring and exclamation points, he recorded hearing of "a man enquiring for it at the *Railway Station!!!* at Waterloo Bridge; and the bookseller said that he had none till the new edition was out."[5] Within eighteen months John Murray had printed 6,250 copies:[6] a figure small enough of itself, but, seen in the frame of reference of contemporary publishing, an impressive testimony to the book's initial impact on thoughtful Victorians. How many of the seminal books of our own age have had a comparable short-term sale?

Not all the best-sellers of 1859, of course, were destined to be remembered. Conspicuous among the ephemeral titles was Harriet Beecher Stowe's *A Minister's Wooing*, issued in monthly parts beginning in January and in book form in October. Its total sale, down to mid-November, amounted to 42,000 copies,[7] two and a half times the sale of *Adam Bede* for the same period; but one must bear in mind that this was a book by the lady whose *Uncle Tom's Cabin* had broken all British sales records only seven years before, and that it was issued in a variety of forms and at a price considerably less than that of *Adam Bede*, which originally appeared in the conventional three-volume form.

No better index can be obtained to the tastes of the middle-class audience in 1859 than the traffic of Mr. Mudie, then at the height of his prosperity and influence. As the year opened, his inventory included 1,000 copies of Bulwer-Lytton's *What Will He Do With It?* and 1,400 of the first two volumes of Carlyle's *Frederick the Great*. As 1859 wore on, he supplied his readers with 2,500 copies of *Adam Bede*, 1,000 of the *Idylls of the King*, 2,500 of Dinah Mulock's *A Life for a Life*, 1,200 of Thomas Hughes' *The Scouring of the White Horse*, and 3,000 of one of the autumn's publishing sensations, Sir Francis McClintock's story of his voyage to discover the fate of Sir John Franklin.[8] These in addition to lesser quantities of countless other titles; for "the insatiable Mudie," as the publisher of *Adam Bede* appreciatively called him,[9] then boasted that he was adding 120,000 volumes a year to his stock. Among the new titles fiction predominated, accounting for about 44 per cent of the total, with history and biography in second place (28 per cent) and travel and adventure in third (13 per cent).[10] So long as Mudie purchased on this scale, his subscribers could be sure that whatever of current literature they were inclined to read, he could provide—if he was at ease about its morality.

The middle-class men and women who borrowed from Mudie's,

and to a limited extent bought copies of first editions for their personal libraries, constituted the central level of the reading audience, just below the small pinnacle occupied by the intellectual élite. As the figures I have mentioned suggest, it was a sizeable public, and it was steadily broadening as prosperity, increased opportunities for education, the expansion of the professions and the new civil service, and other forces of social change enlarged the boundaries of the middle class itself. Publishers tended, understandably, to regard it with affection. "If the public is sometimes a stupid beast," wrote a complacent John Blackwood to his best-selling authoress George Eliot on 30 March, "I am happy to say I have found him a most excellent beast in the main."[11] To this audience belonged the reputation-makers, the people whom the leading novelists of the day (but not Meredith, who detested Mudie's constituency[12]) sought to please. Now that the financial rewards of authorship were becoming ever larger, professional writers wished nothing more than to help that public grow and encourage it to buy more books. Dickens did so, quite deliberately, through the many public readings he gave up and down the island in the season of 1858-59. "Your present correspondent," he observed in a letter of 1 February, "is more popular than he ever has been. I rather think that the readings in the country have opened up a new public who were outside before; but however that may be, his books have a wider range than they ever had, and his public welcomes are prodigious."[13]

The pleasure and profit of catering to this widening audience were not left to Mudie and his confreres alone. For the past decade, certain alert and aggressive publishers had recognized that however large the gross potential of the democratic market was, its individual members, especially the newcomers, had not much money to spend. Hence the yellow-back or railway novel, which sold for a shilling or two at a time when circulating-library novels retailed at 31s. 6d. These highly popular books were mostly reprints. In 1859 the firm of Routledge, a leader in the field, brought out their series of Select Standard Novels—a volume a month, 2s. 6d. in cloth binding, selected from the works of such successful novelists as Marryat, Disraeli, Cooper, Lover, and Mrs. Trollope. And simultaneously (one result of a famous publishing coup by which, for the sum of £20,000, they had secured ten years' exclusive reprint rights to nineteen of the author's novels) Routledge launched a "cheap and complete" edition of Bulwer-Lytton.

This Bulwer enterprise involved, not complete volumes, but parts: weekly numbers at a penny, monthly installments at 5d. Here was another favorite means by which the democratic audience was supplied with what it wanted to read. Certain new works and old ones alike appeared in weekly or monthly segments, priced to suit the contents of the average man's odd-change pocket. Although the practice was declining in favor of magazine serialization, in 1859 some high-quality fiction still made its first appearance in parts; the last ten installments of Thackeray's *The Virginians,* for example, were published during the year. The form was widely adopted for serious non-fiction, including encyclopedic works of one sort or another, ranging from George Henry Lewes' *The Physiology of Common Life* through *Chambers's Encyclopædia* (advertised as "the crowning contribution of its Editors to CHEAP LITERATURE—a work designed in a special manner, equally in its construction and in its price, FOR THE PEOPLE": weekly sheets at 1½ d., monthly parts at 7d.[14]), to Mrs. Beeton's *Book of Household Management,* which began its famous career in the autumn with the issue of the first threepenny part. Older, "standard" literature was re-issued in similar form. Longmans, for example, were issuing "People's Editions" of Thomas Moore's *Poetical Works* and *Irish Melodies* (with the music), Sydney Smith's works, and Macaulay's essays, all in monthly shilling numbers. Meanwhile Routledge brought out fortnightly or monthly installments of Prescott's *Ferdinand and Isabella,* Boswell's *Johnson,* Staunton's edition of Shakespeare, and Charles Knight's popular anthology, *Half-Hours with the Best Authors.*

But the most talked-of aspect of the publishing scene in 1859 was the tremendous increase in the number and variety of periodicals. Among the papers which were born in this year (and for the most part died soon after, for the mortality rate among Victorian periodicals was shocking) were the *Temperance Messenger and Domestic Journal, Good News for the Little Ones,* the *Journal of the Workhouse Visiting Society,* the *Family Treasury of Sunday Reading,* and, at the other end of the moral spectrum, a pornographic sheet called *Fast Life.* In addition there were political journals, such as the one whose title was almost as long as its text, *The Friends of Labour Association's Monthly Educator of General Information and Working Man's Advocate* (it survived under this burden until 1863), and innumerable trade papers. In 1859 alone, new specialized journals claimed the attention of carriage builders, drapers, chemists, stationers, ironmongers, railwaymen, shipping merchants, and dentists.[15]

The birth of *All the Year Round* on 30 April enjoyed ample advance publicity, thanks to Dickens' squabble with his publishers over, among other things, the management of its predecessor, *Household Words.* The new weekly started off with the serialization of *A Tale of Two Cities,* to be succeeded in November by Wilkie Collins' *A Woman*

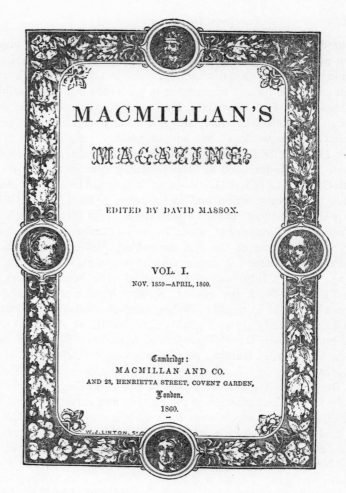

MACMILLAN'S
MAGAZINE.

EDITED BY DAVID MASSON.

VOL. I.
NOV. 1859—APRIL, 1860.

Cambridge:
MACMILLAN AND CO.
AND 23, HENRIETTA STREET, COVENT GARDEN,
London.
1860.

W. J. LINTON, SC.

The title page of one of 1859's important new magazines, engraved by W. J. Linton, a prominent engraver, poet, and political reformer. The figures are King Alfred, Chaucer, Shakespeare, and Milton.

in White, and by its fifth number it reached a circulation of perhaps 120,000 copies[16]—an immense sale for such a periodical, which in addition to its serial fiction published light essays, "personal experience" pieces, and other forms of chatty journalism.

It was undoubtedly Dickens' policy of placing first-rate serial fiction in the front of each issue which made *All the Year Round* so successful. Stories, everybody agreed, were what the new mass audience hungered for beyond all else. But not all editors, even if they were themselves novelists, were happy about this appetite. When he was planning the *Cornhill Magazine* in the autumn of 1859, Thackeray wrote to Anthony Trollope: "One of our chief objects in this magazine is the getting out of novel spinning, and back into the world. Don't understand me to disparage our craft, especially *your* wares. I often say I am like the pastry-cook, and don't care for tarts, but prefer bread and cheese; but the public love the tarts (luckily for us), and we must bake and sell them."[17] And in his form-letter to prospective contributors he desired "as much reality as possible—discussion and narrative of events interesting to the public, personal adventures and observations, familiar reports of scientific discovery, description of Social Institutions—*quicquid agunt homines*—a 'Great Eastern,' a battle in China, a Race-Course, a popular Preacher—there is hardly any subject we *don't* want to hear about, from lettered and instructed men who are competent to speak on it."[18] Luckily Thackeray found a way to deck his table with both tarts and bread-and-cheese. The *Cornhill's* first number, dated January 1860 but published on 23 December to catch the Christmas trade, contained the opening chapters of Trollope's *Framley Parsonage*, Thackeray's own *Lovel the Widower* and the first *Roundabout Paper,* along with a good selection of serious articles. It sold 120,000 copies,[19] and Thackeray, in a happy delirium, treated himself to a spendthrift holiday in Paris.

Overshadowed by the *Cornhill's* success, but symptomatic too of the bright hopes entertained for thoughtful middle-class journalism, was *Macmillan's Magazine,* which began in November with a reported circulation of 10,000.[20] In its two 1859 issues it ran the early chapters of Thomas Hughes' *Tom Brown at Oxford,* an essay by Alexander Smith, articles on the *Idylls of the King* and on Victor Hugo's *Legend of the Ages,* and one of Huxley's discussions of the *Origin of Species.* On the whole, it was too stodgy, lacking the delicate balance between instruction and entertainment that was the early *Cornhill's* special distinction.

II

Thackeray had envisaged the *Cornhill* audience as encompassing learned professors, curates, artisans, and schoolmasters: a mixed clientele, but still essentially middle-class. Dickens' audience for *All the Year Round* overlapped the *Cornhill's* to some extent, but it probably reached lower in the social scale, into the class whose income allowed spending twopence a week but not a shilling a month. Large as they were, these publics were eclipsed by the "unknown public" Wilkie

Collins had described in *Household Words* in August 1858: readers—three million of them, he estimated—who seldom if ever bought a book, but who formed an insatiable market for cheap weeklies of a quality distinctly below that of Dickens'.[21] To most observers, the low literary and intellectual level of these fiction papers, read by servants, unskilled workers, shop assistants, and their families, more than neutralized whatever optimistic conclusions could be reached after contemplating the *Cornhill*'s success. The ominous implications of democracy's encroachment on English literary culture could be read most disturbingly in the pages of periodicals like the *Family Herald,* the *London Journal,* and *Cassell's Illustrated Family Paper,* a class of publications whose five leaders, Collins guessed, had a combined circulation of a million copies.

Below these, in turn, was the true "literature of the streets," the sensational serials typified by G. W. M. Reynolds' *Mysteries of the Court of London,* which had wound up in 1855 after a prosperous penny-weekly run of six years. Unfortunately, since these weeklies were both disreputable and physically frail, they have left but a meagre record. We have no reliable statistics on the quantity in which they were produced, nor do we know how many titles there were; though it is said that about 1859 "sixty publications of a notoriously objectionable character [were] issued by one printing establishment alone."[22] At least we can be certain that the "Salisbury Square" trade was flourishing, unabashed by its exclusion from the company of respectable publishers and by the drum-fire of high-minded criticism.

Like today's pulp magazines, lurid-covered paperbacks, and so-called comic books, the fictional "trash" of 1859—and here I include not only penny serials but cheap sensational and "family" papers of all descriptions, as well as much railway reading—caused alarm by its crudeness, its disregard of all the canons of decent literary art in its anxiety to make sense to the barely literate. Its characters were all flat stereotypes of the most rudimentary sort; heroes were bold, selfless, masculine, yet capable of immense tenderness if the occasion arose; heroines were fragile, easily stirred to tears, dependent, ordinarily incapable of action but blessed with miraculous reserves of fortitude when required; villains were—well, the word used in a Victorian context is self-defining. And all parties, regardless of their moral roles, were sedulously unintellectual. The ordinary reader of 1859 wanted people to whom things happened, and he cared nothing for people who merely thought. A certain amount of sensibility was acceptable, but only if indulged in to pass the time while a new crisis was brewing. Furthermore, in 1859 national and racial stereotypes—the amiable, language-mangling Negro, the lisping, usurious Jew, the phlegmatic Dutchman, the libidinous Latin, and the rest—were far more blatant and pervasive than they now are.

This literature was almost wholly escapist. Not only were the plots contrived to remove the reader as far as possible from the deadly monotony of back-street existence among people as drab as himself, to participate vicariously in adventure and romance; the characters and settings had the least possible resemblance to people and places he himself knew. "What has to be read in the workshop and kitchen," remarked a writer in 1858, "must be enacted at club and boudoir; there must be lackeys at the door, splendid as any macaw of the Zoological Gardens, and stately gentlemen in white neckcloths to usher the visitor upstairs." Not even genteel poverty could be admitted to this dream world. "Even poor superior high-minded governesses, and refined poverty in elegant distress, those staple commodities of fiction, do not flourish in the penny periodicals; *that* public does not care to know how careful gentility makes both ends meet, or how the gentlewoman who has seen better days suffers delicate martyrdom."[23]

Freud was only three years old in 1859, a fact that doubtless explains why people in that year were not disturbed by a quality of sensational literature which figures so prominently in our modern consciousness. Even the severest critics of popular fiction admitted that in sexual matters it was decorous enough. Their test was primarily verbal, and in that regard the critics were quite correct. Seldom, even in the lowest reaches of literature for the multitude, was language used that could bring a blush to the young person's cheek. It is also true that, as Miss Dalziel has noted,[24] apart from G. W. M. Reynolds there were virtually no fictionists whose stock in trade was the uninhibited exploitation of sex, especially sexual violence, and even Reynolds had calmed down considerably by 1859.

But had the Victorians been armed with the instruments of psychoanalysis—a fascinating vision—and concerned themselves not so much with what the printed lines contained but with what might be read between them, they would have been appalled. For if the popular fiction of 1859 was lacking in explicitness, it abounded (as we can see today) in covert symbolism and suggestion. Though its tones were muted and its surface morality unassailable, it was, like ours, a mirror, stimulator, sublimator, and gratifier of its readers' obscure psychological needs. A modern content-analyst could explore its broad tracts with profit to our understanding both of the nature of popular literature itself and of the frustrations and conflicts that were at work in the ordinary Victorian's subconscious. An analysis of the stories in, say, *Rey-*

nolds' Miscellany for 1859, or of a second-rate "society" novel from Mudie's shelves, would be as revealing as any that have been performed on our own mass-circulation fiction.

III

Neither authors nor publishers were aware, of course, of what their product contained in this respect. But they were very conscious of the power they possessed for affecting their readers' attitudes on economic, social, religious, and political issues, and they saw nothing unethical, and indeed much that was admirable, in insinuating their own views into novels and periodicals. This attempt at benevolent thought-control took the form not only of overt and frank propaganda, as in Charles Kingsley's novels, but also of unobtrusive slanting and selection. In July 1859 Alexander Macmillan told Kingsley, apropos of the new shilling magazine the publisher was planning, that "these things have considerable influence, and ought not to be left wholly in hands that use that influence unworthily"[25]—a reference to the fact that cheap periodicals had a deplorable tendency to fall into the hands of people like Reynolds and Edward Lloyd, whose anti-clerical, even republican, sentiments haunted them from the 1840's. Thus, although press lords on the grand scale of Harmsworth and Beaverbrook were still in the future, in 1859 popular periodicals, however disinterested their outward appearance, were often made to serve as the would-be legislators of mass opinion.

Symbolically one of the most significant events of 1859 was the publication, in November, of Samuel Smiles' *Self-Help,* which sold 20,000 copies the first year.[26] Everywhere we look in the popular reading fare of the period, we note a persistent strain of earnestness. Even on the very fringes of the literate public, the proportion of readers who wanted, or flattered themselves that they wanted, information and guidance was larger than it is today. Nowadays the later school-leaving age encourages the assumption that an education adequate for a lifetime has been achieved in the classroom; but in 1859 few readers had any illusion that in their brief and largely profitless period at school they had learned enough to last them through life. Hence the diversity and quantity of self-culture publications was enormous. All periodicals, down to the cheapest and crudest, paid at least lip-service to the age's ideal of democratized learning. Sensational fiction papers like the *Family Herald* sought to cultivate an air of respectability by printing short informational articles, snippets of odd facts, interesting statistics, and sayings of the poets and philosophers. By 1859, however, the incidence of these fillers was sharply declining, and the half-pennyworth of bread was about to be totally lost in the intolerable deal of sack.

This was what worried contemporary observers. It was heartening to find on the bookstalls scores of newly published books bearing titles like *A Sketch Book of Popular Geology, Art and How to Enjoy It, Evenings at the Microscope* (by Philip Gosse), and *A Popular History of the United States*. But these assumed a concentration of purpose that relatively few readers, among the millions who made up the total public, possessed. The books and papers that sold best were the most superficial and the most miscellaneous. It was not surprising that in 1859 John Timbs' *Things Not Generally Known,* a compilation of wildly assorted curious facts, was in its twenty-third thousand, with a sequel doing well also.[27] Samuel Smiles himself—who, despite his present reputation as the embodiment of all that was fatuous in his time, had some eminently sensible things to say about popular literature in 1859—complained that knowledge was "spread so widely, and in such thin layers, that it only serves to reveal the mass of ignorance lying beneath. Never perhaps were books more extensively read, or less studied; and the number is rapidly increasing of those who know a little of everything, but nothing well." The profusion of print, he continued, "doubtless furnishes unprecedented facilities for learning many things easily and without effort; but at the same time it probably tends rather towards superficialism than depth or vigour of thinking."[28]

The popularization of knowledge was well under way, with all its mixed blessings. Superficiality, short cuts, oversimplification were accompanied by persistent and nearly always ill-advised efforts to amuse. "Comic histories" and "comic grammars" were sold on the premise that they made learning pleasant—even, one would be tempted to add, imperceptible. "We may yet possibly," remarked Smiles, "reach the heights of a Comic Euclid and a Comic Prayer-book," or even, as Douglas Jerrold had suggested, a Comic Sermon on the Mount.[29] Though there is nothing "comic," in the genial Victorian sense, in our cartoon-book versions of Shakespeare's plays and other classics, these were clearly foreshadowed in 1859's attempts to prove that "learning can be fun." And while no comic Sermons on the Mount seem in fact to have been composed, the necessity for livening up grave material was felt even (not, of course, for the first time) in religious circles. A writer in the *Athenæum* at the end of the year decried the flippancy, or at best the meretriciousness, of the titles given current tracts: "The Cabman's Dying Cry," "The Bullet in the Bible," "Christ Knocking at the Door of the Soul" (supposedly an effort to trade on the popularity of a Negro song, "Who's That Knocking at the Door?"), and "Pearls from

the Ocean" (the name also of a well-known quadrille).[30] The line between legitimate popularization and mere vulgarization is never very
clearly defined, and in 1859 it was disregarded as blithely as it has been
ever since.

This increasing neglect of the canons of good taste was aided by
the fact that not only were more people—ordinary people—reading;
more were writing, too. They were encouraged to do so by periodical
publishers like John Cassell, who offered prizes of £2 to £5 for essays
by working-class men and women on such topics as "Sanitary Reform,"
"The Advantages of Sunday," "Indiscreet Marriages," and "Labour
and Relaxation." In 1859, too, the Crystal Palace Company's contest
for an ode to mark the centenary of the birth of Burns, the Victorians'
ideal "poet of the people," attracted over six hundred entries. The
winner was one Isa Craig, whom a weekly paper dubbed "the Sappho
of Sydenham."[31] But most significant of all, the multiplication of specialized periodicals created a wholly unprecedented demand for the
services of untrained but purposeful writers, who, however indifferently they managed the pen, were zealous in one cause or another,
or had the advantage of knowing gardening or sailing or the cotton
trade at first hand.

Thus the common writer came into his own, along with the common reader, with results not wholly beneficial to popular enlightenment.
Nothing was more conducive to leveling, to vulgarization, to spreading
mediocrity, than this development, which, while it insured adequate
communication between writer and reader, scarcely elevated the
reader's mind. The typical literature of a democracy became, in a way
appropriately, a conversation between equals. And where the writers
were actually more intelligent and better educated than their readers,
it was essential that they hide the fact behind a matey tone whose cultivation was one of mid-Victorian journalism's proudest achievements.
The mass audience's favorite "literary personalities," writers like John
Frederick Smith in *Cassell's Family Paper* and G. A. Sala in the *Welcome Guest,* specialized in the discursive confiding of their whims and
prejudices and (in Sala's case) the parading of a pseudo-sophisticated
cosmopolitanism that sat very well with the stay-at-homes in Birmingham and Bethnal Green. The very titles of the popular papers, *Welcome Guest, Family Herald, Sunday at Home,* as well as the ubiquitous
"Answers to Correspondents" departments that served as confidantes
and counselors, reflect the great tendency of the time to make the
printed word a natural, indeed indispensable, companion in millions
of crowd-lonely lives. So long as popular journalism had for one of its
principal functions the providing of vicarious friends (at a penny for

a weekly chat), it could hardly fulfill the nobler purposes of literature.

And so, in 1859, popular books and papers had a multiple social role: cinema and television set, pulpit and street meeting, schoolroom and neighborhood club. Because they served so many purposes, it was only to be expected that their significance for the future of English culture could not be clearly discerned. Everybody seemed to agree, at least, that the spread of the reading habit was not an unalloyed boon to the nation. But how was one to read the year's specific portents—and which portents, of the many available, were to be heeded? On the one hand there was the brisk sale of serious instructional works like *Chambers's Encyclopædia* and Cassell's various schoolroom-at-home publications; on the other, the vastly greater demand for the *London Journal,* which, while serializing *Kenilworth* and *The Fortunes of Nigel* for reasons of economy (Scott's novels were then falling out of copyright), protected its circulation by printing the younger Pierce Egan's novels, *The Love Test* and *Love Me, Leave Me Not.* A Victorian reader could select from a wide offering of classics in Bohn's convenient, well-produced volumes at 3*s.* 6*d.* or 5*s.* each. He could also buy a new card game called "Poetry and Literature," which was advertised as combining "the Fun and Laughter of Mischance and Forgetfulness with the higher delights that belong to the gratification of Literary Taste and the enjoyment of Poetry."[32] It is the same conflict of evidence that we have with us today, to complicate every discussion of popular culture. At W. H. Smith's shops and stalls we can choose from hundreds of Penguin titles at 2*s.* 6*d.*; we can also have our pick of the hundreds of low-mentality novels offered for hire at Boots Cash Chemists. For weekend reading there is the *Listener,* which enjoys a circulation that many cheap-fiction papers of the Victorian age only aspired to— and there is also the *News of the World.*

To maintain, with Mrs. Leavis and most other modern critics, that there has been an almost catastrophic decline in the quality of popular literature in the past hundred years is to confess both an ignorance of what the mid-Victorians really read and an excessively dour view of our modern mass reading tastes. It is no less unrealistic than the Victorians' oft-ridiculed idealization of the Middle Ages. But loyally to assert, in reply, that the popular literature of 1859 was fully as bad as ours would be to indulge in a sort of chronological chauvinism. Actually, generalization is hardly possible. Popular literature is so diversified that there are bound to be improvements in some of its categories and deteriorations in others. It seems likely that the literature of an imminent democracy does not change very much either in character or in general quality when the democracy has ceased to be merely imminent. There is simply a great deal more of it, and a great many more people are reading it. For the most conspicuous difference between 1859 and 1959 is less qualitative than quantitative: it is the altered structural proportion of the total audience. Year by year, the pyramid-shaped reading public, for centuries far taller than broad, has bulged wider and wider near the base. The process was well under way in 1859. Since then, the gross population of Great Britain has almost doubled, and the percentage of people able, in some fashion, to read has increased from about seventy to ninety-eight. In sheer numbers, the philistines and the populace have overwhelmed the saving remnant, whose concern is no longer the altruistic one of 1859—throwing out the cultural lifeline to the masses—but rather that of saving itself from being pulled under as well.

In 1859 there were already serious doubts whether the millions of new readers really wanted to be rescued. The various agencies of popular enlightenment had been at work long enough, it was felt, for some effect to be noticeable—and there was none. The further literature spread, and the cheaper and more accessible and more various it be-came, the more confirmed the popular audience seemed to be in its old tastes. It wanted to be delighted, but only in obvious, simple ways; it wanted to learn, but at no expense to the intellect. It had its bursts of virtue, as when it bought 120,000 copies of the first *Cornhill* as a Christmas present to itself, but it soon relapsed into its familiar habits[33] and picked up Sala, Mrs. Southworth, and Mayne Reid instead. Seem-ingly the human constitution contained a strong, instinctual love of mediocrity and worse that was proof against every form of prodding and enticement. Beholding the mass audience's stubborn attachment to reading matter of "a vulgar, exciting, and injurious character,"[34] people could indeed wonder whether progress was a universal principle of life.

Still, they felt, there was hope; this reading public of millions was very new and very ignorant, and it took time for age-old preferences to be corrected. Surely as education spread, and as opportunities for self-improvement multiplied, the level of popular culture would rise? But it did not; or at least it failed to do so in anything like the degree expected. Disenchanted though we are by the failure of the hopes of a century ago, we are not quite ready to admit utter defeat. We are torn, as the men of 1859 were, between two opposing convictions: a residual democratic faith in the possibility of the common man's even-tual improvement, and a haunting suspicion that the old Adam can never, in any cultural sense, be buried.

VICTIMS AND SPOKESMEN:
THE IMAGE OF SOCIETY IN THE NOVEL

T the end of their long and uneasy relation Dickens had the last word upon Thackeray. In February 1864 he described in the *Cornhill Magazine* certain papers and proofs the late editor had left behind him. "The last words he corrected in print," said Dickens, "were, 'And my heart throbbed with an exquisite bliss.'" The heart belongs to Denis Duval, and the sentence, the last in Chapter Six of Thackeray's unfinished novel, expresses the secret feelings of Denis as he nobly reassures little Agnes that he will never be her enemy. As Dickens may have known, Thackeray planned that this exquisite bliss would eventually emerge from the hero's heart into the happy light of marriage. But whatever he knew about the projected outcome of *Denis Duval*, Dickens concluded his eulogy of his old rival with a prayer for the endlessness of that adventure in which the secret throb finds public fulfillment:

God grant that on the Christmas Eve when he laid his head back on his pillow and threw up his arms as he had been wont to do when very weary, some consciousness of duty done and Christian hope throughout life humbly cherished, may have caused his own heart so to throb, when he passed away to his Redeemer's rest!

The consummation here devoutly to be wished is one that any mid-Victorian novel-reader would have understood.

For as he looked through Thackeray's papers Dickens' eye was caught not by a cliché but by an expression that excited the most general and powerful literary expectation of the age, an expectation that existed not only in the insatiable imaginations of a large body of readers but also, most tenaciously, in the imaginations of most novelists good and bad. It is an expectation formed upon an image of society that both reader and writer consulted as they assessed their experience, but an image that was slowly changing its character in the third quarter of the century. Its pervasiveness can be illustrated in countless sources, perhaps most obviously from the many stories of lovers who are temporarily or permanently separated by the barrier of class or rank. We recall the mysterious throes of Pendennis when he meets Fanny, the porter's daughter; or Jane Eyre's feverish awareness of her master, Mr. Rochester; the exalted attraction John Halifax, the tanner, feels for Ursula, the squire's cousin; or the pure, gentle protectiveness felt by the manly middle-class hero of *East Lynne* when he first sees the Lady Isabel. But both the pervasiveness and the shape of the image can perhaps best be shown outside the most conventional situation of the novel, for its features are a good deal larger than are revealed by the happy or unhappy trials of lovers.

I

The image—or, perhaps better, the model—is clearly described in Anthony Trollope's exposition of what he calls his "political theory." This chapter (xvi) of his *Autobiography*[1] was written in 1876, but it expresses certain "feelings and convictions" that Trollope says had always been with him and that he believed must be "present to the minds that create and lead and sway political opinion." The feelings are of "awe and horror at the misery of many of our brethren": we who have been "born to the superior condition," Trollope says, cannot "look upon the inane, unintellectual, and toilbound life of those who cannot even feed themselves sufficiently by their sweat, without some feeling of injustice, some sting of pain." But to these feelings is opposed a powerful conviction: "For the mind of the thinker and the student is driven to admit, though it be awestruck by apparent injustice, that this inequality is the work of God." Moreover, the thinker who is "surely convinced that such inequalities are of divine origin" and who desires to preserve them is a "conscientious philanthropic Conservative," and, obviously, he has God on his side. If Trollope had stopped here, as a good many amateur theorists did before him, the difference between feelings of injustice and the conviction of divine inequality would be a simple opposition, to be resolved only by violence, perhaps, but to be resolved with a fairy-tale simplicity: private feelings and public order are opposed—which will win out?

Trollope, however, goes on to say that the Conservative, "though he sees something, and sees that clearly, sees only a little." And what he is blind to is indeed startling: "The divine inequality is apparent to him, but not the equally divine diminution of that inequality." For it would appear that the God who presides over this society is not only maintaining the "distances between the prince and the peasant" but is also squeezing them together. We might suspect, then, that the "equally conscientious Liberal" in his opposition to the Conservative also has God on his side. But as he moves on, Trollope does not insist on this embarrassing dilemma; indeed the notion that seems to conceal it from him leads directly to the chief expectation of both the novelist and his readers. Trollope's Liberal is "equally aware that these distances are of divine origin," but "he is alive to the fact that these distances are day by day becoming less." And Trollope finishes his exposition of Liberalism by construing "the fact" thus: "What is really in his [the Liberal's] mind is,—I will not say equality, for the word is offensive, and presents to the imaginations of men ideas of communism, of ruin, and insane democracy,—but a tendency towards equality." And armed with "tendency," with a formula that conceals if it does not surmount the difference between divine maintenance and divine diminution of inequality, Trollope takes his final position: "Holding such views, I think I am guilty of no absurdity in calling myself an advanced conservative Liberal." In most reprints of the *Autobiography* this happy solution is rendered by a hyphen: "Conservative-Liberal." The typography is mistaken, but it suggests the desperation of the political theorist who struggles with such a model.

The difficulty is not simply that of reconciling conservatism and liberalism, though of course many writers were directly concerned with Carlyle's "Dandies and Drudges" or Disraeli's "Two Nations." For the novelist the political or economic problem is compounded with that of reconciling the sensibility of the one with the organization of the many. If God diminishes the distances between the ranks of the many in order to satisfy the feeling of sympathy in the heart of the individual, something like "ruin" must indeed result. Yet if God maintains all men in a structure impervious and unyielding to the demands of the individual heart, the world must be an impossibly heartless place. According to either alternative the distinction between private feelings and public order, between Trollope's sympathies and his convictions, is as profound as any distinction a writer can face. Trollope soon turned from his digression into social theory back to the more congenial subject of his novels: he was aware that they rescued him from his political difficulties, but unaware how, and how completely, they did so. For the novel as Trollope and most of his contemporaries practiced it not only filled out with its substance the hyphen that some editors have placed in the middle of Trollope's theory. The novel intervened also to keep the huge forces apart. The dilemma is kept open by tendency, by the slow, gradual shaping of a situation in time.

In a recent autobiography—by a poet, it is true, though by a poet who has written novels and some original novel-criticism as well—there is a reflection which provides a modern counterpart to this passage from Trollope. It occurs in Stephen Spender's *World Within World* and it describes his discovery of "a terrifying mystery of cities" which began to fascinate him as a young man traveling on the Continent in the 1930's. Mr. Spender's "mystery" suggests a relation between self and society very different from Trollope's "theory":

This [mystery] is that a great city is a kind of labyrinth within which at every moment of the day the most hidden wishes of every human being are performed by people who devote their whole existences to doing this and nothing else. Along a road there walks a man with a desire repressed in his heart. But a few doors away there are people utterly devoted to accomplishing nothing but this desire. What has been crushed, never spoken of for generations by his family, revolves there night and day like the wheels of a machine. He has only to know a secret word, open a door, and he may enter into this continuity of things which are elsewhere forbidden. He has only to shut the door again and walk out of the house, and he is again in the locked street where things are scarcely mentioned and unseen. Yet he has in his hands this magic key of entrance into a perpetual stream of fulfillment which he can use whenever he wills. When he even no longer feels desire, he can in an idle, abstract, and unwishing kind of way prove to himself, almost for no reason except a mysterious and remote compulsion to affirm that it is so, that the hidden life of forbidden wishes exists in extravagant nakedness behind mazes of walls.[2]

The strange prurience of this man in the street suggests that he is both separated from and absorbed in the experience of other men, that society is an endless embodiment of one man's fantasy in another man's role. One man's secret wish is another's overt routine, yet even the routines are hidden from each other within the "maze of walls." And it may be that the traveler in the street, whatever his repressed desire, as he walks along is fulfilling the role some concealed watcher from a window longs to play. The distinction made a hundred years ago between private and public, between self and society, has been redrawn. The feelings of the individual are not distinguished from a divinely-instituted order, but from a "labyrinth" within which the individual finds parts of himself mysteriously hidden away in the public but separated lives of others. And each of these others (to enlarge upon the mystery a little) can find his own concealed desires, hidden as they are beneath his dedicated routine, enacted in the routine of yet another.

But the traveler through the maze enters into the "stream of fulfillment" not by any tendency, not by the steady movement of development, but by what can only be called "magic." The maze is not a divinely-maintained barrier to his feelings, nor a barrier melting away under divine pressure exerted in harmony with his feelings. The world of the self, to paraphrase Mr. Spender's title, is "within" the larger world as mysteriously as a feeling is within its expression.

It is of course true that Trollope spoke as one "born to the superior condition" and that his feelings towards the poor are expressed from a position so comfortable that it is hard to take them seriously. And it might well be objected that Trollope's sense of injustice is a good deal less powerful than the myterious compulsions and repressions which trouble Mr. Spender's traveler. But to say so is to emphasize the most important feature of Trollope's image of society, namely that it is a large design, as large indeed as the "divine," and that it may either shrink to the requirements of individual feeling or may in its vastness cause the individual feeling to shrivel away. The feelings of Trollope's individual, whether we call them awe or horror or love, have an appropriate fate: they are either right or wrong, but whether right or wrong is determined by a single large design. Mr. Spender, on the other hand, speaks from no such certainty about the outer world: he has even discarded the certainties of Marxism in which he tried to immerse himself as he marched forward from liberalism. The writer of 1959 addresses himself to a relation between self and society that is a mystery, not a dilemma, and to penetrate this mystery he must rely on many more techniques than that of the slow unfolding of tendency. But the novelist's art in the mid-nineteenth century addressed a dilemma as pervasive as the most insistent literary expectation of both reader and writer. How can the throb of the heart and the order of society be related without the violent reduction of either?

II

We can perhaps most conveniently answer this question by looking at some characterizations of the victim in mid-Victorian fiction. Darwin, who had a great many novels read aloud to him, said there should be a law against unhappy endings and that every novel should contain "some person whom one can thoroughly love, and if it be a pretty woman all the better."[3] But an inspection of some notable victims reveals how difficult the resolution of the happy ending can sometimes be and how irrelevant the reader's attitude towards a character can often be. The victim, of course, is not a villain, and the reader's interest in him will involve considerations larger than an interest in the course of true love. For if he is sufficiently ground down, the victim lying before us condenses the vague oppressiveness of the great world of institutions and groups and makes us believe that whatever else The Law or Greed or Unlawful Passion may be, here at last is what they feel like. And of course if the victim does not lie there for long, but arises to become a triumphant hero or heroine, the reader of Darwin's hopeful persuasion will be pleased. He turns back to that world which is not in words, not in novels, convinced that something momentous has happened and indeed can happen. But it is the victim who stays down that most troubles all readers, for to him our first response will be "If only he . . .," or "But if it had happened that . . ." And as we struggle to assemble our thoughts, to finish the sentence, to re-write if not un-write the novel before us, we are compelled to reflect upon society. Or, if we are interested in history, we try to deduce the idea of society that the suffering implies.

Two such unreclaimable victims, the first in a novel of 1852-53, the second in one of 1871-72, throw some light on the achievements of the years between. The first is Richard Carstone in Dickens' *Bleak House*. The following passage describes him not long before his death. He has so far succumbed to the disease of the vast Jarndyce vs. Jarndyce lawsuit that he has put his affairs into the hands of lawyer Vholes. He has told Vholes the incredible "truth" that to him Mr. Jarndyce, his absurdly self-effacing benefactor who will have nothing to do with the suit of his forebears, has become "the embodiment of the suit; that, in place of its being an abstraction, it is John Jarndyce; that . . . every new delay and every new disappointment, is only a new injury from John Jarndyce's hands."

Richard, emerging from the heavy shade of Symond's Inn into the sunlight of Chancery Lane—for there happens to be sunlight there today—walks thoughtfully on, and turns into Lincoln's Inn, and passes under the shadow of the Lincoln's Inn trees. On many such loungers have the speckled shadows of those trees often fallen; on the like bent head, the bitten nail, the lowering eye, the lingering step, the purposeless and dreamy air, the good consuming and consumed, the life turned sour. This lounger is not shabby yet, but that may come. Chancery, which knows no wisdom but in Precedent, is very rich in such Precedents; and why should one be different from ten thousand?

Yet the time is so short since his depreciation began, that as he saunters away, reluctant to leave the spot for some long months together, though he hates it, Richard himself may feel his own case as if it were a startling one. While his heart is heavy with corroding care, suspense, distrust, and doubt, it may have room for some sorrowful wonder when he recalls how different his first visit there, how different he, how different all the colours of his mind. But injustice breeds injustice; the fighting with shadows and being defeated by them, necessitates the setting up of substances to combat; from the impalpable suit which no man alive can understand, the time for that being long gone by, it has become a gloomy relief to turn to the palpable figure of the friend who would have saved him from this ruin, and make *him* his enemy. Richard has told Vholes the truth. Is he in a hardened or a softened mood, he still lays his injuries equally at that door; he was thwarted, in that quarter, of a set purpose, and that purpose could only originate in the one subject that is resolving his existence into itself; besides, it is a justification to him in his own eyes to have an embodied antagonist and oppressor.

Is Richard a monster in all this,—or would Chancery be found rich in such Precedents too, if they could be got for citation from the Recording Angel? (ch. xxxix)

The second passage comes from Book IV of *Middlemarch* and is part of George Eliot's analysis of the relation between Dorothea and Edward Casaubon, the ardent young St. Theresa and the exhausted scholar who cannot put together the incoherent fragments of his Key To All Mythologies:

Poor Mr. Casaubon! This suffering was the harder to bear because it seemed like a betrayal: the young creature who had worshipped him with perfect trust had quickly turned into the critical wife; and early instances of criticism and resentment had made an impression which no tenderness and submission afterwards could remove. To his suspicious interpretation Dorothea's silence now was a suppressed rebellion; a remark from her which he had not in any way anticipated was an assertion of conscious superiority; her gentle answers had an irritating cautiousness in them, and when she acquiesced it was a self-approved effort of forbearance. The tenacity with which he strove to hide this inward drama made it the more vivid for him; as we hear with more keenness what we wish others not to hear.

Instead of wondering at this result of misery in Mr. Casaubon, I think it quite ordinary. Will not a tiny speck very close to our vision blot out the glory of the world and leave only a margin by which we see the blot? I know no speck so troublesome as self. . . . (ch. xlii)

The similarities are clear enough: the suffering of each victim is "ordinary" or not unprecedented, each has turned against someone near who would save him from the delusion in which he suffers, and each with perversely insistent energy intensifies the delusion that increases his misery. But the differences are equally clear. Richard is "fighting with shadows," and his turning them into the "palpable figure of the friend who would have saved him from his ruin" is sheer madness. The scene of Mr. Casaubon's misery, on the other hand, is not the precincts of Chancery but his own imagination; it is the theme of what we are told is his "inward drama." The "speck" of Mr. Casaubon's self that "blots out the glory" of Dorothea is the inevitable condition of his very consciousness of the world: Dorothea cannot remove it, not only because of the beam in her own eye, but because he would perish of sun-blindness without it. Casaubon's distrust of his wife is not a madness that turns an "impalpable" into an all too palpable enemy; it is his response, in an impalpable drama of the self, to the palpable behavior of Dorothea. The reader of *Bleak House* understands that Richard is the pitiful victim of society, of an endless and hopeless lawsuit that squeezes and shapes into grotesque figures all who labor within it. But the reader of *Middlemarch* must see Casaubon as the victim of himself.

The reader's knowledge is of course the victim's ignorance, and that he cannot overcome his ignorance may well mean that the novelistic victim is less than tragic. In *Bleak House* the separation between the private realm of the throbbing heart and the public realm of the law is so nearly an abyss that Richard's confusion of the one with the other, his identification of Mr. Jarndyce with the suit, is indeed monstrous. But it can be understood so only from a level of knowledge to which no character in this novel can rise, that of the narrator who shows us Richard's misery and suggests its precedents. Earlier, in *Dombey and Son* (1847-48), Dickens had shown his readers something like the reverse of this situation. Mr. Dombey, cold, proud, almost a cartoon of the City Man, arrives at self-knowledge in a catastrophic experience that all but splits him in two—he sees himself as the bearer only of a public, corporate name, and when he sees this he has been saved. But the self-knowledge that brings about this happy ending was not easy for Dickens to express: it involved great violence, as great as a collision between the force that holds the social world rigid and that which would reduce it to the requirements of individual feeling. In the novel constructed upon such a model the happy ending is as difficult—or as factitious—as full tragedy.

But to say that the novelistic victim is ignorant is to say that he is out of communication with those around him. Richard Carstone cannot communicate with Mr. Jarndyce and he is finally isolated even from the sympathies of Esther Summerson. Mr. Casaubon, again, is as unable to communicate with Dorothea as she with him. Lydgate and Rosamond, whose narrative parallels that of Dorothea and Casaubon, suffer a growing private estrangement as their public troubles become more and more generally known. Lydgate finds his credit gone, his wife a silent accuser, his scientific hopes futile. But how he reached his melancholy situation he does not know: he has undergone that "pleasureless yielding to the small solicitations of circumstance, which is a commoner history of perdition than any single momentous bargain" (ch. lxxix). Lydgate, like Rosamond, like Dorothea and Casaubon, even like the wretched banker Bulstrode, lives with his own "inward drama." Its dependence upon his wife, upon the other medical men of Middlemarch, upon his observations of Mr. Casaubon, is impossible for him to know or to utter, for like Casaubon he speaks only from within his own drama. The experience of each character is a nexus of both private feeling and public position. And no character— it may be, no narrator—can add up these inward dramas to find the sum that is society, for the relation of character to character in such a web is in no sense additive. Individual feeling, in the old sense, is greatly qualified here, for Dorothea's inward drama depends upon her response to Mr. Casaubon just as his depends upon his response to her. The provincial society of Middlemarch, moreover, is constituted by a "stealthy convergence of human lots" the "subtle movement" of which is beyond the capacity of any participant to observe (ch. xi). Marriage out of one's rank in such a world is no doubt as impossible as in that of Jane Austen. But rank is subordinated to the interdependence of the inward dramas whose final acts no one can foresee. The most memorable comment in *Middlemarch* is that in which George Eliot describes the necessary blindness in human beings that both separates and connects them:

That element of tragedy which lies in the very fact of frequency, has not yet wrought itself into the coarse emotion of mankind; and perhaps our frames could hardly bear much of it. If we had a keen vision and feeling of all ordinary human life, it would be like hearing the grass grow and the squirrel's heart beat, and we should die of that roar which lies on the other side of silence.   (ch. xx)

III

Of the four major novels of 1859, none is so rich in victims as *The Ordeal of Richard Feverel*. The title itself announces the theme, though Meredith is reticent about who or what victimizes whom. Richard, it will be recalled, is raised under his father's "System," but it fails to subdue his oblivious vitality. He falls in love with Lucy Desborough, the niece of a nearby farmer, and retaliates upon his father's efforts to separate them by secretly marrying her. When Sir Austin discovers that Lucy and Richard are married he fails in his own ordeal by declaring, in the most ironic line of the book, that "it is useless to base any System upon a human being." The irony, of course, is that Richard has constantly been beyond the influence of any system, his father's or that which is invoked by Farmer Blaize—"Baronets' sons were not in the habit of marrying farmers' nieces" (ch. xxvii)—and his destruction must have seemed perverse to many readers. It is at any rate a catastrophe in which the victim is altogether dumb.

For nothing is stranger in *The Ordeal* than the recurring silence of its hero. Lucy gives her solemn attention to Mountfalcon's nightly readings in Roman history while Richard spends long weeks in London waiting for some change of climate to bring his father and himself together. After Sir Austin has finally come to town, though before he and Richard have spoken about what must be spoken about, there is a scene (ch. xlv) as contrived as the anonymous self-immolation of Lady Isabel in *East Lynne*. Richard, Adrian, and Sir Austin are strolling through Kensington; they come upon Lucy and Berry the nurse, who unknown to Richard has brought Lucy to town. But as the two parties approach each other, Lucy is "happily" looking the other way and in a forcible gesture Richard keeps Mrs. Berry silent. The three gentlemen slide by: "Other people intervened. Lucy saw nothing. . . ." Richard says nothing, waiting, apparently, for his honorable attachment to make its own way into his father's understanding.

But Richard is finally engaged in a massive experience of communication in the grandiloquent chapter (xlvi), "Nature Speaks." Having fallen before the startling blandishments of Mrs. Mount, he is in Germany on a tour to forget, or at least to get beyond range of communication. He has ignored letters from home that would have told him not only that his father has taken in Lucy but also that he has become a father himself. Young Austin finds him, breaks the news to him, and Richard sets out into the last conceivable refuge outside society. He goes into the forest accompanied by a little dog and on a "barren corner of the woodland highland" witnesses a huge thunderstorm:

Alone there—sole human creature among the grandeurs and mysteries of storm, he felt the representative of his kind, and his spirit rose, and marched, and exulted, let it be glory, let it be ruin. Lower down the lightened abysses of air rolled the wrathful crash: then white thrusts of light were darted from the sky, and great curving ferns, seen steadfast in pallor a second, were supernaturally agitated and vanished. Then a shrill song roused in the leaves and the herbage. Prolonged and louder it sounded, as deeper and heavier the deluge pressed. A mighty force of water satisfied the desire of the earth. Even in this, drenched as he was by the first outpouring, Richard had a savage pleasure.

The passage has no doubt caught the eye of many a knowing analyst: what's *really* going on here is all too clear—the "savage pleasure" is even a little gross. But this is only the first stage. Richard moves on through the forest and comes upon a tiny leveret. He holds it against his breast and suddenly feels "an indescribable thrill":

The small rough tongue going over and over the palm of his hand produced this strange sensation he felt. Now that he knew the cause, the marvel ended; but now that he knew the cause, his heart was touched, and made more of it. The gentle scraping continued without interruption as on he walked. What did it say to him? Human tongue could not have said so much just then.

What indeed did it say? The pun on "tongue" in the last sentence is perhaps banal but necessary. For this is not simply a "strange sensation"—it is not to be reduced to the reader's memory of his childhood experience with affectionate pets. The secret, remote, ecstatic thrill of this sensation is as far as can be imagined from the society in which human speech functions. Soon Richard comes upon a small shrine in the forest; he looks at the Virgin and Child and walks on.

But not many steps had he gone ere his strength went out of him, and he shuddered. What was it? He asked not. He was in other hands. Vivid as lightning the Spirit of Life illumined him. He felt in his heart the cry of his child, his darling's touch.

Richard, we are told, has achieved "a sense of purification."

Few heroes have moved further away from society to achieve it and few have enjoyed it for so short a time. For though the arrangements for his communication with "other hands" and the "Spirit of Life" are as lavish as can be devised, Richard goes home only to become a victim again. He hears in London that his entrapment by Mrs. Mount was a plot, and after stopping for one of the tenderest—and frankest—scenes of domestic love in any English novel, he tears himself away, duels with the wicked nobleman in France, and awakens from his wounds to find his wife dead from a brain-fever. The message that nature speaks in the tempest, that is rephrased by the leveret's tongue, and that finally penetrates his heart as the Spirit of Life is violently and strangely renounced. This is quite literally the expense of spirit in a waste of shame—with a vengeance.

But of what is Richard the victim? The hugger-mugger ending is certainly not the effect of a collision with Sir Austin's ruined System or with the system Farmer Blaize thinks of. Richard believes that "God [had] spoken to him in the tempest" and that "the finger of Heaven [had] directed him homeward" (ch. lviii). But the grisly conclusion hardly demonstrates that the God-directed heart-throb is absolutely incompatible with the world of civilized society, though it may suggest that "Nature" and "honor" do not precisely agree. The great question here is the status of one who has learned what "no human tongue can say," and Meredith, perhaps altogether appropriately, seems uncertain just what it is. But he seems to have made up his mind some twenty years later, in his masterpiece, *The Egoist*. In the central chapter of that novel, entitled "In the Heart of The Egoist," Meredith shows us Clara Middleton, a mature version of Lucy, revolting in horror from the force of which Richard Feverel seems to be an early and irresolute victim:

she caught a glimpse of his interior from sheer fatigue in hearing him discourse of it. What he revealed was not the cause of her sickness; women can bear revelations—they are exciting; but the monotonousness. He slew imagination. . . . He dragged her through the labyrinths of his penetralia, in his hungry coveting to be loved more and still more, more still, until imagination gave up the ghost, and he talked to her plain hearing like a monster.   (*The Egoist* [1879], ch. xxxix)

The egoist, Meredith goes on to say, is "primeval man," and in him "the primitive is born again, the elemental reconstituted." But the man who talks only to Nature does indeed slay imagination, if he does not induce brain-fever, and the man who knows what no human tongue can tell may indeed sound like a monster when he begins to speak. The primeval man may even live familiarly with an elemental Spirit of Life, but the revelation of a self whose appetites are satisfied by the accommodation of the greatest forces of nature may turn out to be simply monotonous. Richard Feverel, of course, is no monster, but the waste, the untranslatability, of his message from Nature seems a cruel joke.

The silence of its hero is the point of closest similarity between *The Ordeal* and *A Tale of Two Cities*. Indeed, in his portrait of the two young men who so resemble each other, Dickens, like Meredith, seems to have been concerned with a matter far removed from the resources of any contemporary dialogue. When we see Charles Darnay as a prisoner at the bar, there is a mirror over his head to throw light upon him, and in the same scene we meet Sydney Carton as a "wigged gentleman who looked at the ceiling" (Bk. II, ch. ii). A few pages later Carton wins the case: "the wigged gentleman who had all this time been looking at the ceiling of the court, wrote a word or two on a little piece of paper" (Bk. II, ch. iii). By compelling the witness to admit that the prisoner could be mistaken for the barrister, he wins for the defense a case which rests upon evidence of identification. And certainly the major theme of this novel, one that perhaps has kept it alive for the young even more than its account of the French Revolution, is that of suppressed identity.

But the revolution permits if it does not account for the changes and concealments of identity that occur. Mr. Dombey undergoes the most violent turbulence as he changes from a literal company man to a loving father. But Carton in an almost blessed calm, with the turbulence of social revolution around him, takes on himself the identity of the victim of a most unyielding society. And like other victims he communicates with no one. Dickens places him in his last moments in the company of the anonymous little seamstress: her only relative, "an orphan, like myself," knows nothing of her sentence—"for I cannot write—and if I could, how should I tell her! It is better as it is." And how it is better for Carton only the reader can know. He makes no "utterance" as he goes to the scaffold, but his thoughts are given to us in the form of a "prophecy": "It is a far, far better thing that I do, than I have ever done; it is a far, far better rest that I go to than I have ever known." But better for whom or for what, Dickens does not tell us, for this is the end of the novel. In his act of magnanimity Carton completely loses his identity.

The last words of *The Virginians* deliver us to a comfortable hearthside a long distance from Carton's scaffold. Thackeray's vast, gossipy novel, with its portrait of an unbuttoned young George Washington and a diminished old Doctor Johnson, with its account of a family divided, though by no means fratricidally, by another revolution, and with its huge cast of characters, complete even to a young American heiress from Albany who marries a wicked habitué of the wicked Old World—this novel ends with Thackeray's tone at its most domestic. Sir George Warrington, whose narrative constitutes the last twenty-four chapters, is sent off to bed by Gumbo, the faithful body-servant from the old plantation:

> Here my master comes; he has poked out all the housefires, has looked to all the bolts, has ordered the whole male and female crew to their chambers; and begins to blow my candles out, and says, "Time, Sir George, to go to bed! Twelve o'clock!"
> "Bless me! So indeed it is." And I close my book, and go to my rest, with a blessing on those now around me asleep.

Within a tone so cosy even the relation of master and servant can be

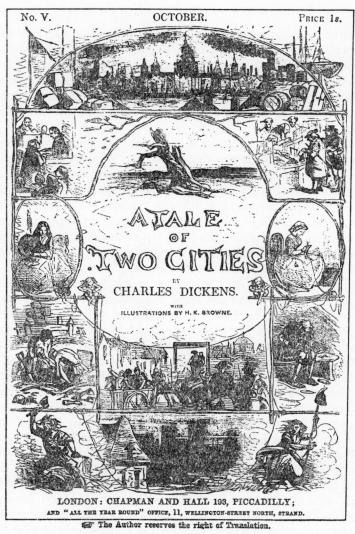

No. V.   OCTOBER.   PRICE 1s.

A TALE
OF
TWO CITIES
BY
CHARLES DICKENS.

WITH
ILLUSTRATIONS BY H. K. BROWNE.

LONDON: CHAPMAN AND HALL 193, PICCADILLY;
AND "ALL THE YEAR ROUND" OFFICE, 11, WELLINGTON-STREET NORTH, STRAND.

☞ The Author reserves the right of Translation.

Cover to the October 1859 number of *A Tale of Two Cities*

coyly reversed, and the cosiness is so insistent that all the large fires
and multitudinous crew of Thackeray's project, including the two
brothers' dangers and trials in fighting the revolution on opposite sides,
can be ordered, subdued, locked up. The villainies of the Castlewoods
are overcome, George marries the girl of his choice over the objections
and schemes of his mother, and all is finally so very well that no victim
is conceivable. The fluency of a thoroughly domesticated memory over-

THE VIRGINIANS

A TALE OF THE LAST CENTURY

BY W. M. THACKERAY.

Author of " Esmond,"
" Vanity Fair,"
" The Newcomes,"
&c. &c.

LONDON:

BRADBURY AND EVANS, 11, BOUVERIE STREET.

1859.

☞ The Author reserves the right of Translation.

Cover to October 1859 number of *The Virginians*. These two covers appeared side by side on bookstalls throughout England during 1859.

comes all obstacles, subdues all terrors. But it did not satisfy Thackeray, and the satisfaction it offered his readers was not very interesting. It was a disappointing product of that talent which had troubled so many in 1848 with the enigmatic portrait of Becky Sharp, the adventuress who was, perplexingly, neither villain nor victim.

But in *Adam Bede,* as its publisher's enthusiastic letters to Lewes and George Eliot attest, many readers found a fresh and at first sight reassuring talent. This novel did not make its readers suffer the agony of Richard Feverel's final departure from his wife, nor did it conceive of magnanimous self-sacrifice as an anonymous beheading. And its robust domesticities, whether at Mrs. Poyser's table or in the sunset glow of Adam's life with Dinah, were subordinate to something like a historical sense of place and region. Even its shocking victim, Hetty Sorrel, whose career is based on a story that Marian Evans heard from an aunt, is brought back into a world of acknowledged acts and consequences by the power of Dinah's words.

But Hetty's ruin is surrounded by more than Dinah's prayers. It is known to every character—to Arthur Donnithorne in perhaps a melodramatic nick of time—and the responses of each character to it, the way in which it is taken into the experience of all the articulate characters, is the substance of this novel. The responses of Adam are of course the most arresting, for as the rude artisan of sturdy but gentle sensibilities he is obviously a new kind of hero. But both his responses and the narrator's comments upon them suggest a novelty more fundamental than the presentation of a working-class hero. Adam's most characteristic response to Hetty's ruin has been noted by many readers and critics: "There's a sort o' damage, sir, that can't be made up for" (ch. xlviii), he says sternly to Arthur Donnithorne. Earlier he is more emphatic: "When a man's spoiled his fellow-creature's life, he's no right to comfort himself with thinking good may come of it: somebody else's good doesn't alter her shame and misery" (ch. xlvi). The doctrine may be as harsh as some features of Marian Evans's early piety, but it affirms a strong sense of the individual consciousness: one man is not another, and Hetty cannot know her own situation as another knows it. But this does not mean that the effects of Hetty's experience must be thrown away. Here, for example, is one comment on Adam's sorrow:

For Adam, though you see him quite master of himself, working hard and delighting in his work after his inborn inalienable nature, had not outlived his sorrow—had not felt it slip from him as a temporary burthen, and leave him the same man again. Do any of us? God forbid. It would be a poor result of all our anguish and our wrestling, if we won nothing but our old selves at the end of it—if we could return to the same blind loves, the same self-confident blame, the same light thoughts of human suffering, the same frivolous gossip over blighted human lives, the same feeble sense of that Unknown towards which we have sent forth irrepressible cries in our loneliness. Let us rather be thankful that our sorrow lives in us as an indestructible force, only changing its form, as forces do, and passing from pain into sympathy—the one poor word which includes all our best insight and our best love. . . . For it is at such periods that the sense of our lives having visible and invisible relations beyond any of which either our present or prospective self is the centre, grows like a muscle that we are obliged to lean on and exert.   (ch. 1)

The voice is unmistakably George Eliot's, and the conclusion, postulating a "sense of our lives having visible and invisible relations beyond any of which either our present or our prospective self is the centre," cumbersome and wordy as it may be, looks towards that vision of society which her best works, in their best parts, were to express. The generalizing and commenting were sometimes clumsy and were often obscure to her contemporaries—Trollope complained that he had to read her sentences over and over—but they bear the marks of intellectual struggle and mastery.

IV

In July of 1859 there was published a story of George Eliot's, "The Lifted Veil," that is one of her strangest productions. It is told in the first person and recounts the adventures of a man who in adolescence discovers that he cannot escape "the obtrusion on my mind of the mental processes going forward in first one person and then another, with whom I happened to be in contact." He miserably endures "the curse of insight—of my double consciousness" in something like a novelist's nightmare. For though Latimer, the "I," knows the inward life of all who surround him, he is miserably blighted. As a youth, though he passed much of his time "in a perpetual sense of exaltation . . . at the presence of Nature in all her awful loveliness," yet this sensibility did not make him a poet:

> . . . my lot was not so happy as that. A poet pours forth his song and *believes* in the listening ear and answering soul, to which his song will be floated sooner or later. But the poet's sensibility without his voice—the poet's sensibility that finds no vent but in silent tears on the sunny bank . . ., or in an inward shudder at the sound of harsh human tones, the sight of a cold human eye—this dumb passion brings with it a fatal solitude of soul in the society of one's fellow-men.

And even when he has attained his terrible insight into the mind behind the tones or the eye, Latimer is still dumb. Years later George Eliot wrote a motto for this story that, she said, was a "sufficient indication" of the "idea which it embodies, and which justifies its painfulness":

> Give me no light, great heaven, but such as turns
> To energy of human fellowship;
> No powers save the growing heritage
> That makes completer manhood.[4]

The rhetoric is no doubt inflated, but the "idea" suggests her attitude towards the "fatal solitude of soul in the society of one's fellow-men." If it is a novelist's nightmare to be cursed with a "double consciouness" that cannot be voiced, it is George Eliot's conception of hell that there should exist a "solitude of soul" on the one hand and "society" on the other.

There is a "parable" in *Middlemarch* that suggests how George Eliot eventually addressed herself to the terrible plight of the hero of "The Lifted Veil":

> An eminent philosopher among my friends, who can dignify even your ugly furniture by lifting it into the serene light of science, has shown me this pregnant little fact. Your pier-glass or extensive surface of polished steel made to be rubbed by a housemaid, will be minutely and multitudinously scratched in all directions; but place now against it a lighted candle as a centre of illumination, and lo! the scratches will seem to arrange themselves in a fine series of concentric circles round that little sun. It is demonstrable that the scratches are going everywhere impartially, and it is only your candle which produces the flattering illusion of a concentric arrangement, its light falling with an exclusive optical selection. These things are a parable. The scratches are events, and the candle is the egoism of any person now absent . . .   (ch. xxvii)

Upon such a model no throbbing heart or burning ego can find its counterpart in the world of events, in society. For the world of events— "that roar . . . on the other side of silence"—consists of minute and multitudinous lines that run in all directions, and their intricacy of relation can be understood only by a vision that is above, or outside, the illusions of egoism. Between such a world and the constant pulsing of individual desire both the happy victory of identity and the unhappy defeat of contradiction are only the concentric circles of "flattering illusion." But to dispel this kind of illusion it is necessary to imagine a relation between self and society both larger and subtler than Trollope's "tendency." And something like that relation George Eliot began to elaborate in 1859. Like the nature discovered by Darwin, the society imagined by George Eliot is so densely woven that even ruin and catastrophe serve only to illuminate the fineness and complexity of the filaments that connect and nourish its cells. And for this imagination the modern novelist, beginning with Henry James, that modern who lived before his time, has been grateful when he could be.

WILLIAM A. MADDEN

THE BURDEN OF THE ARTIST

THE intellectual formula of the modern age was provided some years ago by Bertrand Russell when he observed that the reasons for despair, "if not quite beyond dispute, are yet so nearly certain, that no philosophy which rejects them can hope to stand."[1] There is an impressive amount of evidence in the art of the past hundred years which would indicate that this awareness has touched the creative act itself. A century ago Mallarmé, in describing poetry as "the language of a state of crisis," summed up in a phrase a new attitude toward art that was to be greatly refined but not essentially changed in the years that followed. We have Yeats's complaint early in this century that "Perhaps fifty years ago I had been in less trouble, but what can one do when the age itself has come to *Hodos Chameliontos*," that region, according to Yeats's cabalistic manuscript, in which he himself had become lost, "where image called up image in an endless procession, and I could not always choose among them with any confidence." As Wallace Stevens commented, bringing the problem down to our own day: "we live in an intricacy of new and local mythologies, political, economic, poetic, which are asserted with an ever-enlarging incoherence."[2]

The relation between the comments of Yeats and Stevens and Mallarmé's definition a century ago is not, I think, fortuitous. It is difficult to imagine Wordsworth, for example, defining poetry in terms of crisis, or of Coleridge referring to the world, in Arthur Symons' words, as no longer "the satisfying material object it was to our grandparents."[3] For all the excitement in which the English Romantics saturated the discussion of poetry, they show few signs, either in their poetry or their criticism, of having experienced the special anxiety so familiar as to be almost instinctive to us, those

247

> ledges of our dread
> On whose jellied edges each joy is dandled
> Gently, like danger.[4]

Men became aware of these ledges in a post-Romantic world that seemed less and less satisfying as the nineteenth century advanced. By the middle of the century, as one historian put it, "a mood of aimlessness and despair cast its shadow over Europe's most advanced minds."[5] It was not despair itself, but its ubiquity, depth, and pervasiveness which was something new in human experience. Eventually the term "anxiety" was given popular currency by the new psychology, which in some important respects was simply a response to it: the term identifies a characteristic psychic posture exactly opposite to that which prevails when we are in the presence of what we discover or believe to be good, beautiful, worthy of love. If we accept as our point of departure this general definition of man's response to the ever-enlarging incoherence around him, and to a profound doubt within, we may say that the modern crisis in the arts emerged as an unmistakable phenomenon approximately a century ago.

The reason for the crisis having emerged when it did is suggested by G. M. Young's comment in his seminal study of the Victorian age: "Ruskin's final assurance that it does not much matter to the universe what sort of person you are, was impossible to a generation impressed by its teachers with the infinite importance—and therefore self-importance—of the individual soul."[6] Despair or the "feeling of death" or what William James later described, with special reference to modern instances, as "speculative melancholy,"[7] can be found, of course, in every age and art. But prior to the middle of the nineteenth century such experiences were associated with moods, impulses, transient states of depression that seemed to artists as to their audiences either exotic or morbid, in any case unusual experiences essentially inimical to the creative impulse; they were reactions to factors which were intelligible, if not always controllable, within the context of a certitude that something was in fact good or beautiful. When Coleridge wrote on dejection, he knew, or thought he knew, that joy was the reward of the pure in heart; like the other English Romantics from Blake to the early Carlyle, he was convinced of the infinite importance of the human soul. It was only when this conviction, together with its comprehensive vocabulary of values, came to be either fatally blurred or to seem irretrievably discredited for at least a large minority of thoughtful people, that "modern" art and poetry as a body of works with recognizable themes and techniques made their appearance. A widespread and quasi-permanent condition of existence, the feeling of anxiety is today a significant aspect of our total lives and perhaps the very center of the affective tonality through which we address the universe and our fellow-men.

The primary agent in provoking this sensibility in 1859, the one that directly engaged the artist and most radically altered his public, was the quiet erosion of Christian faith, the gradual evaporation of shared assumptions which had once provided the common consciousness (and unconsciousness) indispensable to ready understanding and sympathy. "It is a terrific problem that faces the poet today," Hart Crane was to remark much later, "a world that is so in transition from a decayed culture toward a reorganization of human evaluations that there are few common terms, general denominators of speech that are solid enough or ring with any vibration or spiritual conviction."[8] This was the literary aspect of the profound crisis which Matthew Arnold first noted in the 1850's:

> Yes! in the sea of life enisled,
> With echoing straits between us thrown,
> Dotting the shoreless watery wild,
> We mortal millions live *alone*.[9]

In England the arrival of this crisis had had its appropriate drama in the 'forties in the unprecedented examination of conscience on a national scale inaugurated by the Oxford Movement, the first of a series of shocks that culminated in the *coup de grâce* delivered by Darwin in 1859. How ill-prepared many Victorians were for Darwin's great work may be guessed from Ruskin's letter written in August to an American friend regarding his doubts "whether Art is a Crime or only an Absurdity; whether Clergymen ought to be multiplied, or exterminated by arsenic, like rats; whether in general we are getting on, and if so where are we going to."[10] If Natural Selection suggested that men were in fact "getting on," it said so in a way that could scarcely have consoled Ruskin and his contemporaries. As the lines from Arnold's poem and Ruskin's letter suggest, the most important fact about mid-Victorian England was that at the very moment when great political, social, and technological changes both furnished the material basis for and placed a premium upon greater mutual understanding and sympathy, the necessary cultural basis for such an exchange was disappearing. So far as the arts were concerned, the resulting uncertainty showed itself first in poetry and affected it most deeply, since language, even when exploited for aesthetic purposes, depends more than do the media of the other arts upon a common fund of emotional, conceptual, and symbolic references, and by 1859 this common fund was no longer available.

Against this background it is possible to see how Tennyson's, FitzGerald's, Arnold's, and Ruskin's 1859 works in particular bear witness to their sense of crisis in that year, suggest in fact their common experience of a situation identical to that described by R. P. Blackmur relative to present-day criticism: tradition was no longer available at either an instinctive or critical level, but had to be "looked for, dug out, and largely recreated as if it were a new thing and not a tradition at all."[11] By 1859 this larger cultural crisis had made itself felt in the arts by imposing an unprecedented burden upon the artist—both in the quality of the experience he had to treat and in the new responsibility which he had to bear: relative to the *Idylls of the King*, the crisis was revealed in Tennyson's sense of a loss of spiritual identity and of a vague and awesome future which this loss portended; in Fitz-Gerald's *Rubáiyát of Omar Khayyám*, there was evident the promise of a new relation to the past that soon expressed itself in the other arts in the search for a new idiom; and in Arnold's and Ruskin's relatively minor efforts, there emerged the first signs of a new kind of criticism, characterized by the tendency to make of poetry and art an absolute as the carriers of sacred values which, they were convinced, had been jeopardized by the breakdown of traditional safeguards against an impending savagery.

I

"Guinevere," one of the initial group of four Idylls published by Tennyson in 1859, contained Arthur's parting words to his sinful queen, "Lo! I forgive thee, as eternal God/Forgives: do thou for thine own soul the rest." The lines have more than once been cited as perfectly expressing the ethos of the middle class which set the tone of Victorian society and Victorian art. Because they embody the "self-importance" referred to by G. M. Young in the passage already cited—which also suggests the rationale behind them—twentieth-century critics were to react strongly against what seemed to them the Victorian public's too reverent and complacent regard for the figure of Arthur. Yet even in 1859 Tennyson's earlier poems were available to warn reviewers against accepting Arthur's words as a sufficient explanation of the poet's vision. These earlier poems had not only exhibited Tennyson's widening range of interests and competence as he labored to forge a language "fit for every mood / And change of my still soul";

they revealed a poet precariously balancing his romantic heritage of
Wisdom and Freedom (evident in "The Poet") above a widening
chasm of doubt and nightmares ("The Palace of Art" is a sketch of
the now familiar image of the artist standing in horrified fascination
on the edge of those "abysmal deeps of Personality" to which Tennyson
refers in the poem). While engaged on the conscious level with a struggle between faith and doubt—a struggle resolved in favor of faith in
In Memoriam (1850)—on a deeper level Tennyson was preoccupied
with impulses which he only dimly recognized as somehow connected
with both. His eventual response was to identify his impulses with his
conscious doubts, thus making it necessary as he thought to stifle both
if he were to preserve his faith in a moral order. Yet in 1859 there still
lurked behind the Poet Laureate who had become an oracle of the
Victorian ethos a sensitive poet who often wrote to greater effect, if
less deliberately and less frequently, out of Ruskin's final assurance that
the universe was not much interested in man.

It is significant that Tennyson's descriptions of nature had much
more of "word painting" about them, of preoccupation with the sounds
of words and the play of metrical patterns, than had Wordsworth's.
In his "pastoral" mood—"you scarce could see the grass for flowers"—
Tennyson supplied for mid-Victorians something analogous to the release that Wordsworth's *anima naturae* had provided for Tennyson's
own generation (notably for John Stuart Mill), but from the mid-1830's
on, nature assumed for Tennyson himself more and more an aspect
which it had never had for the Romantics,* an aspect implicit in the
casual and mindless universe postulated by the skeptical frame of
mind that found its bible in 1859 in the *Origin of Species* and its language of the soul in the new "molecular" psychology. The relation between the poet's response to this demythologized nature—very soon to
be inhabited by Darwin's "favoured" but distressingly amoebic human
species—and Tennyson's search for some sort of spiritual identity
can be discerned in *In Memoriam* in the hope

* Henry Sidgwick, in a letter to Tennyson's son, defined the difference between Wordsworth's and Tennyson's handling of nature as it struck those struggling in the 'sixties with "the great issues between Agnostic Science and Faith."
"Wordsworth's attitude toward Nature was one that, so to say, left Science un-
regarded: the Nature for which Wordsworth stirred our feelings was Nature as
known by simple observation and interpreted by religious and sympathetic intuition. But for your father the physical world is always the world as known to
us through physical science: the scientific view of it dominates his thoughts about
it; and his general acceptance of this view is real and sincere, even when he ut-
ters the intensest feeling of its inadequacy to satisfy our deepest needs" (*Alfred
Lord Tennyson: A Memoir, by his Son* [New York, 1897], 302-303).

> That not a worm is cloven in vain;
>   That not a moth with vain desire
>   Is shrivell'd in a fruitless fire,
> Or but subserves another's gain

which suddenly breaks down into a cry of desolation:

> So runs my dream: but what am I?
>   An infant crying in the night:
>   An infant crying for the light:
> With no language but a cry.

Following Hallam's death in 1833, Tennyson's personal trial had become involved with his poetic function. His task was not merely to reach an expanding public, but in an alien universe to discover who he was and, as a poet, to invent a language commensurate with this self. His poetic achievement was thereafter directly related to his success in rendering the syzygy of his inner life, to his having faithfully if not always consciously reiterated the "cry" which spoke for an important part of the complex totality that he was. Even after the apparent resolution of his struggle in *In Memoriam,* Tennyson returned to poetic consideration of the mid-Victorian threat to a perfectly integrated self in *Maud* (1855), in which the sick lover (a "modern Hamlet," Tennyson called him) confronts the stars and their

> . . . sad astrology, the boundless plan
> That makes you tyrants in your iron skies,
> Innumerable, pitiless, passionless eyes,
> Cold fires, yet with the power to burn and brand
> His nothingness into man.

This was a language of the imagination equivalent to the neutral equations of the physical law of entropy postulated by the succeeding generation. While it was a language powerless to analyze the subtler movements of man's spirit stirred by the threat of annihilation, Tennyson's poetry nevertheless memorably recorded the initial impact of that threat as well as the heroic moral effort provoked by the inevitable "Victorian" reaction to it.

With this earlier poetry in mind, the four 1859 Idylls strike the modern reader as a remarkable feat on Tennyson's part in manipulating recalcitrant material to serve his double vision. The intense moral strain of *In Memoriam* and *Maud* is again evident in these extended narrative poems, and the cause is the same. There was, for example, the significant shift in emphasis in the handling of Malory's Lady of Astolat episode in "Elaine." In the epilogue which Tennyson appended to Malory's story, Lancelot drifts off to the woods to reflect on the events just transpired, falls into a profound melancholy, and ends by putting to himself the question:

> For what am I? what profits me my name
> Of greatest knight? I fought for it, and have it:
> Pleasure to have it, none; to lose it, pain;
> Now grown part of me: but what use in it?

Lancelot's sense of futility derives from his sudden recognition that the chivalric code has proven inadequate to the event, that Elaine's sudden trajectory across the arc of his own destiny, like some random collision of blind comets, has a dimension which the Code of Noble Deeds cannot comprehend. If we substitute "poet" for "knight" in the second line, the passage suggests as well a Tennyson whose moral code has proven similarly inadequate to his personal experience, conveys in fact something of the under-burden of the *Idylls* as a whole and brings us close to those deeps in the poet where some of his finest poetry took shape.

"Enid" and "Vivien" confirm the reader's sense of the vertigo that continually attends the efforts of the Round Table. Horrified by rumors of the Queen's guilty love for Lancelot, Geraint immediately declines into a state of cynical self-righteousness that permits him to see and hear and think only those things which he most hates and fears. His condition indeed passes beyond mere jealously into something like the total cynicism of Hamlet:

> But ever more it seem'd an easier thing
> At once without remorse to strike her dead,
> Than to cry "Halt," and to her bright face
> Accuse her of the least immodesty . . .

And just as the motive for jealousy is irrational, driving the hero into a state suggestive of psychological death, so the motive behind his recovery—Enid's cry "as of a wild thing taken in the trap"—precipitates the hero into violent action and into a resolve equally beyond reason in the manner of his forgiving:

> "I heard you say, that you were no true wife:
> I swear I will not ask your meaning in it:
> I do believe yourself against yourself,
> And will henceforward rather die than doubt."

The irrationality of the belief is unintelligible apart from our recognition of the desperate predicament to which it is a response. Similarly,

Merlin's career in "Vivien" follows the pattern of the Geraint and Lancelot stories, anticipating Arthur's final defeat, in "The Passing of Arthur" (1869), in which high resolve generally gives way before the forces of anarchy and evil. Like Lancelot, Merlin dreads rather "the loss of use than fame" and finds himself possessed of magnificent powers for which he can discern no profitable use in the world of the Round Table. When he finds himself caught in the toils of Vivien's demonic malevolence, he falls, like Lancelot and Geraint, into a "great melancholy," foresees the defeat of noble reason, and succumbs:

> World-war of dying flesh against the life,
> Death in all life and lying in all love,
> The meanest having power upon the highest,
> And the high purpose broken by the worm.

As Vivien departs in a flourish of serpentine imagery, Merlin lies in a hollow oak as one dead, his will to believe and hope gone.

Behind the pattern of Noble Action which dominates the *Idylls* lies the chaos implicit in the poignant question "What am I?" first put by the poet himself in *In Memoriam,* repeated after him by Lancelot in "Elaine," and spoken finally by King Arthur in the terrible closing scene of the *Idylls*: "I know not what I am, / Nor whence I am, nor whether I be King." As in Malory's story, the theme of Tennyson's *Idylls* is a quest,* but the quest in the *Idylls* is for a self that might function in a universe to which the traditional spiritual norms represented by the Grail no longer seemed relevant, and the heroes of the *Idylls* go down one by one to defeat until, at the end, the small circle of light which follows the figure of Arthur goes out, and the world is left in darkness.

Tennyson's poetic quest in the *Idylls* was all but submerged in the rhetoric of duty that became explicit in the late Dedication and Epilogue, a rhetoric that in 1859 was responsible for the Tupperish performances of "Jack Tar" and "Riflemen Form!"[12] in which the poet recommends to the nation as a whole the militaristic ritual of the deed to which the heroes in his epic (as in *Maud* earlier) had also turned to escape the traumas induced by uncertainty within and the ever enlarging incoherence without. The Victorian public hailed the imagery with which the Laureate had, as it believed, adorned its own self-important

---

* As late as 1859 Tennyson's instinct was to avoid the Grail theme: "As to Macaulay's suggestion of the Sangreal, I doubt whether such a subject could be handled in these days, without incurring a charge of irreverence. It would be too much like playing with sacred things. The old writers *believed* in the Sangreal" (*Memoir,* I, 456-457).

morality, failing or refusing to detect behind the rhetoric of the code the "cry" in some of Tennyson's greatest poetry. In 1859 Tennyson wrote, when closest to himself, with the intensely personal stoicism of one for whom sustained contemplation of the sad astrology meant spiritual agony, and for whom cynical resignation was moral catastrophe.

II

Poetry's need for a new mythology and imagery helps to explain the appearance in 1859 of Edward FitzGerald's *Rubáiyát of Omar Khayyám, The Astronomer-Poet of Persia.* Drawing upon the resources of a medieval Persian agnostic who was, probably more than Fitz-Gerald realized, a product of his own imagination,[13] FitzGerald made a new poem and rendered in a far different English idiom the sad astrology which had afflicted Tennyson. There is a suggestion of the deep-seated misgivings at work behind the poem—and among Victorians generally—in the fact that while Tennyson and Thackeray, in their roles as active professional writers, envied FitzGerald's sedentary leisure, FitzGerald himself was bothered in his rural retreat by a vague sense of guilt:

People affect to talk of this kind of life [of mine] as very beautiful and philosophical: but I don't: men ought to have some ambition to stir, and travel, and fill their heads and senses: but so it is. Enough of what is called the subjective style of writing. This word has made considerable progress in England during the years you have been away.[14]

The source of FitzGerald's feeling of guilt and a probable impetus behind the rise of the "subjective style" to which he refers is hinted at in the same letter. Declaring he did not wish to travel when he could abide in a "land so beautiful, as the good sense, justice, and liberality of my good countrymen make this," FitzGerald concluded, "I cling closer to it, because I feel that we are going down hill, and shall perhaps live ourselves to talk of all this independence as a thing that has been." Complacent pride in achievement, linked to uneasy doubts as to its permanence and as to where mankind was going, helps to explain how the devout FitzGerald who in 1840 thought Newman's sermons the best sermons ever written could in 1859 "feel with" what he called an Epicurean Eclogue in a Persian Garden. In his own unostentatious way, FitzGerald was taking the well-trod mid-Victorian path from a comfortable unexamined faith to a disconcerting doubt which neither the securest circumstances nor the deepest pieties could dispel.

It is worth noting that just three years prior to the appearance of the *Rubáiyát* FitzGerald had translated an "orthodox" Persian poem. Whereas the *Rubáiyát* asserted the will to selfhood in the face of cosmic arbitrariness, this earlier translation, *Salámán and Absál* by the "orthodox" poet Jámi, dwelt on the need to efface individuality for the sake of absorption in the Infinite, its theme being the resolution of the dilemma posed by the simple Kurd—

> "I grow perplext, oh God! 'twixt 'I' and '*THOU*';
> If *I*—this Dignity and Wisdom whence?
> If *THOU*—then what this abject Impotence?"

—by way of the ascetic fire of "Self-solitude," ending in the recognition of "How PASSION tires, and how with Time begins / The Folding of the Carpet of DESIRE."[15] But FitzGerald, like Matthew Arnold, dallied with the religious wisdom of the East only to reject it. In the Introduction to his 1859 poem his dissatisfaction with Eastern mysticism expressed itself in a complaint against the orthodox Persian poets' habit of converting Omar's materials

to a mystical Use more convenient to themselves and the People they address'd; a People quite as quick of Doubt as of Belief; quite as keen of the Bodily Senses as of the Intellectual; and delighting in a cloudy Element compounded of All, in which they float luxuriously between Heaven and Earth, and this World and the Next, on the wings of poetical expression . . . Omar was too honest of Heart as well as of Head for this.[16]

Poetry, FitzGerald's spokesman had said in the dialogue *Euphranor* (1851), "will not come at a call, like a Laureate's Odes, but must leap out of its own accord at the unpremeditated contact with Nature (or, at least, the recollection of such contact),"[17] but the reassuring Wordsworthian terminology of 1851 did not prevent FitzGerald's Nature from becoming as disconcerting as Tennyson's in the 1859 *Rubáiyát*.

FitzGerald explained his predilection for Omar to his friend E. B. Cowell in 1857:

in truth I take old Omar as my property more than yours: he and I are more akin, are we not? You see all [his] Beauty, but you don't *feel* with him in some respects as I do. I think you would almost feel obliged to leave out the part of Hamlet in representing him to your Audience: for fear of Mischief.

He went on in the letter to compare Omar's "*free* opinions" with those of Lucretius, a comparison later expanded in a revealing way in his Introduction to the *Rubáiyát*.

Both indeed [Lucretius and Omar] men of subtle Intellect and high Imagination, instructed in Learning beyond their day, and of Hearts passionate for

Truth and Justice, who justly revolted from their Country's false Religion
. . . but who yet fell short of replacing what they subverted by such better
Hope as others, upon whom no better Faith had dawned, had yet made a
Law to themselves.[18]

If we recall that Tennyson wrote and Arnold intended to write a poem
on Lucretius, we may estimate how close FitzGerald was in this passage
to the sources of feeling among sensitive Victorians in 1859, to what
Arnold had referred to in 1853 as "the doubts and discouragements of
Hamlet and of Faust."[19]

FitzGerald's empathy with his theme and the fact of the poem's
startling popularity in the 'seventies are important marks on the chart
recording Victorian emotional disturbances. The *Rubáiyát* created a
self many thoughtful Victorians had sooner or later to come to terms
with, a self in whom the voice of hope, whether of Tennyson or Jámi
or Bishop Butler, had been silenced. As a desperate assertion of human
desire in an indifferent universe, a song sung not in praise of sensual
pleasure, but to honor man's dignity and will to endure, the *Rubáiyát*
touched very nearly the mood of an ostensibly stiff-necked generation;
as embodying the voice of doubt in unqualified purity, it sounded the
cultural death-knell of "the larger Hope" that Tennyson was espousing,
offering in its place the chilling consolation of self-assertion, here and
now. Rossetti's and Swinburne's enthusiastic reception of the poem
was significant, since the *Rubáiyát*'s delayed *succès d'estime* among
these younger poets was a more reliable purport of the future of English poetry than the best-seller success of the *Idylls*. The step was a
very short one from a feeling of alienation in an arbitrary universe to
a feeling of absolute freedom in a dream-world that rejected limitations.
The *Rubáiyát* was but one psychological remove from Swinburne's
hymns to Man as the Master.

In its adoption of the dramatic monologue and in its exploitation
of matter from an older, remote culture, FitzGerald's poem was part of
a growing movement, with Browning at its center, which was to culmi-
nate in this century in Ezra Pound's *Cantos*. Here Yeats's notion of the
poet who would play with all masks was a crucial phase;
man was not merely divided, he was shattered, and the fragments of
various selves were there waiting to be picked up and worn as mood
and interest dictated. An admirer of FitzGerald and Browning precisely for their role in reviving the dramatic monologue, Pound expanded their limited eclecticism and Yeats' masquery to the exploitation of various cosmologies and languages in his effort to "keep the language efficient," ransacking the past for a new idiom commensurate

with the feelings engendered in the artist by a "botched civilization."
Thus Pound bears witness in his poetry to the continuity of the crisis
evident in FitzGerald's poem and exhibits the eclecticism marked by
Sir Herbert Read as characteristic of twentieth-century art generally,
"the tendency to make, both of poetry and painting, a mythological
salad."[20] It is part of the search already present in the early Tennyson
who hoped to explore "every legend fair": the attempt to find imaginative equivalents for various selves in appropriate fragments from
the past.

III

In this context, Matthew Arnold's *England and the Italian Question* and John Ruskin's *The Two Paths* may be seen as the works of
artists *manqués* driven by a sense of urgency to consider the political,
social, and ideological crisis which seemed to them to endanger the
artistic function. As such, their 1859 pamphlets foreshadowed events
and conclusions which proved to be important to the developing crisis
in the arts. Apparently the first fruits of their respective decisions to
abandon the direct criticism of art in favor of political and social criticism, their efforts were in fact motivated by a desire to give to art and
to the artist a new role, a role which they were so successful in imposing that it still powerfully conditions our approach to poetry and art
today. Different though they were in temperament, and even in the
meanings they would attach to the crucial terms, Arnold and Ruskin
were profoundly at one in their insistence that poetry, in the one case,
and art, in the other, were indeed, in Arnold's famous phrase, "a
criticism of life."

In 1859 Arnold had some important poems still to write, but they
were largely a continuation of the sustained threnody of his early poetry
in which he recorded the poet's isolation and melancholy consequent
upon a radical break with a past he could not altogether forget. Acutely
aware of the "strange disease of modern life," Arnold could not as a
poet move beyond the dialogue of the mind with itself which the disease entailed. As late as 1857, in his inaugural lecture as Professor of
Poetry at Oxford, in which he promised to treat the "modern element"
in literature from the time of classical Greece down to his own day, he
was still for the most part lamenting the disease, the "impatient irrita-
tion" which stamped all English poetry of the day, he said, with the
Lucretian qualities of "depression and ennui."[21] To rescue his contemporaries from this "modern feeling" Arnold proposed in this lecture a new function for criticism—an intellectual deliverance; but in
1857 he was still uncertain as to how he should construe the crucial

word "modern."* It was not until 1859, while he was visiting schools in France, reflecting on the French Revolution, and reading Mill's essay *On Liberty* and Renan's *Essais de morale et de critique,* that Arnold announced the important decision which enabled him to solve his dilemma.

The significance of *England and the Italian Question* lay in its serving notice that Arnold had found the key to the "modern spirit," to that *Zeitgeist* which in the late 'forties had driven him to find refuge in the Alps with Senancour, but which he was now bent on applying to unlock the doors of the prison of Puritanism which encaged his countrymen. In his letters home at this date as well as in his pamphlet Arnold indicated that intellectual deliverance was to be had in the "ideas of religious, political, and social freedom . . . which were popularized by the French Revolution," ideas, he added, which "have now leavened for seventy years the populations of Europe."[22] His identification of the "modern spirit" with the liberal, democratic ideas stirring the "masses" on the Continent made overt the radical shift in his interest at this time away from Lucretian ennui and ancient Rome, and toward modern Italy and the affirmations of "modern" authors like Heine and Goethe. "Thereafter," Professors Tinker and Lowry note in their *Commentary,* "the likelihood of his ever completing his Roman play [on Lucretius] grew steadily less."[23] With this shift in interest from past to future, Arnold the melancholy poet retired and the hopeful critic appeared, the critic who was to touch on the "modern" element in politics, education, and religion as well as in poetry.

The significance of this decision for Arnold's later criticism is suggested in a letter written to his friend Arthur Hugh Clough in 1859 shortly after his return from the Continent. "I use *reason,*" Arnold wrote, "for a way of thinking I have about the ancient and the modern or ante Christian and post Christian world, which . . . I am developing in my lectures."[24] This "way of thinking"—based on a concept of history which allowed, indeed required, analogous roles for periods remote from one another in time and culture—Arnold had inherited from his father, Dr. Thomas Arnold.[25] It made itself evident all through the important *Essays in Criticism,* which were composed in

* Arnold's confusing use of the word "modern" was noted by a reviewer in the *Spectator* when the inaugural lecture was first printed in 1869. Arnold attempted to explain what he was driving at in a letter to his mother about this review (*Letters of Matthew Arnold 1848-1888,* ed. George W. E. Russell [1895], II, 4). The lecture itself makes clear that he was fluctuating between equating modernity with the *thought* of classical Greece, a modernity which he urgently recommended, and with the *feeling* of Virgilian Rome, which he was attacking.

the early 'sixties. In "The Function of Criticism at the Present Time,"
which set the standard and tone of the volume, Arnold classed the
French Revolution with "the stir of the great productive time of
Greece" and placed its ideas among "the prescriptions of reason"
which are "absolute, unchanging, of universal validity." In concluding
that the French Revolution was "the greatest and most animating event
in history,"[26] Arnold provided a rationale for his praise of Goethe and
Heine in the same volume as "modern" poets, and for his reservations
regarding the inadequate "content" in the poetry of Dante and Milton.
Here too was the assumption behind Arnold's equation, in his later
religious criticism, of Christianity with other poetic mythologies. The
note of progressive intellectual liberation was struck in *Essays in
Criticism* in the following passage:

The modern spirit is now awake almost everywhere; the sense of want of
correspondence between the forms of modern Europe and its spirit, between the new wine of the eighteenth and nineteenth centuries, and the old
bottles of the eleventh and twelfth centuries, or even of the sixteenth and
seventeenth, almost everyone now perceives.[27]

This was the point of view which first found expression in the
1859 pamphlet, in which Arnold's immediate object was to warn the
English aristocracy that the French Revolution had ended the reign
of "aristocracy and character" and had ushered in the reign of "the
people and ideas." But he wished to do more than merely announce
the fact; his ultimate goal was to counteract the political anarchy latent
in the new society by proposing a "symbol of force and order," just as
he was to propose a few years later a National Academy to counteract
the capricious standards of taste. This concern for standards, for order,
in a society which had lost its center motivated Arnold's attempt over
the next thirty years to establish a new basis for culture, or rather to
offer Culture itself to all classes as the true safeguard against anarchy.
It soon became clear that the use of Napoleon III as a symbol of order,
in *England and the Italian Question,* was merely the first tentative step
in Arnold's efforts to bring together, through the instrumentality of
criticism in the broadest sense, the several interests of education in a
democracy, international *Realpolitik,* classical literature, and moral
sensibility.*

* The key argument in Arnold's education reports following his 1859
visit to France rested on an analogy between a poetic masterpiece and the body
politic. "It is the chief virtue of a healthy and uncorrupted aristocracy," he wrote
in 1861, "that it is in general, in the grand style," the style which, presumably,
Arnold was defining in his lectures on Homer. The value of the English aristocracy's influence on the people, he repeated, was its ability to fashion the

In coming to terms with the ideology behind the French Revolution Arnold in effect sanctioned the intellectual ideals of an "open society," a society to be kept in perpetual ferment through the continual and free exercise of critical analysis, although for this very reason it was a society also, Arnold insisted, requiring the conservative and morally formative inspiration of great poetry to stabilize it. It was impossible to find for poetry a more impressive task. The 1859 pamphlet proved to be a prolegomenon to Arnold's famous conclusion that in the realm of intellectual inquiry there was "Not a dogma that does not threaten to dissolve, not a tradition that is not shaken, not a fact which has its historical character free from a question,"[28] while in the order of political and moral action the "touchstones" from the world's great poetry provided man's last hope and stay. The 1859 pamphlet thus paved the way for the Arnold who was to become most familiar to his contemporaries and to be most influential on the future course of English and American criticism and education. What survived of his message was a sense that poetry was somehow related to the salvation of society. His critical program rescued the poet from the isolation with which a new civilization threatened him by bringing him onto the center of the stage, where, as spokesman for man's best self, he has since remained in the imaginations of many who have cared for civilization.

By 1859 Ruskin too had decided that the preservation and elevation of the social order required the extension of the values implicit in art to every form of social activity. Entitled *The Two Paths: Being Lectures On Art and Its Application to Decoration and Manufacture,* his 1859 book brought together five lectures delivered between January 1857 and March 1859 in which Ruskin's aim was to hold before the aspiring artist the "responsibility for choice, decisive and conclusive, between two modes of study, which involve ultimately the development, or deadening, of every power he possesses."[29] The narrower context of this choice was the Battle of Styles in architecture which resulted in the dramatic public encounter in 1859 between Lord Palmerston and the architect Gilbert Scott over whether the design of the Foreign Office building should be Gothic (Christian) or Classic (Pagan).[30] Within this narrower context Ruskin's pamphlet was a defense of the Gothic style against the "geometry and legalism" of the Classical style,

---

masses after its own pattern into "peoples in the grand style" (*The Popular Education of France* [1861], pp. xv-xvi). This view of history in the Grand Style permitted Arnold to exalt the fact of change on the one hand, while, on the other hand, retaining the moral and imaginative standards of a poetic ideal by which to evaluate the currents set moving by the *Zeitgeist.*

and, implicitly, of the artist's integrity against the pretensions of the politician. But—as with Arnold's pamphlet—the importance of *The Two Paths* lay less in its *ad hoc* relevance to a local argument than in its anticipation of new modes of thought and feeling regarding the place of the arts in a democratic society and a technological civilization.

The larger context behind Ruskin's choice was the debate over what constituted the true tradition of art, and his significant verdict favored neither classicism nor medievalism, but Nature. The theme common to all five lectures derived from Ruskin's belief in "the dependence of all noble design, in any kind, on the sculpture or painting of Organic Form." "This is the vital law," he said, "lying at the root of all that I have ever tried to teach respecting architecture or any other art."[31] In these words Ruskin distilled the essence of his many-sided campaign to introduce the Romantic view into the discussion of painting, sculpture, and architecture, doing as an art critic for Turner's painting and Gothic architecture what Coleridge had done as a literary critic for Wordsworth's poetry and German metaphysics, and in general saturating art criticism with a new intensity and purpose.

But if Ruskin was prophetic of an "Organic" theory which was to be extremely influential in architectural aesthetics,* his romantic naturalism lacked the kind of metaphysical vindication which his comprehensive claims for it required. Even "nature" needs a coherent mythology if it is to be a useful concept, and there was an element in Ruskin's work, to some extent neutralized by the pragmatic limitations of architecture, which revealed an "organic" world quite unlike the one he referred to consciously, and which we can now see gave to his message a significance for the plastic arts of which he himself could not be aware. Behind his explicit judgments, often heavily Victorian and occasionally chauvinistic in their bias, lay Ruskin's intuition of the absolute claims of art upon the artist. This intuition was at odds with

---

* For Ruskin's influence on American architectural practice and theory, and the opposition to that influence exerted by T. H. Huxley, see Albert Bush-Brown, " 'Get an Honest Bricklayer!': The Scientist's Answer to Ruskin," *Journal of Aesthetics and Art Criticism*, XVI (1958), 248-356. R. H. Wilenski has shown how prescient Ruskin was at times regarding the possibilities of new materials in architecture (*John Ruskin* [New York, 1933], p. 224). Wilenski argues that *The Two Paths* was Ruskin's last effective art criticism (p. 193), but it might be argued that even in his later economic and social criticism Ruskin was moved by something of the *élan* which inspires contemporary town-planners, a faith in the redemptive powers of an art of the metropolis which educates the sensibilities of the masses. His aesthetic comprehended a complete social, economic, and political program not unlike those espoused in our day by Lewis Mumford and Sir Herbert Read.

his strict moral intent, and the inner conflict that resulted, in addition
to contributing to Ruskin's personal tragedy, proved to be prophetic
of the toll exacted of all modern artists whose intuition runs counter to
received canons of feeling and behavior in a democratic society.

One of the most compelling passages drawn up by Ruskin for
The Two Paths was eventually cancelled in favor of another, quite different statement. The context called for the clear definition of a criterion by which the art student might know whether or not he was a true
artist. In the innocuous passage which he chose to publish, Ruskin
advised the students to "love that which your work represents," explaining that the landscape painter should love hills and trees, the
figure painter love the human soul, and so on. The cancelled passage on
the other hand enlarged upon the true artist's "instinctive craving":

It is not, observe, a feeling to be described in any exalted terms; it is a sort
of hunger, an instinct more like that of the young of a wild beast for its
prey, than anything else; it has hardly anything to do with conscientious or
religious feeling. I am sorry to say that very pious and good people don't
generally make good painters . . . the real feeling is just an unreasonable,
unaccountable, insatiable fury for seeing things and setting them down. If
there were no other living being in the world, still your real painter would
go on painting . . . He doesn't paint for any good purpose, but because he
can't help it; he doesn't think it the best thing to be done, but he can't do
anything else; nothing can stop him, nothing comes amiss to him; if he were
going to be hanged, he would sketch the gallows.[32]

To speak of an "unreasonable, unaccountable, insatiable fury" in connection with art was to strike out on unexplored paths in English art
criticism; the language has a compulsive urgency drawn from depths
which neither Ruskin nor his hearers were accustomed to recognizing.

The difference in emphasis in the two passages may be traced to
Ruskin's "conversion" in 1858 while studying Veronese's "Queen of
Sheba" at Turin, an experience which came as the climax to his years
of restless inquiry, travel, and reflection, and after which he began to
seek in art the moral imperatives, spiritual ecstasies, and ordering
vision which he had hitherto thought the prerogatives of religious experience.* The cancelled passage went beyond the largest Romantic

---

* Ruskin deduced from his study of Veronese that "to be a first-rate
painter—*you must n't* be pious; but rather a little wicked, and entirely a man of
the world" (*Letters to C. E. Norton,* I, 67). Much later Ruskin claimed that
after this experience at Turin in 1858 "my evangelical beliefs were put away,
to be debated no more." Norton's comment on this admission ran, in part: "It
was a hard, an unsettling revelation, and from the effects of it I believe that he
never recovered" (p. 71).

claims, liberating art from all utilities and postulating an instinctive urge in the artist which would save both self and society. In this way, although it never deliberately challenged Victorian domestic morals, Ruskin's aesthetic provided the basis for a new kind of religion, which can only be described as a religion of art, by shifting the spiritual center of art criticism away from moral imperatives toward the artist's self-justifying passion. Convinced that the values implicit in art and in the artist's integrity, if extended to "the comfort or the relief of the mass of people," could save the state, Ruskin in effect extended Arnold's notion of the saving power of poetry to all the arts—in a word, to Art, and placed a burden on the artist corresponding to the one which Arnold placed on the poet.

Ruskin's cancellation of the passage in *The Two Paths* in 1859 was indicative of a split paradigmatic of the modern sensibility. Unable to control the inner movements which more and more encroached upon his mental and emotional life, Ruskin was obliged to undertake their exploration involuntarily and we begin to find in his prose studies of animal symbolism and Greek myths and, very strikingly in a late sketch, the flow of images characteristic of twentieth-century poetry and art (his sketch of Amiens in 1880, we are told, passing "beyond all the skill he had so patiently acquired into a strange childish primitivism"[33]). With his furious attack in the 1870's on Whistler's impressionistic paintings, provoked by inner needs he did not understand, Ruskin's personal bewilderment entered the public domain of art criticism. A new generation had arisen without that vested interest in the Victorian sense of moral identity which characterized Ruskin, and it had already set about deliberately exploring other possibilities. By this time architecture in particular had begun to display the cultural eclecticism evident earlier in poetry, Whistler's architect, Edward William Godwin, designing Celtic, Gothic, Greek, and Japanese houses in his search for an "organic" and "natural" style expressive of the modern sensibility, while in America Frank Lloyd Wright, whose architectural theory is remarkably akin to Ruskin's, was beginning a similar search that eventually led him out into the desert and to Mayan architecture. The artist's victorious fight to free himself from the purposes imposed by public opinion so that he might follow his intuition unimpeded, begun in England by Ruskin, was not without its pyrrhic element, however. "The stylistic possibilities open to the painter and sculptor of to-day seem so limitless," an art historian has recently said, "that he is bewildered and even stultified by his own freedom."[34]

The paradoxical effect of Ruskin's and Arnold's great influence, both in England and America, was to hasten the break-up of the old

Ruskin's copy of the "incorrigible Angel," from Westwood's *Palaeographia Sacra*

"The Aristotelian principles of the Beautiful are, you remember, Order, Symmetry, and the Definite. Here you have the three, in perfection, applied to the ideal of an angel, in a psalter of the eighth century . . . Here you have the most pure type possible of the principles of idealism in all ages: whenever people don't look at Nature, they always think they can improve her."

". . . this fellow does not want scales, nor coils; he wants the serpent's heart—malice and insinuation . . . note the eyes slightly askance, the lips compressed, and the right hand nervously grasping the left arm: nothing can be declared impossible to the people who could begin thus—the world is open to them, and all that is in it; while, on the contrary, nothing is possible to the man who did the symmetrical angel."

Ruskin's copy of the "corrigible Eve," from St. Ambrogio of Milan

Two passages from Ruskin's lecture on "The Deteriorative Power of Conventional Art over Nations," published as Lecture I in *The Two Paths*.

order, leaving the poet and artist in his private *Angst* to master the Age of Violence alone. Less certain perhaps than Ruskin and Arnold about the efficacy of poetry and art in a mass-culture, distinguished artists who came after them—Yeats and Emily Dickinson and Dylan Thomas and Wallace Stevens come to mind—have looked to their own work and have lived by it as a private religion, a personal liturgy offering a world of hope and beauty apart from, and a "criticism" of, the world of metaphysical uncertainty and of moral and material ugliness from which it arose. "I am prepared to assert," a British poet has recently said, "that so far from poetry being without power or value in the modern world—that is, precisely, in the lives of you and me today in the fifth decade of the twentieth century—it is one of the very few things which can save us from the ultimate catastrophe that threatens our civilisation, perhaps the only thing in the long run."[35] But there is considerable evidence which suggests, as do Arnold's and Ruskin's own careers, that the burden of saving society must seriously interfere with the creative act for those poets and artists who take the burden literally, and that when it becomes too oppressive the artist either will reject all social relevance in his art, seeking in the depths of "subjectivity" a meaning the external world cannot give, or, refusing to abandon society, will turn to the more direct work of criticism.

The turn to criticism is related to Arnold's postulate of a constantly evolving *Zeitgeist* from which the artist must draw his "content" if he is to be a "modern" artist.* Granted the need to follow the Time-Spirit with a criticism *ondoyant et divers,* it was not improbable that the artist would find himself devoting a major portion of his energy to the enormous task of sifting the confused currents of his age in an effort to dig out a tradition which would enable him to articulate his insights, while an unregenerate public found less arduous ways to deal with its mass anxieties. One thinks of the creative talents, more or less fully realized, which have expended themselves in the discussion of problems similar to the ones which engaged Arnold and Ruskin. T. S.

* John Wain has invoked Arnold to explain why in recent years "every good English poet has been a practicing critic." The continuance of the problem is suggested in the fact that while Wain, like Arnold, sees the function of criticism as one of preparing an audience for poetry, Philip Larkin, whom Wain considers the best of the younger English poets, is described as exhibiting in his poems an "I" which is "quite deliberately presented as reticent, elusive, and uncommitted" ("English Poetry: The Immediate Situation," *Sewanee Review,* LXV [1957], 353-374). Here is the problem introduced by Arnold, of the disinterested poet who must assimilate the *Zeitgeist* and still create in the midst of an indifferent public. Larkin's "Church Song" is the contemporary version of Arnold's "Stanzas from the Grande Chartreuse."

Eliot, William Empson, E. M. Forster, and Lionel Trilling are reminders of the persistence of this "critical" function in contemporary letters, and there are corroborative instances in the other fields of art.

Rejection of all social concern on the other hand is implicit in Julian Symons' statement: "The poet, in society as it is now constituted, has no 'duty'; the poet is not of necessity concerned with the alteration of society; he may accept or reject or remain indifferent to the effects of war."[36] Unexceptionable, even Arnoldian, in its protest against a narrowly utilitarian view of poetry, the statement's conclusion altogether withdraws the poet from the human community into an isolation from which Arnold had hoped to rescue him and places him at the disposal of that private insatiable fury which in the end destroyed Ruskin.

IV

There is, of course, more to be said about the work of the Victorians whom we have discussed, and about Victorian art generally, than the perspective of "crisis" that is almost normal in a nuclear age permits. Art forms expressive of other sensibilities—the humorous, the satiric, the popular, the academic, the genteel—all continued to flourish alongside of and sometimes even within the sensibility shaped by anxiety. But if the latter was, as I believe, at the center of mid-Victorian feeling and if it conditioned the other art forms more perhaps than was recognized at the time, awareness of the possibility may help us to read the mid-Victorians more sympathetically and, at the same time, in a truer historical perspective than we can enjoy from a vantage point which sets that age apart from us by references to compromise, smugness, and prudery. If the mid-Victorians handed down to us not only their fair share of superficialities and cant, but also, especially among the more sensitive, their deep anxieties, their sense of spiritual crisis, and their faith in art, these too are part of our Victorian inheritance and in the long run the more significant part. It has recently been said, "True definition, for any period, can come when the nature and especially the objective of the self—with its hope, its memory, and its consciousness of the present—are truly identified and humanly defined. Out of such definition arises the sense of identity which is style."[37] The energetic, moral, and resourceful middle-class culture which shaped whatever common life there was in Europe and America for over a century, provided a definition—and in Victorian England one that was in many ways enviably successful—but not a common, complex, and adequate identity which, from the point of view of the artist, is the basis of a great and unifying style. The values of what we call Victorian culture lingered on as the substratum of English and American life, with steadily diminishing strength, until the inherent limitations of its moral identity became evident in a new psychology of the unconscious and a catastrophic "world" war. Since then the "multitude of voices counselling different things" of which Arnold complained has grown, while the desolation described in the *Idylls* and the vatic gloom of Ruskin's prose have been vindicated.

MICHAEL WOLFF

VICTORIAN REVIEWERS AND
CULTURAL RESPONSIBILITY

THE challenges faced by a popular culture are many. One of the most pressing, in a largely egalitarian and only partly educated democracy, is that of discovering and using the highest products of civilization. The public whose opinions, attitudes, responses, and ideas shaped the history of England in 1859 was, of course, not yet a democratic one. Political power in 1859 was no longer in the hands of the aristocracy or great mercantile families, but on the other hand it had not yet begun to be dispersed through even the lower middle classes. Nevertheless, the patterns of English culture in the 1850's were no longer straightforwardly determined, as a generation earlier, by the most eligible of the University men or their intellectual equivalents.

Where should one look for the great debate by which the "national" mind and imagination were nourished in 1859? It seems to me that there is no better place than the periodicals, in particular, of course, those which were written for and were most widely read by the fairly well educated minority which still ruled the England of 1859. In the wide variety of magazines and reviews, there was opportunity, whether in half-a-column or in thirty pages, for the expression of an equally wide variety of opinions. The pervasiveness of the periodicals was remarked on all sides. Wilkie Collins in 1858 spoke of "this age of periodicals," and another writer talked in 1859 of the age as luxuriating "in a copious stream of journals and hebdomadals, monthlies and quarterlies"; later one of the better contemporary critics was confident that it was "the enormous development of periodical literature of one sort or another which is the great feature of our time."[1]

Everybody wrote for the periodicals. In their pages for 1859, for example, appeared Dickens, Thackeray, George Eliot, Trollope, Collins, Tennyson, Ruskin, Maurice, Mill, Bagehot, Gladstone, Huxley,

Spencer, Lewes, Acton, Buckle, Hutton, and Newman, all engaged
in characteristic and representative work. It is here that we see the
sweep and power, and a little of the character, of the organs written by
and for "the articulate classes, whose writing and conversation make
opinion,"[2] and the history of whose opinion *is* Victorian history.

I

That the word "review" is so closely linked to the nineteenth-
century periodicals is no accident, for each article in the early quarterlies
was, ostensibly at least, a book review, and book-reviewing continued
as the focus of the better Victorian periodicals. Moreover, as periodical
literature became increasingly widespread and important, book-reviewing assumed an increasingly important role as a channel of information
and opinion. One journalist in the spring of 1860 commented on this
phenomenon and on contemporary attitudes toward it:

In the literature of the present day the most remarkable feature is the por-
tentous dimensions to which Reviews and Review-writing have attained.
. . . Not a book is published, from the annual volume of *Reynolds' Miscellany* up to *Darwin on Species,* which is not seized by the reviewer. . . .
No literary effort is too humble, none too erudite, for a review. History,
poetry, fiction, are all laid under contribution for the weekly, monthly, or
quarterly periodical; . . . review-writing has become the avocation of a numerous class, comprehending almost every grade of social rank and literary
ability; and review-reading is the amusement, too frequently the sole source
of instruction, of a large majority of the intelligent public. . . . in spite of
declamation against shallowness and superficiality, it is by no means impossible that a comparatively imperfect acquaintance with a large variety
of subjects is better calculated than an abstruse knowledge of any one of
them to fit a man for meeting the varied demands of social converse, and,
further than that, is more likely to confer that large-mindedness and general breadth of view which are so constantly found missing in deeply-read
theologians, in erudite philologists, and profound philosophers. . . . Many
. . . who would never have acquired any knowledge at all, may now, through
this much-abused medium, become fairly acquainted with the leading subjects in science and general literature.[3]

It is, indeed, in the reviews that we can say that all the second speeches
in the national debate were made. A book, a pamphlet, a column of
Hansard made a statement; the first comment on that statement then
appeared in the reviews, which were thus a national forum for that discussion from which effective action developed.

II

What were the "better" periodicals of 1859 like? Their contents were, with very few exceptions, unsigned; this anonymity gave each periodical a corporate identity, usually expressed, hardly ever contradicted, by every contributor. Many were characterized by particular religious or political commitments, although the political ones were less directly organs of the parties than the religious ones were organs of the churches. Some were primarily concerned with literature, some too general to classify; almost all had a variety of interests, political, religious, literary, and so on. Some were quarterly, some monthly, some weekly, some tri-weekly, some daily.* In this essay I have confined myself to an examination of some twenty-five magazines and reviews chosen first for their educated readership and secondly for their relatively wide circulation.[4] Of these, ten are quarterlies, six are monthlies, eight are weeklies, and one, *The Times,* is a daily. The quarterlies, with their longer, fewer articles tended to be informative and sensible when good, tedious and stale when bad.† The following are typical critiques of individual issues of the quarterlies for 1859: "The 'Edinburgh' is, as usual, to be reckoned amongst the 'heavy-armed' troops of the periodical press"; "The 'Quarterly' gives us one of the dullest numbers we have read for a long time": "That omnivorous but lamentably superficial personage, 'the general reader,' will find more entertainment in this number of the 'North British' than is usually to be met with in that able and well-conducted, but occasionally heavy, quarterly."[5] A few monthlies were very similar to the quarterlies, but most

* The pace of the times seemed to encourage shorter intervals of publication: "the weeklies and the monthlies were swallowing up the quarterlies" (*Literary Churchman,* VI [16 Jan. 1860], 35).

† Briefly characterized, the *Edinburgh Review,* the Whig-Liberal journal, was the oldest; the *Quarterly Review,* second but with a little larger circulation, was as solidly Anglican as the *Edinburgh,* but Tory; the *Westminster,* third of the great reviews of the earlier period, was Philosophical Radical in politics and rationalistic in religion; *Bentley's Quarterly Review,* the other mainly political quarterly, was Conservative, though less formally so than the *Quarterly.* The other quarterlies were, in origin, organs of religious bodies: the *Christian Remembrancer* was an Oxford Movement offshoot and in 1859 still a High Church periodical; the *Dublin Review,* founded by Wiseman, was the leading Roman Catholic paper; the *National Review,* originally Unitarian, had a strong interest in literary, political, and philosophical matters; the *North British Review,* originally Evangelical, was by 1859 broadly liberal both in religion and politics; the *London Quarterly Review* was written chiefly for Methodists, and the *British Quarterly Review* for Congregationalists and Baptists.

were magazines rather than reviews.* The latter were journals of entertainment as well as opinion (although some of the magazines, *Bentley's Miscellany, Once A Week,* and Dickens' periodicals, for example, were almost entirely "entertainment" and appealed to an audience less educated than the one with which we are concerned). None of the monthlies written for an educated audience was as determined to entertain as the *Cornhill Magazine* (put on sale just before Christmas 1859); all regarded themselves as influential in the formation of opinion, and are therefore relevant to our purposes. The weekly papers were coming increasingly into their own. Although most weeklies were only newspapers, some of them did effectively combine criticism with information and gossip; some even gave the major emphasis to criticism, and we are interested in these.† *The Times,* though still perhaps more the Thunderer than the Old Lady of Printing House Square, was, then as now, the self-appointed representative of the educated classes.

One way of seeing how the periodicals contributed to the national debate is to examine the treatment by Victorian reviewers of some of the books of 1859 still important enough to figure in *this* book: Darwin's *Origin of Species* and Mill's *On Liberty,* the four novels by Dickens, Thackeray, George Eliot, and Meredith, Tennyson's and FitzGerald's poems, Arnold's and Ruskin's booklets, and the various books in the controversy between Mansel and Maurice. How were these books received by the periodicals of their day? How many reviews and

* The two monthly "reviews" were almost purely religious: the *Eclectic Review* appealed to the smaller Dissenting sects; the *Christian Observer,* "conducted by members of the Established Church," chiefly to the Evangelicals. *Fraser's Magazine,* primarily an organ of opinion, and an important one, was very serious and liberal both in politics and religion. More liberal in religion though not in politics and with more emphasis on entertainment than *Fraser's* was the new *Macmillan's Magazine.* There was greater stress on fiction and light reading in *Blackwood's Edinburgh Magazine,* but it was nevertheless the chief monthly organ of conservatism. Consciously similar to *Blackwood's* but liberal-conservative rather than Tory was the *Dublin University Magazine,* in 1859 very un-Irish.

† Among the more critical was the *Saturday Review,* probably the most colorful and perhaps the most influential (after *The Times*) of all the periodicals. The *Spectator* and the *Athenæum* had both improved under competition from the *Saturday,* but the *Examiner* seems not to have retained its once high standing. More specialized were the *Literary Gazette* and the *Critic* (also literary), but both were in their last stages. Also with influential and valuable general sections were the *Economist,* the financial and commercial journal, and the *Guardian,* a religious paper.

notices did they get? What elements were singled out for comment? In short, how did the organs of educated opinion treat, at their first appearances, the volumes which the contributors to this book have felt called upon to treat a century later?

Some of these books received a great deal of attention, some almost none. Tennyson's *Idylls of the King* was reviewed in twenty-two of our twenty-five periodicals;[6] FitzGerald's *Rubáiyát*, on the other hand, was reviewed by only one. Darwin's *Origin* was noticed at least in twenty-two periodicals and *Adam Bede* was, for a mere novel, exceptionally widely noticed, scoring twenty out of twenty-five. Mill's *On Liberty* comes next with sixteen out of twenty-five possible reviews, then the Mansel-Maurice controversy with fourteen. Ruskin's *Two Paths* had eleven reviews or notices, Meredith's *Richard Feverel*, rather surprisingly, had nine. Arnold's pamphlet on the Italian question, review copies of which were probably not widely distributed, received only four notices. Dickens' and Thackeray's novels were hardly noticed when published, for they had been running in parts, Dickens' since April 1859 and Thackeray's since November 1857, although *The Virginians,* issued independently, not (as was *A Tale of Two Cities*) as part of a rival magazine, was mentioned part by part in some of the miscellaneous columns. Finally there was the lone review of FitzGerald.*

Over half the periodicals did a reasonably good job in giving space to a selection of the important books of 1859, and (if we take our count down to Ruskin's eleven reviews) half the books received a reasonable share of attention.

III

This analysis has so far been numerical; it remains to be asked what sort of reviews these books received in the better periodicals. Almost unanimously praised and that most lavishly were *Idylls of the*

---

* One more count should be made. Which periodicals did best by these eleven books (that is, taking the Maurice-Mansel controversy as one item)? From the evidence above, it may be suggested that a periodical should have reviewed Tennyson, Darwin, and Eliot and at least one of the Ruskin, Mill, or Mansel and Maurice books to be considered a perceptive book-reviewing organ. Fifteen of the twenty-five were so qualified. The *Saturday* reviewed ten out of eleven; the *Literary Gazette* nine; the *Westminster* eight; the *Athenæum,* the *British Quarterly*, the *Critic*, the *Dublin University Magazine*, the *Examiner*, the *Guardian*, and the *Spectator* seven; the *Eclectic*, the *National*, the *North British*, and *The Times*, five; and the *Christian Observer* four.

King by the Laureate and *Adam Bede* by an unknown novice. These
two books were among the great hits of the year, both best-sellers,
Tennyson's receiving only one bad and George Eliot's only two mildly
disapproving notices. The next most favorably received book was *The
Virginians,* which, though sparsely noticed, enjoyed the momentum of
Thackeray's reputation as the first novelist of the day. Next, rather
astonishingly, came *The Ordeal of Richard Feverel,* hardly recommended for family reading, but clearly recognized as a work of great
originality and promise. Arnold's pamphlet on the Italian crisis was
received with respect though mostly respectful disagreement. Ruskin's
The Two Paths had extremely varied treatment; a bare majority of reviews were in its favor despite everything Ruskin's manner had done to
antagonize the reviewers. In descending order of acclaim, then, the
1859 books generally approved (regardless of the quantity of attention
they received) were Tennyson's, Eliot's, Thackeray's, Meredith's,
Arnold's, and Ruskin's.

The *Origin of Species* and *On Liberty* both had very mixed re-
ceptions. They did, in fact, receive more unfavorable than favorable
reviews (though both had their enthusiastic advocates), and it is plain
that only the authors' reputations saved the books from even harsher
treatment. Neither Mansel nor Maurice emerged from the pages of the
reviews as clearly victorious in showing the way from man to God.
Mansel had perhaps a slight edge, but both on the whole fared badly;
the conclusion seemed usually to be that the writers of the notices
(though hardly ever neutral) knew more of the secrets of Heaven than
either of the controversialists. At the bottom of the scale comes *A Tale
of Two Cities,* scarcely noticed but, where noticed, almost uniformly
scorned.

I have not taken into account the single review of the *Rubáiyát.*
Despite the accepted view that the poem was thoroughly neglected and
indeed not reviewed anywhere until 1869 and not in England until
1870, there was not only a two-column notice in the *Literary Gazette,*[7]
but the notice was such as to arouse the curiosity of the reader and to
provoke interest in the poem. As was perhaps to be expected, the reviewer was thoroughly out of sympathy with the content of the *Rubáiyát,* whose "crushing fatalism" seemed to him intolerable, but (and in
the light of his disapproval of the creed his praise must be valued
highly) he was impressed with the excellence of the verse. He offered
a very generous selection of extracts, and concluded that the "Gospel
of Despair" had never been preached so fervently. All in all, then, this
one review cannot be blamed for the fact that FitzGerald's poem had
to wait over ten years for recognition.

If despite a favorable review, the *Rubáiyát* remained unsold, there is no question but that *A Tale of Two Cities* was a popular success despite the critics. The famous onslaught in the *Saturday Review,* "the most violently abusive to appear in Dickens' lifetime,"[8] was echoed in two other notices I have found, one in the *Critic,* the other in the *Dublin University Magazine.* The *Saturday* reviewer was particularly concerned with Dickens' "incurable vulgarity of mind and of taste"; and both the other reviewers felt this: the *Critic* found Dickens had power only in the "heightening and intensifying" of commonplaces; the *Dublin University* reviewer, " Christopher Grim," thought Dickens was sinking "lower and lower into that vein of caricature in which his talent resides." As for the *Saturday*'s second charge—"an intolerable arrogance of temper," and in particular, a cheap distaste, "insolent and unbecoming," for the England of the second half of the eighteenth century—this the *Critic* found especially offensive: Dickens had no right to his "jaunty scorn"; the world then was not essentially different from the world of 1859; England is still imperfect; indeed "how jaunty and severe may 1959 be upon this then!" "Christopher Grim" spoke for all three reviewers, I believe, when he said that he had "a great dislike to this writer's works," and attested "to a great sense of relief when I got to the end of the book, and of regret at having been fool enough to begin it."[9]

If Dickens' unpopularity with his reviewers seems surprising to us, so does the corresponding popularity of a book called *The Limits of Religious Thought Examined in Eight Lectures before the University of Oxford,* the Bampton Lectures for 1858. Of this book it was written that "few works of the present century, perhaps, have attracted so large an amount of criticism from writers competent to deal with the questions on which they treat. Scarcely one of the many Reviews, monthly and quarterly, possessing any reputation, has omitted to notice it."[10]

The "great literary event of the year" was what one review[11] called the controversy between the Bampton Lecturer, the Reverend Henry Longueville Mansel, Reader in Moral and Metaphysical Philosophy at Magdalen College, Oxford, and the Reverend Frederick Denison Maurice, Chaplain of Lincoln's Inn, not too long before dismissed from his Professorship of Divinity of King's College, London, for doctrines of "dangerous tendency." Maurice's reputation for orthodoxy was none too high; he was linked by one church paper with Baden Powell and Jowett as one of "the three leaders of the Rationalistic movement," and by another with the secularists, "Mr. Hennell and his friends Mr. Holyoake and others of the 'Reasoner' school."[12] Mansel, on the other hand, was one of these rare Oxford men, neither a Puseyite nor a Rationalist; here was at least one who had "not bowed the knee either to the idol of superstition or of reason" and who was prepared "to sustain the claims of evangelical truth."[13] He was therefore welcomed with enthusiasm as a "safe" Oxonian who was able to foil German philosophers and Rationalists with their own weapons. *The Times* gave the Lectures two enthusiastic reviews; the religious papers, especially the orthodox ones, hailed them.[14]

Gradually, however, objections began to be raised. Mansel had attempted to place orthodox belief on an unassailable foundation by showing that the mysteries of religion were not strictly available to human understanding and can be neither defended nor attacked. He was forced therefore to rely upon the external evidences. But in the course of his demonstration, it seemed to many of his contemporary reviewers, he left the general impression that "really after all Atheism and Pantheism have a great deal to say for themselves," that his line of argument undermined "completely the very foundations of all religious faith" and that "once placed on such an inclined plane as Dr. Mansel glides upon, there is no logical break that can prevent our descent into sheer scepticism."[15]

The third stage in the reception of the Bampton Lectures (after the first enthusiastic welcome and the subsequent nervous retreat) lay in the discussion of Maurice's reply to Mansel. It was indeed strange as *Fraser's* remarked, to "have one eminent man of the day . . . on the point of being accepted . . . as the champion of orthodoxy; and another, on whom it has been commonly thought that orthodoxy . . . looks askance, denouncing the former as the enemy of all faith."[16] The hostile reviewers fastened on Maurice's incomprehensibility, his indifference to verbal precision, and his inadequate logic. Those who were worried over the effect of Mansel's line of argument had expressed themselves with great caution and respect; but even where they used Maurice's arguments to point up Mansel's weakness, there was no question but that their sympathies lay with the reserved, logical, and evangelical Mansel and against the passionate and not always articulate Maurice who was struggling to save what he felt was the whole meaning of his spiritual life.

The *Spectator,* with no special theological interests, thought that the affair was to be regretted, for laymen had great need of spiritual reassurance and "infirm belief or religious unbelief, yearning to become belief, saddens as it sees two 'masters in Israel,' each declaring the other's truth falsehood, and each stigmatizing the other's method as unsound." The *Saturday Review,* on the other hand, more modern and more at ease in its new world, recognized the basic incompatibility of the two temperaments without dismay and was ready to rise above the controversy, finding it "a battle between dog and fish, in which it is hard to say which has the best."[17]

One of the factors which prevented the reviewers from doing justice to Maurice's work was his reputation as a heterodox and difficult thinker. But the 1859 books of both Charles Darwin and John Stuart Mill appear to have benefited from the earlier reputation of their authors. The reception of the *Origin of Species* has, understandably enough, been given greater study than has the reception of any other of the books of 1859.[18] It is necessary here only to make one point, to correct an emphasis, and to exhibit some of the eccentricities of the reviewers.

The point which I believe not to have beeen sufficiently regarded refers to Darwin's reputation in 1859. It is true enough that the *Origin of Species* burst upon a startled public, but it was not as the product of an unknown hand. Darwin was already known as "one of the first naturalists of the day,"[19] and because of this many unfavorably disposed towards the theories of evolution and natural selection were ready to give his work serious consideration. The comment of the *Guardian,* the High Church weekly, is worth citing at some length, not only for the view it offers of Darwin's standing, but also for the impression it conveys both of the theory and of the shock that accompanied it:

There are forms of speculation so wild and improbable, or, at any rate, so alien to our ordinary habits of thought, that they can only obtain a fair consideration under the protection of some illustrious name. If an anonymous author, or one only known as amateur in natural science, were to propound the startling theory, that all the various tribes of living creatures which people earth, air, and water with an infinite diversity of form and habit, are descended from some four or five progenitors, whose progeny have, by small successive degrees of difference in the lapse of ages, developed into the manifold divergence of the countless species now in existence, a busy man would be justified in turning from the unread volume with a smile of incredulity. But the case is widely different when this theory is put forward by Mr. Darwin, a man confessedly in the foremost ranks of natural philosophy, a Fellow of the Royal, Geological, and Linnaean Societies, honoured among his scientific peers (as was publicly shown not long ago in the assignment to him of the medal of the Geological Society), and already favourably known to the outer world by his celebrated *Journal of the Beagle.*[20]

Darwin's reputation was not the only extraneous factor in his favor. Many journals, not at all friendly to the *Origin,* were struck both by the twenty years or more of labor behind the book and by the candor and moderation of the exposition. Furthermore, one reviewer was struck by Darwin's "classic beauty of style" and explained the effectiveness of some important statements in their reading "so pleasantly that we don't wonder they have been found attractive and unanswerable by amateur naturalists."[21]

It is also interesting to note the disagreement among the non-religious periodicals as to whether or not the book should be reviewed on theological as well as on scientific grounds. The decision was strongly against what the *Dublin University Magazine* called "the use of the theological tomahawk in the discussion of a matter in which science alone has a right to speak." The *Saturday Review* and the *Economist* supported this; the *Athenæum* alone felt a positive interest in what "Theologians will say—and they have a right to be heard. . . ." The bitter attacks on theological grounds by magazines like the *Eclectic Review* and the *Christian Observer* and by reviewers like the Bishop of Oxford and the Reverend Mr. Dunns loom very large in one's impression of the reception of the *Origin,* but it seems to me unlikely that these carried great weight with the general educated public.[22]

Nevertheless it is from the religious reviews that the clash between two worlds most clearly emerges. The reviewer in the *Christian Observer* took up Darwin in the hope of finding errors in the objections brought against "the details of the ark of Noah"; the *Dublin Review* went further and accepted the account of the struggle for survival in part because it "diminishes the number of fellow voyagers with the patriarch in the ark."[23] It is in the *British Quarterly,* however, that we find the best example of the ridicule which we associate with the contemporary reception of Darwinism. That reviewer asked "whether, in case an exaggerated nose were to appear in a family, there would be any reason to expect that it would continue to increase in bulk, as it was handed down from parent to child, until it attained treble the ordinary dimensions?" Again, although Darwin makes little enough of man and the monkeys in the *Origin,* the *British Quarterly* reviewer indulged in a monstrous fantasy in which a monkey in the zoo proposes to a pretty Victorian *filia familias,* "Yes, my dainty young lady (you with the gay parasol and copious crinoline), pray don't look so indignant when I venture to suggest that there would be nothing particularly outrageous (that's my candid opinion) in your selecting a husband from this very menagerie. I am willing to make you an offer myself"—no doubt an attempt to arouse the deepest feelings of the

Victorian psyche against the Darwinians by that standard question of bigotry "Would you want to see your sister married to one of them?"[24]

The most forceful impression one gets after reading the reviews of *On Liberty* is of a hostility repressed or softened in an acknowledgment of "a writer who has perhaps exercised more influence over the formation of the philosophical and social principles of cultivated Englishmen than any other man of his generation." The book was only twice praised with any great determination—by Henry Buckle in a signed article in *Fraser's* and by Fitzjames Stephen in the *Saturday*. For the rest, though their tone was mostly respectful, the reviewers were likely to recommend the book as interesting and suggestive rather than as true (this recommendation being habitually accompanied by a rather hollow compliment). For the *British Quarterly*, "A book from Mr. Mill on such a subject is sure to be worth reading. Even where his conclusions may not be sound, his conception of facts is sure to be suggestive." And again, the *London Quarterly* "thought it necessary to take exception to several of the statements and theories of this book; but we regard it nevertheless as a most suggestive and valuable one, and one which is worthy of the high reputation which Mr. Mill has achieved in the department of pure science as well as in that of practical economics." Only the *North British* launched an outright attack: "with the exception of the gross ignorance and audacity of his attack on the morals of Christ's teaching, and on the system of Calvinism, and a few other outrageously absurd opinions, his book consists of flat and thread-bare commonplace."[25]

The main grounds of objection were that the book ignored social interests in its concern for the individual, that its advice—that people should carefully examine all sides of a question before coming to an opinion—was hopelessly impractical, that England was not as intolerant of spontaneity or originality as he supposed, and, finally, that the book was irreligious.

The idea that society was more than an "aggregate of individuals"[26] and that Mill had "profoundly under-rated the significance and value of social liberty" was put forward by the Coleridgeans of the *National Review* ("there is no element so utterly absent . . . as any indication of sympathy with the free play of a national or social character in its natural organization"), the Burkeans of *Bentley's Quarterly* (Mill fails to understand those questions "which society must close, or go to pieces"), and the Comtists of the *Westminster* ("in recognising in society a real and natural existence, finding its expression in a positive law, we inevitably differ from . . . Mr. Mill"). As for Mill's contention that, according to one reviewer, in order for our opinions to be really our own we should "first dissolve them in a universal scepticism, and wait till they rearrange themselves according to our own individuality," this was neither desirable nor possible. Mill's view here was mere "logical Quixotry."[27]

The *Literary Gazette* made more than its colleagues of the claim that Mill was "scarcely just to modern society, and does not recognize the noble elements to be found even in the very tendencies he so much condemns." The *North British* was even more indignant, demanding: "Are we to suffer it to be insinuated that the right [to free discussion and thought] is not enjoyed to the full in these lands?"—this demand following immediately upon a panegyric of modern British institutions. The *North British* was equally indignant at "the gross ignorance and audacity of his attack on the morals of Christ's teaching" mentioned earlier and at his "avowal that the Bible is not a complete rule of moral conduct." This last is an extreme statement of a very generally held view that Mill should not be allowed to escape unscathed for his unbelief. It was intolerable for the *Christian Remembrancer,* for instance, that Mill's infidel principles might spread "from the intellectual few, who may be above the grosser forms of temptation, to the reckless many, who are but too likely to prove in such cases wholly enslaved to them."[28]

Mill's *On Liberty,* then, despite Morley's enthusiastic memories,[29] sold well because it was thought that whatever Mill had to say was worth reading, certainly not because it at all hit off the mood of the educated public.

Mill was called the Don Quixote of political science, and it was Ruskin, the *Athenæum* claimed, who was "the Don Quixote of heretical Art." His five lectures, gathered in the *Two Paths,* the reviewer found "arrogant, subtle, paradoxical, rhetorical, and illogical." Ruskin abused works of art he had never seen and eulogized "small side-alley marvels abroad which no one else has seen." He could not bear to be found inconsistent, he would "rather lose all his reputation than be discovered in a deviation, change, or contradiction." Ruskin, in fact, was not temperamentally suited to fulfill his chosen task as High Priest of the criticism of art.[30]

It is clear indeed from the notices, of which the *Athenæum*'s is by far the most unrelievedly harsh, that the Victorian reviewer found Ruskin very difficult to criticize in terms of what he had to say. His originality and eloquence were acknowledged, but his manner was such that even those inclined to sympathize with his teaching could not praise him unreservedly. The *Literary Gazette* admitted that "no other writer of our day has earned so fair a title to be heard on the subject of Art" and yet it had to regret his "persistence in the tone of arrogant superiority and dogmatism which so grievously blemishes his style and impairs his influence." Even the *Eclectic,* whose review began "Every rift of these noble lectures is loaded with precious ore" and continued to talk of the "pure celestial aspect" and "highest moral lustre" of Ruskin's writing, had to mention his "quick, explosive . . . supercilious tone." *Fraser's,* the other thoroughly favorable review, called Ruskin perhaps "one of the most remarkable men of this—may we not say any?—age" and claimed that he has done "more for art" perhaps than "has ever yet been done by man." Nevertheless the reviewer felt compelled to concede that Ruskin is "not seldom dogmatic, self-contradictory, conceited, arrogant and absurd."[31]

Of these two favorable reviews, that in *Fraser's* seems the more thoughtful. The *Eclectic* was enthusiastic because in Ruskin "the highest teaching of art . . . is in beautiful accord with the doctrines of revealed religion," hardly a point which Ruskin could in 1859 have thought relevant. *Fraser's,* on the other hand, was excited because "No one before him had seriously attempted to treat the study of art as that which it really is—a philosophy—the least trodden and the most delightful of all the walks of science." This type of analysis was rare. Most of the reviewers were unable to bypass the problem of "the manifold evidences of conceit," "the audacity of the confident egotism," and his "inborn propensity for dogmatizing."[32] It was Ruskin's personality, not his argument, that was, for the most part, under consideration.

The *Ordeal of Richard Feverel* was perhaps the most remarkable novel of 1859; certainly it was the most modern and the least conventional. How was it received? "Sparsely and unperceptively," says Meredith's biographer[33]—but it was noticed upon publication in the leading weeklies, the *Athenæum,* the *Critic,* the *Examiner,* the *Literary Gazette,* the *Saturday,* and the *Spectator,* as well as later in *The Times* and the miscellaneous sections of the *Westminster*—and that was as much as a little known author could expect. Fiction was not widely received outside of the weeklies, although "important" novelists like Bulwer-Lytton and Thackeray occasionally received general appraisals from the quarterlies. What sort of notices did the literary weeklies give Meredith's book? None of them damned it; all recognized the presence of an unusual author; none, in the light of its sexual frankness, could recommend it.

The *Athenæum* reviewer found it "about as painful a book as any reader felt himself inexorably compelled to read through"; he could not put the book down despite his protests and hoped the author would use "his great ability to produce something pleasanter next time." The *Critic* found Meredith a deep thinker but believed that his mind was "none of the purest"; the book was a clever one but it was rather "meat for strong men than food for babes"—in short, "this work has great merits and great defects." The *Literary Gazette* particularly praised the scene between Mrs. Mount and Richard (which had led the *Critic* to talk of Meredith's "gloating over what had better be only hinted at"), and concluded that the *Ordeal* was a book of "great merit." The *Saturday Review* was very impressed; here at last was a bold, original book "distinguished from the novel of the day by having something in it." When your subject is an intriguer with a man in her grasp there is no use shrinking from the handling of it. It is dangerous to literature in general if men get the impression that "life" in novels is hypocritical and superficial. There should be "men's novels" and Meredith's was one of them. If this "is all that Mr. Meredith can do, it is a failure"; but, the reviewer ended, "it gives us hopes that it may prove the prelude to a work that will place Mr. Meredith high in the list of living novelists." For the *Spectator* there was more "vigorous thought, imagination, wit, humour, and pathos, than would suffice to make the fortune of a score of average novels."[34]

The *Times* and *Westminster Review* notices are special instances, for the *Times* reviewer was a friend and publisher of Meredith's and Meredith was, or until recently had been, a contributor to the *Westminster*. Even so it is worth noting that, although Meredith's friend was not prepared to say more of the novel than that there was "such purity mingled with its laxness, such sound and firm truth in the midst of its fantastic subtleties, that we hesitate whether to approve or condemn," he defended the book strongly against the charge of impurity, which had led to its being tabooed "in some quarters by the over-fastidious." These quarters were, of course, Mudie's, the great subscription library, which controlled "the British Matron's" reading. The *Times* review seemed very "eulogious" to chatty "Christopher Grim," who described in his column in the *Dublin University Magazine* how he picked up the book on the strength of that review. The book, he acknowledged, is "written with extraordinary power, and betrays talent of the highest order," but it "leaves an unpleasant taste in the mouth." The columnist was forced to regret *The Times's* advocacy of such a book and therefore (tacitly) to accept Mudie's ban, for the ladies in the Feverel home, he remarked, felt hot whenever the "apple-disease" was mentioned, and "this is just the feeling which comes over one repeatedly in perusing the 'Ordeal'."[35]

It seems to me that the journalists of 1859 did as well as they could by Meredith. They may not have seen genius; they certainly did not see the verdict of posterity. But if they praised the book for its originality and power and blamed it (though not unanimously) for its unconventional morality, surely we can understand the strength of the inhibitions behind the blame and give them credit for the praise.*

I have said that novels were not widely noticed outside the pages of the literary weeklies. *Adam Bede* was one of the exceptions. *Adam Bede,* not *Richard Feverel,* was the novel of 1859 acclaimed by its contemporary reviewers as enlarging the scope of fiction and bringing the novel to readers who ordinarily could not be bothered with such a plebeian form. According to the *Eclectic* it marked "a new and welcome advance in the aim and morale of fiction"; for *Bentley's Quarterly, Adam Bede* had "found its way into hands indifferent to all previous fiction"; the *Saturday Review* spoke of it to those "who do not wish to read novels unless they are really good," saying in February that those who only read one novel a year ("and rarely does a year produce more than one that is really good") may venture to make this year's selection *Adam Bede.* The book was lavishly praised and widely read. *The Times* began its review, "There can be no mistake about *Adam Bede.* . . . its author takes rank at once among the masters of the art" and the *Edinburgh* noted that the universal question in men's mouths in the pause between topics of war and politics, is "Have you read 'Adam Bede'?"[36]

It seems to have been the moral (or, for some reviewers, the religious) tone of the book that most recommended it. "If we must have works of fiction it is well that they should have a tendency so plainly moral as this," said the *Christian Observer.* "It is a fact that the most absorbing and original novel we have had for many a year is also the most sternly moral" concluded the review in *Bentley's Quarterly.* It is not that the artistry of the book was neglected. Once the reviewers elected to discuss *Adam Bede,* they praised Mr. Eliot's "truly Shakesperian" power to adapt his thoughts to "every nature and every situa-

---

* The following criticism from the *Literary Churchman,* V (1 Sept. 1859), 324, deserves recording here: *"The Ordeal of Richard Feverel,* by George Meredith, (Chapman and Hall, 31s. 6d), is also a remarkable book, so remarkable indeed for the eccentricity of its story, the absorbing interest which characterizes it, and the unusual vigour of its writing, that one feels bound to give our readers one caution respecting it,—it is not a moral book. This caution is the more necessary, because were it not for the forbidden ground on which it treads, and the extreme license the author allows to his pen, it would probably make a greater sensation than any work that has appeared this season.

tion"; they noted the book's unequalled depth of pathos, its wit, its realism, its minuteness, its power, its style. But they chose to review it because it was more than a mere novel ("With fashionable novels, as our readers know, we give ourselves no concern. We should as soon think of reviewing *The Sporting Calendar*."), because the tone of the book, though moral rather than doctrinal, was serious and, apparently, orthodox in religious matters.[37]

Who was George Eliot? *"Adam Bede*. By the Rev. George Eliot," said the *National Review* confidently. "Evidently a country clergyman," said the *Saturday*; "either a clergyman or a dissenting minister," said the *Dublin University Magazine*. The *Economist* (which rarely reviewed fiction) was glad to meet with a good novel written by a man, for such novels are "nearly always more in keeping with the actual world, have a wider outlook, and embrace a greater variety of interests. . . . 'Adam Bede' is one of the best of this best class of novels." There were indeed those who suspected a woman's hand, even "a lady who was brought up among the Baptists." But the *Edinburgh* reviewer who was glad that Mrs. Poyser, for all her biting tongue, did not belong "to that race of strong-minded women of whom we think with a goose-skinned shudder" must have been startled to discover that Mrs. Poyser's creator was, as the *Critic* put it, "simply a Miss Mary Ann Evans, already known in this strong-minded generation as the translator of Strauss's 'Life of Jesus'," herself as strong-minded and as heterodox (both in her life and her thought) as, in reputation at least, she could be.[38]

Adam Bede was highly praised, but not without condescension as being written in a form not yet fully established. But the *Idylls of the King* hinted at the possibility of that highest of forms, a national epic, and the praise was mingled with awe. For the *Quarterly* reviewer (none other than Gladstone) the poem "of itself raises the character and the hopes of the age and the country which have produced it"; Tennyson had added to the "permanent wealth of mankind." For *Fraser's* the *Idylls* called to mind the power of Dante and was to be matched only in the greatest scenes of Shakespeare. There appeared through many of the reviews the feeling that the excellence of the *Idylls* was a justification of the time. As the *Blackwood's* reviewer put it, "we tremble now and then for the fate of the nineteenth century in the hands of some future Macaulay," but this poem was evidence that "the age which produced it could not be wholly corrupt."[39]

This last comment referred in particular to what was generally considered the high point of the poem. Of the four idylls, "Enid" was least liked for it seemed to the reviewers commonplace and rather low in style; "Elaine" was thought better but flawed by the impropriety of showing a woman's declared but unrequited love; "Vivien," with its seduction of Merlin, was matter for scandal at the worst, distant praise at the best; but it was "Guinevere" which was acclaimed as the climax of the poem. And the interview in the Abbey between Arthur and the prostrate Queen was the climax of "Guinevere." It was in dealing with this section that the critics told themselves that the work surpassed comment, that the only response was "silence with a sense of Awe, and thoughts that lie deeper than tears." Those who were nevertheless articulate found Arthur an ideal, "the very type and model of restored humanity," "the great pillar of the moral order, and the resplendent top of human excellence."[40] The portrait of Arthur itself was at its finest in those speeches to Guinevere in which Arthur forgives her "as God forgives"; that is, contemporary praise was highest at precisely the point in the poem which separates the *Idylls of the King* from many of its modern readers.

Apart from the reviewers who protested that "Enid" was the best or that "Guinevere" was the least good, disagreement arose over the propriety of "Vivien" (passages which *Blackwood's* ranked with the Divorce Bill and the popularity of "La Traviata" as evidence of the bad character of the time) and even of the whole poem (of which the *Christian Observer* commented that "Stories of matrimonial unfaithfulness will never, we believe, become part of our popular literature.").[41]

A more vital discussion lay in the validity of the antique setting. The *British Quarterly* saw many a Crimean soldier in Lancelot; the *Literary Gazette* was glad to leave "these hard days of cash and currency . . . throbbing with a heated and unhealthy life"; *Bentley's* felt there was not enough antiquity about Guinevere: "pages of talk . . . might pass in a modern drawing-room"; the *Edinburgh* that Tennyson had not been able to turn "the knights and ladies of King Arthur's court into living men and women." For some the *Idylls* were happily remote and unhappily remote, happily modern and unhappily modern. The *Westminster* reviewer who posed an alternative wanted Tennyson to exchange the simplicity of the past for the challenging complexity of today. The great epic-subject was London, the great city: "Surely, beneath its repulsive exterior, amidst the turmoil and confusion, the myriad sights and sounds which make up its glare and gloom, lie richly scattered the yet unwrought materials for modern tragedy."[42]

The romance of Arthur, with all the possibilities for idealization that it presented, was seen by Tennyson's reviewers and presumably by the public as a portrayal of national aspirations. The collapse of

Arthur's court and the defeat of the King were hardly seen as warnings, let alone as modern realities. There were few critics who reached into the poem for the questioning and pain which we can see there. But one reviewer saw something in the poem other than nobility and chivalry. The *Dublin University Magazine* was able to recognize that the time was painted not in the King but in the sinful Queen, and consoled itself for this gross vision by commenting: "Arthur's hope for Guinevere is ours for ourselves."[43]

IV

We have seen how some of the works of 1859 still important in 1959 were introduced by their first reviewers to the educated public. There is nothing startling about the quality of the reviewing; from the perspective of a hundred years, some of the books seem to have got more, some less than their due. And yet, seen as a representative sampling of the journalism of the mid-Victorian period, these book reviews do have a special significance. For they can not only make for a better understanding of prevalent and general attitudes toward the important writing of 1859, they can also cast light upon what may be happening to important writing in 1959. A study of them underlines a critical challenge posed by a democratic culture, namely, its need to know about ideas and imaginings beyond its ordinary range of interests and comprehension.

In discussing book reviews we have dealt with a relationship in which the reviewer operates primarily as a mediator between the writer and his readers. The great importance of this mediation in 1859 is clear from the ubiquity among educated people of those periodicals devoted, in part at least, to book reviewing. This interposition of the reviewer between the important writers and the significant audience was a phenomenon of the middle third of the nineteenth century. Prior to that period there had been no need for an intermediary; subsequent to it, the mediation has been relatively ineffective. Moreover, there was good cause then for the emergence of the reviewer, and there is good reason now to hope for his return to effectiveness.

Such a conclusion rests on three assumptions. The first is a very simple one about the nature of the class of minds and imaginations capable of important writing, of seminal work (I would say that all the authors treated above are members of this class). It seems clear that the presence in a given place and at a given time of a member of this class, of what we call a genius, is a matter of accident to which factors of, say, education and political opportunity are irrelevant. Sup-

plementary to this notion is one claiming that genius is seldom immediately recognized. No age succeeds perfectly in identifying those
who will survive as the heroes of posterity. It is not, however, the age's
ability to prophesy with which we are concerned, but its ability and its
willingness to hear all those who are candidates for posterity's more
considered honors.

The second assumption is that the actions and climate of a society
are ultimately based upon ways of behaving which are first suggested
or practised by the remarkable scientists, theologians, philosophers,
and poets. These are the people who first view the world in new ways,
who first capture and express man's new view of himself in a new world,
and within whom the sparks of future ideologies first light. These are
the people whom a generation ignores at its peril.

The third assumption has to do not with these remarkable men,
but with the nature of their possible audience. The people who should,
ideally, be paying attention to these critical writings are all those whose
opinions and whose political, moral, and intellectual decisions constitute a culture. Now, if the number of important writers varies from one
age to the next only haphazardly, the number of people responsible for
the course of the civilization in which they live has increased startlingly
within the last two hundred years.

To confine ourselves to the England of the last two centuries, we
can observe that the seminal writing of the 1750's, say, the work of
Adam Smith, David Hume, Edmund Burke, and Samuel Johnson (all
of whom published in 1759), was an integral part of the aristocratic
and homogeneous culture of the 1750's. For the middle of the
eighteenth century, as perhaps for all previous history, the ideational
and imaginative content of the important writing was generally, practically, comprehensible to the comparative few who were effectively in
command of the tone and motion of their culture. The people who, so
to speak, ran the England of the mid-eighteenth century formed a social
and cultural group to which the seminal writers (whatever their personal origins) naturally addressed themselves. To put it simply, they all
"spoke the same language."

By the 1950's what has happened? The equivalent work being
done now, by nobody knows whom, is probably not a part of today's
culture. Such work is available to only a minute portion of those now
responsible for the shape of our history, and that slight fraction has a
correspondingly slight influence.

Apart from our inability to lay our finger on the writers who will
seem a hundred years from now (if there is anyone to care) to have
been those we should have most seriously read, what is the significant

difference between the attentive audience of the 1750's and the in-attentive audience of the 1950's? It does not lie in the mere growth of populations nor in that breaking of barriers which forces us to consider half a world in 1959 where we could consider an island in 1759 and even in 1859. The difference lies rather in a qualitative change concomitant upon the growth of the idea of popular responsibility, and upon the actual economic, social, and political growth of democratic power. For during the nineteenth and twentieth centuries not only has the community grown, but more and enormously larger sections of the community have come to participate in its governing. We have now not only a mass audience but a mass audience in a democracy. This development in the sharing of power has not been accompanied by a comparable development in the intellectual and imaginative capabilities or even pretensions of the new holders of power. Hence the lack of useful influence within modern society of the best that society may be capable of saying or thinking. This is not at all to deplore democracy, but to regret that one of the values of an aristocratic society, its cohesiveness, does not yet have its place in ours to the extent that we may benefit promptly from whatever powerful new ideas our thinkers may throw out.

What has this to do with 1859? Where do the mid-Victorians fall along this line from a society to whose ears the sounds of intellectual and imaginative genius were, however, unwelcome, at least intelligible, to a society which, willing or not, hardly hears the voices of its sages and prophets and understands little of what it does hear.

By the middle of the nineteenth century, the audience responsible for the national destiny had expanded beyond the reach of the great men writing for it. By 1859, those writers whose cultural task it was to initiate the dialogue of the national mind with itself were no longer at one with the people they were writing for. But this crucial audience was not yet beyond feeling the loss in this separation, nor was it so far away that the gap could not be bridged. This bridging the gap was, I take it, the grand role of the book reviewers. The reviewers made it possible for a while longer, until after the Reform Acts of 1867 or 1884 or the Education Acts of 1870 or 1902 became effective, say, for English society to ensure itself a prompt opportunity of using an idea, a poem, or a discovery.

There has always to be dilution before a new idea, a new mode of poetry, or a new concept of nature can become part of a popular ideology. What seems to me vital to the health of a democracy is that its members be presented as rapidly as possible (and with whatever dilutions are necessary) with all the new attempts that men make to understand themselves and their surroundings. The responsibility lies thereafter with the democracy to make the best use of what is offered it. This mediating role was, I believe, fulfilled by the intellectual journalists of 1859, some of whose efforts we have just examined. To explain important things in ways "understanded of the people" is still the role of all whose task it is to serve the mind and imagination of society.

Houses of Parliament (S. C. Hall, *Book of the Thames*, 1859).

NOTES ON CONTRIBUTORS

(The editors of this book are members of the faculty of Indiana University and editors of *Victorian Studies*.)

Richard D. Altick, Professor of English at The Ohio State University. Among his books are *The Cowden Clarkes, The Scholar Adventurers,* and *The English Common Reader.*

Noel Annan, Provost of King's College, Cambridge, and University Lecturer in Politics. Author of *Leslie Stephen: His Thought and Character in Relation to His Time.*

W. O. Aydelotte, Professor of History, State University of Iowa, has published on the social, intellectual, and political history of Victorian England; now engaged on a detailed study of the Parliament of 1841-47.

J. A. Banks, Research Lecturer in Industrial Sociology at the University of Liverpool. Author of *Prosperity and Parenthood: A Study of Family Planning Among the Victorian Middle Classes.*

Derek Beales, Fellow of Sidney Sussex College, Cambridge. Now completing a book on the Italian crisis of 1859-60.

J. B. Conacher, Assistant Professor of History, University of Toronto. General editor of Champlaign Society publications and former editor of the *Canadian Historical Review.*

G. Armour Craig, Professor of English at Amherst College. Now finishing a book on the novel from Jane Austen to Henry James.

George Haines, IV, Charles J. MacCurdy Professor of American History at Connecticut College. Author of *German Influence upon English Education and Science, 1800-1866.*

J. R. T. Hughes, Associate Professor of Economics at Purdue University. Author of the forthcoming *Fluctuations in Trade, Industry and Finance: A Study of British Economic Development 1850-1860.*

Howard Mumford Jones, Professor of English at Harvard University. Books include *America and French Culture 1750-1848, Ideas in America, Education and World Tragedy,* and *The Theory of American Literature.*

R. B. McCallum, Master of Pembroke College, Oxford. Books include a *Life of Asquith* and an edition of Mill's *On Liberty* and *Considerations on Representative Government.*

R. V. Sampson, Lecturer in Government, University of Bristol. Author of *Progress in the Age of Reason.*

Basil Willey, King Edward VII Professor of English Literature at Cambridge University. Among his books are *Nineteenth Century Studies, Christianity Past and Present,* and *More Nineteenth Century Studies.*

NOTES

In all notes the place of publication is London unless otherwise stated.

I. SCIENCE, RELIGION, AND THE CRITICAL MIND
INTRODUCTION *by Noel Annan*

1. W. A. Leigh, *Augustus Austen Leigh* (1906), pp. 133-134.
2. F. P. Cobbe, *Broken Lights* (1865), pp. 36-37.
3. See E. M. Forster, *Marianne Thornton* (1956), pp. 162-163.
4. J. H. Newman, *Lectures and Essays on University Subjects* (1859), pp. 278-280.
5. Newman, pp. 234-236.
6. Newman, p. 309.
7. J. M. Keynes, *Essays in Biography* (1933), p. 163.
8. A. R. Vidler, *Witness to the Light* (New York, 1948), pp. 4-5.
9. Vidler, p. 34.
10. B. F. Westcott, *Characteristics of the Gospel Miracles* (Cambridge, 1859), pp. 3-4.
11. A. J. Ayer, *Language, Truth and Logic* (1946), p. 115.
12. Paul Tillich, *Systematic Theology* (1953), I, 263.
13. *Religion and Culture,* ed. Walter Leibrecht (New York, 1959), pp. 3 and 355n.
14. Norman Birnbaum, "An Agnostic Looks at the Church," *Frontier,* II (1959), 8-13.
15. David Lack, *Evolutionary Theory and Christian Belief* (1957).

THE LIMITS OF RELIGIOUS THOUGHT: THE THEOLOGICAL CONTROVERSY
by R. V. Sampson

1. Goethe, *Sämtliche Werke* (Jubiläums-Ausgabe), V, 247-248.
2. Quoted by C. Kingsley in *Charles Kingsley: His Letters and Memories of his Life,* ed. by his wife (1877), I, 142.
3. Goldwin Smith, *Lectures on the Study of History,* 2nd ed. (1865), p. 176; from the lecture, "The Moral Freedom of Man," delivered in Nov. 1861. Cf. the observations by Benjamin Jowett in the essay "On the Interpretation of Scripture" in *Essays and Reviews,* 10th ed. (1862), pp. 421-422.
4. J. W. Burgon, *Lives of Twelve Good Men* (1888), II, 185.
5. F. D. Maurice, Preface to 1873 edition of *Moral and Metaphysical Philosophy,* p. xlii.
6. H. L. Mansel, *A Lecture on the Philosophy of Kant* (1856), p. 40.
7. H. L. Mansel, *The Limits of Religious Thought Examined in Eight Lectures* (1858), p. 57.
8. *The Life of Frederick Denison Maurice,* ed. by Frederick Maurice (1884), II, 498.
9. *The Life of F. D. Maurice,* I, 135.
10. *The Life of F. D. Maurice,* I, 136. Cf. the treatment of this subject by William Temple in *Nature, Man and God* (1956), pp. 299-300.

11. H. L. Mansel, *An Examination of the Rev. F. D. Maurice's Strictures on The Bampton Lectures of 1858* (1859), p. 106.

12. Søren Kierkegaard, *The Sickness Unto Death*, trans. by Walter Lowrie (1941), p. 140.

13. *The Life of F. D. Maurice*, I, 139.

14. F. D. Maurice, *What is Revelation? A Series of Sermons on the Epiphany; to which are added Letters to a Student of Theology on the Bampton Lectures of Mr. Mansel* (1859), p. 336.

15. F. D. Maurice, *The Kingdom of Christ* (1842), I, 41.

16. *What is Revelation?*, p. 249.

17. Quoted by A. M. Ramsey, *F. D. Maurice and the Conflicts of Modern Theology* (1951), p. 14.

18. G. Lowes Dickinson, *Religion: A Criticism and a Forecast* (1905), p. 38.

19. *An Examination of Maurice's Strictures*, p. 100.

20. See Mansel, *Man's Conception of Eternity: An Examination of Mr. Maurice's Theory of a Fixed State Out of Time* (1854), pp. 23-24.

21. *What is Revelation?*, p. 203.

22. *What is Revelation?*, p. 434.

23. *The Life of F. D. Maurice*, II, 348.

24. J. S. Mill, *Autobiography*, World's Classics, pp. 129-130.

25. F. D. Maurice, *What is Revelation?*, p. 197.

26. F. D. Maurice, *Sequel to the Inquiry, What is Revelation?* (1860), p. 290.

27. *The Life of F. D. Maurice*, II, 137.

28. *The Life of F. D. Maurice*, I, 13.

29. *The Life of F. D. Maurice*, I, 14.

30. See Letter VIII of *What is Revelation?*

31. F. D. Maurice, *Sequel*, p. 185.

32. L. Susan Stebbing, *Ideals and Illusions* (1941), p. 200.

33. J. P. Sartre in *The Republic of Silence*, ed. A. J. Liebling (New York, 1947), p. 499.

34. *L'Express*, 4 Dec. 1958.

DARWIN, PATER, AND A CRISIS IN CRITICISM *by Philip Appleman*

1. Thomas Wright, *The Life of Walter Pater* (1907), I, 174, 203.

2. *Appreciations*, p. 66; latter italics mine. This and all quotations from Pater are from the Library Edition (1910).

3. Wright, I, 170.

4. "Confidence in the particular alone . . . hardly began to be exploited in European thought until the advent, in the seventeenth century, of Baconian experimentalism and especially of British empirical psychology" (Walter Jackson Bate, *From Classic to Romantic* [Cambridge, Mass., 1949], p. 93).

5. *Appreciations*, p. 68.

6. *Appreciations*, p. 68.

7. *Appreciations*, p. 68.

8. Introduction to Charles Lancelot Shadwell, *The Purgatory of Dante Alighieri* (1892), p. xviii.

9. *Renaissance*, p. vii.

10. *Renaissance*, pp. vii-viii.

11. *Renaissance*, p. 233.

12. *Renaissance,* p. 235.
13. *Renaissance,* p. 236.
14. *Renaissance,* pp. viii, x.
15. See pp. 486, 494, and 281-282.
16. *Renaissance,* p. 223; *Appreciations,* p. 153; *Guardian,* p. 55; *Appreciations,* pp. 187, 203; *Renaissance,* p. 157; *Miscellaneous,* pp. 138-139.
17. *Greek Studies,* p. 111.
18. *Renaissance,* p. 199.
19. *Plato and Platonism,* p. 9.
20. *Plato and Platonism,* pp. 19-20; latter italics mine.
21. See, *e.g.,* Ruth C. Child, "Is Walter Pater an Impressionistic Critic?" *PMLA,* LIII (1938), 1172-1185, and René Wellek's balanced estimate, "Walter Pater's Literary Theory and Criticism," *Victorian Studies,* I (1957-58), 29-46.
22. "Walter Pater" in *Inspiration and Poetry* (1955); Bowra's metaphor is borrowed from Paul Bourget whom he quotes as having described Pater as "ami de Circé transformé en dogue" (p. 199).
23. *Walter Pater: The Scholar-Artist* (Cambridge, England, 1955), *passim.*
24. Wimsatt and Brooks, p. 541.
25. *Renaissance,* pp. 33-34.
26. *Marius the Epicurean,* I, 101.
27. *Renaissance,* p. 166.
28. *Appreciations,* p. 261; *Renaissance,* pp. xiv-xv.
29. *Renaissance,* p. 34.
30. Hyman, *The Armed Vision* (New York, 1948), p. 14; Eliot, "Tradition and the Individual Talent," in *Selected Essays* (New York, 1950), pp. 13-14; Trilling, "The Sense of the Past," in *The Liberal Imagination* (New York, 1957), p. 176.
31. John Crowe Ransom, *The New Criticism* (Norfolk, Conn., 1941), pp. 138-139.
32. See chapters vii-xi of René Wellek and Austin Warren, *Theory of Literature* (New York, 1949).
33. "History and Criticism: A Problematical Relationship," *PMLA,* LXVI (1951), 25.
34. "Criticism and Literary History," *Sewanee Review,* LV (1947), 200.
35. *The Well Wrought Urn* (New York, 1947), pp. 197, 205.
36. *The Well Wrought Urn,* p. 199. Cf. Wellek and Warren's comment (*Theory of Literature,* p. 260): "Theorists as different as the Richards of *Practical Criticism* and Brooks and Warren (*Understanding Poetry*) think of a single standard for poetry and exactly stress that one should not try to 'place' the poem as to author, period, or school before judging it."
37. *The New Criticism,* p. x.
38. Geoffrey Tillotson, *Essays in Criticism and Research* (Cambridge, England, 1942), p. xi.
39. Trilling, p. 181.
40. Tillotson, pp. xx-xxi.
41. Tillotson, p. xviii.
42. Tillotson, p. x.
43. "The 'New Criticism': Some Qualifications," in *Literary Essays* (New York, 1957), p. 172.

44. "The Scholar-Critic," in Lewis Leary, ed., *Contemporary Literary Scholarship* (New York, 1958), pp. 7-8.

45. Wimsatt and Brooks, p. vii.

46. See Eric Bentley, ed., *The Importance of Scrutiny* (New York, 1948), pp. xiii-xiv and xviii-xix; see also Ransom on Eliot's "perception" and his transmission of the term "sensibility" (*The New Criticism*, pp. 175, 184).

47. Bodleian Library, MS Eng. letters, d. 120, fol. 9. Quoted by permission of Mr. D. Sturge Moore.

48. Cleanth Brooks and Robert Penn Warren, *Understanding Poetry* (New York, 1950), p. xi (Letter to the Teacher, 1938) and p. xxi (Postscript, 1950). There are numerous indications of this change of attitude in the text itself; for instance, in discussing "The Going," Brooks and Warren now offer the information that Hardy and his wife had been estranged, on the grounds that this "piece of information may be useful" (p. 216); and in a new section on "Intention and Meaning," they point out that "we can presumably understand *Hamlet* without knowing Shakespeare's private life or the steps in the composition of the play, but we cannot understand the play unless we know something of the heroic tradition that revenge is honorable" (p. 592).

49. Hazard Adams, "Criticism: Whence and Whither?" *The American Scholar*, XXVIII (1959), 238.

50. "Criticism and Literary History," p. 222.

51. "History and Criticism," p. 21. Some New Critics have of course been speaking to this point all along; see R. P. Blackmur's comment in "A Critic's Job of Work" (1935): "It is not surprising to find that the great scholars are sometimes good critics . . . and it is a fact, on the other hand, that the great critics are themselves either good scholars or know how to take advantage of scholarship" (in *Form and Value in Modern Poetry* [Anchor Books: New York, 1957], 362-363).

52. Teachers are forced constantly to be aware of this unyielding fact. Two incidents, both of which occurred in my own classes within a month of this writing, will serve as examples. In the one case it developed during class discussion of Randall Jarrell's poem, "The Death of the Ball Turret Gunner," that many in the class did not know, and had been unable to learn, what a ball turret was. In the other case students had been asked to examine the imagery of Elizabeth Barrett Browning's sonnet, "What can I give thee back, O liberal / And princely giver, who hast brought the gold / And purple of thine heart . . ." One student wrote, "In line three there is a metaphor, 'And purple of thine heart.' . . . In the war a person who receives the purple heart shows that he has performed a task of generosity, perhaps with his life. Here, the man had been very generous and liberal. The image of the purple heart is very appropriate."

53. Trilling, p. 181.

54. Eiseley, pp. 330-331; latter italics mine.

55. Gates's statement in full (*Studies and Appreciations* [New York, 1900], pp. 218-223) holds that the critic "is persuaded that in all the art and all the literature that reach the present out of the past, spirit speaks to spirit across a vast gulf of time; that he can catch the precise quality of one of these voices that come down the years only through the aid of delicate imaginative sympathy with the life of an elder generation; but the mood of the modern critic is something far subtler than any mere repetition of the mood of the original creative artist; it contains in itself a complexity and a richness of suggestion and *motifs*

that correspond to all the gains the human spirit has made since the earlier age. . . . Always, then, in the complete appreciation of a work of art there is this super-imposition of other moods upon the mood of the creative artist—there is a reinforcement of the original effect by the delicate interfusion of new tones and strains of feeling."

56. Eliot's context is as follows: "the historical sense involves a perception, not only of the pastness of the past, but of its presence; the historical sense compels a man to write not merely with his own generation in his bones, but with a feeling that the whole of the literature of Europe from Homer and within it the whole of the literature of his own country has a simultaneous existence and composes a simultaneous order. This historical sense, which is a sense of the timeless as well as of the temporal and of the timeless and of the temporal together, is what makes a writer most acutely conscious of his place in time, of his own contemporaneity. . . . No poet, no artist of any art, has his complete meaning alone. His significance, his appreciation is the appreciation of his relation to the dead poets and artists. You cannot value him alone; you must set him, for contrast and comparison, among the dead. I mean this as a principle of aesthetic, not merely historical, criticism" (*Selected Essays 1917-1932* [New York, 1932], pp. 4-5).

57. Trilling, p. 181.

58. *Kenyon Review,* XX (1959), 555-556. See also Wellek and Warren's discussion of "Perspectivism" in *Theory of Literature,* p. 35: "We must be able to refer a work of art to the values of its own time and of all the periods subsequent to its own."

59. *Miscellaneous Essays,* p. 117.

60. Eiseley, p. 352.

TECHNOLOGY AND LIBERAL EDUCATION *by George Haines, IV*

1. The Prince Consort, *Principal Speeches and Addresses* (1862), p. 227.

2. See his "Education and National Development," in T. Mary Lockyer and Winifred Lockyer, with assistance of Herbert Dingle and others, *Life and Work of Sir Norman Lockyer* (1928), p. 440.

3. See Charles Hunter Van Dusen, *Contribution of the Idéologues to French Revolutionary Thought* (Baltimore, 1935). After a purge of the faculty, the Normale was re-opened.

4. John Emerich Edward Dalbert-Acton, First Baron Acton, *Historical Studies,* ed. J. N. Figgis and R. V. Laurence (1907), p. 370.

5. John Theodore Merz, *A History of European Thought in the Nineteenth Century* (Edinburgh and London, 1904), I, 160-161, 167.

6. Alfred North Whitehead, *Science and the Modern World* (New York, 1926), p. 120.

7. Robert C. Binkley states this well in the first chapter of *Realism and Nationalism, 1852-1871* (New York, 1935), Vol. XVI in *The Rise of Modern Europe,* ed. William L. Langer, Cf. Merz, I, 91 ff.

8. Cf. Whitehead, p. 122. The conscious realization of this can be seen in the thought of Werner von Siemens. See his *Personal Recollections,* tr. W. C. Coupland (New York, 1893), pp. 43-46. An early technological entrepreneur, Siemens was the founder of the great electrical firm of Siemens and Halske.

9. A bureaucracy is "a hierarchy of appointed, paid, and removable servants,

equipped with definite commissions to perform certain special functions. Its essence is accountability and control. It implies a complicated administrative mechanism based on the principles of division of labor and specialized skill." (Walter Dorn, *Competition for Empire, 1740-1763* [New York, 1940], p. 21; this is volume IX in *The Rise of Modern Europe* series.) See also in Robert K. Merton, Ailsa P. Gray, Barbara Hockey, Hanan C. Selvin, eds., *Reader in Bureaucracy* (Glencoe, Ill., 1952), the following: Max Weber, "The Essentials of Bureaucratic Organization," pp. 18-27; Karl Mannheim, "Orientations of Bureaucratic Thought," p. 360; and Robert K. Merton, "Bureaucratic Structure and Personality," pp. 361-377.

10. See Friedrich J. Paulsen, *German Education, Past and Present,* tr. Theodor Lorenz (New York, 1908); the same author's *The German Universities,* tr. Frank Thilly and William W. Elwang (New York, 1906); Johannes Conrad, *The German Universities for the Last Fifty Years,* tr. John Hutchinson (Glasgow, 1885). On the school system generally, see I. L. Kandel, "Germany," in Peter Sandiford, ed., *Comparative Education* (London and New York, 1928); and M. E. Sadler, "The History of Education," in *Germany in the Nineteenth Century* (Manchester, 1912). In their recent study, *Education and Society in Modern Germany* (1949), p. 4, R. H. Samuel and R. Hinton Thomas observe that "bureaucratic control remained the characteristic feature of Prussian education," and "Prussian influence . . . continued to radiate out to other parts of Germany . . ."

11. Among many acounts, see, on the industrial development, Earl Dean Howard, *The Cause and Extent of the Recent Industrial Progress of Germany* (Boston, 1907); on British awareness of the threat, Ross J. Hoffman, *Great Britain and the German Trade Rivalry* (Philadelphia, 1933).

12. On science and education in this period, see George Haines, IV, *German Influence upon English Education and Science, 1800-1866* (New London, Conn., 1957).

13. The quotation is given in D. L. Burn, "The Genesis of American Engineering Competition, 1850-1870," *Economic History,* II (1930-33), 296. This whole paragraph is based on Burn's essay. Cf. Roger Burlingame, *Backgrounds of Power* (New York, 1949), pp. 158-165.

14. From the "Special Reports of Mr. George Wallis and Mr. Joseph Whitworth," *Parliamentary Papers,* 1854, XXXVI, cited by Burn, pp. 309-310.

15. Cited by Wemyss Reid, *Memoirs and Correspondence of Lyon Playfair* (1899), p. 312.

16. See Sir Theodore Martin, *Life of His Royal Highness the Prince Consort* (1880), esp. Vol. II; Sir F. A. Abel's and Lord Playfair's respective Hofmann Memorial Lectures in *Memorial Lectures before the Chemical Society, 1893-1900* (1901); and C. R. Fay, *Palace of Industry, 1851* (Cambridge, 1951), pp. 106 ff.

17. Masses of mostly unreliable statistics are available, but Matthew Arnold's statement, made in his report to the Newcastle Commission, *Parliamentary Papers,* 1861, XXI, Part IV, p. 69, will serve here: "I should mislead him [the reader] if I let him think I found in France, or that I believe to exist in France, a schoolless multitude like the 2,250,000 of England."

18. See Hansard, *Parliamentary Debates,* 3rd Series, CLVII (1857), 1211. In the same debate A. J. B. Beresford Hope, 1217-1218, linked compulsory education to the German bureaucracy and compulsory military training.

19. See W. F. Connell, *The Educational Thought and Influence of Matthew Arnold* (1950), chs. iii-vi. The first Manchester society appears to have been a successor to the Anti-Corn Law League. See Connell, p. 55.

20. Matthew Arnold, *Schools and Universities on the Continent* (1868), p. xx.

21. The phrase is quoted from W. W. Thornton, "Technical Education in England," *Cornhill Magazine,* XXIX (1871), 323-341. See also the Fifth Report of the Commissioners for the Exhibition of 1851, Appendix O, *Parliamentary Papers,* 1867, XXIII, esp. pp. 117-143.

22. "Upon the speedy provision of elementary education depends our industrial prosperity. It is of no use trying to give technical teaching to our artizans without elementary education; uneducated labourers—and many of our labourers are utterly uneducated—are, for the most part unskilled labourers, and if we leave our work-folk any longer unskilled . . . they will become over-matched in the competition of the world" (Hansard, 3rd Ser., CXIX [1870], 466).

23. S. J. Curtis, *Education in Britain Since 1900* (1952), p. 8.

24. The need of better secondary schools both for the middle and the lower classes was continually pointed out in the evidence given before every investigating committee and in every report from the Taunton School Inquiry Commission of 1867 to J. C. Smail's report, *Trade and Technical Instruction in France and Germany,* to the London County Council in March, 1914.

25. The Institute of Chemistry of Great Britain and Ireland, *History of the Institute: 1877-1914* (1914), p. 163. See also J. H. Reynolds, "Fifty Years of Technical Education," *Nature,* CIV (1919), 259.

26. On the secondary boarding schools see Edward Clarence Mack, *Public Schools and British Opinion Since 1860* (New York, 1941).

27. John Henry Newman, "University Teaching," first published in 1852, in *The Idea of a University* (1891), p. 152.

28. See Charles Edward Mallett, *A History of Oxford University* (New York, 1928), III; D. M. Winstanley, *Early Victorian Cambridge* (Cambridge, 1940); and A. I. Tillyard, *A History of University Reform* (Cambridge, 1913). Only the last offers a critical analysis.

29. Adam Sedgwick, *A Discourse on the Studies of the University* (Cambridge, 1834); William Whewell, *On the Principles of English University Education* (1838); John Henry Newman, *University Teaching* (1852); E. B. Pusey, *Collegiate and Professorial Teaching* (1854).

30. In addition to the biographies of the leading figures, see Klaus Dockhorn, *Der Deutsche Historismus in England* (Göttingen and Baltimore, 1949), and Duncan Forbes, *The Liberal Anglican Idea of History* (Cambridge, 1952).

31. Evelyn Abbott and Lewis Campbell, *Life and Letters of Benjamin Jowett* (1897), I, 190.

32. See the comments of a writer in the *Quarterly Review,* XCIII (1853), 155.

33. See J. A. Venn, *Oxford and Cambridge Matriculations, 1544-1906* (Cambridge, 1908), pp. 16-17 and the Graphic Chart.

34. See the Oxford University Commission Report, *Parliamentary Papers,* 1852, XXII, 256-260, paragraphs 23, 25, and 30; and *P. P.* 1852-53; XLIV, 101-102, and 116-119.

35. Mark Pattison, *Suggestions on Academical Organization* (Edinburgh, 1868), cited extensively by Tillyard, pp. 160-197.

36. Margaret Goldsmith, *Florence Nightingale* (1937), pp. 231, 234.

37. A. M. Carr-Saunders and P. A. Wilson, *The Professions* (Oxford, 1933), p. 240.

38. See the comments of Mr. Ackroyd in the Commons, Hansard, 3rd Series, CLVIII (1857), 1211.

39. "What Knowledge Is of Most Worth?" in *Education* (New York, 1860). The essay first appeared in the *Westminster Review* in July 1859.

40. Connell, *Educational Thought . . . of Matthew Arnold,* p. 281.

41. See D. M. Turner, *History of Science Teaching in England* (1927), esp. ch. viii. It should be supplemented by Edward Frankland's communication to *Nature*, III (1870-71), p. 445, quoted in part in Haines, pp. 53-54.

42. On the scholars, see Diderick Roll-Hansen, *The Academy, 1869-1879* in *Anglistica,* VIII (Copenhagen, 1957), esp. chs. ii, iii, iv.

43. On the scientists, see my essay, "German Influence upon Scientific Instruction in England, 1867-1887," *Victorian Studies,* I (1957-58), 215-244. See also Cyril Bibby, "Thomas Henry Huxley and University Development," *Victorian Studies,* II (1958-59), 97-116.

44. J. C. Smail, *Trade and Technical Education in France and Germany,* Report to the London County Council (March 1914), p. 11.

45. Sir William Tilden, *Sir William Ramsay* (1918), p. 198. See also Morris Travers, *A Life of William Ramsay* (1956).

46. In his presidential address to the Mathematical Association of England, reprinted in *The Aims of Education* (1929). Quotation cited from 1955 reprint, p. 25.

47. "The scholar becomes a technologist instead of an explorer," Alexander Vucinich, *The Soviet Academy of Science,* Hoover Institute Studies (Stanford, 1956), p. 48. But see the whole discussion.

48. See, for example, Alexander G. Korol, *Soviet Education for Science and Technology* (New York, 1957), esp. ch. xii.

II. PATTERNS OF NATIONAL DEVELOPMENT

INTRODUCTION *by William O. Aydelotte*

1. Bernard Cracroft, "The Analysis of the House of Commons, or Indirect Representation," in *Essays on Reform* (1867); Elie Halévy, *A History of the English People in the Nineteenth Century,* Eng. tr., III (New York, 1950), 60-70; William O. Aydelotte, "The House of Commons in the 1840's," *History*, XXXIX (1954), 251-262.

2. G. S. R. Kitson Clark, "The Electorate and the Repeal of the Corn Laws," *Transactions of the Royal Historical Society,* 5th ser., I (1951), 118, 124-125; George L. Mosse, "The Anti-League, 1844-1846," *Economic History Review,* XVII (1947), 134-142.

3. Kitson Clark, *passim;* Norman Gash, *Politics in the Age of Peel: a Study in the Technique of Parliamentary Representation, 1830-1850* (1953), *passim.*

4. Gash, pp. 109-110; Halévy, III, 64.

5. Rowland E. Prothero (Lord Ernle), *English Farming Past and Present,* 2nd ed. (1917), ch. xvii.

6. Kitson Clark, "The Repeal of the Corn Laws and the Politics of the 'Forties," *Economic History Review,* 2nd ser., IV (1951), 12.

7. John Morley, *The Life of Richard Cobden* (1881), II, 232.

8. Queen Victoria to Viscount Palmerston, 2 July 1859, *The Letters of Queen Victoria* . . . , 1st ser. (1907), III, 446.

9. Some examples of businessmen who became M.P.'s for their counties are: William Brown the merchant banker in South Lancashire; Thomas Houldsworth the Manchester cotton spinner in North Nottinghamshire; Abel Smith the banker in Hertfordshire; William Thompson the ironmaster and shipowner in Westmoreland.

10. James Caird, *English Agriculture in 1850-51* (1852), p. 526.

11. Herbert C. Bell, "Palmerston and Parliamentary Representation," *Journal of Modern History,* IV (1932), 210.

12. Bell, pp. 191-197, 202-213.

13. Disraeli to General Grey, 15 Mar. 1867, *The Letters of Queen Victoria* . . . , 2nd ser. (1926-28), I, 409.

14. *The Speech of C. N. Newdegate, M.P., at the Annual Meeting of the Rugby and Dunchurch Agricultural Association, November 26th, 1858* (1859), p. 6.

15. Asa Briggs, *Victorian People: a Reassessment of Persons and Themes, 1851-67* (Chicago, 1955), p. 201.

16. John Stuart Mill, *Thoughts on Parliamentary Reform* (1859), p. 30.

17. Francis H. Herrick, "The Second Reform Movement in Britain, 1850-1865," *Journal of the History of Ideas,* IX (1948), 174-182.

18. Samuel H. Beer, "The Representation of Interests in British Government: Historical Background," *American Political Science Review,* LI (1957), 615-618, 628-629.

19. Bell, p. 196.

20. Queen Victoria to Lord John Russell, 3 Dec. 1851, *The Letters of Queen Victoria* . . . , 1st ser., II, 403.

21. Herrick, p. 190.

22. To support constitutionalism abroad and to oppose further political reform at home did not of course necessarily involve an inconsistency. Mr. Bell points out that Palmerston simply preached to continental rulers the adoption of existing British institutions. See Bell, p. 187.

23. Harold Temperley, "British Policy Towards Parliamentary Rule and Constitutionalism in Turkey (1830-1914)," *Cambridge Historical Journal,* IV (1933), 157.

24. Temperley, pp. 156-191.

25. Gavin Burns Henderson, *Crimean War Diplomacy and Other Historical Essays* (Glasgow, 1947), pp. 123-152; Briggs, pp. 213-220.

26. R. W. Seton-Watson, *Britain in Europe, 1789-1914: a Survey of Foreign Policy* (Cambridge, 1937), pp. 221-222, 416; Henderson, pp. 128, 137; John Howes Gleason, *The Genesis of Russophobia in Great Britain* (Cambridge, Mass., 1950), pp. vii, 2-3, 272-274, 276, 284-290; B. Kingsley Martin, *The Triumph of Lord Palmerston: a Study of Public Opinion in England Before the Crimean War* (New York, 1924), *passim.*

27. Seton-Watson, pp. 301, 357, 374n., 375.

28. Donald Stuart Owings, *English Anti-Judaism, 1800-1879,* unpublished M.A. thesis, State University of Iowa, June, 1957.

29. Hansard, 3rd ser., CXLIV, 1785.

30. George Macaulay Trevelyan, *The Life of John Bright* (1913), pp. 285-286.

31. Seton-Watson, p. 370.

32. It must be added that Roebuck became much less of a radical in his later days, and also that he did at times take a strong stand against British aggression, as in his motion on the Afghanistan War of 1 Mar. 1843, or in his speech on the bombardment of Canton in 1857, which has been quoted above.

PROBLEMS OF INDUSTRIAL CHANGE *by J. R. T. Hughes*

1. A fuller description of these events will be found in J. R. T. Hughes, "The Commercial Crisis of 1857," *Oxford Economic Papers,* VIII (1956), 194-222.

2. Arthur Redford, *The Economic History of England 1760-1860* (1931), p. 200.

3. See G. D. H. Cole, *A History of Socialist Thought* (1954), II, 89-90 for this episode.

4. G. D. H. Cole, *A Short History of the British Working Class Movement* (1926), II, 81-84. The democratic character of the League may be seen in its Rules of 1865, reproduced in G. D. H. Cole and A. W. Wilson, *British Working Class Movements, Select Documents* (1951), pp. 532-534.

5. Except where otherwise indicated these population data are taken from *Accounts and Papers,* LIII, Parts I and II.

6. A. K. Cairncross, "Internal Migration in Victorian England," *Manchester School,* XVII (1949), 70.

7. William Page, *Commerce and Industry* (1919) II, 3.

8. For comparison see Sir John Clapham's analysis of the 1851 Census in *An Economic History of Modern Britain* (Cambridge, 1942), II, 22.

9. The contribution of manufacturing industry may have been two-thirds as large as that of agriculture as early as the 1830's. See R. C. O. Matthews, *A Study in Trade Cycle History* (Cambridge, 1954), p. 3.

10. The American figures are here converted at the rate £1 = $4.867; for British imports, see A. H. Imlah, *Economic Elements in the Pax Britannica* (Cambridge, Mass., 1959).

10a. See Werner Schlote, *British Overseas Trade from 1700 to the 1930's* (Oxford, 1952), pp. 48-49, for growth of trade in the 1850's compared to other periods. Walter G. Hoffman's *British Industry 1700-1950* (Oxford, 1955) contains a well-known index of industrial production, table 54, part B (exclusive of building construction), which shows a more rapid rate of growth in the 1850's than in other decades of the Victorian era.

11. James Caird, *The Landed Interest* (1878), p. 160, for harvests.

12. For a discussion of these factors in the business cycle of the 1850's, see Hughes, "Commercial Crisis," pp. 205-207.

13. Walter Bagehot, *Lombard Street* (1878), pp. 41-42; for a sharp discussion of the Bank's activities in this period see Jacob Viner, *Studies in the Theory of International Trade* (New York, 1937), pp. 254-255.

14. Sauerbeck's price index for the period is reproduced (rebased) in Schlote, *British Overseas Trade,* table 26.

15. G. H. Wood, "Real Wages and the Standard of Comfort Since 1850," *Journal of the Royal Statistical Society,* LXXII (1909), 93; R. S. Tucker, "Real Wages of Artisans in London 1729-1935," *Journal of the American Statistical Association,* XXXI (1936), 79.

16. L. H. Jenks, *Migration of British Capital to 1875* (1938), pp. 192-224.

17. Schlote, *British Overseas Trade,* table 19.

18. *Manchester Guardian,* 3 Jan. 1859.

19. For details of the cotton boom in the years just before the American Civil War see: Karl Marx, *Capital,* ed. Glaisher (1918), I, 458; Andrew Ure, *The Cotton Manufacture of Great Britain* (1861), II, 362; and W. O. Henderson, *The Lancashire Cotton Famine* (1934), pp. 11-12.

20. Hughes, "Commercial Crisis," pp. 208-213.

21. A. L. Dunham, "The Development of the Cotton Industry in France to 1860," *Economic History Review,* I (1928), 291, table showing reduction of stocks at expense of imports.

22. Hughes, "Commercial Crisis," pp. 208-213.

23. An early appraisal of the importance to Lancashire of the new India Market is: J. C. Ollerenshaw, "Our Export Trade in Cotton Goods to India," *Transactions of the Manchester Statistical Society,* Session 1867-68.

24. Hughes, "Commercial Crisis," pp. 204-205.

25. James S. Jeans, *Notes on Northern Industry* (1879), p. 59; *Memoirs of the Geological Survey of Great Britain, Mineral Statistics,* 1857.

26. Data from yearly tabulations in *Mineral Statistics.*

27. Isaac Lowthian Bell, *The Iron Trade of the United Kingdom* (1886) p. 9.

28. Hughes, "Commercial Crisis," pp. 215-217.

29. *Mining Journal,* 10 Dec. 1859.

30. Hughes, "Commercial Crisis," p. 205.

31. *Mineral Statistics.*

32. *Statistical Abstract* for tonnage of ships built and first registered in the U. K. For a general discussion of shipbuilding in the period and the problems associated with the Crimean-War boom in shipbuilding and the rise of the steamship, see J. R. T. Hughes and Stanley Reiter, "The First 1,945 British Steamships," *Journal of the American Statistical Association,* LIII (1958), 360-381.

33. Discussions on this problem are abundant in the contemporary press; for example, *Building News,* 23 Jan. and 3 Apr. 1857; *The Times,* 27 Jan. 1857.

34. *The Times,* 9 Feb. 1857.

35. *The Times,* 9 Feb. 1857.

36. Hughes, "Commercial Crisis," p. 214 and sources cited there.

37. *Select Committee* on the Bank Acts, *Accounts and Papers,* 1857 (Session 1), X (220). Evidence of Edward Capps, London Builder, esp. QQ. 5413-5467. For details of the application of machinery in building construction, see the public statement of the strike committee, which is reproduced in the *Economist,* 6 Aug. 1859, "Rights and Wrongs of the Building Strike."

38. G. Shaw Lefevre and Thomas R. Bennett, "Account of the Strike and Lock-Out in the Building Trades of London in 1859-60," *Trade Societies and Strikes* (1860), p. 53. This is the most thorough and factual account of the strike I have seen.

39. Cole, *Short History,* II, 65-68 on the builders' strike.

40. Cole and Wilson, *Documents,* pp. 486-488; also Sidney and Beatrice Webb, *The History of Trade Unionism* (1902), pp. 209-214 on the London builders generally. The strike is treated in feature articles in the *Economist,* 6, 13, 20 Aug., 17 Sept., 22, 29 Oct., 26 Nov., and 17 Dec., 1859. The strike is also given extensive space in the trade journals, e.g., *Building News,* 22 July 1859—17 Feb. 1860.

41. Cole and Wilson, *Documents,* p. 488.

42. Webb, *History of Trade Unionism,* p. 212.

43. Cole, *Short History,* II, 78.

44. Taken from the *Annual Report* of May 1867 of the London Trades Council, Cole and Wilson, *Documents,* p. 528.

45. On Marx and the First International, its origins and connection with British Labor in the period see Cole, *Socialist Thought,* II, ch. vi, also *Short History,* II, chs. ii and iii; Webb, *History of Trade Unionism,* ch. v, "The Junta and Their Allies."

46. V. I. Lenin, *Marx-Engels-Marxism* (Moscow, 1951), pp. 18-19.

THE INDIVIDUAL IN THE MASS: MILL ON LIBERTY AND THE FRANCHISE
by R. B. McCallum

1. Michael St. John Packe, *Life of John Stuart Mill* (1954), p. 36.

2. John Stuart Mill, *Thoughts on Parliamentary Reform* (1859), p. 8.

3. *Parliamentary Reform,* p. 17.

4. *Parliamentary Reform,* p. 18.

5. Ruth Borchard, *John Stuart Mill the Man* (1957), p. 128.

6. John Stuart Mill, *On Liberty,* ed. R. B. McCallum (Oxford, 1946), p. 4.

7. *On Liberty,* p. 5.

8. *On Liberty,* p. 6.

9. *On Liberty,* p. 21.

10. *On Liberty,* p. 9.

11. *Parliamentary Reform,* p. 9.

12. *Parliamentary Reform,* p. 21.

13. *Parliamentary Reform,* p. 23.

14. *Parliamentary Reform,* p. 26.

PARTY POLITICS IN THE AGE OF PALMERSTON *by J. B. Conacher*

1. From Tennyson's "The War" printed in *The Times,* 9 May 1859, reprinted in the *Annual Register . . . 1859* (1860), p. 556.

2. *Annual Register,* pp. 186-187.

3. I am indebted to Mr. John Kenyon for making available to me his analysis of Dod's *Parliamentary Companion* for 1857, where the votes on such topics as Church rates, Roman Catholicism, and the ballot lend support to my statement.

4. See Norman Gash, *Politics in the Age of Peel* (1953), ch. xv, *passim*; also "Peel and the Party System, 1830-1850," *Transactions of the Royal Historical Society,* 5th ser., I (1951), pp. 47-69.

5. Dod's *Parliamentary Companion* (1859) lists as members 148 out of 236 Conservative or Liberal-Conservative peers and 206 Conservative or Liberal-Conservative M.P.'s.

6. H. F. C. Bell, *Lord Palmerston* (1936), II, p. 370.

7. Lord Stanmore, *Sidney Herbert* (1906), II, 93.

8. G. Saintsbury, *The Earl of Derby* (1906), pp. 100-101.

9. See the list of "Ayes" on this motion printed in S. Maccoby, *English Radicalism, 1832-1852* (1935), Appendix A, pp. 449-451.

10. See J. H. Whyte, *The Independent Irish Party 1850-1859* (Oxford, 1958).

11. W. F. Monypenny and G. F. Buckle, *The Life of Benjamin Disraeli* (rev. ed., New York, 1929), I, 1476.

12. Sir Stafford Northcote was perhaps typical of this group when he wrote to Gladstone in 1856: "I don't think anybody is naturally more inclined to partisanship than I am, and I hope against hope for the time when I may find myself fairly in the ranks of an undivided party. At present it is exceedingly difficult to know what one is to do, and I don't see much light out of the wood yet. What I feel is, I know, felt by a large number of those who usually sit near me, and who could, I think, easily be moulded into a powerful and independent party if fate would only send them a leader" (British Museum, Add. MS. 44,217, ff. 5-6). The Reverend Whitwell Elwin, then editor of the *Quarterly Review*, took the same line in his correspondence with Gladstone (Add. MS., 44,152, ff. 13-79).

13. Of the other Peelite peers it may be noted that the Duke of Argyll, the Earl of Dalhousie, and Viscount Canning had all joined the Liberals, Argyll as a continuing member of Palmerston's first Cabinet, Dalhousie and Canning as successive Governors General of India, 1847-55 and 1855-62. The Duke of Newcastle had temporarily withdrawn from active politics after his discomfiture in 1855. For the early history of the Peelites see my article, "Sir Robert Peel and the Peelites, 1846-1850," *English Historical Review,* LXXIII (1958), 431-452.

14. British Museum, Add. MS. 44,747, f. 80.

15. *Annual Register . . . 1859,* pp. 3-4.

16. Lytton Strachey and Roger Fulford, eds., *The Greville Memoirs, 1814-1860* (1938), VII, 404-407.

17. Stanmore, II, 177.

18. C. S. Parker, *Life and Letters of Sir James Graham* (1907), II, 365.

19. *The Times,* 21 May 1859. These figures include a double return for Aylesbury, where a Liberal and a Conservative candidate each obtained the same number of votes.

20. *Greville Memoirs,* VII, 417-418.

21. Monypenny and Buckle, I, 1635-44.

22. What follows is based on correspondence printed in Stanmore, II, 181-198; Parker, *Graham,* II, 381-388; Lord Edmund Fitzmaurice, *The Life of Lord Granville* (1905), I, 327-331; Spencer Walpole, *The Life of Lord John Russell* (1891), II, 313-315; and *Greville Memoirs,* VII, 419-422.

23. R. A. J. Walling, ed., *The Diaries of John Bright* (1930), pp. 237-238.

24. Stanmore, II, 198.

25. *The Times,* 7 June 1859.

26. Stanmore, II, 198.

27. Horsman, Lindsay, and Roebuck, the unpredictable Philosophical Radical, who had taken umbrage at Russell's failure to inform him of a change of plan with regard to the Reform debate of the previous session.

28. Monypenny and Buckle, I, 1650.

29. *The Times,* 8 and 9 June 1859.

30. *The Times,* 13 June 1859; Dod's *Parliamentary Companion* for 1859 and 1861. *The Times* does not recognize the category "Liberal-Conservative" and, in its election results of 21 May, it lists six of those supporters of the motion whom Dod calls "Liberal-Conservative" as "Liberals" and two as "Conservatives." No wonder it was impossible to be sure of divisions ahead of time!

31. British Museum, Add. MS. 44,152, f. 83. "I have a good many friends who are thorough Austrians and they attacked me vehemently for the views put forth in the Q.R.," Elwin, the editor, wrote to Gladstone on 5 May 1859.

32. W. D. Jones, *Lord Derby and Victorian Conservatism* (Oxford, 1956), p. 255.

33. Parker, II, 388.

34. Stanmore, II, 196-197.

35. Herbert Maxwell, *The Life and Letters of . . . the Fourth Earl of Clarendon* (1913), II, 196.

36. Fitzmaurice, I, 294.

37. Fitzmaurice, pp. 304-341.

38. Stanmore, II, 200.

39. *Bright Diaries*, p. 241.

40. *Bright Diaries*, p. 242.

41. Granville sharply forecast that Gibson would lose the character of a middle-class representative in office (Stanmore, II, 189).

42. Lord Granville, the Duke of Somerset, Lord Campbell (as Lord Chancellor), and the three baronets, Wood, Lewis, and Grey.

43. John Morley, *The Life of William Ewart Gladstone* (1903), I, pp. 627-628.

44. Fitzmaurice, I, 344.

45. Bell, II, 404.

46. In a series of three articles entitled "Parliament in Danger," which appeared in the *Observer* on 11, 18, and 25 Jan. 1959.

47. See R. T. McKenzie, *British Political Parties* (1955), pp. 598-599.

AN INTERNATIONAL CRISIS: THE ITALIAN QUESTION *by Derek Beales*

1. Cavour to Victor Emmanuel (*Il Carteggio Cavour-Nigra dal 1858 al 1861* [Bologna, 1926-29], I, 103-113, 24 July 1858). A formal treaty was not signed until the end of Jan. 1859, when the federation proposal was dropped.

2. In this passage on Cavour I have relied heavily on the recent work of D. Mack Smith, especially *Cavour and Garibaldi 1860* (Cambridge, 1954) and his article "Cavour and Parliament," *Cambridge Historical Journal*, XIII (1957), 37-57.

3. See C. W. Hallberg, *Franz Joseph and Napoleon III, 1852-64* (New York, 1954), esp. ch. vii, and J. M. Thompson, *Louis Napoleon and the Second Empire* (Oxford, 1954), esp. ch. vi.

4. The phrase is Valsecchi's. See F. Valsecchi, *La Mediazione Europea e la definizione dell'aggressore alla vigilia della guerra del 1859* (Rome, 1938).

5. See Hallberg, esp. pp. 187-192, and F. Engel von Janosi, *L'Ultimatum Austriaco del 1859* (Rome, 1938).

6. See Hallberg, pp. 196-200, and A. J. P. Taylor, "European Mediation and the Agreement of Villafranca," *English Historical Review*, LI (1936), 52-78.

7. Comte de Hübner, *Neuf Ans de souvenirs d'un ambassadeur d'Autriche à Paris . . .* (Paris, 1904), p. 244. This would seem to be the most authentic of the many versions of this remark.

8. Earl of Malmesbury, *Memoirs of an Ex-Minister* (1885), one-vol. ed., p. 457. *Correspondence Relating to the Affairs of Italy, January to May 1859* (State Papers. Session 31 May-13 Aug. 1859. Vol. XXXII. Command Paper No. 2524), pp. 4-10.

9. *Correspondence*, pp. 208 [refusal of guarantee to Austria] and 133, 172, 186, 234, 247 [negotiations with France on guarantee of Piedmont]. The second

Austrian request was omitted from the Blue Book (H. Hearder, "La Politica di Lord Malmesbury verso l'Italia nella Primavera del 1859," *Rassegna storica del Risorgimento,* XLIII [1956], 53-54). For French feelers see especially M. B. Urban, *British Opinion and Policy on the Unification of Italy, 1856-1861* (Scottdale, 1938, chs. ix-x, and Hon. F. A. Wellesley, *The Paris Embassy during the Second Empire* (1928), ch. viii.

10. H. W. V. Temperley and L. M. Penson, *Foundations of British Foreign Policy* (Cambridge, 1938), pp. 201-202; Derby's speech in the House of Lords on 18 Apr. Cf. Malmesbury, p. 482.

11. Malmesbury to Hudson, 12 Feb., *Correspondence,* p. 45.

12. Malmesbury to Loftus, 21 Apr., *Correspondence,* p. 276.

13. See *Further Correspondence Respecting the Affairs of Italy* (State Papers. Session 31 May-13 Aug. 1859. Vol. XXXII. Command Paper No. 2527), *passim.* Dr. Hearder kindly allowed me to read his unpublished thesis on "The Foreign Policy of Lord Malmesbury, 1858-59," which, with his article cited above, is the main source for this discussion of Malmesbury's attitude.

14. Russell to Bloomfield, 7 July, *Further Despatches . . .* (State Papers. Session 31 May-13 Aug. 1859. Vol. XXXII. Command Paper No. 2550).

15. See *Correspondence Relating to the Affairs of Italy, from . . . Villafranca to the Postponement of the Congress* (State Papers. Session 24 Jan.-28 Aug. 1860 Vol. LXVIII. Command Paper No. 2609).

16. [W. E. Gladstone] "War in Italy," *Quarterly Review,* CV (1859), 531, 532.

17. Wellesley, pp. 174-175, end of Jan., Palmerston to Cowley.

18. "War in Italy," p. 563.

19. *The History of* The Times (1935-52), II, 331-332.

20. Malmesbury to Cowley, 20 Apr., Cowley Papers, F.O. 519/196, Public Record Office, London.

20a. Queen Victoria to the King of the Belgians, 26 April, ed. A. C. Benson and Viscount Esher, *The Letters of Queen Victoria . . . ,* 1st ser. (1908), III, 328.

21. Derby to the Queen, 1 May, *The Letters of Queen Victoria,* III, 330.

22. Malmesbury to Cowley, 4 Apr., Cowley Papers.

23. Derby's remark was made during a speech in the City on 25 Apr., Malmesbury, p. 488.

24. Derby to the Queen, 2 June, *Letters of Queen Victoria,* III, 337.

25. See Hon. E. Ashley, *The Life of . . . Viscount Palmerston* (1876), II, 174-180; Gladstone to Russell, 3 Jan. (Gladstone Papers, British Museum Add. MS. 44,291, ff, 289-290.

26. Argyll to Russell, 6 Jan., Russell Papers, PRO 30/22/25, Public Record Office, London.

27. C. Sebag-Montefiore, *A History of the Volunteer Forces* (1908), p. 373n. and *passim.*

28. The Prince Consort to the Prince Regent of Prussia, 18 May, K. Jagow, ed., *Letters of the Prince Consort* (1938), p. 322.

29. J. P. Baxter, *The Introduction of the Ironclad Warship* (Cambridge, Mass., 1933), chs. vii-viii.

30. Malmesbury to Bloomfield, 2 May (*Correspondence . . . Jan. to May 1859,* p. 377).

31. C. C. F. Greville, *A Journal of the Reign of Queen Victoria from 1852 to 1860* (1887), II [*The Greville Memoirs,* VIII], 254.

32. Clarendon to Cowley, 27 Jan. 1860, Wellesley, p. 196.

33. Granville to Palmerston, 7 Jan. 1860, Lord Edmond Fitzmaurice, *The Life of 2nd Earl Granville* (1905), I, 368.

34. E. d'Azeglio to his father, 29 Oct., A. Colombo, ed., *Carteggi e documenti diplomatici inediti di Emanuele d'Azeglio*, II (privately printed), 229-230.

35. See W. E. Mosse, *The European Powers and the German Question 1848-1871* (Cambridge, 1958), esp. chs. iii-iv.

III. THE CHALLENGE OF POPULAR CULTURE
INTRODUCTION *by J. A. Banks*

1. For changes in the meaning of the word "culture" over the past 200 years, see Raymond Williams, *Culture and Society, 1780-1950* (1958), Introduction.

2. These figures have been calculated from the data given in G. T. Griffiths, *Population Problems of the Age of Malthus* (Cambridge, 1926), Table 3, p. 18. Since only rough numbers are given there is no point in suggesting a spurious accuracy by writing 1751, 1801, and 1851.

3. Data taken from the Census of 1951 *Preliminary Report,* Table 1, p. 1.

4. These essays were inspired by Emerson's second visit to England, in 1847, when he was invited to lecture to Mechanics' Institutes in Lancashire and Yorkshire.

5. The May family first appeared in *The Daisy Chain,* published as a book in 1856, after being issued as a series of sketches in *The Monthly Packet,* a High Church magazine edited by Charlotte Yonge. This novel has been claimed to be the first to lay down the pattern of middle-class family life in the nineteenth century which we usually think of today as typical of that period, largely through the influence of the children's writers who carried on the tradition. See Marghanita Laski, *Mrs. Ewing, Mrs. Molesworth and Mrs. Hodgson Burnett* (1950), pp. 15-17. The Underwood family appeared in *The Pillars of the House* (1872).

6. Anthony Trollope, *An Autobiography* (1883), ch. xii: "On Novels and the Art of Writing Them."

7. W. E. H. Lecky, *History of European Morals* (1869), ch. v.

8. O. R. McGregor, *Divorce in England: A Centenary Study* (1957), p. 71. ch. iii of this book—"The Victorian Family: Illusion and Reality"—is one of the few good general accounts of family life in Victorian England.

9. William Acton, *Prostitution, considered in its Moral, Social and Sanitary Aspects, in London and other large cities, with Proposals for the Mitigation and Prevention of its Attendant Evils* (1857).

10. Patricia Thomson, *The Victorian Heroine: a Changing Ideal, 1837-1873* (Oxford, 1956), ch. v, "The Social Evil." *Lizzie Leigh* was first published in *Household Words* and reprinted with other short stories in book form in 1855.

11. H. L. Beales, "Victorian Ideas of Sex" in *Ideas and Beliefs of the Victorians, an Historic Revaluation of The Victorian Age* (1949).

12. W. E. Houghton, *The Victorian Frame of Mind, 1830-1870* (New Haven, 1957), p. 343. The whole of Houghton's ch. xiii—"Love"—is relevant to this point.

13. Quoted in Thomson, p. 140.

14. *SOCIAL versus POLITICAL REFORM. The Sin of Great Cities: or, the Great Social Evil, a National Sin, illustrated by a brief enquiry into its extent, causes, effects, and existing remedies* (1859).

15. See F. W. Newman's attack on Oxford undergraduates in his "Remedies for the Great Social Evil," 1869; quoted in Houghton, pp. 365-366.

16. George Eliot, *Adam Bede* (1859), ch. xlvi.

17. For evidence that a double standard of sexual conduct still prevails in England, see the *Report of the Committee on Homosexual Offenses and Prostitution* (1957), Cmnd. 247, and the debate in the House of Commons, 26 Nov. 1958, Hansard, 596 (22).

18. "The Social Science Association," *Saturday Review,* 14 June 1862. The *Saturday Review* maintained a consistently anti-feminist line for most of the century.

19. *A Century of Family Law,* ed. R. H. Graveson and F. R. Crane (1957).

20. McGregor, pp. 18-19.

21. J. S. Smith, *Social Aspects* (1850), p. 45.

22. C. W. Cunnington, *The Perfect Lady* (1948), ch. iii.

23. J. A. Banks, *Prosperity and Parenthood: A Study of Family Planning among the Victorian Middle Classes* (1954), pp. 41-47. Details of incomes and expenditure patterns, 1851-71, are given in chs. iv-vii of that work.

24. S. W. Partridge, *Upward and Onward: a Thought Book for the Threshold of Active Life* (1857), quoted in Banks, p. 36.

25. *How to Woo, When, and to Whom* (1855), p. 6.

26. M. E. Perugini, *Victorian Days and Ways* (1946), p. 49.

27. Florence Nightingale, *Suggestions for Thought to Searchers of the Religious Truth* (privately printed but not published, London, 1859). A section from the second volume of this work is reprinted as Appendix I to Rachel Strachey, *"The Cause": a Short History of the Women's Movement in Great Britain* (1928).

28. E. C. Mack, *Public Schools and British Opinion, 1780 to 1860* (1938), p. 400.

29. Francis Davenant published a book under this title in 1870 with the subheading, *Hints to Parents on the Choice of a Profession or Trade,* but similar books had appeared earlier: *e.g.,* J. C. Hudson, *The Parent's Handbook* (1842), Banks, ch. xi.

30. See particularly *The Book of Household Management* (1861).

31. Nightingale, p. 397.

32. *My Life and What Shall I do with it* (1860).

33. Strachey, ch. v.

34. Anthony Trollope, *Can You Forgive Her?* (London, 1864), ch. xi. See also the title of the last chapter of *Framley Parsonage* (1861).

35. Horace Mann, "On the Statistical Position of Religious Bodies in England and Wales," *Journal of the Statistical Society of London,* XVIII (1855), 159. A comparison of 1851 with 1952 shows an increase in religious affiliation of 53% as against a total population increase of 145% (A.M. Carr-Saunders, D. C. Jones, and C. A. Moser, *A Survey of Social Conditions in England and Wales as Illustrated by Statistics* [Oxford, 1958], p. 256).

36. Margaret Hewitt, *Wives and Mothers in Victorian Industry* (1958), ch. vi.

37. G. M. Trevelyan, *British History in the Nineteenth Century and After, 1782-1919* (1937), p. 241.

38. Trevelyan, p. 275.

39. Hermann Levy, *Large and Small Holdings* (trans. and rev., Cambridge,

1911), p. 91. Levy is at pains to show that the distinction had nothing to do with the size of the holding, other than that no gentleman farmers had small holdings. Both might employ the same number of men.

40. Archer Polson, *Law and Lawyers* (1840), I, 145.

41. Report of the Select Committee on Legal Education, *British Parliamentary Papers*, 1846, Vol. X, p. 1963—evidence of Sir George Stephen; see also the commentary on this evidence in E. B. V. Christian, *A Short History of Solicitors* (1896), p. 190.

42. Mack, pp. 324-333; *Tom Brown's Schooldays* appeared in 1856 and *Tom Brown at Oxford* in 1861, having first appeared in *Macmillan's Magazine* in 1859-60. Mack argues that the influence of Hughes' anti-intellectualism "was unfortunate. It gave sanction to a tradition which Arnold had tried, with some success, to break down" (p. 330).

43. John Ruskin, "Pre-Raphaelitism" (1851), quoted in Houghton, p. 187; italics in the quotation. See also pp. 201-206 of Houghton for an excellent description of the squirearchy's worship of force.

44. Noel Annan, "The Intellectual Aristocracy" in *Studies in Social History: a Tribute to G. M. Trevelyan*, ed. J. H. Plumb (1955).

45. She also thought "shoppy people" pretentious. Elizabeth Gaskell, *North and South* (1854), chs. ii and iii.

46. Beatrice Webb, *My Apprenticeship* (1926), ch. i, italics in the original.

47. Reinhard Bendix, *Work and Authority in Industry: Ideologies of Management in the Course of Industrialization* (New York, 1956), ch. ii.

48. *Advice to Clerks, and Hints to Employers, by an Experienced Clerk* (1848), pp. 6-7.

49. David Lockwood, *The Blackcoated Workers: a Study in Class Consciousness* (1958), ch. i.

50. From a speech by one of them in the late 1850's, quoted in Asher Tropp, *The School Teachers* (1957), p. 40. Chs. ii and iii of this study are invaluable for information on the social pressures on this class and the development of professional trades unionism.

51. "People who keep a carriage, but are silent respecting their grandfathers" were placed at the top of a "Transition" class in "High" life by *Punch* in 1841; see Perugini, pp. 31-35.

52. J. L. and Barbara Hammond's *The Bleak Age* (1934), especially in its 1947 edition, revised for publication by Pelican Books, was largely their *Age of the Chartists* (1930) written from the angle of an age of leisure.

53. See, for example, G. J. Holyoake, *Self-Help by the People: History of Co-operation in Rochdale* (1858) and his later book, *Self-Help, a Hundred Years Ago* (1888).

54. Quoted from the Address to the Trades by the Metropolitan Trades Conference, the *Operative*, 27 Mar. 1852 in *British Working Class Movements: Select Documents*, ed. G. D. H. Cole and A. W. Filson (1951), p. 483.

55. John Glyde, *The Moral, Social and Religious Condition of Ipswich in the Middle of the Nineteenth Century* (Ipswich, 1850), pp. 69-70.

56. Glyde, pp. 65-66.

57. J. M. Robertson, *A History of Freethought in the Nineteenth Century* (1929), ch. xi, and John Eros, "The Rise of Organized Freethought in Mid-Victorian England," *Sociological Review*, II (1954), pp. 98-120.

THE LITERATURE OF AN IMMINENT DEMOCRACY *by Richard D. Altick*

1. "Popular Literature—the Periodical Press," *Blackwood's Magazine,* LXXXV (1859), 98-99. This article (pp. 96-112) and its continuations (LXXXV, 180-195, 515-532, and LXXXVI, 681-689) are perceptive treatments of various aspects of popular literature in 1859. Three other contemporary discussions are [Wilkie Collins], "The Unknown Public," *Household Words,* XVIII (1858), 217-222; "The Byways of Literature: Reading for the Million," *Blackwood's,* LXXXIV (1858), 200-216; and "Cheap Literature," *British Quarterly Review,* XXIX (1859), 313-345.

2. These sentences are borrowed from an earlier essay of mine, "English Publishing and the Mass Audience in 1852," *Studies in Bibliography,* VI (1954), 4-5. That article (pp. 3-24) offers a much more detailed survey of the publishing scene and the character of the democratic reading public in the 'fifties than is possible in the present space.

3. *The George Eliot Letters,* ed. Gordon S. Haight, III (New Haven, 1954), 234 n.

4. Charles Tennyson, *Alfred Tennyson* (New York, 1949), p. 319. (Charles Morgan, however, in his *House of Macmillan* [New York, 1944], p. 52, says that 10,000 copies were sold in the first *month.*) Another indication of the public's receptivity to poetry is the fact that by June 1859 a cheap one-volume edition, issued a year earlier, of Barham's *Ingoldsby Legends* had sold 21,000 copies (*Publishers' Circular,* 15 June 1859, p. 282).

5. Francis Darwin, *The Life and Letters of Charles Darwin* (New York, n. d.), II, 1, 31, 61.

6. After the first edition of 1,250 copies, there was a second of 3,000, published 7 Jan. 1860, and a third of 2,000 copies in April 1861 (*Life and Letters,* II, 51, 149).

7. Advertisement in *Athenæum,* 12 Nov. 1859, p. 623.

8. This material is taken from Mudie's advertisements in the *Athenæum,* various dates, 1859.

9. *George Eliot Letters,* III, 33.

10. Of the 200,000 volumes Mudie bought between Jan. 1858 and Oct. 1859, 87,780 were fiction, 56,472 history and biography, and 25,552 travel and adventure (*Athenæum,* 22 Oct. 1859, p. 538).

11. *George Eliot Letters,* III, 40.

12. With good reason, because it was in this year that Mudie, after ordering 300 copies of *Richard Feverel,* yielded to the outrage of certain patrons and banned the book from his shelves (Lionel Stevenson, *The Ordeal of George Meredith* [New York, 1953], p. 72).

13. *Letters of Charles Dickens,* ed. Walter Dexter (1938), III, 92.

14. Advertisement in *Athenæum,* 12 Mar. 1859, p. 366.

15. See [*The Times*] *Tercentenary Handlist of English and Welsh Newspapers, Magazines and Reviews* (1920), pp. 91-92.

16. Edgar Johnson, *Charles Dickens: His Tragedy and Triumph* (New York, 1952), II, 946.

17. *Letters and Private Papers of Thackeray,* ed. Gordon N. Ray, IV (Cambridge, Mass., 1946), 158-159.

18. *Letters and Private Papers of Thackeray,* IV, 160.

19. George M. Smith, "Our Birth and Parentage," *Cornhill Magazine,* N.S., X (1901), 9.

20. *George Eliot Letters,* III, 207.

21. See note 1.

22. *Publishers' Circular,* 31 Dec. 1866, p. 988.

23. "The Byways of Literature" (see note 1), pp. 207-208.

24. Margaret Dalziel, *Popular Fiction 100 Years Ago* (1957), p. 36.

25. Charles L. Graves, *Life and Letters of Alexander Macmillan* (1910), p. 130.

26. Smiles, *Autobiography* (New York, 1905), p. 223.

27. Advertisement in *Athenæum,* 5 Mar. 1859, p. 336.

28. *Self-Help* (1859), pp. 249, 265-266.

29. *Self-Help,* p. 268.

30. *Athenæum,* 31 Dec. 1859, p. 888.

31. *Athenæum,* 29 Jan. 1859, p. 153; *George Eliot Letters,* III, 15 n.

32. Advertisement in *Publishers' Circular,* 1 Dec. 1858, p. 593.

33. For the decline in the *Cornhill*'s fortunes after its brilliant beginning, see Leonard Huxley, *The House of Smith Elder* (privately printed, 1923), pp. 119-120.

34. *Publishers' Circular,* 31 Dec. 1866, p. 988.

VICTIMS AND SPOKESMEN: THE IMAGE OF SOCIETY IN THE NOVEL
by G. Armour Craig

1. *An Autobiography,* ed. Frederick Page (1950 [The Oxford Trollope]), pp. 291-295.

2. *World Within World: The Autobiography of Stephen Spender* (1951), p. 120.

3. *The Autobiography of Charles Darwin,* ed. Nora Barlow (1958), pp. 138-139.

4. *The George Eliot Letters,* ed. G. S. Haight (7 vols., New Haven, 1954-55), V, 380.

THE BURDEN OF THE ARTIST *by William A. Madden*

1. Bertrand Russell, *Philosophical Essays* (New York, 1910), p. 61.

2. Mallarmé is cited in Arthur Symons, *The Symbolist Movement in Literature,* rev. and enlarged ed. (New York, 1919), p. 188. The Yeats quotation is from *The Autobiography of William Butler Yeats* (New York, 1953), p. 226. Wallace Stevens is cited by Henry A. Murray in *Daedalus* (Spring, 1959), p. 217.

3. Symons, p. 202.

4. From W. R. Rodgers' poem "The Fall" in *Europa and the Bull and Other Poems* (New York, 1952).

5. Karl Löwith, *The Meaning of History* (Chicago, 1949), p. 96.

6. G. M. Young, *Victorian England: Portrait of an Age* (1936), p. 76.

7. William James, *The Will to Believe and Other Essays* (New York, 1907), p. 42.

8. From "General Aims and Theories" (1925) reprinted in Philip Horton, *Hart Crane* (New York, 1937), p. 324.

9. "To Marguerite—continued," *The Poetical Works of Matthew Arnold,* ed. C. B. Tinker and H. F. Lowry (1950).

10. *Letters of John Ruskin to Charles Eliot Norton* (Boston and New York, 1905), I, 85.

11. "A Burden for Critics," reprinted in *Essays in Modern Literary History,* ed. Ray B. West (New York, 1952), p. 159.

12. Martin Tupper was widely credited with the authorship of "Riflemen Form!" (originally titled "The War"). See Derek Hudson, *Martin Tupper: His Rise and Fall* (1949), pp. 191-192.

13. A. J. Arberry, *The Romance of the Rubáiyát* (New York, 1959), p. 18.

14. *Letters of Edward FitzGerald* (1901), I, 67.

15. Variorum edition, *Poetical and Prose Writings of Edward FitzGerald,* ed. George Bentham (New York, 1903), I, 127.

16. *Writings,* I, 11.

17. *Writings,* I, 216.

18. *Writings,* I, *xxx* and 13-14.

19. *Poetical Works,* from the 1853 Preface. FitzGerald thought Tennyson's "Locksley Hall" was "far more like Lucretius than the last Verses put into his mouth by A. T." (*Letters,* II, 105).

20. *The Tenth Muse* (1958), p. 321.

21. *Essays in Criticism, Third Series,* ed. Edward J. O'Brien (Boston, 1910), pp. 35-36 and 70-71.

22. *England and the Italian Question* (1859), pp. 25-26 and *Letters,* I, 89.

23. C. B. Tinker and H. F. Lowry, *The Poetry of Matthew Arnold: A Commentary* (1949), pp. 343-344.

24. Letters of Matthew Arnold to A. H. Clough, ed. H. F. Lowry (1932), p. 149.

25. "We shall see that there is in fact an ancient and a modern period in the history of every people; the ancient differing, and the modern in many essential points agreeing with that in which we live now" (Thomas Arnold, "On the Social Progress of States," *Miscellaneous Works* [1845], p. 108).

26. *Essays in Criticism,* edition de luxe (1903), III, 10-13.

27. *Essays in Criticism,* III, 174.

28. "Introduction" to *The Hundred Greatest Men* (1879), p. iii.

29. *The Works of John Ruskin,* Library Edition, ed. E. T. Cook and Alexander Wedderburn (1905), XVI, 253.

30. For a summary of the issues involved in the Battle of Styles and its resolution in the "curious combinations" of late-Victorian architecture, see William Gaunt, *Victorian Olympus* (1952), pp. 136-146.

31. *Works,* XVI, 251.

32. *Works,* XVI, 290-291.

33. A passage from the *Cestus of Aglaia* (1867) supplies impressive evidence of the breakdown in Ruskin's control over his thought (see ch. iii, "On Modesty"). The comment on the 1880 sketch is made by Joan Evans, "John Ruskin as Artist," *Apollo,* LXVI (1957), 145.

34. Eric Newton, *European Painting and Sculpture* (Pelican Art Series), 4th ed. (Baltimore, 1956), p. 235.

35. John Lehmann, *The Open Night* (1952), pp. 117-118.

36. Cited in Geoffrey Bullough, *The Trend of Modern Poetry* (Edinburgh, 1949), 210.

37. Vincent A. Scully, Jr., "Modern Architecture," *College Art Journal,* XVII (1958), 159.

VICTORIAN REVIEWERS AND CULTURAL RESPONSIBILITY *by Michael Wolff*

1. [Wilkie Collins], "The Unknown Public," *Household Words,* XVIII (21 Aug. 1858), 222, quoted by Richard D. Altick, *The English Common Reader: A Social History of the Mass Reading Public, 1800-1900* (Chicago, 1957), p. 6; H., *Fraser's Magazine,* LX (July 1859), 97; T. H. S. Escott, *England, Her People, Polity, and Pursuits* (New York, 1880), p. 572.

2. G. M. Young, *Victorian England: Portrait of An Age* (1936), p. 6.

3. *Literary Gazette,* n.s. IV (5 May 1860), 554-555.

4. For information about most of the twenty-five periodicals, see Alvar Ellegård, *The Readership of the Periodical Press in Mid-Victorian Britain* (Göteborg, 1957). Mr. Ellegård gives the life-span of each periodical and its price and estimated circulation in 1860. See also H. R. Fox Bourne, *English Newspapers: Chapters in the History of Journalism* (1887), Vol. II; J. D. Jump, "Weekly Reviewing in the Eighteen-Fifties," *Review of English Studies,* XXIV (1948), 42-57; *The Tradition Established, 1841-1884,* The History of *The Times,* II (1939); Leslie A. Marchand, *The Athenaeum: Mirror of Victorian Culture* (Chapel Hill, 1941); Merle Mowbray Bevington, *The Saturday Review, 1855-1868* (New York, 1941); and Oscar Maurer, "Froude and *Fraser's Magazine,* 1860-1874," *University of Texas Studies in English,* XXVIII (1949), 213-243. I am also indebted to the Wellesley Index to Victorian Periodicals and to its General Editor, Walter E. Houghton.

5. *Economist,* XVII (23 April 1859), 454; (22 Oct. 1859), 1182; (26 Feb. 1859), 230.

6. I have included here reviews published in 1860 as well as in 1859. The quarterlies especially were not always prompt with their notices. Since Darwin's book, for instance, was published at the end of November, to have confined myself to 1859 reviews would have been needlessly limiting (I have not, however, counted as eligible reviews such as *Blackwood's* 1861 review of the *Origin of Species*).

7. *Literary Gazette,* n.s. III (1 Oct. 1859), 326.

8. George H. Ford, *Dickens and His Readers: Aspects of Novel-Criticism Since 1836* (Princeton, 1955), p. 103. The reviewer is identified as Sir James Fitzjames Stephen.

9. *Saturday Review,* VIII (17 Dec. 1859), 741; *Critic,* XIX (17 Dec. 1859), 602; *Dublin University Magazine,* LV (Feb. 1860), 238-239. Was the enthusiastic review in the *Examiner,* 10 Dec. 1859, pp. 788-789, by John Forster, the editor and Dickens' close friend?

10. *Christian Remembrancer,* XXXIX (June 1860), 283.

11. *Literary Churchman,* V (16 Dec. 1859), 451.

12. *Christian Remembrancer,* XXXIX (June 1860), 285; *Literary Churchman,* V (1 Sept. 1859), 313. Both Baden Powell and Benjamin Jowett were to be contributors to the highly controversial *Essays and Reviews* (1860); "Mr. Hennell" is probably George Eliot's friend Sara Hennell (who published as S. S.

Hennell); George Jacob Holyoake was editor of the *Reasoner*, the avowed organ of the Secularists.

13. *Eclectic Review*, CIX (March 1859), 227.

14. See F. G., *Fraser's Magazine*, LX (Nov. 1859), 563; *London Quarterly Review*, XIV (July 1860), 363; and *British Quarterly Review*, XXX (July 1859), 199.

15. *Guardian*, XIV (12 Jan. 1859), 32; *Christian Observer*, LIX (7 Feb. 1859), 121; [William Smith], *Blackwood's Edinburgh Magazine*, LXXXVI (July 1859), 66.

16. F. G., *Fraser's Magazine*, LX (Nov. 1859), 564.

17. *Spectator*, XXXII (19 Nov. 1859), 1187; *Saturday Review*, VIII (22 Oct. 1859), 486.

18. See especially Alvar Ellegård, *Darwin and the General Reader: The Reception of Darwin's Theory of Evolution in the British Periodical Press, 1859-1872* (Göteborg, 1958).

19. *Literary Gazette*, n.s. III (24 Dec. 1859), 609.

20. *Guardian*, XV (8 Feb. 1860), 134.

21. *North British Review*, XXXII (May 1860), 457.

22. "Christopher Grim," *Dublin University Magazine*, LV (Feb. 1860), 235; *Saturday Review*, VIII (24 Dec. 1859), 775; *Economist*, XVIII (12 May 1860), 511; [J. R. Leifchild], *Athenæum*, 19 Nov. 1859, p. 660. The *Eclectic Review* article is CXI (March 1860), 217-242; the *Christian Observer*, LX (Aug. 1860), 561-574. Bishop Wilberforce's review was in the *Quarterly Review*, CVIII (July 1860), 225-264; and Mr. Dunns's in the *North British Review*, XXXII (May 1860), 455-486.

23. *Christian Observer*, LX (Aug. 1860), 561; *Dublin Review*, XLVIII (May 1860), 78.

24. *British Quarterly Review*, XXXI (April 1860), 416, 399.

25. *National Review*, VIII (April 1859); Henry Buckle, *Fraser's Magazine*, LIX (May 1859), 509-542; [Sir J. F. Stephen], *Saturday Review*, VII (12 Feb. 1859), 186-187; *British Quarterly Review*, XXIX (April 1859), 547; *London Quarterly Review*, XIII (Oct. 1859), 275; *North British Review*, XXX (May 1859), 400. See also J. C. Rees, *Mill and His Early Critics* (Leicester, 1956).

26. See G. M. Young, *Victorian England*, p. 68, n. 2: "S. T. C[oleridge] once said to Miss Martineau: 'You seem to regard society as an aggregate of individuals.' 'Of course I do,' she replied. There is much history implicit in that encounter, and by 1850 Coleridge had won."

27. *National Review*, VIII (April 1859), 407; *Bentley's Quarterly Review*, II (Jan. 1860), 457; *Westminster Review*, LXXII (Oct. 1859), 405; *Guardian*, XIV (20 April 1859), 351; *British Quarterly Review*, XXXI (Jan. 1860), 189.

28. *Literary Gazette*, n.s. II (26 Feb. 1859), 265; *North British Review*, XXX (May 1859), 399-401; *Christian Remembrancer*, XXXVIII (July 1859), 195.

29. John Morley, *Recollections*, Works of Lord Morley, I (1921), I, 55.

30. [G. W. Thornbury], *Athenæum*, 28 May 1859, p. 703. See also E. T. Cook and Alexander Wedderburn (eds.), *The Works of John Ruskin* (1905), XVI, 247.

31. *Literary Gazette*, n.s. II (4 June 1859), 665; *Eclectic Review*, CX (Sept. 1859), 326-327; *Fraser's Magazine*, LX (July 1859), 105-106.

32. *Critic*, XIX (20 July 1859), 104.

33. Lionel Stevenson, *The Ordeal of George Meredith* (New York, 1953), p.

71. See also René Galland, *George Meredith and British Criticism* (Paris, 1923).

34. *Athenæum,* 9 July 1859, p. 48; *Critic* XIX (2 July 1859), 6-7; *Literary Gazette,* n.s. III (20 Aug. 1859), 187; *Saturday Review,* VIII (9 July 1859), 48-49; *Spectator,* XXXII (9 July 1859), 718. The *Examiner,* 9 July 1859, p. 437, said, "Judged by every-day standards, it is one of the best novels of the year."

35. *Westminster Review,* LXXII (Oct. 1859), 627-628; [Samuel Lucas], *The Times,* 14 Oct. 1859, p. 5; "Christopher Grim," *Dublin University Magazine,* LV (Feb. 1860), 237. For Mudie's, see Stevenson, pp. 72-73; and R. A. Colby, " 'The Librarian Rules the Roost': The Career of Charles Edward Mudie (1818-1890)," *Wilson Library Bulletin,* XXVI (1952), 623-627.

36. *Eclectic Review,* CIX (March 1859), 332; [J. B. Mozley?], *Bentley's Quarterly Review,* I (July 1859), 439; *Saturday Review,* VII (26 Feb. 1859), 250; [E. S. Dallas], *The Times,* 12 April 1859, p. 5; [Mrs. Norton?], *Edinburgh Review,* CX (July 1859), 246. See also Gordon S. Haight (ed.), *The George Eliot Letters,* III (New Haven, 1954).

37. *Christian Observer,* LX (Jan. 1860), 29; [J. B. Mozley?], *Bentley's Quarterly Review,* I (July 1859), 441; *Christian Observer,* LX (Jan. 1860), 21.

38. *National Review,* VIII (April 1859), 565; *Saturday Review,* VII (26 Feb. 1859), 250; *Dublin University Magazine,* LIII (April 1859), 484; *Economist,* XVII (5 March 1859), 256-257; [Mrs. Norton?], *Edinburgh Review,* CX (July 1859), 235; *Critic,* XIX (6 Aug. 1859), 126.

39. [W. E. Gladstone], *Quarterly Review,* CVI (Oct. 1859), 485; *Fraser's Magazine,* LX (Sept. 1859), 302, 311; *Blackwood's Edinburgh Magazine,* LXXXVI (Nov. 1859), 625. See also Hallam Tennyson, *Alfred, Lord Tennyson, A Memoir* (1897), I, 443-444.

40. [John Nichol], *Westminster Review,* LXXII (Oct. 1859), 519; *London Quarterly Review,* XIII (Oct. 1859), 75; [W. E. Gladstone], *Quarterly Review,* CVI (Oct. 1859), 477.

41. *Blackwood's Edinburgh Magazine,* LXXXVI (Nov. 1859), 625; *Christian Observer,* LX (April 1860), 246.

42. *British Quarterly Review,* XXX (Oct. 1859), 483; *Literary Gazette,* n.s. III (23 July 1859), 81; *Bentley's Quarterly Review,* II (Oct. 1859), 185; [Coventry Patmore], *Edinburgh Review,* CX (July 1859), 263; [John Nichol], *Westminster Review,* LXXII (Oct. 1859), 525.

43. *Dublin University Magazine,* LV (Jan. 1860), 65.

INDEX

Aberdeen, Earl of, 166, 168-69
Acton, Lord, 98, 270
Adam Bede, 14, 216-17, 243-45, 273-74, 283-84
Albert, Prince Consort, 26, 97-98, 103-5, 109, 188, 193
All the Year Round, 14, 219, 220
America, 14, 102-3, 106, 110, 112, 149
Annual Register, 183
Argyll, Duke of, 171, 178, 191
Aristotle, 32, 58
Arnold, Sir Edwin, 16
Arnold, Matthew, 14, 16, 32, 35, 91, 104, 108, 155, 199, 200, 210, 249, 250, 256-61, 266-68, 272-74
Arnold, Dr. Thomas, 39, 43, 62, 103, 106, 259
Art, 16, 26, 250, 258-67, 280-81; see also Ruskin
Athenæum, 225, 272-73, 278, 280-81
Austria, 13, 109, 173, 175, 181-96

Bacon, Francis, 16, 32, 99
Bagehot, Walter, 121, 269, 271
Bampton Lectures, 14, 40, 275; see also Mansel
Baudelaire, Charles, 257
Beeton, Isabella, 206, 218-19
Bell, Clive, 257
Benn, A. W., 44
Bentham, Jeremy, 32, 34, 155
Bentley's Miscellany, 272
Bentley's Quarterly Review, 271, 279, 283, 285
Bernal, J. D., 40
Bible, 35, 51-62, 82; see also Biblical Criticism
Biblical criticism, 34, 35, 60, 64, 67, 106; see also *Essays and Reviews*
Birmingham, 134, 141, 226
Bismarck, 183, 195
Blackwood's Edinburgh Magazine, 215, 284-85
Blake, William, 32, 90, 248

Bleak House, 234-36
Book reviews, 60, 269-89
Bowra, Sir Maurice, 84-85
Bright, John, 118, 121, 127, 129, 167, 171-72, 174, 177, 179-80, 209, 211
British Association, 56, 97
British Quarterly Review, 271, 273, 278-79, 285
Broad Church, 38, 41, 106-7; see also Arnold, T., and Maurice
Brooks, Cleanth, 84, 88-89, 92-93
Browning, Robert, 35, 257
Buckle, Henry, 34, 270, 279
Bulwer-Lytton, Edward, 103, 217-18, 281
Bureaucracy, 100-101
Burke, Edmund, 32, 154, 279, 287
Butler, Bishop, 18, 37, 68, 257
Butler Samuel, 54, 60

Cambridge University, 32-33, 40-41, 54, 154, 251
Cardwell, Edward, 168, 178
Carlyle, Thomas, 14, 152, 155, 217, 231, 248
Cassell, John, 222, 226-27
Cavour, Count, 175, 181, 183-88, 194-95
Cecil, Lord David, 85
Chambers, Robert, 52, 60
Chambers's Encyclopædia, 219, 227
Chartists, 120-21, 132, 148, 213
Christian Observer, 273, 278, 283, 285
Christian Remembrancer, 271, 280
Church of England, 37, 49, 158, 271; see also Broad Church, Evangelicalism, Tractarians
Civil Service, 36, 154, 218
Clarendon, Earl of, 177, 193
Clough, Arthur Hugh, 35, 259
Coal production, 136, 140-41
Cobbett, William, 128, 209
Cobden, Richard, 118, 127-29, 167, 177-80, 209, 211

Colenso, Bishop, 23, 35, 60-61, 82
Coleridge, Samuel Taylor, 62, 74, 82-
  83, 106, 247-48, 262, 279
Collins, Wilkie, 219, 222, 269
Colonialism, 13-14, 16; see also India
Comic literature, 225-26
Communism, 231; see also Marx
Comte, Auguste, 34, 279
Conservatives, 165-66, 168, 171-72,
  230-31
Copernicus, 39, 57, 81
Corn Laws, 118, 136, 148, 164, 209
Cornhill Magazine, 221, 222, 228-29,
  271-72
Cotton, 132, 135, 137, 139, 145
Crimean War, 107, 127, 136, 139, 141,
  150, 166, 192-93, 285
Critic, 272-73, 275, 281-82, 284
Criticism, 43-44, 81-95, 250, 258-67,
  280-81; see also New Criticism
Cuvier, Georges, 52

Dante, 83, 260, 284
Darwin, Charles, 14, 17-23, 27, 28, 32,
  35-37, 42-44, 50, 56, 58, 60, 81-95,
  216-17, 246, 249, 251, 270, 272-73,
  277-78; see also Evolution, Natural
  selection, *Origin of Species*
Democracy, 148-49, 158-59, 161, 193,
  201, 208, 231, 260, 269, 286, 288
Derby, Earl of, 126, 166, 169, 171,
  173, 175-76, 178, 187, 190-91
Descartes, René, 59, 99
Dickens, Charles, 14, 26, 218, 222,
  229, 234-36, 240-41, 269, 272, 275;
  see also *Bleak House, A Tale of Two
  Cities*
Dickinson, G. Lowes, 43, 74
Disraeli, Benjamin, 25, 119, 121, 129,
  147, 150, 153, 165-69, 171, 173, 175,
  180, 189, 218, 231
Divorce, 204, 285
Dublin Review, 271, 273, 275, 278
Dublin University Magazine, 278, 282,
  284, 286

Eclectic Review, 273, 278, 281, 283
Economics, 34, 132, 137-40, 152, 167;
  see also Free Trade, Industrialism
Economist, 272, 278, 284

Edinburgh Review, 59, 102, 108, 271,
  283-85
Education, 25, 97-112, 157, 159, 161,
  209-10, 214, 260-61, 286, 288; see
  also Public Schools, Universities
Eliot, George, 14, 16, 19, 26-27, 35,
  218, 235-37, 243-46, 269, 272, 274;
  see also *Adam Bede, Middlemarch*
Eliot, T. S., 87, 91, 94, 255, 258, 266,
  273, 274
Empiricism, 17, 23, 31-37, 82-84; see
  also Positivism, Rationalism
Empson, William, 46, 267
Englishwoman's Journal, 204
Essays and Reviews, 23, 39, 41, 60-61,
  74, 82, 109; see also Biblical Criti-
  cism
Evangelicalism, 37-42, 271, 276
Evans, Marian, see George Eliot
Evolution, 16, 34-35, 81, 277; see also
  Chambers, Darwin, Lamarck
Examiner, 272-73, 281

Family Herald, 222, 224, 226
Family life, 201-7, 209; see also Di-
  vorce, Marriage, Servants
Feminism, 204, 206-8
Feuerbach, Ludwig, 41
Fiction, 14-16, 215-46, 281-84; see also
  Novel
"Field, Michael," 91-92, 95
FitzGerald, Edward, 14, 16, 26-27, 43,
  200, 255-58, 268, 272; see also *Ru-
  báiyát*
Foreign affairs, 25, 126-30, 181-96;
  see also America, Austria, France,
  Germany, Italy, Bismarck, Napo-
  leon III
France, 98, 104, 139, 149, 181-96, 241,
  259-61
Franchise, 14, 115-23, 147-61, 151,
  153, 156-57
Fraser's Magazine, 272, 276, 279, 281,
  284
Free Trade, 165, 167
French Revolution, 241, 259-61
Freud, Sigmund, 70, 223

Galileo, 22, 39
Gaskell, Mrs., 203, 211

Germany, 34, 60, 145, 183, 185, 238, 276; see also Prussia
Gibson, Milner, 174, 177
Gladstone, W. E., 119, 120, 128, 154, 164, 166, 168-70, 172, 175-76, 178-80, 188-89, 191, 269, 284
Glasgow, 134, 150
Goethe, J. W., 63, 259-60
Gosse, Philip, 225
Graham, Sir James, 168, 171-74, 176-77
Granville, Lord, 173-77, 194
Gray, Asa, 51, 54
Great Exhibition, 102-4, 226
Greville, C. C. F., 171-72, 193
Grey, Earl, 124
Guardian, 272-73, 277

Hamilton, Sir William, 16, 40
Hamlet, 90, 252, 253, 257
Hegel, G. W. F., 84, 154
Heine, Heinrich, 23, 259, 260
Heraclitus, 82, 84
Herbert, Sidney, 166, 168, 171-78
History, 23-25, 47-48, 87-91, 260, 270, 275; see also Benn, Buckle, Mill, J.
Hobbes, Thomas, 32
Hort, F. J. A., 41, 62
Household Words, 219, 222
Hughes, Thomas, 210, 217, 221
Hugo, Victor, 23, 221
Hume, David, 32, 37, 39, 287
Hume, Joseph, 120
Humor, 19-20; see also Comic literature
Hutton, R. H., 123, 270, 271
Huxley, T. H., 35, 45, 56, 59, 62, 70, 109, 155, 221, 262, 269

Idealist philosophy, 34, 70, 101; see also Hegel, Kant
Idylls of the King, The, 14, 16, 26, 216-17, 221, 250-55, 268, 273-74, 284-86
India, 13, 32, 138, 145, 147, 150, 153, 158, 163, 170
Industry and industrial change, 24, 35, 48, 131-46, 158, 211; see also Coal production, Cotton
Invention, 99-100

Ireland, 14, 134, 150, 165, 168
Italy, 13-14, 25, 170, 183, 189-95; see also Cavour, Piedmont-Sardinia

James, Henry, 22, 27, 246
James, William, 248
Jewish emancipation, 170
Johnson, Samuel, 90, 215, 219, 241, 287
Journalism, 23, 269-89; see also Magazines, Periodicals
Jowett, Benjamin, 39, 40, 43, 60, 62, 107, 109, 275

Kant, Immanuel, 47, 68, 76
King, Locke, 120, 167
Kingsley, Charles, 55, 62, 71-72, 224
Kropotkin, Peter, 22, 81

Labor, 133-45
Lamarck, Jean Baptiste, 52, 81
Leavis, F. R., 88
Leavis, Q. D., 227
Leighton, Sir Frederick, 26-27
Lewes, George Henry, 219, 243, 270
Liberal Party, 125, 163-80
Liberalism, 24, 169, 179, 180, 231, 233
Literary Churchman, 271, 283
Literary Gazette, 272-74, 280-82, 285
London Journal, 222, 227
London Quarterly Review, 71, 279
Lowe, Robert, 123, 129, 269
Lucretius, 256-59
Lux Mundi, 41-42, 62
Lyell, Charles, 34, 60, 82

Macaulay, Lord, 18, 39, 43, 128, 219, 254, 284
Macmillan's Magazine, 59, 219, 221, 224, 271-72
Magazines, 202, 269-89
Malmesbury, Lord, 126, 167, 175-76, 187-89, 191, 193
Malory, Sir Thomas, 27, 252, 254
Manchester, 134, 138, 143, 150
Manning, Cardinal, 40
Mansel, H. L., 14, 23, 40-41, 46, 63-80, 272-77
Marriage, 203-7

Marx, Karl, 17, 23, 44, 46, 133, 145, 154, 233, 268
Maurice, F. D., 14, 23, 37-42, 63-80, 269, 272-77
Medical Act of 1858, 107, 211
Meredith, George, 16, 155, 203, 218, 237-40, 272, 274, 281, 283; see also *Ordeal of Richard Feverel*
Merz, J. T., 98, 100-101
Middle class, 204-8, 212, 217-18
Middlemarch, 235-37, 246
Mill, James, 147-48
Mill, John Stuart, 14, 16-17, 33-34, 36, 38, 40, 75, 77, 115, 119, 121, 147-61, 251, 259, 269, 272-73, 277, 279-80; see also *On Liberty*
Morley, John, 152, 154-55, 280
Mudie's Subscription Library, 217-18, 224, 282
Mundella, A. J., 105, 109

Napoleon III, 13, 22, 129, 181-96, 260
National Review, 59, 271, 273, 279, 284
Natural selection, 35, 50, 53; see also Darwin, *Origin of Species*
Nature, 97
New Criticism, 81, 91-93
Newman, Francis, 35
Newman, John Henry, Cardinal, 32, 39-40, 48, 50, 57, 64, 72, 106, 108, 255, 270
News of the World, 214, 227
Newton, Isaac, 32, 33, 57, 59, 71
Niebuhr, Barthold, 34
Nightingale, Florence, 107, 205, 206
Nonconformists, 271, 284; see also Evangelicalism
North American Review, 59
North British Review, 58, 271, 273, 279, 280
Novel, 200, 202, 218, 229-46, 283-84; see also *Adam Bede, Bleak House, Middlemarch, Ordeal of Richard Feverel, A Tale of Two Cities, The Virginians*

On Liberty, 14, 16-17, 36, 147-61, 259, 272-74, 279-80
Once a Week, 272

Ordeal of Richard Feverel, The, 14, 16, 216, 237-40, 273-74, 281-83
Origin of Species, The, 14, 17-23, 27, 32, 35-36, 81-96, 109, 129, 200, 216, 221, 251, 272-74, 277-79; see also Darwin, Natural selection
Oxford University, 32, 82, 154

Paley, William, 54, 67
Palmerston, Lord, 13, 118, 120, 121, 123, 125, 127-29, 154, 163-80, 187-89, 191, 194, 261
Papacy, 182, 186
Parliament, 148-49, 150, 157, 165, 179
Parliamentary Companion, 165, 167
Pascal, Blaise, 48, 59
Pater, Walter, 43, 44, 81-95
Pattison, Mark, 104, 107
Peel, Sir Robert, 118, 123, 164, 165, 168
Peelites, 164, 167-69, 171, 178-79
Periodicals, 201, 203, 215-28, 269-89
Persia, 16, 27, 256, 257
Piedmont-Sardinia, 13, 173, 181-96
Plato, 43, 82
Playfair, Lyon, 104, 109
Plombières pact, 181, 184-85, 189
Poetry, 247-68, 274, 284-86
Political parties, 123-26, 163-80; see also Conservative, Liberal, Radical
Popular culture, 119-228, 269-70, 286-89
Population, 134-38, 199
Positivism, 32-37, 70-71; see also Comte, Empiricism, Rationalism
Powell, Baden, 35, 59, 275
Prose style, 17-22, 278; see also Fiction
Prostitution, 202-3
Prussia, 109, 185-86, 193
Psychology, 248, 251, 268; see also Freud
Public Schools, 36, 206, 210, 211
Publishing, 23, 24, 199, 213
Punch, 128, 202
Pusey, E. B., 39, 41, 51, 57, 58, 106

Quarterly Review, 56, 164, 168, 175, 189, 271, 284

Radicals, 154, 156, 165, 167, 177; see also Bright, Chartists, Hume, J., King, Roebuck

Rambler, 58

Rationalism, 33-34, 37, 276; see also Empiricism, Positivism, Scepticism, Secularism

Reading public, 199-228, 287-89; see also Mudie's

Realpolitik, 183, 195-96, 260

Reform, 133, 166, 183; see also Franchise, Parliament

Reform Acts of 1832, 1867, and 1884, 104, 164-65, 171, 209, 269, 288

Reform Bill of 1859, 147, 150, 153, 170-72

Relativism, 17, 27, 43, 82

Religion, 51-80, 160, 275-76, 278-80; see also Broad Church, Church of England, Evangelicalism, Nonconformists, Roman Catholicism, Tractarians

Renan, Ernest, 259

Reviews, 60, 269-89

Reynolds' Miscellany, 223, 270

Roebuck, John Arthur, 128-29, 167

Roman Catholicism, 14, 48, 58-59, 152, 271

Romanticism, 32, 43, 200, 247-48, 251, 262-63

Rossetti, Dante Gabriel, 216, 221

Rubáiyát of Omar Khayyam, The, 14, 16, 43, 216, 250, 255-58, 273-75

Ruskin, John, 14, 16, 32, 200, 248-51, 258, 261-64, 267-69, 272-74, 280-81

Russell, Lord John, 107, 119-21, 123-25, 150, 164, 166-68, 170-77, 179, 187-88, 191, 194-95

Russia, 148, 152, 186, 189-93

Sala, G. A., 226, 228

Sargent, John Singer, 26, 27

Saturday Review, 59, 75, 167, 272-73, 275-77, 281-82, 283-84

Scepticism, 276, 280

Science, 82-87, 97-112, 161, 251, 277; see also Darwin, Lyell, Technology

Scotland, 134, 135, 150

Scott, Gilbert, 261

Scott, Sir Walter, 16, 227

Secularism, 49-50

Sedgwick, Adam, 59, 106

Seeley, J. R., 109

Self-help, 213, 224-28; see also Smiles

Servants, 204, 206, 208, 213

Sexual morality, 202-4, 281-82

Shakespeare, 90, 283, 284

Shipbuilding, 136, 141

Smiles, Samuel, 35, 211, 213, 224-25

Smith, Adam, 287

Smith, Alexander, 221

Smith, Goldwin, 64, 109

Smith, Sydney, 219

Sociology, 45-46, 232-33

Spectator, 59, 259, 272-73, 276, 281-82

Spencer, Herbert, 35-36, 55, 108, 155, 270

Sporting Calendar, 284

Stanley, A. P., 39, 62

Stanley, Lord, 172

Stephen, Fitzjames, 152, 155, 279

Strauss, David Friedrich, 34, 284

Sullivan, Sir Arthur, 26

Swinburne, Algernon, 43, 155, 257

Symons, Arthur, 43, 247

Tale of Two Cities, A, 14, 219, 240-43, 273, 275

Taxation, 154, 157

Technology, 25, 28, 97-112, 161; see also Science

Tennyson, Alfred, Lord, 14, 16, 26-27, 33, 60, 163, 192, 200, 250-58, 268-69, 272-74; see also *Idylls of the King*

Thackeray, W. M., 14, 219, 221, 229, 241-43, 255, 269, 272, 274, 281; see also *Virginians*

Times, The, 59, 75, 168, 175, 189, 192, 205, 271-73, 276, 281-83

Tractarians, 39, 64, 249, 271

Trade Unions, 132-33, 144, 158

Trilling, Lionel, 87, 93-94, 267

Trollope, Anthony, 27, 160, 202, 206, 209, 221, 230-32, 245, 269

Tupper, Martin, 216, 254

Two Paths, The, 16, 258, 261-64, 273-74, 280-81

Unitarians, 271
Universities, 36, 97-112, 152, 159,
    210; see also Cambridge, Oxford
Utilitarianism, 34, 106, 123, 151-54;
    see also Bentham, Mill

Victor Emmanuel, 181, 183
Victoria, Queen, 13, 118, 121, 123,
    125, 174, 176-77, 188-89, 191
Villafranca, 183, 185-86, 188
Virginians, The, 14, 219, 241-43, 273-
74
Volunteer Rifle Club movement, 192
Von Humboldt, Wilhelm, 98, 155, 158

Wales, 134-35, 140, 150, 199
Wallace, Alfred Russel, 17-18
Weekly Political Register, 128

Welcome Guest, 226
Westcott, B. F., 41, 47, 62
Westminster Review, 203, 271, 279,
    281-82, 285
Whewell, William, 106
Whitehead, A. N., 99, 110
Wilberforce, Bishop, 56-57, 278
Wimsatt, W. K., Jr., 84, 86, 88, 93
Wiseman, Cardinal, 271
Wittgenstein, Ludwig, 47, 70
Wordsworth, William, 21, 22, 247, 251,
    262

Xenophobia, 14, 128-29

Yeats, W. B., 32, 247, 266
Young, G. M., 248, 250